# EXPLORATIO

# EXPLORATIO

Military and political intelligence in the
Roman world from the Second Punic War
to the battle of Adrianople

*N.J.E. Austin and N.B. Rankov*

London and New York

First published 1995
by Routledge
11 New Fetter Lane, London EC4P 4EE

Simultaneously published in the USA and Canada
by Routledge
29 West 35th Street, New York, NY 10001

©1995 N.J.E. Austin and N.B. Rankov

Typeset in Baskerville 10/12 by Florencetype Ltd,
Stoodleigh, Devon

Printed and bound in Great Britain by Biddles Ltd,
Guildford and King's Lynn

*British Library Cataloguing in Publication Data*
A catalogue record for this book is available from the British Library

*Library of Congress Cataloguing in Publication Data*
A catalogue record for this book has been requested

ISBN 0-415-04945-8

# CONTENTS

# FIGURES

# PLATES

1 The northern frontier: Hadrian's Wall at Walltown Crags (*photo N.B. Rankov*)

2 The eastern frontier: a view across the Euphrates from Dura Europos (*photo Richard Stoneman*)

3 Trajan's Column (scene ix): the mushroom message. A man fallen from a mule grasps at what appears to be a large mushroom attached to his saddle; this is perhaps the incident referred to in Dio LXVIII 8.1 (see p. 65) (*photo German Archaeological Institute, Rome*)

4 Segment II of the *Peutinger Table*, a copy of a fourth-century map of the world showing routes, rivers, natural features and towns, and also marking distances between stages. This segment depicts Germany, part of Gaul, the Alps and Liguria in northern Italy and, at the bottom, part of North Africa (see p. 115) (*photo Österreichische Nationalbibliothek, Vienna*)

5 A wooden writing-tablet of the late first/early second century AD found at Vindolanda, just south of Hadrian's Wall. It contains what may be an intelligence report from the field describing British cavalry and their method of fighting (*Tab. Vindol. II* 164; see pp. 171–2) (*photo The Trustees of the British Museum*)

6 Trajan's Column (scene xxxvii): two *exploratores* gesture to the emperor Trajan to follow them during a campaign of the First Dacian War against the Roxolani (*photo German Archaeological Institute, Rome*)

7 Memorial of Tiberius Claudius Maximus, who, as a junior officer of *exploratores*, captured the body of the Dacian king Decebalus whose suicide is shown on the relief panel. Found at Philippi in Macedonia (*AE* 1969/70.583; see p. 190) (*photo Prof. M.P. Speidel*)

8 Trajan's Column (scene cxlv): the death of Decebalus. The rider just failing to prevent the suicide can now be identified as the *explorator* Tiberius Claudius Maximus (see Plate 7) (*photo German Archaeological Institute, Rome*)

9 Altar dedication of the *Exploratio Halic(ensis)* dated to the reign of Severus Alexander (AD 222–35). Found at the Feldbergkastell in Germany (*CIL* XIII 7495 = *ILS* 9185; see p. 192) (*Saalburg Museum; photo N.J.E. Austin*)

10 A *beneficiarius*-lance found alongside a group of *beneficiarius*-inscriptions in the sacred enclosure at Osterburken on the Upper German frontier (see p. 200) (*photo Landesdenkmalamt Baden-Württemberg*)

11 The insignia and command of the *dux Britanniarum* (Duke of the Britains), as listed in the *Notitia Dignitatum*, an administrative document of the early fifth century preserved in a number of fifteenth- and sixteenth-century copies (*Not.Dig.Occ.* XL). The Duke has under his command the prefect of a *numerus exploratorum* based at Lavatris (Bowes) (*photo The Bodleian Library, Oxford, MS. Canon. Misc. 378, fols 164v–165r*)

# PREFACE

*Exploratio* has had a long genesis. Too long, perhaps; but given the facility of humans to shift responsibility, an explanation in our case would be that conditions within the Universities in the 1980s and 1990s have been directly or indirectly to blame. But for its two authors the subject has retained its freshness, fascination and even controversy as the ramifications of what we were working on have widened.

The idea for the book arose out of Norman Austin's doctoral thesis on the military knowledge of Ammianus Marcellinus for the University of London. The thesis was subsequently modified into a book *Ammianus on Warfare*, published in the Collection Latomus in 1979. Work on the new project was slowed by his move to New Zealand and the inevitable upheaval such things occasion in domestic and academic affairs. A Commonwealth Study Grant in 1981 held at the Institute of Classical Studies in London gave very great impetus to the project's revival, and first public exposures of some of its ideas took place at 'work-in-progress' seminars there and at the University of Nottingham, and subsequently elsewhere in developing forms. An apparently simple question from the chairman of the London seminar, Professor Fergus Millar, turned out in effect to be seminal in the longer term: he asked, 'What evidence is there for the existence of a filing cabinet marked *Intelligence* in a provincial governor's headquarters?'

That question started to be answered properly only as the result of the completely coincidental meeting with Boris Rankov over a desk at the British School at Rome in 1985. He was in the last stages of writing his Oxford doctoral thesis on the *beneficiarii consularis*, and what started out as social conversation about each other's work rapidly became close discussion and eventually collaboration, since what Norman Austin was looking for was material linking intelligence to administration, and Boris Rankov for some aspects of the work the *beneficiarii* were doing out on station. Boris Rankov's work on the intelligence project was subjected to stresses in turn by a move first to Western Australia, with comparable domestic and academic pressures, and then back to Britain. He too has exposed central parts of the project to a number of seminars in Oxford, London and Australia.

*Exploratio* then is the result of our collaboration. Readers will note the differences in style, and even very occasionally of viewpoint. But since no analysis is ever definitive or final, we felt that such issues should only illustrate the fact that healthy academic debate will continue. Norman Austin was mainly responsible for the chapters on operational intelligence, Boris Rankov for the historical and administrative development chapters; and both for the introduction and conclusions. Both of us had very substantial input into each other's sections, naturally.

We should like to acknowledge with a real sense of gratitude the help given to us which has contributed to the project. Institutional support and hospitality have been very valuable indeed, from Massey University, the University of Western Australia (including two Australian Commonwealth Research Grants), Royal Holloway and Bedford New College, the Institute of Classical Studies (London), the British School at Rome, the Humanities Research Centre (Canberra), Clare Hall (Cambridge) and the Ashmolean Museum. But fellow-scholars have also helped at various stages, by probing, critically questioning, just listening, suggesting ideas and sometimes even approving: in particular Professor Fergus Millar, Professor Sheppard Frere, (the late) Professor Frank Goodyear. None of these can be held guilty by association of the errors or heterodoxies these pages may contain. Finally, our thanks must go to our wives, Anne and Kati, and other close departmental colleagues too, for their patience in putting up with the strategies and tactics of *Exploratio*.

Norman Austin
*Massey University*

Boris Rankov
*Royal Holloway and Bedford New College*
*University of London*
October 1994

# ABBREVIATIONS

| | |
|---|---|
| *AE* | *L'Année Épigraphique* |
| *ANRW* | H.Temporini (ed.), *Aufstieg und Niedergang der römischen Welt* (Berlin/New York, 1972–) |
| *BAR* | *British Archaeological Reports* |
| *BGU* | *Aegyptische Urkunden aus den staatlichen Museen zu Berlin, griechische Urkunden* (Berlin, 1892–1937) |
| *BMC* | H. Mattingly *et al.* (eds), *Coins of the Roman Empire in the British Museum* (London, 1923–75) |
| *BMCRR* | H. A. Grueber (ed.), *Coins of the Roman Republic in the British Museum* (London, 1910) |
| *BRGK* | *Bericht der Römisch–Germanischen Kommission* |
| *Chronica Minora* | *Chronica Minora saec. iv, v, vi, vii* (ed. Th. Mommsen, Berlin, 1892–8, vols. i–iii) *Monumenta Germaniae Historica (Auctores Antiquissimi)*, IX, XI, XIII |
| *CIG* | *Corpus Inscriptionum Graecarum* (ed. A. Boeckh, Berlin, 1828–77) |
| *CIL* | *Corpus Inscriptionum Latinarum* (Berlin, 1863-1986) |
| *CIRB* | V.V. Struve (ed.), *Corpus Inscriptionum Regni Bospori (Korpus Bosporskih Nadpisei)* (Moskva and Leningrad, 1965) |
| *CJ* | *Codex Justinianus* (ed. P. Krüger, Berlin, 1877) |
| *CPR* | *Corpus Papyrorum Raineri* (Wien, 1895–1987) |
| *CTh* | *Codex Theodosianus* (ed. Th. Mommsen, Berlin, 1905) |
| *Digest* | Justinian, *Digesta seu Pandectae* (ed. Th. Mommsen, Berlin, 1870) |
| *FGrHist* | F. Jacoby, *Die Fragmente der griechischen Historiker* I–III (Berlin, 1923–54) |
| *FHG* | C. Müller *et al.* (eds), *Fragmenta Historicorum Graecorum* (Paris, 1841–70) |
| Fink | R.O. Fink, *Roman Military Records on Papyrus*, American Philological Association Monograph 26 (Cleveland, 1971) |
| *HSCP* | *Harvard Studies in Classical Philology* |
| *IG* | *Inscriptiones Graecae* (Berlin, 1873–1972) |

| | |
|---|---|
| *IGBulg.* | G. Mihailov (ed.), *Inscriptiones Graecae in Bulgaria Repertae* (Sofia, 1956–70) |
| *IGRR* | R. Cagnat (ed.), *Inscriptiones Graecae ad Res Romanas Pertinentes* (Paris, 1901) |
| *ILS* | H. Dessau (ed.), *Inscriptiones Latinae Selectae* (Berlin, 1892–1916; 2nd ed. 1955; 3rd ed. 1962) |
| *IRT* | J.M. Reynolds and J.B. Ward Perkins (eds), *The Inscriptions of Roman Tripolitania* (Rome/London, 1952) |
| *JRS* | *Journal of Roman Studies* |
| *MAAR* | *Memoirs of the American Academy in Rome* |
| *Not. Dig.* | *Notitia Dignitatum* (*Occ.* = *Occidentalis*; *Or.* = *Orientalis*) (ed. O. Seeck, Berlin, 1876) |
| *Nov. Th* | Theodosius II, *Novellae* in *Codex Theodosianus* Vol. II (ed. P. Meyer, Berlin, 1905) |
| *OGIS* | W. Dittenberger (ed.), *Orientis Graeci Inscriptiones Selectae* I–II (Leipzig, 1903–5) |
| *P.Abinn.* | H.I. Bell, V. Martin, E.G. Turner and D. van Berchem (eds), *The Abinnaeus Archive: Papers of a Roman Officer in the Reign of Constantius II* (Oxford, 1962) |
| *P.Amh.* | B.P. Grenfell and A.S. Hunt (eds), *The Amherst Papyri* (London, 1900–1) |
| *P.Brem.* | U. Wilcken (ed.), *Die Bremer Papyri* (Abhandlungen der Preussischen Akademie der Wissenschaften) (Berlin, 1936) |
| *P.Brux.* | G. Nachtergael (ed.), *Papyrologica Bruxellensia* (Bruxelles, 1974–) |
| *P.Cair. Isid.* | A.E.R. Boak and H.C. Youtie (eds), *The Archive of Aurelius Isidorus* (Ann Arbor, 1960) |
| *P.Dur.* | C.B. Welles, R.O. Fink and J.F. Gilliam (eds), *The Excavations at Dura-Europos. Final Report V* (ed. A. Perkins) *Part i: The Parchments and Papyri* (New Haven, 1959) |
| *P.Flor.* | D. Comparetti and G. Vitelli (eds), *Papiri greco-egizii* (Milan, 1906–15) |
| *P.Grenf. II* | B.P. Grenfell and A.S. Hunt (eds), *New Classical Fragments and Other Greek and Latin Papyri* (Oxford, 1897) |
| *P.Laur.* | R. Pintaudi (ed.), *Dai papiri della biblioteca Medicea Laurenziana* (Firenze, 1976–83) |
| *P.Lond.* | F.G. Kenyon and H.I Bell (eds), *Greek Papyri in the British Museum* (London, 1893–1917) |
| *P.Lugd. Bat. VI* | B. A. van Groningen (ed.), *A Family – Archive from Tebtunis* (*P. Fam. Tebt.*) (Leiden, 1950) |
| *P.Mich.* | C.C. Edgar, A.E.R. Boak, H.C. Youtie *et al.* (eds), *Michigan Papyri* (Ann Arbor, 1931–82) |
| *P.Oxy.* | B.P. Grenfell, A.S. Hunt *et al.* (eds), *The Oxyrhynchus Papyri* (London, 1898–) |

| | |
|---|---|
| *P.Panop. Beatty* | T.C. Skeat (ed.), *Papyri from Panopolis in the Chester Beatty Library, Dublin* (Dublin, 1964) |
| *P.Petaus* | W. Hagedorn, D. Hagedorn, C.C. Youtie and H.C. Youtie (eds), *Das Archiv des Petaus* (Köln/Opladen, 1969) |
| *P.Ryl.* | A.S. Hunt, J. de M. Johnson, V. Martin and C.H. Roberts (eds), *Catalogue of the Greek Papyri in the John Rylands Library, Manchester* (Manchester, 1911–52) |
| *P.Vindob.* | Papyri in the Papyrussammlung der Österreichischen Nationalbibliothek zu Wien, cited by inventory number |
| *PBSR* | *Papers of the British School at Rome* |
| Peter | H.W.G. Peter (ed.), *Historicorum Romanorum Reliquiae* I², II (Leipzig, 1906–14) |
| *PIR* | E. Klebs and H. Dessau (eds), *Prosopographia Imperii Romani Saeculi I, II, III* (Berlin, 1897–8; 2nd ed. by E. Groag and A. Stein, Berlin, 1933) |
| *PLRE* | A.H.M. Jones, J.R. Martindale, and J. Morris (eds), *The Prosopography of the Later Roman Empire*, Vol. I (Oxford, 1971) |
| *PSI* | G. Vitelli, M. Norsa *et al.* (eds), *Papiri greci e latini* (Pubblicazioni della Società Italiana per la ricerca dei papiri greci e latini in Egitto) (Firenze, 1912–) |
| *RE* | A. Pauly, G. Wissowa and W. Kroll (eds), *Real-Encyclopädie der Klassischen Altertumswissenschaft* (Stuttgart, 1893–) (*Suppl. = Supplement*) |
| *REL* | *Revue des Études Latines* |
| *RIB* | R.G. Collingwood and R.P. Wright (eds), *The Roman Inscriptions of Britain* Vol. I. The Inscriptions on Stone (Oxford, 1965) |
| *RIU* | L. Barkóczi, A.S. Burger, F. Fülep, A. Mócsy and S. Soproni, *Die römischen Inschriften Ungarns* (Budapest/Bonn, 1972–90) |
| *SB* | F. Preisigke *et al.* (eds), *Sammelbuch griechischer Urkunden aus Aegypten* (Strassburg, etc. 1915–) |
| *SEG* | *Supplementum Epigraphicum Graecum* |
| SHA | Scriptores Historiae Augustae |
| *Stud. Pal.* | C. Wessely, N. Reich and T. Hopfner (eds), *Studien zur Palaeographie und Papyruskunde* (Leipzig, 1901–24; Amsterdam, 1974) |
| *Tab. Vindol. I* | A.K. Bowman and J.D. Thomas (eds), *Vindolanda: the Latin Writing-Tablets*, Britannia Monograph 4 (London, 1983) |
| *Tab. Vindol. II* | A.K. Bowman and J.D. Thomas (eds), *The Vindolanda Writing-Tablets (Tabulae Vindolandenses II)* (London, 1994) |
| *ZPE* | *Zeitschrift für Papyrologie und Epigraphik* |

# 1

# INTRODUCTION
## The other side of the hill

How did Roman military and political intelligence work? How effective was its contribution to Roman operations in the field? How was it linked to the formation of frontier policies? How did its structures develop and change? How good was it? These questions appear never to have been posed and certainly in the last fifty years or so there has been no systematic examination of the subject. It is an important one in the history of military affairs and its neglect seems inexplicable.

The point at which we start is a standard, training-manual, definition of what forms the basis of military intelligence: 'that which is accepted as fact, based on all available information about an actual or potential enemy or area of operations'. It is a definition which we find useful and it forms the basis of much of this book. Behind it lies the perhaps obvious truism that without intelligence, an armed force, regardless of its size, operates with a much reduced hope of success. At all periods military strength and the maintenance of power in defensive and offensive situations have depended to varying degrees on a regular flow of intelligence provided by a wide variety of agencies and sources. The Romans, one would think, were no different in their intelligence needs.

## THE EVIDENCE

Our survey of Roman military and political intelligence, covering some six centuries from the Second Punic War to the battle of Adrianople, discusses two main types of evidence – literary and epigraphic. The literary side necessarily tends to be concentrated around information derived for the most part from historians who themselves had had practical experience in the field. Practical experience was considered in antiquity a prime qualification for a historian (which partly accounts for the habit of memoir-writing of leading commanders): the great second-century BC Greek historian Polybius in a critique of his predecessor Timaeus emphasized the value of experience for the insights it gives.[1] The most important writers who meet the criterion are Caesar, Tacitus, Dio Cassius, Ammianus Marcellinus and, beyond the limits of our period, Procopius. In many other writers, of course, there is useful information to be found, as there is from the compilers of military handbooks. The reason for the low profile here normally accorded to writers such as Livy (except where he is usefully reflecting a better-qualified source such as Polybius) is precisely that of lack of personal experience, which can lead, in the case of the treatment of many episodes, to either a muddled approach or an over-simplified one. For detailed work on intelligence, this lack will vitiate much of the value of what is transmitted.

While experience is perhaps the most important virtue in the writers under examination, it is equally important to be aware of the pressures on them of literary convention: historiography in antiquity was an art, not a science. The direct consequence of such a convention is that many expressions or items of vocabulary or even circumstantial details that are specifically technical in their application are omitted, or else their presentation is modified to fit the expectations of their cultivated, serious, audience. It is not difficult to give an example of the process: in an article on Caesar's methods of literary presentation,[2] Pelling points out that there is strong evidence that Caesar made considerable simplifications to topography in order to help his audience to follow more easily the essential lines of the events as they unfolded. In itself this is not seriously objectionable. Topography of course forms a central aspect of intelligence; it is also a technical one. Thus, if it should be simplified, there is no reason to doubt that other technical aspects will be similarly diluted. Further, there is no reason to limit this process to Caesar alone – it is clearly applicable to all. Discussing Caesar's campaign against Ariovistus, Pelling goes further: 'the strategy of a campaign, the course of the fighting and the nature of the terrain may all have been more complex than Caesar's language would suggest; and these complications may have led both generals to act (or to allow their enemy to act) in ways which we find hard to understand'. Again, this point can easily be applied to all the historians. The intellectual and physical difficulties of selecting the important moments, shaping the material and then writing down an ordered account of confusing action, should not be underestimated. In spite of the problems, there is still glamour and excitement to be found in the historical evidence and much detail on the workings of intelligence can be extracted from it.

The four main writers who meet Polybius' criterion of experience need little introduction here, apart from a note on the relevance of their experience to our study. In the first century BC, most of Caesar's career was inextricably tied up with the exploitation of military power for political ends but his knowledge of intelligence processes and the use he made of them is presented with a care and clarity that makes his *Commentarii* virtually a textbook of intelligence practice. His continuator Hirtius had the benefit of Caesar's reports and notes, which make his material almost equally valuable as a source. The unknown authors of the rest of what is called 'the Caesarian corpus' have at least the advantage of eye-witness participation, though they lacked the actual entrée to Caesar's headquarters itself. As for the second author, Tacitus, who wrote one hundred and fifty years after Caesar, it seems likely that, in the early part of his career,

he served as a *tribunus laticlavius* (a junior officer post for a man starting a senatorial career) and after his consulship in AD 97 was perhaps governor of one
of the Germanies. Tacitus qualifies under this section's heading not only by
reason of his personal experience but also by his evident application of it in his
access to the reports of governors and commanders submitted to the Senate, to
actual leading participants in military action (and their families), as well as to
first-hand historical-ethnographical material such as the elder Pliny's *German
Wars*.[3] On occasion Tacitus' evidence on intelligence matters is very valuable –
hence his prominence as a contributor to this study. Mommsen's old canard
about his being the most unmilitary of historians needs to be discarded in the
context. The third writer under this rubric is the third-century historian Dio
Cassius. He was consul twice – his second tenure, in AD 229, was shared with
the emperor himself – and in the final stages of his career, after the bulk of his
history had been completed, he was one of the most influential men in the
empire and was chosen to govern the key frontier province of Upper Pannonia.
It is clear that he was familiar with the ways of the imperial court and the
administration of the empire even before then and the immense and valuable
detail that his history displays in the areas of diplomacy, external relations,
frontier policy and strategic issues (in spite of the fragmentary state of the text)
suggests considerable first-hand knowledge.[4] In the fourth century AD,
Ammianus Marcellinus served as a *protector domesticus* (imperial guardsman) during
the active part of his military career, when he had access at various headquarters to the reception of intelligence and the implementation of planning
that resulted from that intelligence. An important feature of his career was actual
participation in many aspects of intelligence work. It is clear too that in the
later part of his career, after he had left the army, he maintained contacts with
senior military figures.[5]

Within the literary field there are a number of further authors who possess
the requisite criterion of personal experience. Polybius is one but he is something of a disappointment despite his long-standing close association with Scipio
Aemilianus and his reputation in modern critics' eyes as the best military historian of the middle Republic. He may have been present with Scipio Aemilianus
at Carthage in 146 BC and at Numantia in 133 but the contribution that such
detailed experience could have made to the present study is negligible. He
exhibits a marked aversion to the technical (except in one or two cases where
he does show real interest in specialized, applied, technical matters): he is much
more interested in the social, political and diplomatic aspects of warfare where
he shows himself to good advantage. Nevertheless it is what little he does give
us, either directly where his work survives, or through the mediation of Livy,
which allows us to begin the present study with the outbreak of the Second
Punic War.[6] A substantial amount of material of exceptional interest unexpectedly occurs in the letters of the very unmilitary figure of Cicero: in particular
one should note his clear description and analysis of the different kinds of information that came into his headquarters during his successful governorship of

Cilicia in 51–50 BC. Sallust is another in this category but in general terms his military material is thin and subordinate, not unexpectedly, to the theme of corruption weakening the fabric of Roman achievement. But the *Jugurthine War* does have the advantage that Sallust was active as the propraetorian governor of a closely relevant area in Africa and so should have been well informed about climate and geography. One would expect Velleius Paterculus, with an extensive military background acquired in service under Augustus and Tiberius, to have an important contribution to make to our knowledge but apart from a few vague generalities, such as could be made by any armchair historian, he is uninformative and disappointing on intelligence. The Jewish historian Flavius Josephus, one would think, would have had some valuable relevant material in the area, since he had experience as a commander on one side and adviser on the other in the Jewish revolt of AD 66–70, quite different from any other category of historian. He is however hampered by a serious lack of precision in this side of his work, as of course in others. Though there are items of value, they are less numerous than they should be. Only that part of his work which involves personal experience is surveyed here, i.e. *Jewish War III* onwards. Frontinus had considerable practical experience of field operations, acquired during his governorship of Britain in the mid-70s and a campaign against the Silures of southern Wales. He is best known for his technical treatise on aqueducts; his surviving work on military matters, the *Stratagems*, preserves none of his own war experience. It is no more than a rather simple compendium of historical *exempla* of lateral thinking, mostly drawn from the classical age of Greece, Alexander's campaigns and the early and middle Roman Republican period. Only a small handful of these could be called contemporary or relevant and they are mainly obsequious references to the emperor Domitian's recent actions on the frontiers; they contain practically no usable information on intelligence. Flavius Arrianus (Arrian) was Hadrian's governor of Cappadocia in Asia Minor who in AD 135 successfully beat off an attack by the Alani upon his province, as well as being a prolific writer and historian (he is our principal source for the life of Alexander the Great). Two of his minor works provide details of considerable interest for our subject: his *Ektaxis kata Alanon* (*Deployment against the Alani*) is a fragment which describes his deployment of the province's army to meet the Alani in battle; and his *Periplous Euxeinou Pontou* (*Circumnavigation of the Black Sea*) is a Greek literary version of a Latin dispatch to Hadrian describing his initial inspection-tour of Cappadocia's defences, together with an itinerary for a proposed tour of the Black Sea by the emperor. Despite the literary pretensions of these works, both are firmly grounded in real activities carried out by the author as part of his duties and so give us an invaluable insight into the military side of a Roman governor's work.

Much less literary are the handbooks. Onasander's *Strategikos* (*Art of Generalship*), with its introduction of a moral element into the conduct of warfare, is a manual written in the mid-first century AD. It reads like a stylishly elaborated checklist and contains a selective unspecific amalgam of past and present practices.

On intelligence, its material is simple but sensible but it does not deal with structural matters. It makes no claim to completeness, either. Much more strikingly perceptive and commonsense is the fourth-century AD *Epitome De Re Militari* (*Epitome of Military Science*) compiled by Flavius Vegetius, which shows intelligence as a basic requirement of any campaigner and illustrates the use of it in Roman enterprises by laying emphasis on its universal applicability. It is difficult to overestimate the value of this work for showing the practical importance of intelligence but its lack of specific details of intelligence organization is a severe limitation. There is a short section dealing with intelligence-gatherers in the anonymous Byzantine manual *Peri strategikes* (*On Strategy*), generally ascribed to the sixth century (although recent work has suggested a later date, up to the tenth century, for all or part of it). This work reflects past and present experience and has much of the flavour of the practical to recommend it, in spite of its abbreviated nature.[7]

The physical evidence is traced more concretely through the substantial epigraphic material and papyrus fragments, though this relates almost entirely to the period of the Principate. The inscriptions and papyri cover not only matters of organization that concern bodies involved in collecting intelligence but also their locations and, occasionally, the length of time these bodies were stationed at a place. That continuity of operation is instructive, since it shows that the Romans came to feel that long-term familiarity with an area and its inhabitants was a necessary qualification for useful intelligence. Some of this material even allows one to reach down to the level of an individual's operational activity and is extremely interesting for this feature. Taken in combination with recent work on the duties and activities of other kinds of officials, it now seems possible to define the links between intelligence-collecting bodies with the headquarters of provincial governors in many areas and the reporting and archival structures that supported the system; and so the way towards establishing how a response to a threat was formulated can also be reached.

Similar to the inscriptions are the official lists which were compiled by government agencies for a variety of reasons at various dates. Best-known of these lists are the strip-maps and lists of staging-posts known as *Itineraria*, which preserve occasional records of the existence of other places where permanent intelligence-gathering personnel were stationed. They also acted as guides to the road and sea distances between towns, settlements and facilities that could be used for civil and military purposes, as for example that preserved in Arrian's *Circumnavigation of the Black Sea* (*Periplous Euxeinou Pontou*), which describes the rim of the Black Sea in geographic, military and strategic terms for the emperor Hadrian. Besides this, there are the better-known *Peutinger Table* (*Tabula Peutingeriana*) (see Plate 4) and *Antonine Itinerary* (*Itinerarium Antoninianum*). Information from the *Itineraria* is supported and supplemented by the controversial list of official and military appointments called the *Notitia Dignitatum* (see Plate 11) – it was compiled around AD 400 and is the last formal or semi-official document of the Roman world to reveal the existence of well-defined bodies of intelligence-gatherers. Whatever its shortcomings and incompletenesses and intractability, the *Notitia* does at least give some indications of possible deployments of these troops.

## THE INTELLIGENCE PROCESS

In ancient warfare where sophisticated weaponry of mass destruction and sophisticated means of communication are absent, the contact between combatants is a great deal closer than in modern conventional warfare. While that may seem perhaps another obvious point, it has an influence on the analysis of strategic and tactical intelligence that follows. In this context, we have attempted to define strategic intelligence as the analysis of everything that happens before the arrival at the battlefield and this would include any long-term information that would influence the conduct of a whole campaign, the capacity of an enemy to wage war and his intention to do so. Tactical intelligence would take over at the point where the two sides are nearly in sight of each other and includes short-term material influencing the choice of a battlefield, the positions taken up on that battlefield and the conduct of the fighting itself. This convention is adopted in our text for analytic purposes but it must be stressed that in practice the two shade off into each other and are treated as such in the later chapters.

An army in the field vitally needs intelligence in order to be able to build up a picture of its own situation and operations in relation to those of its opponents. A single piece of information may be useful to a commander but its value is much improved if it is subjected to tests of its accuracy, mainly by comparing and collating it with other relevant information that has already been acquired: it requires a context. That context is provided first by a flow of information into a headquarters and second by a spread of sources from which information is derived. Only where information has been processed in these areas does it become intelligence. Intelligence is not a fixed unchanging entity – its shape and relevance change as it is modified by successive inputs of information. This constant modification is essential to a commander as he comes to grips with the enemy. He must know as much as he can about all aspects of his enemy in order to be prepared for defence or attack, and indeed must be able to imagine himself into his enemy's thought-processes. If he knows what his opponents are capable of doing, he can avoid making unnecessary concessions and even mistakes and will be able to counter any moves they may make to prevent him from fulfilling his own intentions and instructions. His responses will require accurate knowledge.

Vegetius' manual shows this quite clearly. In a passage on the background requirements for the planning of operations, he alludes to the kind of material needed for the briefings that form part of the process. First, enemy strengths and weaknesses, which will dictate the selection of battleground, tactics and timing; then food supplies; then the nature of the opposition's leadership and the quality of its manpower (*Epitome of Military Science* III 9). Considerable emphasis is placed on the necessity for detailed prior reconnaissance of the terrain over which progress to the battlefield takes place as well as of the battle-field itself in the light of the criteria mentioned above. All this must be a continuous process checked against information coming in from as wide a spread of sources as possible (*Epitome of Military Science* III 6). Vegetius stresses that knowledge of the enemy, his *modus operandi* and his daily routines is an indis-pensable adjunct to the skill and experience of the commander in the field (*Epitome of Military Science* IV 27). Tacitus provides an illustrative example: he confirms the drift of Vegetius' requirements in a well-known passage dealing with the military ineptitude of Vitellius, whose ignorance of the need for intel-ligence (among other things) rendered him more than usually incompetent (*Histories* III 56) – but the point is made through an essentially negative presen-tation. Sallust shows the positive aspect in his favourable picture of the great commander C. Marius at the opening of his African command in 107 BC: Marius is portrayed as paying extremely close attention to a whole range of intelligence issues before re-starting the Jugurthine War.[8] It may be a general-ized or conventional picture but it accurately sums up what is required of a commander who is balancing the enemy's aims and point of view with his own.

Of course limitations to such an ideal situation have to exist in the reality of military operations (and therefore in the transmitted versions of the his-torians), since the availability of the raw information that feeds the intelligence cycle fluctuates widely and forces a commander to base decisions on guesses that supplement the gaps in his knowledge. As Wellington put it, 'All the busi-ness of war, and indeed all the business of life, is to endeavour to find out what you don't know by what you do; that's what I called "guessing what was at the other side of the hill".' The gaps in knowledge must thus be filled by informed speculation, based on previous intelligence plus likelihood or past experience. But since such gaps will always exist, the duty of the intelligence staff is to work continuously to reduce them to a minimum.

Modern military training manuals use a five-point diagram to clarify the way information is turned into intelligence and to illustrate what they term the intelligence cycle. While it may be a simplified and conventionalized way of presenting the process, it is by no means simplistic, since it can be devel-oped into a very complex picture indeed. In its easy-to-follow form it looks like this:

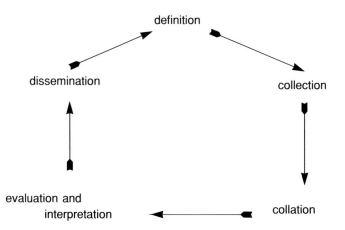

Presentation in this manner allows one to see how the successive stages in the process influence and depend on each other. Definition of the problem and collection of information need no comment but the others may. Evaluation of intelligence material and its interpretation are impossible without collation with other material coming in or with pre-existing information already in the hands of a staff. Then dissemination is vitally important, since without intelligence that is relevant and opportune and timely to use in the field, a force can be almost ineffective: intelligence may be first class but if it is not disseminated to those who need to use it, it is wasted. Operating with knowledge allows a force to collect additional and more appropriate information, so further refining and sharpening the definition of the task in hand and the approach to it.

It is not easy to find evidence in the Roman historians we survey here for the essential stages in the intelligence cycle between collection and any resultant action: there are only a few passages that point to their existence. Caesar shows an evaluation and redefinition process taking place during the campaign against Ambiorix in 52 BC. Here, working with the certainty that Ambiorix would not fight immediately, he carried out a detailed review of all the relevant back-ground and present circumstances which could indicate where next to apply military and diplomatic pressure. That review is a good example of strategic policy analysis based on intelligence (*Gallic War* VI 5.3ff.). Ammianus too describes a meeting where interpretation was discussed at length. It followed the receipt in Amida in AD 357 of an allusive quasi-cryptographic message from Roman negotiators at the Persian court warning of the massive preparations being made for invasion of the eastern Roman provinces. This formed the basis for planning new responses to the threat (XVIII 6.17ff.). The disastrous defeat the Romans sustained at the hands of the Goths at Adrianople in 378 can probably be attributed to a failure in one of these intermediate stages: the information that Gothic infantry in the immediate area of Adrianople was unsupported by the cavalry was correct but it would certainly have been known from previous experience that the Gothic cavalry would only be away for a short period; thus the Roman attack, to be successful, had to be carried out within a very short time-frame. It was not (Ammianus XXXI 12.12). These examples all illustrate that the intermediate stages in the intelligence cycle are usually passed over in our literary sources. The reason for it is possibly because of their self-evident technical nature but more probably because of the processes of selection and editing either by the historian himself (if he is using a primary source), or by his predecessors (if he is relying on secondary material). Those processes mean that all the cloud of unfocused information that may exist during the cycle in the field is trimmed to the relevant essential elements in the finished text.

## THE OPERATION AND ORGANIZATION OF MILITARY INTELLIGENCE

The basic methods by which Rome acquired both strategic and tactical intelligence remained fairly constant throughout the period under consideration. They were indeed methods which would have been familiar both to Alexander the Great and to any subsequent ruler or general up to the mid-nineteenth century. Only with the advent of the railway, the telegraph and the balloon during the American Civil War did the essential nature of military intelligence (as of course of warfare itself) begin to change; in our own century, the field has been further transformed by the development of wireless telegraphy and aerial and satellite photography, radar and sophisticated imaging processes.

Strategic intelligence, collected in anticipation of hostilities and during them, has always been obtained through a variety of means, both active and passive: diplomacy, especially with client princes, and espionage (the two are closely linked), the use by the military of frontier forts and markets as listening posts, occasional military expeditions into unknown territory; the dissemination of disinformation to induce the enemy to take a desired course of action; and more passively, informal contacts with individual members of the opposing forces, sheer good luck, captured documents and even drawing the right conclusions from not being able to obtain intelligence at all.

Likewise, tactical intelligence, once hostilities have broken out, always required the exploitation of as many different types of collectors as possible, both Roman and non-Roman. These included troops operating in a reconnaissance role immediately ahead of a force in the field, normally referred to in our sources as *procursatores* (or close variants). There were also bodies of scouting troops operating further afield, the *exploratores*, who are attested by a sufficiently substantial body of literary and epigraphic evidence to allow the range of their activities to be examined in some detail. In addition, there were more covert operators, undercover agents known as *speculatores*, who do not have independent inscriptional evidence, for reasons to be discussed later (note however that the word *kataskopoi* and its variants used in the Greek sources covers the work of *procursatores*, *exploratores* and *speculatores*). Very important but quite unquantifiable, is autopsy, the practice of bolder (or more foolish) Roman generals to go and see for themselves. On the fixed frontiers of the Principate some forts were provided, where necessary, with advance watch- and signal-towers to give early warning of a hostile attack. All these standard means of obtaining battlefield information were further supplemented by some ingenious approaches to particular problems. Equally valuable, however, were the non-Roman sources whose use is widely attested. They included prisoners (both prisoners of war and kidnapped civilians), refugees and their military counterparts, deserters and local informers (*indices*). The much less definite *rumor* or *fama* (unsubstantiated rumour) are not really sources but in warfare where accurate identification of the origin of a piece of information is not always practicable, they can acquire some solid standing in certain circumstances.

The very wide array of methods and agencies used by the Romans for collecting intelligence of both a strategic and tactical nature shows quite clearly that any method was good enough provided it could be exploited to get the information needed. The variety employed also facilitated the comparison and collation of information which we have already noted as being essential to the proper operation of the intelligence cycle. Most of these methods and agencies were in use throughout our period but that is not to say that they were always used in exactly the same way or with the same efficiency. Indeed, over the six centuries this study covers, the organization and infrastructure of intelligence-gathering underwent profound change, mostly in direct response to the enormous changes in political and military administration experienced by the Roman world, not least the concentration of supreme command in the hands of one man.

On the strategic side, embassies sent out by the Republican Senate for purposes of investigation or negotiation had a different composition, different powers and different aims from those sent out by the emperors. Imperial governors were more constrained than their Republican predecessors in what they could do, whilst the ossification of Rome's frontiers under the Principate created entirely new problems in and approaches to obtaining and processing intelligence; and the administrative reorganization of the Late Empire took responsibility for these tasks out of the hands of the governors altogether and gave it to purely military officials, some of them of the same racial or ethnic origins as the enemy they faced.

On the tactical side, the Second Punic War saw very little or very poor use of scouting until Scipio Africanus and other Roman commanders learned from the most painful experiences at Hannibal's hands; a century and a half later, Caesar's brilliant handling of intelligence work (admittedly by his own account) was the product not just of his genius but also of the development of a much greater level of professionalism in the Roman army in the intervening period. Augustus' eventual establishment of a truly professional army paved the way for the emergence of specialist, if temporary, campaign scouting units, and later even of permanent local units for patrolling the frontiers. Finally, the great improvement in the number and quality of the Roman cavalry arm in the Late Empire made possible still more efficient scouting and an even more rapid response to intelligence as it was delivered.

The study which follows will consider in detail both the operation of the intelligence-acquisition methods and agencies employed by the Romans and the ways in which their organization and exploitation changed between the late third century BC and the late fourth century AD. In this way we hope finally to be able to make a guess at what was at the other side of the hill and provide tentative answers to the questions with which we began.

# 2

# THE HOSTILE HORIZON
## Strategic intelligence

### DEFINITIONS AND SCOPE

Strategic intelligence aims at acquiring long-range military information for a commander, information that affects the conduct and direction of a whole campaign in a region or theatre of war; and in an environment where the frontiers are fixed, strategic intelligence serves to provide the basis for the long-term planning and management of resources deployed on frontier defence. Its scope does however extend beyond the purview of the purely military. In his attempt to wage war effectively in offensive or defensive conditions, a commander in the field or a provincial governor must have a knowledge of the enemy that extends beyond the military into the social, political and economic structures that condition the way his opponents will act in the field.

The scope of strategic intelligence is the subject of precisely defined approaches in sections of Caesar and Ammianus. Both authors in these passages exhibit a strikingly comprehensive understanding of the need for such material and of its range. Even so, a caveat should be entered: the literary sources as a whole on strategic intelligence are demonstrably thin, a fact which lends weight to an observation made by Millar that the literary sources are oriented less towards strategic interests than towards the tactical.[1] There are good reasons for the thinness: strategic matters are more remote and less immediately obvious in their effects on the outcome of the drama of battles and sieges; they are also often technical matters and thus to be consciously avoided in the canons of literary historiography. There is a further reason, with more serious connotations. The presentation of the literary evidence as a whole strongly suggests that the Romans did not usually initiate action in response to strategic intelligence, such as would for instance be demonstrated by pre-emptive strikes against an enemy. The majority of cases show the Romans taking action only in response to incidents, that is, after they have occurred. The phenomenon is widespread throughout the history of the Republic and Principate; the conclusion to be drawn from it seems to be that a deeply ingrained belief existed that Roman forces were quite adequate to deal with any military problem that might occur: the occasional battle might be lost but the war would inevitably be won.

We can trace for example in the Principate only one properly documented series of actions based on strategic intelligence that can be termed pre-emptive: in AD 62 Nero's general Domitius Corbulo received positive information about Parthian plans to expel the Roman nominee from the throne of Armenia and to attack Syria; he immediately sent two legions to Tigranocerta before any serious incident could take place and took extensive emergency measures to strengthen the Euphrates frontier (Tacitus *Annals* XV 3). The Roman attitude can be documented through examination of what evidence we possess for the workings of strategic intelligence-collection processes, where it will become obvious that the present authors' division of the evidence into active collection and passive collection shows the latter category largely predominant. That passivity however comes to an end with the crises of the later second century, when the inevitable winning of wars receded from the Romans' grasp. From then on, to at least the end of the fourth century, intelligence was collected much more actively and aggressively.

The parameters given by Caesar can be found in an analysis of the strategic information he needed for background planning leading up to the invasion of Britain in 55 BC: the geography, the harbours, the approaches and the nature of the inhabitants – information, then, on levels that were both physical and psychological. This rather wide and loosely defined initial list was further clar-ified when he brought in people who conducted trading activities across the Channel. He asked them about the geographical extent of the island, the ethnic divisions, size of tribal populations, techniques of war, social and political insti-tutions and the location of harbours suitable for substantial numbers of ships (*Gallic War* IV 20.2–4; Suetonius, *Julius Caesar* 58.1). These requirements cover just about every aspect that could conceivably need reporting on and, if they could be fulfilled, detailed information about all of them would represent an ideal situation. From his subjects Caesar got little satisfactory response. He there-fore sent a tribune, C. Volusenus, to find out the answers to his questions but Volusenus failed to land and discovered almost nothing. Caesar sailed anyway but his landing in Britain was only barely successful (*Gallic War* IV 21–6). There is a distinct gap in the account between the expert statement of aims and needs and the surprising lack of effective acquisition of intelligence to meet them. Polybius would be very unhappy with Caesar's opportunism and dangerous risk-taking: he makes it clear that a really experienced and responsible general (in his case, Hannibal) simply does not move into a region which he knows next to nothing about without having first obtained thorough and detailed geographi-cal, political and social intelligence (Polybius III 48; cf. in particular Vegetius *Epitome of Military Science* III 6 init.).

A more psychological approach to the understanding of opponents emerges from Caesar's treatment of a theme mentioned by Vegetius. Vegetius notes that habit and routine are and must be, identifiable in a hostile force and that knowledge of them is very helpful if not essential in the planning process (*Epitome of Military Science* III 6 fin.; IV 27; cf. also Procopius *Wars* II 18.17). His observation refers principally to tactical contexts; Caesar however sees habit and routine in much more of a strategic context in those sections of his work where he discusses the mental and emotional make-up of, particularly, the Gauls (*Gallic War* III 19.6; IV 5.1–3; VI 11.2–5; VII 42.2; cf. *Civil War* III 59.3; 79.6) but also, to a degree, of the Germans (*Gallic War* VI 21ff.). He indicates those areas of weakness he thinks can be exploited to Roman advantage because they will have important effects on the capacity of the tribesmen to organize and fight – Gallic volatility and consequent unreliability; their boastfulness; their lack of resilience after a setback; the factional conflicts visible in all levels of their society. The weaknesses are of course seen from a Roman point of view. Features of this type may have politico-cultural origins or have been inculcated by tribal social and military discipline but whatever their source, awareness of them would contribute to the background fund of knowledge about the enemy which must be used for the successful development of strategic intelligence. To some extent, as Caesar's material displays, this knowledge can be simplified by a process of ethnic stereotyping. If a commander and his intelligence staff are, as we noted earlier, to be able to put themselves into the enemy's position in order to see what damage can be done to their own side and if the *modus operandi* and predispositions of the enemy to act in certain ways are to be exploited, then ethnic and other stereotyping processes (and even comments on particular individuals as exhibiting national traits) are useful: they help in the formation of an analytic appraisal and may provide a framework on which to hang further pertinent information. Tacitus expresses the idea in a memorable epigrammatic formulation applied (rather exaggeratedly) to an operation of Germanicus': 'all of this had been identified by [Germanicus] Caesar: he knew the plans, the positions, the obvious and the covert, and was to turn his opponents' stratagems to their own ruin' (*nihil ex his Caesari incognitum: consilia, locos, prompta, occulta noverat, astusque hostium in perniciem ipsis vertebat*) (*Annals* II 20.1). Polybius too notes the need to probe for the weaknesses of one's opponent but in his case he lays less emphasis on the physical aspects and more on the psychological and moral defects of the enemy leadership. Those are the weaknesses which lead to mistakes being made by an opponent during a campaign and the efficient and imaginative commander can turn them to his own advantage (Polybius III 81).

The most detailed statement found in Ammianus on the kind of information that should be covered by strategic intelligence puts less emphasis on the sociopolitical information and more on the purely military – this in an account of the defection to Persia in AD 359 of a former senior government official with important information, the *apparitor* Antoninus. By dint of careful enquiries and analysis of his information, this official had been able to arm himself before his departure with details of unit manpower figures, designations, locations, timings for operations, as well as comprehensive material on weapon and stores supplies and the resupply situation (XVIII 5.1). Here again is a thorough exposition of the needs that strategic intelligence is designed to fill. Such material is clearly of enormous value to an enemy: its worth to the Persians in this particular case was demonstrated by a special reception for the defector, an immediate grant of the insignia of high social status and the conferral of the right to dine with the king and to advise him (XVIII 5.6) – and the advice was used (XVIII 7.10f.; XIX 1.3). Interesting too in this case is the fact that before he had joined the service of the government, he had been a merchant who had travelled widely throughout the East – and across the border, because he was already known to the local Persian satrap before his defection (XVIII 5.3). His knowledge therefore of local sympathies, geographical detail and wider economic issues, quite apart from military information, would have been extensive – and useful.

We are fortunate in possessing a reasonably full example of how the principles that the strategic intelligence requirements just mentioned involved could be applied in practice. A complementary and detailed passage in Polybius traces the steps taken by P. Cornelius Scipio (the future Africanus) in planning the campaign of 210/209 BC that led ultimately to the surprise capture of Nova Carthago (Cartagena) in Spain (X 6.11–9.1). This striking passage is the earliest such formulation that we possess (it is one of the very few from the period of the Republic) and underlines the spectacular originality of Scipio in the Republican military context. Polybius, it will be remembered, was imbued with the Scipionic tradition through his long association with the family.

Immediately on taking up his command in Spain, Scipio launched a thorough examination of the complicated strategic issues that would influence the war in Spain and thus the planning of his campaign: these covered the diplomatic relations between Spanish tribes and the Romans or the Carthaginians; then the military dispositions and internal problems of the Carthaginians. Polybius' account does not give the actual sources for the information, apart from saying that Scipio explored all avenues to gain it. Arising out of this careful survey emerged the question of whether he should pick off each of the three widely separated Carthaginian armies one at a time. But then the importance of Nova Carthago started to become prominent: this place was the centre for the Carthaginian administration, war *matériel* and communications and Scipio decided on a bold and imaginatively conceived strike against it. And the action was possible, given that no Carthaginian force of any size was within ten days' march of it.

Once the strategic aim of capturing Nova Carthago had been established, Scipio then moved on to investigate more tactical aspects of intelligence that would affect the implementation of his strategic plan – the town's large population was considered, the small number of Carthaginian defenders, the local topography and in particular the characteristics of the encircling tidal lagoon; information on the lagoon came from local fishermen. Even escape routes were worked out, in the event of a failure.

Though incomplete, Polybius' picture is a model of the intelligence processes that underpin the creation of a strategic plan. The rarity has been noted but it illustrates particularly well many of the issues that need to be taken into account when the structure of a campaign is being set up. When these issues are combined with those detailed by Caesar and Ammianus, a framework for strategic intelligence becomes clearer.

All these cases cover the prime requisites. As an aside, however, it should be observed that the acquisition of strategic intelligence is an exercise which must go on all the time, even in peacetime. For the purpose, it does not matter whether a local commander is present or absent for some reason, as can be gathered from the instructions left behind for T. Labienus by Caesar during the second invasion of Britain: Labienus among other things was ordered to continue close monitoring of the situation in Gaul, a wide-ranging and demanding instruction given the complexity of intra-Gallic politics and the Gauls' relationships with the Romans and the volatile nature of their military alliances (*Gallic War* V 8.1). The problems for a field commander or provincial governor start when information that fulfils these intelligence requisites needs to be translated into reaction.

# THE ACQUISITION OF STRATEGIC INTELLIGENCE

The methods used by the Romans to acquire strategic intelligence were understandably as diverse as the intelligence sources themselves: they also reflect the very wide range of activity within which the administration and exploitation of strategic intelligence took place. For the purposes of discussion and for qualifying and exemplifying the preceding introductory material, we divide the sources and methods into active and passive areas. It is important to remember that the division between them is arbitrary, because in actual operations they are to a great extent mutually interdependent, where one contributes to or modifies the other. The Roman side of this required the active organization of manpower to collect the information that was needed and involved the penetration of hostile environments by Romans or Roman agents in a variety of guises; it also involved the active encouragement of people 'on the other side' to provide information. The process applied equally to campaign-type situations and to more static ones on the fixed frontiers.

## Active methods

### Diplomacy and espionage

Perhaps, therefore, the place where strategic intelligence begins is with diplomacy. In modern states the processes of diplomacy still retain overtones of espionage and the Romans were no different in finding and exploiting opportunities to get their own side into the midst of the opposition with immunity on the pretexts of negotiation or investigation. At every period in Rome's history, there was a constant flow of diplomatic envoys from peoples across the frontiers, wherever the frontiers were conceived to be; the level at which they negotiated varied of course but the fact is that the contacts were omnipresent. At what we call 'national' level, the Senate during the period of the Republic and the imperial court under the emperors received embassies made up of envoys of high rank from all kinds of states and peoples and sent envoys out in their turn. This was also done throughout the Roman period by individual Roman governors or other officials acting as the representatives of Senate or emperor. The diplomatic process at this level almost by convention involves the trading and acquisition of information between both sets of negotiators as a *quid pro quo* and the information that was gained formed part of the background store of strategic intelligence. Accompanying individuals or groups on embassies came attendants and support staff and all of them possessed information and were capable of discovering information. It is for this reason that in a section on embassies, the Byzantine manual *On Strategy* suggests that even the attendants of foreign negotiators should be kept under surveillance in order to avoid their being able to wander about asking questions or just looking so as to gain information (43.2; cf. Livy XXX 4.1–3; Procopius *Wars* VIII 15.20). Many of the individual cases we examine concentrate on exemplifying the strategic intelligence component that inevitably accompanies diplomatic negotiations. But espionage is a logical adjunct to the process: it ensures the penetration of potentially hostile activity by personnel who have been specifically instructed to acquire information.

While the active acquisition of intelligence through Roman agencies was prosecuted vigorously in all periods, much the same could be said of the simultaneous complementary systematic exploitation of sources of intelligence that were non-Roman. Just as in the case of the Roman sources, all levels of source from the client kings down to deserters were used for the purpose. It goes without saying that the non-Roman sources effectively allowed a substantial extension to the Roman ones in terms of manpower and range of operations. Range of operations was an important issue in that in some areas it would clearly have been impossible to infiltrate Romans or their agents – hence one of the tangible benefits of careful diplomacy not only at the level of external leaders but also with individuals lower down in their hierarchies.

There are numbers of cases from all periods that can be adduced in support and that illustrate the conduct of Roman embassies in probing for strategic intelligence. When, for example, Caesar himself entered direct negotiations with Ariovistus in 58 BC over the advance of the Helvetii into Gaul, the face-to-face interviews nearly ended in fighting; but on Ariovistus' unexpected suggestion next day that discussions should continue, Caesar realized that if Roman officers took part they would not be safe, so he sent two trusted men, a Romanized Gaul whom the Helvetii would find acceptable and a Roman who was well known to Ariovistus through bonds of hospitality with him. The chief accused the two of being spies (*speculatores*) and threw them into chains: this is undoubtedly what they were, so even though Caesar's apologetic account may suggest it, it was not simply a matter of the arbitrary and unreliable conduct of the Helvetic leader extending even into diplomatic matters (*Gallic War* I 47). Very similar principles form the background to Caesar's description of the negotiations between Ambiorix and the local Roman commanders in 54 BC in north-eastern Gaul, again conducted through trusted intermediaries: in this case, though, the Gauls' strategic situation and intentions, as well as the sources of support to implement those intentions, did not have to be discovered: they were made the subject of an explicitly assertive and aggressive statement forcefully delivered by Ambiorix and this is what the negotiators reported back (*Gallic War* V 27.1ff., esp. 5–8). An item reported by Ammianus as occurring during the Caesar Julian's campaign in 359 on the Rhine frontier gives a later example relating to strategic intelligence collection from across the frontiers in a diplomatic context: Hariobaudes, a *tribunus vacans* (an officer without formal posting), was sent across the river ostensibly for routine discussions with the German chieftain Hortarius but covertly to check what the neighbouring tribes were organizing. The particular requirements for this operation are specified by Ammianus – that Hariobaudes was an extremely reliable officer and one completely familiar with the local German dialect. In this case a total lack of distinguishing features was necessary for what was also an espionage mission to gain strategic intelligence (XVIII 2.2). The familiarity and acceptability to the other side that are features of these diplomatic contacts are stressed as important prerequisites: here it is clear that Hariobaudes' linguistic skills, as well as his origins as a German, smoothed the path to penetration of hostile activity. The so-called 'barbarization' of the Late Roman army gave ample opportunity for the employment of men such as Hariobaudes in this kind of role but the advice given in the manual *On Strategy* is strongly against it: the anonymous author makes it clear that undercover *kataskopoi* should not have the same tribal origins as their opponents because of the risks associated with personal ties on the enemy side (*On Strategy* 42.8). Nevertheless, Julian's action seems sensible given the divided and factional nature of Germanic society in contact with the Roman frontiers and the increased numbers of Germans in all ranks of the army.

Ammianus covers two high-ranking missions into Gothic territory across the Lower Danube frontier carried out by Victor, Valens' *magister equitum*, a few years later. In 366 the diplomatic purpose was to seek a formal explanation for the Goths' support for the usurpation of Procopius but behind it lay the intelligence aim of assessing their evident war-readiness following earlier warning reports of restlessness. The campaigns which followed were long and inconclusive but were supported by the total exclusion of Goths from Roman border markets; so Victor's second mission, in 369, in association with the *magister peditum* Arinthaeus, could examine the level of war-weariness and now exploit the fact that the Goths had been so severely affected by military pressure and economic disruption that they were ready to enter into negotiations. The ability to compare conditions at the beginning and at the end of the period was, we think, the more important purpose of this mission, the purely diplomatic being much less so (XXVII 5.1,7,9). Victor is no different from earlier examples in being one of a number of very senior men from the emperor's entourage who were regularly used for combined diplomatic and intelligence purposes. His case can be paralleled in a civil war context, for example: Constantius II sent his highly trusted eastern Praetorian Prefect Flavius Philippus to Magnentius in 351 – again ostensibly to work on truce and peace-treaty negotiations with the usurper but in reality to examine Magnentius' preparations and discover his intentions and which routes he would be using and to report back in detail (Zosimus II 46.2). The value of diplomatic operations of this nature for the acquisition of important strategic intelligence cannot be overestimated.

On the Mesopotamian frontier in 359 the historian Ammianus himself undertook, as an imperial guardsman (*protector domesticus*), a dangerous espionage mission that contributed eye-witness information to an evolving strategic intelligence analysis at the beginning of that year's confrontation with the Persians. As part of his account of the developing emergency, he quotes in full a document sent back to the command headquarters of his chief Ursicinus at Amida. It came on parchment hidden in a sword-scabbard smuggled back from a high-level diplomatic team that was already negotiating in Ctesiphon, in what was presumably a response to earlier information that the Persians were making preparations for a significant action against the eastern Roman frontier provinces. The message came from an imperial secretary, Procopius, who had accompanied the *comes* Lucillianus on an embassy to Sapor II. Procopius had discovered that the *apparitor* Antoninus, a Syrian with a grievance against various influential Romans, had collected a host of information on military dispositions in the East and had defected to Persia; then he had been successful in persuading Sapor to invade Syria. Procopius' message was a virtual cryptogram, *obscurius indicantem*. Further, it was read with real difficulty because it was also written in code, *notarum figuris*, says Ammianus, which presumably means shorthand since Procopius was a *notarius* or shorthand secretary: 'Now that the envoys of the Greeks have been sent far away and perhaps are to be killed, that aged king, not content with Hellespontus, will bridge the Granicus and the Rhyndacus and come to invade Asia with many nations. He is naturally passionate and very cruel and he has as an instigator and abetter the successor of the former Roman emperor Hadrian; unless Greece takes heed, it is all over with her and her dirge is chanted.' According to Ammianus, who was almost certainly one of the officers who decoded it, the message indicated that Sapor, urged on by Antoninus ('the successor of the former emperor Hadrian'), would invade Syria crossing the rivers Anzaba and Tigris. Thus it gave an idea of the route the Persians were to follow; then of very large numbers, which indicated the force levels that would be needed for defence; then how much of Roman defence information was already in Persian hands. The document gave more form and shape to a long build-up of information that had been received by both the imperial court and Ursicinus and his staff, which included Ammianus: it had started with rumour, then confirmatory reports; it had been given urgency by the defection of the former senior functionary with a great deal of strategic information (see above, p. 14f.) and was then being followed by specific reports of advance parties raiding into Roman Mesopotamia.

At his headquarters in Amida, Ursicinus' next response to all this was to dispatch Ammianus himself on an espionage mission deep into Persian territory. His first task was to make contact with the satrap of Corduene, Iovinianus, whom Ammianus knew personally. The satrap had been educated in Antioch and may easily have been acquainted with other senior men in the upper levels of the Roman administration based in Antioch. As a result of his earlier experiences, he was favourably disposed towards Rome and Ammianus made use of this entrée. In this particular case, there is no evidence to suggest that Ammianus gained any information directly from him; rather he was placed in a position where he could find out what he wanted through the assistance and co-operation of the satrap (XVIII 6.20–1; 7.1–2). The next part of the task involved being sent on to the high country overlooking the two indicated rivers to assess more exactly the size and speed of the invasion. Ammianus' report to Ursicinus on his return caused a range of defensive responses to be set in train: in the event, however, they turned out to be not particularly useful since unseasonable flooding of the Euphrates forced the thrust of the invasion further north and brought about the lengthy siege of Amida. In this substantial episode there is a remarkable series of pieces of strategic intelligence, each of which confirmed and modified the previous state of knowledge; Ammianus provides a masterful illustration of the process of its development, a good example of the intelligence cycle (XVIII 6.17ff.).[2]

The secret espionage mission carried out by identifiable and relatively senior men may not be as uncommon as the apparently isolated episode involving Ammianus above suggests. The cases of Hariobaudes and of Flavius Philippus are two such but so also is one just touched on in a letter of Libanius. He mentions the mission of one Clematius, an *agens in rebus* (an official normally active only in internal security), who in 356 is reported as having made a secret crossing of the Euphrates to examine Persian activity across the frontier. It was clearly strategic information that he was looking for, because on his return he reported to the *praefectus praetorio per Orientem* in Antioch, Strategius Musonianus, and not to any frontier commander for reaction (*Letters* 430.7). Not much further information can be got out of the story beyond its connection with attempted peace negotiations conducted by Musonianus over the next year or two (Ammianus XVI 9.2–4; 10.21) but the serious strategic purpose of this episode is emphasized by Clematius' evident seniority: even though his rank at the time remains uncertain, he was soon after appointed governor of Palestine (see *PLRE* I, s.v. Clematius 2). Clematius' mission fits into the context of a curious mixture of high- and low-level diplomatic and intelligence activity that took place on the Mesopotamian frontier in 356. Following a long series of local border incidents, deep-penetrating *speculatores* with particular disguise and *agent provocateur* skills were sent to operate across the border under special instructions from the Praetorian Prefect and local *dux* Cassianus to discover if there was anything of deeper significance that lay behind the Persians' actions: they were able to report, reliably, that King Sapor was heavily committed with frontier problems else-where and that the raids were only of a local character. Generally, this type of information was not easy to acquire given the exceptionally good security of the Persians but the pressing need to find it out may underlie what seems to be an additional special task for the *speculatores* in question. Knowing now that the king was well out of the way, the Roman commanders set about exploiting the situation by using low-level soldiers to put about peace indications which Tamsapor, the local satrap, would pick up through his own intelligence service (obviously known to exist, e.g. Ammianus XVIII 6.16; Libanius *Orations* XVIII 213; Julian *Letters* 402A; cf. Procopius *Wars* II 18.5, and for the pre-Sassanid period, perhaps Tacitus *Annals* II 58.1) and thus be induced to enter into secret negotiations where he could be invited to help persuade the king into accepting a treaty and so put an end to friction in the region. In this case, the diplomatic solution that was envisaged for the local border problems and that soon involved consideration of ways to keep Persia occupied on other frontiers, was inextri-cably linked to strategic intelligence activity and could not have occurred without the link (Ammianus XVI 9.2–4; XVII 5.15).

Several letters of Cicero throw particular light – more so than any other evidence apart from Caesar – on the way in which intelligence on a single large strategic problem could be derived from non-Roman sources. He exemplifies how good contacts with client kings could ensure access to intelligence that could not have been obtained otherwise. Now Cicero was hardly a major mili-tary figure and his period of office as proconsul in Cilicia in 51–50 BC was in his eyes almost a form of exile; but the carefully spelt out detail about the sources and content of his information about Parthian invasion movements and about the responses he was making to them, gives the Cilician section of his corre-spondence an exceptional value and interest. In passing, it is perhaps worth pointing out here that Cicero's correspondence with his friends and acquain-tances meant that through their letters to him he could be kept very well briefed about many areas of Roman military activity (even as an individual) and notice-ably so in the Gallic War and Civil War periods. This reflects an important part of the process by which Roman strategic policy was formulated at the level of the Senate (see pp. 104ff.).

His correspondence from Cilicia demonstrates how over a period of time a provincial governor obtained intelligence about external activity that could have had a serious effect on the security of his province and how he reacted to it. Cicero was acutely aware of the threat to his province in the context of the aftermath of the Crassus disaster at Carrhae in 53 BC, where a full-sized Roman army had been wiped out, with the loss of its commander and several standards. He had an extremely difficult strategic programme to carry out as his contri-bution to the defence of the frontier region: to keep himself well informed on any developments, to garrison strongpoints with the limited forces at his disposal, to exert tough control over the recalcitrant tribes in the border mountains, to try to keep the client kings of the region on side and all the time to be ready to go to the aid of the neighbouring province of Syria if requested. How he did this, with some considerable success, will be considered in detail in chapter 4.

In conditions of campaign warfare which entailed the co-operation of allied clients, the process of gathering intelligence through diplomatic contacts with them could be expanded. It was certainly done on a wide scale by Caesar, who used reliable allied leaders to acquire information and so contribute to the formation of strategic policy. It also entailed exploiting inter-tribal tensions to gain the information he needed. Two instances from early 57 BC can be quoted as representative examples. Labienus had shortly before sent through early warnings about serious trouble developing with the Belgae. As a result, the Senones and other tribal groups living on the borders of Belgic territory in northern Gaul were given a specific commission to report on how far the preparations for war had advanced there. Caesar does not usually mention the means used by pro-Roman Gauls to acquire their information but they were able to tell him that the Belgae were raising and assembling an army and on this information the subsequent planning and prompt response was based (*Gallic War* II 2.3–4). A point Caesar makes about the quality of the information reported by the Gallic allies is that it was self-consistent; it was also accurate and reliable, since, as is clear from the wording of the text, he had of course been careful to involve several tribes in its collection – thus built into the original request was an automatic confirmation mechanism. He was also fifteen days' march away from Belgic territory when the initial intelligence work was being completed by his allies, a situation which allowed great latitude in the planning of the resulting action. Then, once he was much closer to the trouble area, the Remi as his chief allies were asked for more detailed information, which they readily divulged: full background on the recent history and relevant national characteristics and also detailed statistics of the Belgic war potential, to which, as members of the Belgic common council, they had access. They provided all this very detailed strategic intelligence, which was then used by Caesar to create and exploit divisions among his opponents and to avoid direct confrontation until still more strategic and, later, tactical information and confirmation became available (*Gallic War* II 4.1–10; 5.1–4). In roughly the same area during the harsh winter of early 51 BC, it was through frequent diplomatic contacts (*crebrae legationes*) that the Remi passed invaluable information to him about the congregation of large new forces of rebels led by the Bellovaci and where they were (Hirtius *Gallic War* VIII 6.2). As Hirtius makes clear, the link in this case would have been less effective if Caesar had not used it in the context of his assessment that the overall strategic situation in Gaul was not so explosive as to prevent him dealing with the Bellovaci. Hence, the diplomatic connection was both a contributor to the intelligence process here and an integral part of it: the close link between intelligence and diplomatic activity is inescapable and sharply demonstrated by the frequent use made of it.

There are many further cases of the use of diplomatic contacts for just these ends in the Gallic War. For example, there were at least three occasions when the Ubii on the west bank of the Rhine were encouraged at a high level to pass on to Caesar all information they had gained about the hostile activities of the Suebi just across the Rhine to their north-east (*Gallic War* IV 19.2, 55 BC; VI 10.2–4 and VI 29.1, 53 BC); and in 54 BC, five tribes from south-east Britain who came over to the Roman side, as part of the diplomatic package, supplied Caesar with detailed information about a fortified settlement held by Cassivellaunus in force (*Gallic War* V 21.2). It is clear that once intelligence had begun to be acquired in this way, other information right down to the tactical level could readily be obtained, as can be seen at, for example, *Gallic War* II 5.4 (57 BC), where the proximity of a unified Belgic force was identified by information provided by the friendly Remi as well as through Roman *exploratores*. In this last case, it should be noted that the confirmation process is carefully observed in order to maintain the spread of sources. A further case which illustrates the process of detailed confirmation of information that had been obtained from diplomatic negotiations (and shows that the process was very much part of Caesar's practice) can be seen in the description of the campaign of 53 BC against the Germanic support recruited by Ambiorix. Caesar was faced with a claim by the Segni and Condrusi that they had never joined Ambiorix (they were two small German tribes who occupied territory between that held by the hostile Eburones and the Treveri); he used information coming from his own sources to confirm the version from the other side: thus the loyalty of the two tribes, which was asserted by their own negotiators, was separately confirmed by questioning some captured prisoners. It was a sophisticated investigation technique, in that the prisoners were not actually Eburones themselves but would have known if the forces they had been part of had counted Segni, Condrusi or Eburones in their number and the kind of responses they made would have revealed the truth or otherwise of the official negotiators' claim (*Gallic War* VI 32.2).

There is more to be said about strategic intelligence under the heading of diplomatic contacts. Caesar, for example, does not disguise the fact that in the course of diplomatic activity with key tribes he was interfering in tribal political processes and structures for intelligence-gathering purposes. The Aedui form a case in point, though they had for many years cultivated good relations with Rome (*Gallic War* I 11.2–3). When the Romans had become closely involved in Gaul in 58 BC, for instance, Caesar convened a meeting of leading men from the tribe to complain about their lack of co-operation in making food supplies available; under pressure one of them hinted at and later confirmed in detail the resentment felt by Dumnorix over the preferential treatment given to his brother Diviciacus and the ambiguous if not actually hostile actions that had resulted from that (*Gallic War* I 16.5–18.10). In a later incident, during the rebellion of Vercingetorix, it was revealed to Caesar by the young noble Eporedorix that the Aeduan infantry under his rival Litaviccus was about to defect to the

Gallic revolt (a precious piece of strategic intelligence which affected the whole of Caesar's approach to this part of the campaign). It is clear that the roots of that rivalry lay back in earlier tribal conflicts that had been adjudicated by Caesar as *patronus*, the patron or special advocate of the tribe; no doubt, too, the conflicts had been developed by him within the tribe against the eventuality that one of the sides in a dispute would give him information in order to get one-up on the other (*Gallic War* VII 39.3ff.). Both episodes suggest that long-term preparation would eventually bring results in intelligence. In another case, the tensions allowed to develop in the Treveri over rival claims by Cingetorix and Indutiomarus to the chieftainship in 54 BC follow a similar pattern for similar ends (*Gallic War* V 3.2-4). Caesar was thus forewarned about the problems which Indutiomarus caused later in the year; and the man on the spot, Labienus, made use of the carefully cultivated Cingetorix to gain information which, first, allowed a successful tactical trap to be developed, into which Indutiomarus fell and, second, led to the rebel's death during his escape (*Gallic War* V 56–8). The chief of the Pictones at the time of the great Gallic revolt in 50 BC, a man called Duratius, had also been cultivated in the same way. Hirtius remarks that he remained loyal to Rome while numbers of his fellow-tribesmen had joined the rebellion; Duratius demonstrated his loyalty by sending strategic information by letter and courier to C. Caninius Rebilus about the gathering of rebels in his territory. Conflict between the chief and many of his people would therefore have predated an incident of this kind (and certainly would have been cemented in place by his actions) but the intelligence generated as a result of the conflict allowed prompt Roman reaction to crush the concentration of opposition moving north from Lemonum (Poitiers) (Hirtius *Gallic War* VIII 26.1ff.).

Caesar's actions in this field were clearly deliberate. The long-standing hostility between Arminius and Segestes, the leading men in the Germanic Cherusci in the first decades of the first century AD, is a prime example of the lack of a co-ordinated policy, even in the early Principate. Segestes repeatedly passed on first-rate strategic intelligence to the Romans, in particular the warning about Arminius fomenting rebellion. It was a pity that the information from this excellent source was ignored by Varus in AD 9. This is representative, however, of an attitude which apparently saw the vast amount of valuable information that Segestes possessed remain untapped by Roman authorities and not used for military purposes after he had been settled in 'the old province', presumably the left bank of the Rhine, in AD 15 (Tacitus *Annals* I 55.2–3; 58.1–5; Velleius Paterculus II 118.4; cf. Dio LVI 19.3). Similar strictures can be sustained about the apparent non-utilization of the Marcomannic king Maroboduus and Bato the Pannonian chieftain, both of whom ended up in comfortable retirement in Ravenna, under the eyes of the prefect of the fleet (Tacitus *Annals* II 63.5; Suetonius *Tiberius* 20), of the Hermundurian Goth Catualda, who succeeded Maroboduus, at Forum Iulii (Fréjus) (Tacitus, *Annals* II 63.6), and others (see pp. 135f.). Maroboduus did however serve as a weapon in Tiberius' diplomatic

armoury, the threat that he would be restored as king seemingly being sufficient to keep the Suebi toeing the Roman line. In such circumstances, it may
be that he still possessed useful information on tribal issues, geography and
personalities which could be exploited over the period of his detention. It should,
however, be recalled that all information becomes dated and in the case of these
leaders, their usefulness may have ceased by the time of their settlement/deten-
tion. It appears, however, that a rather different situation obtained in the
mid-fourth century. The exemplar here is the case of Hormisdas, brother of the
long-reigning Persian king Sapor II; he had defected from Persia in 324 and
spent the rest of his days as an intimate of the court close to the reigning
emperor and evidently performing useful services. They included the actual
command of Roman troops before and during Julian's Persian expedition and
even a covert intelligence mission (*ad speculandum exiturum*) near Ozogardana on
the Euphrates in 363. It is inconceivable that the prince, who clearly maintained contacts within the Persian establishment, should not have been a prime
source for strategic background information over the period of nearly forty years.
The clever witticism he is reported as making to Constantius II during that
emperor's first visit to Rome in 357 not only suggests familiarity between them
but also contains politico-military advice, no doubt a reference to Trajan's
conquest of Mesopotamia: while they were looking at the great equestrian
statue of Trajan in the atrium to his Forum, Hormisdas said, 'the horse you
propose to create should have as much space to range over as the one before
your eyes' (Zosimus II 27; III 11.3; Ammianus XVI 10.15–16; XXIV 1.2; 2.4,
11, 20; 5.4).[3]

### Frontier posts, markets and their associated personnel

All the foregoing deal with the acquisition of intelligence during a campaign or
from some distance across the frontiers. But along the actual line of the frontiers,
once they had become fixed, towards the end of the first century AD, where
the presence of Roman troops and administrative activity was often concentrated, there were many opportunities for such information to be collected,
rather than actively sought out. There is often an unwritten assumption even
in specialist works on Roman frontiers that wherever there was a line of forts
deployed along a military road or *limes* (which by the Late Empire had become
the usual term for a border or a frontier district itself),[4] there was patrolling not
just along the line of the *limes*, but also well beyond it.

The extent of such patrolling has, however, been overestimated. While there
is good evidence to suggest that on some land frontiers – the Lowlands
of Scotland north of Hadrian's Wall for example – regular patrols deep into
barbarian territory were maintained at some periods, it appears that over much
of the length of the empire's frontiers the installations which would have
permitted this activity were never provided. It is particularly true of the great
river frontiers along the Rhine, the Danube and the Euphrates, which were

regarded as the definitive frontiers of the empire (cf. Josephus *Jewish War* II 16.4/363, 377; Statius *Silvae* V i 89–90; Tacitus *Annals* I 9; IV 5).[5] On these frontiers under the Principate, with only a few exceptions, hardly any permanent forts or bridges or landing places have been found on the external banks, while the same structures have readily been identified on the Roman banks and within the frontiers; more of them are from the Late Empire but even then they were sited only to provide access to the far bank, presumably for the purpose of allowing mobile striking forces access to attack or counter-attack. At no period were military structures permanently maintained away from the rivers to provide the advance bases essential for continuous deep patrolling. This is not to say that Roman troops never visited barbarian territory before then: there is sporadic archaeological and epigraphic evidence for a military presence at a few points, especially opposite legionary bases and provincial capitals, immediately beyond the Rhine and the Danube – though rather less than there is for Roman-style civilian building – and also some literary evidence for the occasional maintenance of a strip of land empty of native settlements on some sections of the far banks of the same rivers. This required both diplomatic contact and apparently the presence from time to time of Roman centurions (Tacitus *Annals* XIII 54–5; Dio LXXI 15–16; LXXII 2.4; cf. Tacitus *Annals* IV 72–3). But it is important to realize that the lack of provision for sorties in strength or of bases beyond the frontier line effectively precludes regular patrolling more than half a day's ride – say 20 or 30 km at most – from the river bank; in fact the 15 km exclusion zone, later reduced to 7.5 km (38 stades), which was imposed on the Marcomanni north of the Danube in the early 170s (Dio LXXI 15; cf. LXXII 3.2), probably represents a more practicable figure. We shall return to argue these points in chapter 7 (pp. 173ff.).

There were, however, methods and opportunities by which strategic intelligence could be picked up over a long distance at frontier posts even on frontiers where long-distance patrolling was not provided for. They would have arisen from the movement of trade and travellers both ways across the frontiers, which was invariably channelled and controlled by Roman forts situated either at established river crossing points served by small boats or ferries, or on traditional land routes across the frontier zone.

Markets were a central feature of Roman frontier control and were enabled to become so as an aspect of external policies that caused many cross-frontier peoples to become at least partially dependent on Rome even for staples, let alone for luxuries. To judge from recent assessments of the archaeological evidence, in Europe economic domination extended over a 200 km-wide zone ahead of the actual frontier line and some economic–political influence for some 200 km beyond that; and this situation obtained from Augustus' time until the late fourth century. The markets could therefore be used as a means for exerting pressure: if, for instance, there were difficulties over an issue between the Roman side and the local tribal authorities, the markets could be closed for a period to cross-frontier trade, an action that could cause economic dislocation and even severe hardship for a tribe (e.g. Tacitus *Germania* 41.1; *Histories* IV 64; Dio LXXI 11.3; 15; 16; *Ammianus* XXVII 5.7; Procopius *Wars* II 28.29).[6]

In an intelligence context, markets and trading-stations are also listening posts. Country people go to market mainly for economic reasons but there is also a very important social aspect: they use the opportunity for talk, the exchange of gossip and news. Roman frontier society was without any real means of mass communication and so in the course of ordinary social interchange, information on current issues within the tribe and beyond was frequently revealed and it was part of the duties of the market supervisors to pick it up and pass it back. Again, at this kind of occasion, not only is much information traded but also any change in the composition of people coming into the markets or in their attitudes can readily be noticed and reported back. In this context, it is interesting to find a member of the governor of Lower Pannonia's headquarters staff, which was based at Aquincum (Buda), making a dedication to the 'Spirit of Commerce' (*Genio Commercii*) across the Danube at Transaquincum (Rákospalota) (*CIL* III 3617) and later a fortified tower (*burgus*) built by Valentinian in 371 at Esztergom, opposite the junction of the River Hron with the Danube, was named *Commercium, qua causa et factus est* ('Commerce, which was also the reason for its construction') (*CIL* III 3653 = *ILS* 775). The great importance of markets as an environment where intelligence can be gathered easily is strongly emphasized in the manual *On Strategy* and its author goes on to give special attention to markets and trading as a front for covert intelligence activity (42.7). This cut both ways, however: Dio tells us that the Quadi were refused access to markets on the Danube even after they had sued for peace from Marcus Aurelius, for fear that the still-hostile Iazyges and Marcomanni would be able to mingle with them unnoticed and so spy on the Romans (*ta te ton Romaion kataskeptontai*) and buy themselves provisions (Dio LXXI 11.3). It is important to keep in mind that while traders and markets were valuable sources of information about activity beyond the line of the frontiers – look, for example, at the fact that information about Ireland was obtained from traders by Agricola (Tacitus *Agricola* 24.2) – that information was often, as Wells puts it, 'vague, imprecise and lacunose on the very points where the soldier would most desire full and accurate intelligence; [it] was in any case no substitute for that to be derived from military reconnaissance'.[7] As noted earlier, Caesar's inability to obtain usable information from cross-Channel traders illustrates the point. But even so, the intelligence network would at least have been alerted to the need for further investigation.

With the trade and travellers undoubtedly came information. But it is not clear to what extent this information was actively collected at ordinary frontier forts – the evidence is lacking. The development, as attested by inscriptions, of small units of specialist *exploratores* (scouts) garrisoning or attached to the garrison of some forts on the land frontiers, mostly from the late second century AD onwards, implies that in the aftermath of the Marcomannic Wars greater interest was shown than before in patrolling the immediate vicinity of the frontiers, although only on some frontiers do we find the occupation of outpost forts which would suggest anything more extensive (see pp. 185ff.). Likewise the appearance at the same time at many frontier forts and provincial capitals in several provinces of *beneficiarii consularis* (officers of the provincial governor's staff) may be connected with a greater interest in the co-ordination of intelligence-gathering there rather than with civilian policing, as is usually assumed (though the two may not be mutually exclusive) (see pp. 195ff.). But if these suggestions are correct, they may equally imply that before the growth of the external threat in the late second century, there was relatively little if any active intelligence collection at the ordinary frontier forts, even though alert commanders would undoubtedly have reported and investigated any overt hostile action or anything suspicious which happened to come to their notice.

On the other hand, there is evidence to indicate that at a more senior level, provincial governors did themselves make a direct effort from the second century onwards to obtain cross-frontier information, especially from trading activity. We have already seen that it was an officer of the provincial governor's staff, a *beneficiarius consularis*, who made the dedication to the 'Spirit of Commerce' at Transaquincum (Rákospalota). Also found on either side of the Danube at Aquincum and Transaquincum (both within the modern Budapest), were two second/third-century inscriptions recording the presence of *interpretes* (interpreters): one individual, of unknown date, was attached to the staff of the local governor and was clearly an expert in German dialects, being termed *interpres Germanorum officii consularis* (*CIL* III 10505); the second, in perhaps the third century, also on the staff of the governor, noted his expertise in Sarmatian (?) (*interprex Sarmatarum* (?) *ex officio consularis*, *CIL* III 14349[5]). Men of this kind would seem on the surface of it to have been occupied with translation work in contacts with the tribes across the frontiers. Ammianus refers to two such officials (*interpretes*) sent across the Danube by the emperor Constantius II in 359, accompanied by *tribuni*, to question the Limigantes about breaches of the treaty struck only the year before. Their detailed knowledge of the language, perhaps native knowledge, would be particularly valuable for picking up the nuances such negotiations entailed, a useful adjunct to the tribunes' view of the situation (XIX 11.5). The epigraphic evidence attests the existence of more such officials. One, the old legionary centurion Q. Atilius Primus, appears on a funerary inscription of the late first century AD, found (though not *in situ*) at Boldog in Slovakia on the left bank of the Danube across and downstream from Carnuntum, the probable capital of the as yet undivided province of Pannonia. He was both an *interprex* (because of his expert knowledge of Quadic) and a *centurio negotiator* (i.e. a centurion trader). His title suggests employment in procuring supplies for the local garrison but a slight expansion of the wording, to *centurio negotiator(um)* (i.e. a centurion of traders), could imply a role in supervising local trading activity in the markets. Equally, he may have been first a *centurio*, then later a *negotiator*. In whichever case, he would have been in frequent contact with the locals and thus was in a peculiarly advantageous position for picking up information

(*AE* 1978.635).[8] Another three military *interpretes* are attested: one of the early third century, who could speak Dacian, is recorded at Brigetio, the base of his legion *I Adiutrix*, but his linguistic speciality is more likely to have been employed at the capital of Lower Pannonia, Aquincum, which faced Dacia across the Great Hungarian Plain (*AE* 1947.35; cf. *CIL* III 10988 for date); another two, whose language is not indicated, appear on a long list of discharged veterans, dated to AD 195 and found at Viminacium, the base of legion *VII Claudia* and capital of Upper Moesia (*CIL* III 14507 *dextr.* a 11; *sinistr.* 40). The existence of these officials (and certainly more of them will have existed), taken with the kind of places where they are recorded, some of them across the frontier, demonstrates a policy of using the languages of the local inhabitants. One of the intentions underlying the policy would have been the early detection of changes of attitude which could have an effect on frontier security. It is significant that of the six epigraphically attested interpreters, five are recorded at or near the seats of their respective provincial governors and the sixth may likewise have served at the provincial capital: this implies that the contact envisaged may have been mainly at a high level. Provincial capitals did of course also tend to be situated facing the most likely avenue of threat.

Presenting a rather higher profile than *interpretes* but with similar ends in view, are those men here termed the 'political' centurions. Dio records the imposition of limitations on political activity after 180 on the Marcomanni, among which was the prohibition of meetings of the tribe except at monthly intervals at a fixed place and only in the presence of a Roman centurion (LXXII 2.4). Such an individual would have had to be a fluent speaker of Marcomannic German. The effects of these restrictions on an assembly of course would have been immediate: they entailed Roman knowledge of the content of any discussion at tribal level, if not actual control over what matters were discussed or suppressed. Coupled with this go all the features mentioned earlier: a first-hand view of attitudes, of the composition of the assembly and of the presence of known individuals at it and so on. We do not know how widespread the practice was – this one may have been a single *ad hoc* arrangement, though there seems to have been some similar supervision of *loca*, meeting places, throughout the Scottish Lowlands in the Commodan and Severan periods;[9] there seem also to be similarities between this kind of political centurion and, for example, a version from the early first century AD, the *primipilaris* Olennius, who was appointed to supervise the Frisians on the Lower Rhine and whose duties (until he grossly exceeded his brief in AD 28) must have been comparable (Tacitus *Annals* IV 72).[10] The pattern just outlined, of supervision by an experienced Roman (with its implicit intelligence function), now seems to fit an appointment made by Tiberius in AD 18: the post of regent in the semi-client kingdom of Thrace was assigned to Trebellenus Rufus, a former praetor, whose task it was to run the state during the minority of its young princes (Tacitus *Annals* II 67.4; III 38.4). All these cases demonstrate aspects of frontier management that were clearly implemented in order to gain the intelligence that was a necessary precondition for strategic readiness.

One of the more striking manifestations of this kind of policy comes from the end of Hadrian's reign. In 135 the Iberian kingdom of Pharasmanes II suddenly became a great deal more pliable, quiescent and reliable, apparently following an intervention by Flavius Arrianus (the writer Arrian), who was consular legate of Cappadocia between 131 and 137. Pharasmanes had allowed the Sarmatian Alani to raid through his territory into neighbouring Media and Albania; and on the way back, laden with their plunder, they had crossed into Roman Cappadocia but had been diverted by Arrian away from the Roman area of interest. Then, in connection with the settlement of wider regional issues following this diversion, Arrian had successfully installed a Roman officer, Publicius Agrippa, as chief adviser to the king; Publicius' post was permanent too, since he was called *pitiax*, the native title for the incumbent and he also married into the local aristocracy. Around the same time also, Pharasmanes was presented with a 500-man auxiliary cohort as a mark of courtesy (*SEG* XVI 781; SHA *Hadrian* 17.11–12). In combination these events look like pressure and surveillance to ensure compliance from an ambivalent frontier monarch and undoubtedly created an effective channel for intelligence.[11] Not altogether different would be the interest displayed towards the Bosporan kingdom in Crimea, also during Hadrian's reign. Cotys II was being maintained as a client king in 123/4 but in the next decade, more material support was accorded to his successor Rhoemetalces: a Roman force was stationed at his court and it too was not there purely for ceremonial purposes (Arrian *Circumnavigation* 17.3; Phlegon of Tralles *FGrHist* II B no. 257 F 17/20; *CIRB* 47).

### Strategic reconnaissances

Actual evidence for Roman forces setting out to acquire geographical, topographical or other information in anticipation of a major expedition is scarce. No such mission is known to have been ordered by the Republican Senate, which is hardly surprising in view of its annual magistracies and intense political rivalries which made long-term strategic planning virtually impossible. Even the dispatch by Scipio Aemilianus of the historian Polybius and philosopher Panaetius with ships to reconnoitre the African coast during the Third Punic War seems to have been a private scientific venture (Pliny *Natural History* V 9–10; *Index Stoicorum Herculanensis;* see p. 88 with n. 3).

Only with the advent of the Principate and the rule of one man did the sort of forward planning implied by this sort of undertaking become viable. Significantly, however, the bulk of the evidence for such reconnaissances relates to the reign of Augustus before the Varus disaster of AD 9 turned the tide of Roman imperial expansion, even if it did not put a complete end to it. Aelius Gallus, Prefect of Egypt from *c.* 27 until 25 BC, probed with an army into Arabia and the elder Pliny notes specifically that he recorded strategically useful information about the tribal and agricultural infrastructure of the region (Pliny *Natural History* VI 160–1); his successor C. Petronius made a similar foray into

Ethiopia, penetrating some 1,400 km from Aswan up the Nile (*Natural History* VI 181–2). Around the same time in the late 20s BC, a proconsul of Africa, L. Cornelius Balbus, staged a successful invasion into the heart of the Fezzan (*Natural History* V 36–7). And sometime in Augustus' reign, an exploration of the Baltic area took place (*Natural History* II 167; cf. Strabo *Geography* VII 2.4/294). All these reconnaissances were done in force and, though none achieved or led to permanent or further subjugation, most if not all seem to have aimed at the acquisition of geographical information and some form of preliminary conquest. More interesting, therefore, is the dispatch by Augustus in 1 BC, ahead of Gaius Caesar's planned expedition to Armenia, of one Isidore (or Dionysius) of Charax to investigate details of the area to be invaded (Pliny *Natural History* VI 141). This is a very rare but important exception to our general position about prior strategic reconnaissance.

After the reign of Augustus only a few other advance reconnaissances are recorded, all carried out under the later Julio-Claudians, who to an extent reacted against Tiberius' strict adherence to the principle of avoiding further expansion after AD 9. Gaius Caligula's personal foray across the Rhine in AD 40 may have been one, in anticipation of the subsequent successful campaigns of Ser. Sulpicius Galba: he is said by Suetonius to have rewarded the cavalry who accompanied him with a new type of decoration, scouting crowns (*coronae exploratoriae*) (Suetonius *Caligula* 45.1; 51.2; Dio LIX 21.1–3; cf. LX 8.7). Another reconnaissance may have been carried out in AD 42 under Claudius by Suetonius Paullinus, who campaigned in Mauretania in and across the Atlas mountains towards the south, certainly beyond the Roman area of interest at the time (Pliny *Natural History* V 14–15). More clearly a reconnaissance rather than a preliminary campaign, since it was carried out only by a detachment of the Praetorian Guard under a tribune, was the expedition ordered beyond the far southern boundary of Egypt into Ethiopia by Nero. They recorded exactly what the distances were between settlements and staging-posts – and there is a clear indication of contemplated future military activity, another exception to our earlier general assertion (Pliny *Natural History* VI 181, 184–6; XII 18–19; cf. Seneca *Natural Researches* VI 8.3–4).

Thereafter, however, we hear no more from the literary sources about re-connaissances ahead of a campaign. There were in any case fewer campaigns beyond the borders of the empire after the Julio-Claudian period and those seem to have been conducted without any such preparation, like Septimius Severus' Parthian campaign of AD 198, which foundered after his capture of Ctesiphon 'through ignorance of the country and inability to obtain supplies' (*to men agnosiai ton chorion to d'aporiai ton epitedeion*) (Dio LXXV 9.4; see below p. 38). Only in the aftermath of this disaster can we perhaps find in inscriptions some evidence of preliminary reconnaissance being organized, in advance of Severus' next and last campaign, in northern Britain, in 208–11 (see pp. 193f.). This may, however, be viewed as an exception which proves the rule.

## Disinformation

Perhaps surprisingly, the principal literary sources do not reveal much in the way of disinformation affecting the Romans, at least in the period we are surveying. On the other hand, we do possess evidence for a small number of occasions when the Romans exploited disinformation emanating from their own side.

A good example of this occurs in the context of Caesar's operations in north-west Gaul during the course of 56 BC. In a sideshow exercise against the Venelli of the Cherbourg peninsula, his legate Titurius Sabinus initially avoided an open battle and carefully developed a scenario of hiding behind his camp's fortifications, which made him appear fearful and incompetent and allowed a sense of confidence to develop among his Gallic opponents. He reinforced this impression after a few days by sending across a Gaul in the guise of a deserter, well-briefed with a nicely spurious story about Sabinus' nervousness and his imminent departure to help Caesar with the serious difficulties he was experiencing further to the south-west. The tribesmen seized on the information (because it not only fitted their perceptions of the situation but also was what they wanted to hear) and attacked, to be met with a disciplined charge which inflicted heavy losses (*Gallic War* III 18.1ff.). Another case is discussed in perhaps the only passage in Frontinus' *Stratagems* that contains more than a bare mention of a name and related incident. During operations against Parthia in 38 BC across the Euphrates from Cappadocia, Antonius' general Ventidius deliberately leaked information about his supposed weak points, fears and the routes he would have to take to avoid Pacorus. As expected, Pacorus reacted to the news: he spent the next six weeks committing resources to building a bridge across the Euphrates and moving troops into an area where Ventidius wanted him to be. The time gained by setting up this elaborate scenario allowed Ventidius to collect his own dispersed forces together in time to ensure a victory on his chosen terms (*Stratagems* I 1.6). All these incidents, as Caesar would have been aware, illustrate a psychological truism which inevitably influences all interpretation of intelligence and which therefore lies behind disinformation: people hear what they want to hear and react to it (*Gallic War* III 18.6). It is an important concept, though one often overlooked by historians, in understanding how intelligence is used in reality and it is one to which we shall have to return on several occasions in this book.

## Passive methods

### Informal external contacts

The satrap Iovinianus discussed earlier in this chapter (p. 20) is representative of a phenomenon more noticeable in the fourth century and later: informal personal contacts beyond the frontiers who could be exploited in an active (if *ad hoc*) way in order to acquire strategic intelligence. Since they took place outside the formal framework of Roman diplomacy, how sophisticated the networks of contacts were and how much they were the result of previous cultivation, is not now knowable (cf. Procopius *Wars* III 14.1–13). Nevertheless, it was sometimes the contacts who took the initiative in providing information which would not have been available in any other way.

More unusual than the Iovinianus episode, because it is a case where an individual appears to have been in direct contact with enemy leadership and planning, is that of Vincentius in North Africa, related by Ammianus in connection with the suppression of the widespread revolt of Firmus in 373–5 by the elder Theodosius. When Theodosius arrived to restore the loyalty of the inhabitants of the region, Vincentius had disappeared from his post as second-in-command to the governor of Tripolitania, no doubt afflicted by a conscious-ness of imminent punishment for earlier abuses of his authority. However, after the campaign had opened with inconclusive preliminary guerrilla warfare, a temporary peace was patched up, during which Vincentius and some other provincial administrators came out of hiding and made their way to Theodosius, now in Caesarea (Cherchel), with extremely valuable information about Firmus' plans and methods of operation: it was revealed that under cover of this peace Firmus was organizing a sudden extensive attack on the Romans; and it seems clear too that Vincentius and his associates also informed Theodosius which actual Roman troops and officials in charge of allied frontier tribes were deeply implicated in giving the rebels support (XXIX 5.19–21). Until the moment this senior defector returned, Theodosius apparently had not made a great deal of progress – here the redirection of the strategy of a campaign was dependent on the existence of a person in the right position to acquire information. A second important redirection, perhaps a year later, took place when a single *explorator* brought in the news that Firmus had joined yet another hostile tribe in the region, the Isaflenses (XXIX 5.40). His report seems to have been of as great strategic importance as Vincentius' information, because it allowed Theodosius to focus all the pressure he was able to muster on this one tribal group and so avoid dispersing effort as he had done earlier in the campaign. In both these cases Ammianus appears to indicate that in such guerrilla warfare conditions chance intelligence can have important effects on the whole subsequent strategic direction of the campaign. The problem brought to light by the reception and exploitation of the substantive pieces of intelligence in the account is that from the beginning Theodosius' intelligence-collecting operation did not work effec-tively. Intelligence is a fragile thing and the heavy-handed methods employed by Theodosius to bring the region back into line (implicitly harshly criticized by Ammianus) would not have created an atmosphere conducive to the devel-opment of a flow.[12]

### *Adventitious intelligence*

There is no question that good fortune is a factor in warfare and throughout antiquity generals had to be known as fortunate if they were to retain their reputation and status. Sulla's agnomen 'Felix', the 'Fortunate', is of course one

of the best-known manifestations of the genre. In the intelligence field, the importance of fortuitous and adventitious elements that occur in the process of
acquiring information (for example, individuals or commanders just happen to
encounter particularly useful items which could not have been expected or
planned for in the normal course of events but which have a central bearing
on subsequent planning and action) should not be underestimated even if it
cannot be quantified. Caesar in particular recognizes the role played by luck in
war and connects it with intelligence, in an admittedly rather rhetorical passage:
while he refers mainly to a tactical context, the pursuit of Ambiorix (*Gallic War*
VI 30.2ff.), luck in intelligence-gathering can easily be extended to the strategic.

It is when chance reports are investigated more thoroughly for even longer-
term information that they can reveal most important and detailed material
which may affect planning to a remarkable extent. A notable case in point (of
51 BC) takes us back to the Remi and their information about the Bellovaci
and their allies: once Caesar had arrived in the area, cavalry snatches of people
found lurking in farm buildings led first to the discovery that they were on
spying missions but further investigation into their stories allowed very considerable items of information to emerge about the present tactical defence activity
and intentions of the hostile groups as well as much detailed wide-ranging background explanation of the regional tribal alliances; also divulged were the
possible involvement of massive German support and the fact that the Bellovaci
and their allies would commit themselves to fight a battle if Caesar appeared
with only three legions but if he came with a larger number would resort to
extensive guerrilla-style denial of food and fodder supplies, aided by the weather
and time of the year and the sheer weight of demand from Caesar's troops
(Hirtius *Gallic War* VIII 7.1–8). Hirtius' account here illustrates that the
intelligence gained showed Caesar that this was not a mere *temeritas barbarorum*,
which suggests rashly conceived reckless behaviour expected in barbarians but
a thoroughly worked-out and very skilful strategic plan of action with dangerous
connotations (*Gallic War* VIII 8.1). The importance of the episode in the present
survey is emphasized by the very detailed analysis of the information which had
been discovered that Caesar accorded to it; it is a model example of the ramifications of strategic intelligence into personal, diplomatic and military areas.

On occasion information collected by an agency for tactical purposes or in
tactical contexts turns out to have unexpected and important long-term strategic
implications. A very marked case is provided by Tacitus in the account of
Cn. Domitius Corbulo's assault on Artaxata in AD 58. Routine tactical intelligence by *exploratores* around the site was supposed to confirm that King Tiridates
would, after a series of feinting movements, finally face Corbulo from inside the
fortifications of the city; but he was in fact found not to have retired into Artaxata
at all but to have moved away some considerable distance to deal with frontier
trouble in Media or Albania: a question no doubt of strategic alternatives. Thus
the strategic centre of Artaxata was left undefended for the Romans to destroy
(*Annals* XIII 41).

## *Captured documents*

Captured documents revealing actions or intentions that required a strategic response do not figure largely in the sources. Nevertheless, the Second Punic War does furnish two famous examples. In 215 BC a Roman fleet intercepted the ship of an Athenian, Xenophanes, returning from Capua where he had negotiated a treaty with Hannibal on behalf of Philip V of Macedon. Captured with Xenophanes and the Carthaginian officers accompanying him were correspondence and the draft text of the treaty. The envoys and documents were sent to Rome, whereupon the Senate reinforced the fleet at Tarentum and ordered further investigation of whether Philip planned to join the war. Should it be confirmed, the praetor M. Valerius Laevinus was to take command, cross to Macedonia and contain Philip there (Polybius VII 9; Livy XXIII 33.4–34.9; 38; Appian *Macedonian Wars* 1.2–3). Eight years later, in 207, six messengers sent by Hasdrubal to his brother Hannibal to inform him of his arrival in Italy crossed almost the whole length of the Italian peninsula before they were finally caught quite fortuitously by Roman foragers near Tarentum. Forced to speak under threat of torture, they admitted that they were carrying a letter from Hasdrubal to Hannibal and were sent to the consul C. Claudius Nero, who was able to read the letter through an interpreter. Nero forwarded the document to the Senate and at the same time informed them of his plan of action. Having arranged for provisioning along his route, Nero took a picked force north to join up with his fellow-consul M. Livius Salinator. Together they destroyed Hasdrubal's army at the River Metaurus and Nero returned south to face Hannibal before the latter even knew he had gone. Hannibal only learned of what had taken place when his brother's head was thrown into his camp and two of the captured messengers were sent in to explain (Polybius XI 1–3.6; Livy XXVII 43–51). In both instances the timely capture of documents together with personnel who could be interrogated proved to be of the greatest possible value and allowed appropriate and highly effective action to be taken.

Captured documents were not always quite so useful. Caesar reports the finding of a complete list of military manpower and other population statistics, all written in Greek letters (*litteris Graecis*), in a plundered camp of the Helvetii in 58 BC: evidently a census document, which is unusual for such a tribe. Had the list been found before the defeat of the Helvetii, it would of course have been a strategic coup (*Gallic War* I 29.1). As a general rule though, except in civil war conditions and on the Persian frontier, the Romans were dealing with pre-literate peoples among whom documents that would serve the purposes of strategic intelligence did not exist.

The paucity of evidence for actual written documents as sources of intelligence in the literary evidence makes it generally clear that almost all intelligence material gathered from informants of whatever type across the frontiers was oral; information was picked up by combinations of autopsy and hearsay and was only committed to writing, if necessary, at the frontier. But the existence of documents that had been intercepted even in literate Roman civil war contexts is not very widespread, to judge from the evidence: the author of the Caesarian *Spanish War* quotes the purported text of a captured letter from Sex. Pompeius to the inhabitants of Ursao but it reveals no more than that Pompeius intended to defend the towns that supported him (a cloudy generality) and that Caesar's inexperienced troops could not fight on difficult ground (which in the event they did, so upsetting Pompeius' defence arrangements) (*Spanish War* 26.3–6).

Several of the correspondents in the Ciceronian corpus mention that letters between protagonists in the Civil Wars were being intercepted and their contents exploited. Asinius Pollio for instance, writing to Cicero from Spain in 43 BC, blames ill-defined *dispositi*, inspectors or agents posted along the main routes by both sides, for inflicting delays on dispatches and for opening them (*Letters to his Friends* X 31.1; 33.1). An official dispatch (*relatio*) from P. Lentulus Spinther in Lycia addressed to the Senate, again from 43 BC, reveals that a captured letter gave him the information about Dolabella's intention to abandon Syria and Egypt with his 'ruffians' and to move on Italy supported by requisitioned ships now collecting in Lycia; Spinther made use of this in negotiations with the Rhodians to attempt to bring them over to the Republican side and to forestall Dolabella's lieutenants from finding more ships (*Letters to his Friends* XII 15.2).

Captured correspondence with a strategic intelligence content affecting the security of the frontiers is also relevant here. When covering the opening phase of the confrontation between Julian and Constantius II in AD 361, Ammianus reports that Julian was able to intercept correspondence between the Alaman chieftain Vadomarius and Constantius, along with Vadomarius' secretary. Ammianus is uncertain about the actual details of the contents but clearly the mere existence of such correspondence was taken to mean that Vadomarius was being encouraged to raid or create incidents that would distract Julian and so allow more time for Constantius to organize his response to Julian's elevation to the purple. The capture was an intelligence coup, because it alerted Julian and allowed him to take very firm action to prevent the problem occurring in his rear. Vadomarius was kidnapped at a dinner during a routine visit to his nearest frontier post and was shipped off to Spain after an interview with Julian (and, interestingly, is later attested as leading Roman troops in the East in 366 and 371) (XXI 3.4–4.6; cf. XXVI 8.2; XXIX 1.2).

*Negative intelligence*

When strategic intelligence usually involves the handling of concrete evidence for broad situations, it can be called positive intelligence; however, the converse, negative intelligence, which is the absence of indications of hostile activity, can be equally informative for a headquarters staff attempting to plan a reaction. Caesar shows how it is possible to use both information and lack of information in the context of establishing what an enemy is intending to do. His brief comment on how he worked out the likely course of events in connection with the near-disaster in Britain in 55 BC is important. He recognized that he had no positive knowledge of British intentions; but with his ships severely damaged by a storm and spring tides, he realized that taken together with the negative information that the British had stopped handing over hostages, it was likely that some attack would occur. What modern manuals call an 'essential element of information' was here the ending of the hostage-giving, a negative: but when it was taken together with his losses of equipment, that information became a strong positive indicator (*Gallic War* IV 31.1). A somewhat similar example of negative intelligence can be seen in Ammianus' account of what was happening in Constantius' headquarters at Edessa during AD 361, an almost textbook example of the flow of intelligence and the responses to it. Reports from *speculatores* in Persian territory, taken together with those from *exploratores* and information from refugees and deserters, were expected to indicate when and where a Persian invasion would be launched against Roman territory, following a massive troop build-up on the Tigris under the command of the king himself. That Persian force remained at the Tigris because the auspices for its advance were not favourable. For the Romans, however, there was a problem – because of excellent Persian security, the information received from all the sources of intelligence and from senior Roman commanders on the spot was contradictory, with no piece of evidence predominating clearly enough to be conclusive. The absence of conclusive evidence, of essential pieces of information, meant that the Persians had not been making final preparations for the advance (e.g. the positioning of supply-dumps, the building-up of boat numbers for bridge construction, or even unusual activity) in the eastern part of the area between the Tigris and the Euphrates (or they would have been observed) and thus no invasion could occur that year. Perversely in a case of this type, no intelligence turned out to be good intelligence. The whole episode is one of those where single items of local tactical information pieced together produced an overall strategic picture: a good example of the close relationship between tactical and strategic intelligence (XXI 7.7; 13.1ff.).

While on this occasion the particular set of strategic circumstances exhibited characteristics that the headquarters involved could make something of, it should, however, be pointed out that not always is negative intelligence or lack of intelligence so useful. A prime case of lack of intelligence affecting the conduct of a campaign can be seen in the tantalizingly abbreviated surviving version of Dio's account of events following his contemporary Septimius Severus' capture of Ctesiphon in southern Mesopotamia at the beginning of 198. The campaign was initially another moderate success in the long series of Roman invasions of the Parthian Empire involving attempts to reach the Persian homeland. But the captured city was held only briefly, as together with a supplies shortage there was a lack of intelligence about the state of the surrounding country. No doubt itineraries from Trajan's campaigns in 115–17 and from L. Verus' in the 160s were used (see pp. 115ff.) but they could not provide the kind of immediately relevant intelligence that would be needed. Since the expedition was so far from the frontier bases, both the supply issue and the state of the countryside around Ctesiphon were critically important and affected the whole range of Severus' strategic options (LXXV 9.4). The problems that confronted Severus would have become visible earlier and would have allowed modifications to the invasion plan if any serious preliminary intelligence work had been carried out. The case is an important one. It is one of those which appear to support the contention made earlier in this chapter, that very extensive strategic intelligence work did not generally take place before major military actions were undertaken.

# 3

# MAKING CONTACT
## Tactical intelligence

## DEFINITIONS AND SCOPE

The capacity and intention of the opposition to wage war is the purview of strategic intelligence, the acquisition of which may be pursued even in peacetime; the immediate problem of how to find the enemy and face them in operations once hostilities have broken out is that of tactical intelligence. Even so, one should not lose sight of the fact that both kinds are always so closely connected that what happens in one area will have results in the other. Tactical intelligence and its ramifications are, by contrast with strategic intelligence, given a much greater coverage in the literary sources, a situation which allows the various agencies that do the actual collection to be more clearly differentiated. One reason for the greater coverage may be because the results of tactical intelligence are more conspicuous; another may be that at a tactical level the relationships between the phases of the intelligence cycle are clearer, closer and therefore easier to grasp. This holds true both for the soldiers involved, down to the lowest level, and for the historians who record their activity.

The spread of the evidence allows the groups and individuals involved in tactical intelligence collection to be separated into well-differentiated bodies with relatively defined functions. In field practice, however, some overlaps occurred, not unexpected of course, given the rather *ad hoc* nature of much Roman campaigning, as is particularly demonstrated in the immediate antecedents to difficult military engagements. The sophistication in intelligence procedures seems to have improved after the later second century right down to the fourth century but throughout the key concepts in this pre-technological intelligence remain individual flexibility and ingenuity, especially where commanders are concerned, and the use of a variety of sources. Corresponding to our division of strategic intelligence-gathering into active and passive areas, the procedures are here divided between Roman sources – guards, scouts, spies, autopsy by generals and also some ingenious approaches; and non-Roman sources – prisoners, deserters, locals and even rumour.

# THE ACQUISITION OF TACTICAL INTELLIGENCE

## Roman sources

### *Advance guards:* Procursatores

The troops who appear in the ancient writers under the generic name *procursatores* and allied terms from the same root, and their close Greek equivalent *prodromoi*, need consideration first; they were, however, never formally organized on a standing basis and it would seem that their functions may not have been primarily the collection of intelligence. For the most part, they appear to have been a detachment of ordinary cavalry skirmishers posted immediately ahead of an army on the march. Ammianus approaches a definition of such troops when describing the order of march that Julian adopted on the advance down the Euphrates in 363. Once across the border at Circesium, the army marched in full readiness, preceded by a body of 1,500 *excursatores* who operated on both flanks as well, moving with great care and attention to detail so that no sudden or unexpected attack could occur (XXIV 1.2). Close similarities exist between this deployment of troops (and the purpose for doing so) and that laid down by Arrian for his *kataskopoi hippeis*, scouting cavalry, apart of course from the numbers involved (*Deployment* 1). In these descriptions of their duties, two things are implicit – first, there is a flushing-out purpose, which, because their numbers are high enough, allows them to do any skirmishing that may be needed (as for example at Ammianus XXIV 5.5); and second, a subsidiary intelligence purpose in that if they ran into any opposition or obstacle, it could be quickly referred back to the main force for action. Ammianus' definition is obliquely confirmed in almost exactly similar terms by Josephus in describing the standard Roman order of march (*Jewish War* III 6.2/116): Vespasian set out for Galilee from Ptolemais with light-armed auxiliaries and bowmen ahead to protect the main force from sudden ambush and to check over suspect wooded areas. Not specifically named as *procursatores*, they certainly had similar ends in view. Better for our purposes here are the *prodromoi*, advance skirmishers, reported as ranging ahead of M. Licinius Crassus' force as it began the invasion of Parthia in 53 BC. Once the main force had crossed the Euphrates at Zeugma, *prodromoi* were deployed to clear the route east, towards Carrhae ultimately: they reported finding the tracks of large numbers of horses turning away from the Romans but had encountered no actual people (Plutarch *Crassus* 20.1). The *prodromoi* were operating in a full reconnaissance role, as the immediate context reveals but clearly, in the circumstances, they had sufficient numbers to defend themselves if a brush with the Parthian cavalry had occurred.

In Caesar the role of *procursatores* is mostly attributed to simple *equites*, horsemen, operating at some distance, as, for example, in the Helvetian campaign of 58 BC, where for a while the whole of Caesar's cavalry force, 4,000 strong, which for the purposes seems very large, kept the Helvetii under observation from a distance so as not to lose contact (*Gallic War* I 15.1–2). But one passage reveals the fact that forces of any size utilized them. In the haste to relieve Q. Cicero during the Nervian rising of 54 BC, Caesar had sent an urgent message to M. Crassus, the triumvir's son, to join him with his one legion immediately from his base 25 *milia passuum* away (about 36 km): Crassus left at midnight and by about 9 a.m. Caesar was being informed by Crassus' *antecursatores* that he was about to arrive (*Gallic War* V 47.1). Their function was very much that defined by Ammianus above. More closely associated with an intelligence operation are the *speculatores et antecessores equites*, cavalry scouting skirmishers, who, at a point in the African theatre of the Civil War when Caesar had landed at Ruspina, reported to him that they had seen the enemy encamped not far off, and had then moved out to secure the local countryside – and the moment he received the report that Labienus was imminent, it was confirmed, the author goes on to say, by everyone seeing a large dust-cloud rising (*African War* 12.1). Further north, in the area round Utica in 49 BC, Curio's cavalry brought news of the imminent arrival on the scene of King Juba, the ally of his opponent Attius Varus; they came in from outpost patrolling (*ex statione*), and at the same time an identical dust-cloud feature confirmed their message. In this case, the intelligence content was very significant, sufficient to surprise Curio into a makeshift but unexpectedly successful running battle (*Civil War* II 26.2–3).

All the rest of the examples dealing with *procursatores* come from Ammianus, which may suggest that regular bodies for armed reconnaissance in force developed late in the Roman army. On the other hand, given Ammianus' reluctance to use technical terminology, the point must be made that these units could well be no more than bodies of *exploratores*, scouts, working ahead of the main force. Two of these examples deal with encounters with armed opposition and the need to fight their way out when carrying out the duties mentioned earlier (XXIV 3.1; 5.5). The others all have a much stronger intelligence component. Ammianus indicates that the signal for dividing the army that Julian had assembled in 363 for the invasion of Persia at Carrhae was the news of irruptions by Persian cavalry groups across the nearby desert frontier. It was brought in by *procursatores*, who were already operating and quite clearly separately from the normal intelligence services along the frontier (XXIII 3.4). Julian himself accompanied a body of *procursatores* patrolling near Coche-Seleucia on the Tigris in order to reconnoitre a deserted town but what they found there was the grim scene of numbers of public figures impaled, doubtless *pour encourager les autres* not to fail in their duty and help the Romans (XXIV 5.3). After Julian's death and the negotiated peace-treaty between Jovian and the Persians, when the army was attempting to return to Roman territory, it appears that standard reconnaissance patrols by *procursatores* went on – they were responsible for the discovery that the Persians were putting together a pontoon bridge at a considerable distance from the Romans for undoubtedly hostile ends. Once the discovery had been made and reported, the work was stopped (XXV 8.4).

Valentinian's campaigns across the Rhine in 368, which ended in the big success at Solicinium, show *procursatores* obtaining both factual and topographical intelligence. In one incident, they reported a presence of Germans at some distance (XXVII 10.8); in a second, they worked out a route up to the Solicinium plateau, held by a large force. The sequel, however, is illuminating – Valentinian was not happy with their indications and went forward himself to trace a different path. But this led to his nearly losing his life in an ambush and so the route that had been surveyed earlier was used (XXVII 10.10–11).

*Procursatores*, moreover, had a direct role in what was arguably the most serious defeat the Romans ever suffered, at Adrianople in 378, serious perhaps not so much in terms of numbers lost but in its effects (see pp. 241ff.).

## *Scouts:* Exploratores *and* kataskopoi

More important for our study are the troops who are designated *exploratores*, scouts. This term tends to be used by the literary sources for men who are operating further ahead of an army than is implied by the designation *procursatores* and who are more clearly involved in gaining advance intelligence than in providing a forward force of skirmishers. The Greek equivalent term is *kataskopoi*, or less frequently its cognates *proskopoi* or just *skopoi*. These words do, however, tend to be used more broadly than the Latin *exploratores* and sometimes seem to cover as well both *procursatores* and *speculatores* (see next section, pp. 54–60) – which should warn us not to draw too fine a distinction between the Latin terms. No surprise should be occasioned, since the functions of these groups do overlap and may even at times have been carried out by the same troops.

Unlike *procursatores*, however, who were always, perhaps, simply part of the general cavalry contingent of an army, formal units of *exploratores* appear to have been raised for campaigning purposes, at least under the Principate, though initially on a temporary basis. By the later second century AD inscriptions reveal that some standing units were in existence; the reasons for their development will be considered later (pp. 189ff.). Nevertheless, the literary sources, unlike military inscriptions, are not normally technical in the use of terms such as *exploratores* or *kataskopoi* and do not necessarily draw the distinction between *ad hoc*, temporary or permanent units. Here we are concerned only with the functions carried out by any troops so described.

First of all, the manuals make considerable play of the role of *exploratores* in acquiring topographical intelligence about the route to be followed by an army on the march. Not only must they be fully briefed about the general direction to be taken but, in keeping with the necessity to ensure maximum security on the march, they must keep their eyes open for anything that looks remotely suspicious (Vegetius *Epitome of Military Science* III 6; Onasander *Art of Generalship* 6.7). The whole thrust of the section of Vegetius' handbook that deals with them is directed in particular towards illustrating the necessity for *exploratores* to be used to find out as much as possible about the intended route. Its purpose is that the commander be enabled to develop a mental pictorial map of the way ahead and that all the inherent problems of 'going' – the condition and security of routes in an area – can be clearly acknowledged. This aspect of their duties, however, receives surprisingly little attention from the historians in passages devoted to campaign movement: Polybius for example discusses the matter, quite briefly, as part of a section of his work devoted to the art of gener-alship and does not relate it specifically to any operation (IX 14.2–3). Much more frequently, though, mention is made of somebody or some vaguely defined group of cavalry going forward, sometimes at considerable distances, to check and clear a route of march for their own side (e.g. Caesar *Gallic War* VII 56.4; Tacitus *Histories* III 52; and cf. Livy XXII 4.4), or to identify an enemy's (e.g. Polybius III 41.8–9; Caesar *Civil War* III 38.2). Clearly, on a number of these occasions the cavalry referred to must be *exploratores* (e.g. Sallust *Jugurthine War* 53.7) but in the absence of specific detail about them it would be unwise to be too definite. The checking and clearing duties are underlined by Arrian in a recommendation at the very beginning of the *Deployment*, where the two prongs of his force's advance were to be formed by scouting cavalry (*kataskopoi hippeis*) (*Deployment* 1). Suetonius makes reference to a centurion of the senior cohorts on a march acting as route scout (*explorator viae*), presumably to avoid local ob-stacles along a predetermined itinerary (*Tiberius* 60).

In certain campaign conditions, where local topography required it, *exploratores*, in association with more regular troops, were used to help site camps for the best offensive and defensive purposes. A passing note in the elder Pliny provides incidental evidence that this was part of their function. He mentions that once *exploratores* had selected a site, they were required to get fires going, for which they would use flints or rubbed sticks. This may have been done to signal where the site was, although the primary function is likely to have been to provide an immediate source of fire for food-preparation and warmth as soon as the main body of troops arrived (*Natural History* XVI 208; XXXVI 138). For a more substantial confirmation, witness Caesar on the Sambre in 57 BC where *exploratores* and centurions went forward to fix a site for a camp at a point where maximum pressure could be exerted on the Nervii (*Gallic War* II 17.1). The fact that Caesar's account of the topography of the subsequent battle is suspect does not affect the role here described for the *exploratores*.[1] More significant were the *exploratores* who reconnoitred a flat crest outside Gergovia in 52 BC, following apparently unexplained movements of Vercingetorix' Gallic forces off the crest: once their report on its topography and these movements had been reinforced by a string of deserters from the town, Caesar successfully exploited the tactical possibilities of the site during the opening stages of his siege (*Gallic War* VII 44.1–3). Much clearer is Tacitus' remark on the role of *exploratores* guiding Agricola to the position of the hard-pressed Ninth Legion in AD 83: the infor-mation they provided on the Caledonians' line of march enabled him to follow their path right to the battleground and retrieve the disastrous situation (created, it should be said, by what seems an amazing lack of judgement in having divided

his army into three in very hostile conditions and thus having allowed an opportunity for the Caledonians to pick legions off piecemeal) (*Agricola* 26.1). It can
be seen how indispensable in the circumstances the *exploratores* were.

Much more attention is, however, devoted to the collection of detailed information about factual events and situations on which could be based a particular
kind of response. Some of the theoretical basis for this is made clear by Arrian
in a passage where *kataskopoi* are specifically to be sent forward to check for
possible indications of hostile activity at or near a battlefield, while the main
force remains in a tight defensive formation (*Deployment* 11). Failure to carry out
this function leads to situations where it is difficult to extricate a force without
grave risks – Velleius, for instance, contrasts the careful and thorough Tiberius
with his subordinates Caecina and Plautius during an incident in AD 7 during
the Pannonian Revolt, emphasizing the critical role of *exploratores* in preventing
a surprise and unwelcome encounter, unprepared, with large enemy forces. The
negligence and incompetence of the two consular commanders on this occasion very nearly led to a disaster for their five legions (II 112.5). Even though
it is in a rhetorical context, one dealing with Constantius' fighting in the Singara
area in 343/4, Libanius depicts with unusual clarity the role of *kataskopoi* in
closely observing and then reporting accurately without guesswork a range of
Persian activity leading up to the first of two important engagements. Here these
troops provided a full picture of the developments as they occurred (these being
the crossing of the Tigris in several places and the establishment of a strongpoint perhaps 30 km east of Singara) and allowed Constantius to respond with
initiatives that both conserved his resources and allowed a fully thought-through
series of tactical manoeuvres to take place: the Romans enticed the Persians
into a trap and then pursued them back to their strongpoint (Libanius *Orations*
LIX 101ff.). Ammianus makes a similar kind of observation in the course of his
account of the chaos in the Balkans brought on by the Gothic incursions
of 377. The *dux* Frigeridus was able to withdraw from his defensive position
at Beroë (Stara Zagora) in Thrace westwards towards Illyricum in an ordered
way with no losses, because he had been given proper advance warning by his
*exploratores* about the progress of a large Gothic force against him. His experience and his use of *exploratores* to confirm his suspicions prevented his being
forced into a confrontation and his success in thus conserving his manpower
earned him commendation from Ammianus as *dux cautissimus*, a very prudent
and wary commander (XXXI 9.2, 4).

*Exploratores* work at distances beyond that covered by the reconnaissance
of larger groups of mounted troops, if the bald statement by Tacitus referring
to the Flavian general Antonius Primus in the Bedriacum area in 69 is to
be accepted at face value. In the course of a tart vignette Tacitus relates
that Antonius left Bedriacum, taking 4,000 cavalry with him towards Cremona,
to provide support for the plundering activities of some auxiliary cohorts sent
out earlier and adds 'while his *exploratores*, as is usual practice, looked after things
at a greater distance away'. Such a remark suggests that their normal operations

would be expected to take place beyond the 12 km range of his cavalry that Tacitus notes and so would naturally provide Antonius with a deeper screen within which intelligence could be gathered. Proof, here, is provided by the fact that next day the *exploratores* located the advancing Vitellians, at which stage planning for the ensuing contact could begin (*Histories* III 15–16).

Rather less informative for this purpose are two passing references from Tacitus dealing with contacts along the Po in the Placentia region shortly before the above. The first notes the Vitellian Caecina's German and Batavian troops moving along the north bank of the river at one point and then making a sudden crossing to snatch a number of Othonian *exploratores* on the opposite bank. As these *exploratores* were working only about 4 km from their base Placentia, this action caused inflated alarmist reports to get back to the Othonians in the town (*Histories* II 17). Here the working range was very close. Then, after the Othonians' reaction to the situation and a night away practising unfamiliar encampment procedures, Vestricius Spurinna calmed his unseasoned troops, led them back to Placentia and shortly after returned a number of *exploratores* to the same area. Note that the conditions described by Tacitus were exceptional and not standard operating conditions (*Histories* II 19). The second reference mentions constant clashes between groups of Othonian and Vitellian *exploratores* in which Caecina's side came off less well. While it illustrates the point that both sides were making serious attempts to get intelligence, it serves no informative purpose: it is only made by Tacitus to heap obloquy on Caecina (*Histories* II 24).

The least ambiguous piece of evidence for the working distance of *exploratores* on campaign is in Caesar's account of his move from Vesontio (Besançon) to confront Ariovistus and the Helvetii in 58 BC: after six days of forced march by the legions, *exploratores* ahead reported that Ariovistus and his forces were 24 *milia passuum* away (about 35 km). This may seem at first sight to be a considerable distance ahead for an army on the march, but it is by no means inconsistent with the urgency Caesar says was necessary at this stage; again, the *exploratores* knew what they were looking for, and had some idea of where to find it. The distance Caesar gives represents a cross-country ride of about three hours (*Gallic War* I 41.5). A second case which involved earlier extensive shadowing of Ariovistus by *exploratores*, but from a closer distance (about 11 km, an hour's ride), is dealt with below in the next paragraph (*Gallic War* I 21.1; cf. I 15.5). Further, in the immediate antecedents to the famous battle of Strasbourg in AD 357, Ammianus notes that *procursatores* had exactly located the concentrated Alaman invasion force some 21 *milia passuum* (about 30 km) away from Julian's last position. Identification of this force was made easier because in their confidence that they would easily finish Julian off, the Alamanni had actually prepared the battleground with tactical obstructions. If, as we suggested earlier (p. 41), such *procursatores* were no more than *exploratores* sweeping ahead of the main force, then they too can be used as indicators of working distance (Ammianus XVI 12.8, 23).

The principle of instant access to the commander himself at all times by anyone with information is strongly recommended in Onasander's manual, where there is a warning that delays in receiving information can easily lead to disaster (*Art of Generalship* 11.6). It is clear that the very accessibility of the commander to his *exploratores* allowed them to act as his eyes at a distance. A good short example of this from AD 69 concerns Caecina in the midst of a bridge-building inspection and preparing to listen to peace proposals from two tribunes from Otho's Praetorian Guard, when *exploratores* arrived in haste with the news of how close Otho's forces were. The inspection was abruptly ended, the interview abandoned and battle preparations begun (Tacitus *Histories* II 41; cf. also Suetonius *Caligula* 45.1; *Vitellius* 16). But the more detailed account that Caesar gives, of a series of events during the Helvetian campaign of 58 BC, shows this access even better. After an initial victory over the Helvetii as they crossed the Arar (River Saône) (discussed below, p. 47), Caesar had been following them at a distance of a few kilometres. Eventually, the *exploratores* indicated that the Helvetii had stopped 8 *milia passuum* (about 12 km) ahead. A check was made on the nature of a ridge in the immediate vicinity and whether it could be climbed (a topographical check perhaps carried out by the same *exploratores* who had reported the halt in the march). Labienus was led up the ridge by the same group during darkness while Caesar himself moved closer to the Helvetii. Constant reconnaissance round them was carried on by *exploratores* under the command of the experienced P. Considius – who galloped in early in the morning to report that Labienus' ridge was held by Gauls whose equipment he had recognized. Caesar formed into battle order and waited, while patrols continued to check the situation and eventually revealed that Labienus was still on the ridge also waiting for action to start. At this point it became clear that the Gauls knew nothing of what the Romans were doing and that Considius' report had been the result of panic and that he had seen what was in fact not there. Needless to say, he does not reappear in Caesar's work. What is of particular interest here is the constant flow of intelligence from his *exploratores* into Caesar's command post, each piece of which added more information to the pool already held and modified it, so bringing about a change in Roman responses. Caesar's receptiveness and sensitivity to that intelligence flow show the ideal link between information and action that good intelligence work should assist (*Gallic War* I 21–2). Even more interesting is Caesar's comment that prisoners were afterwards questioned on what the Helvetii were doing during all this activity: it emerged that they knew nothing about it nor where the Romans were. This process indicates a policy of debriefing after significant actions to find out where weaknesses and errors were and shows a high degree of sophisticated organization of the intelligence establishment (*Gallic War* I 22.1). A second, supporting, passage in Caesar that deals with subsequent de-briefing occurs in the aftermath of Q. Cicero's valiant defence of his camp during the revolt of late 54 BC in north-eastern Gaul. Here the details of the events that had led to the defeats and death of Cicero's co-officers Sabinus and Cotta were elicited from prisoners and very clearly had been discussed in the headquarters: in contrast to Cicero, they had attempted to escape from their winter quarters but had been ambushed; then when they had surrendered, they were attacked and killed during negotiations (*Gallic War* V 52.4).

A similar stage-by-stage use of *exploratores* occurs in Hirtius' discussion of the campaign in 51 BC against the Senonian Drappes in the area round Uxellodunum. Caninius Rebilus' smallish force was occupied in trying to encircle Gallic strongpoints, which were in need of fresh supplies. Movement was heard one night by sentries and detailed information on what was happening was brought back by *exploratores* sent out to investigate. Prompt reaction by Caninius based on their information resulted in disruption of the Gauls' efforts at dawn. More information about Drappes' situation was discovered from prisoners (Hirtius emphasizes that it was carefully corroborated) and Caninius was able to respond quickly by sending a fast-moving cavalry contingent to start the action: he himself was kept informed through *exploratores* of the situation as it developed, including a move by the Gauls off high ground to a river, while he was bringing up a legion. This process ensured the end of Drappes' efforts – it is a small object-lesson in itself of the substantial contribution made by a flow of information straight to a commander. Intelligence material arrived in time to be exploited by quick reactions, yet proper safeguards to ensure its accuracy were implemented (Hirtius *Gallic War* VIII 35.4–36.4).

Caesar, again, gives a good example of an action where this process involving a flow of information must have taken place: at the beginning of the campaign of 58 BC against the Helvetii mentioned earlier, the River Arar (Saône) had to be crossed for the whole tribe to move west into fresh territory. Using his *exploratores* to identify the right moment, Caesar waited until some three-quarters had crossed, then made an effective attack on the last quarter, while they were still preparing to cross. The exact timing for an operation of this kind was dependent on a regular flow of reports on the situation as it developed and could not have been contemplated without the careful pre-planning implied in Caesar's narrative here (*Gallic War* I 12.2). There are few differences between this incident and one from much later in the Gallic campaign where Caesar was preparing to attack Cenabum (Orléans) during the revolt of Vercingetorix in 52 BC: here Caesar had arrived too late in the day to begin the assault and so encamped next to the town while *exploratores* kept the place under observation in case the inhabitants should try to escape across the Loire bridge. During the night the *exploratores* reported that the Gauls had in fact started to cross the river and so the Roman troops were sent into action. Here, again, the importance of timing for the success of the operation can be seen, in that the beginning of the action was dependent on the reporting of the *exploratores* (*Gallic War* VII 11.8). In a roughly similar situation but one requiring days rather than hours, Caesar describes the need for *exploratores* to keep Afranius and Petreius under continuous observation in the area round Ilerda (Lérida) in the early part of the Civil War in Spain: it occurred in the context of the very difficult movements occasioned by floods, bridge damage and lack of suitable river-crossings nearby and was made particularly necessary by Caesar's initial lack of manpower, supplies and physical command of the terrain. Every move of the enemy needed to be reported and analysed so that any advantage, however small, could be exploited; and at the same time, in a complementary effort to improve his position Caesar pushed on with the extreme course of diverting part of the River Sicoris (Segre) to lower its level for easier crossing (*Civil War* I 62.1–3).

In the case of partly subdued areas, too, it is to be expected that patrols of *exploratores* would continue to operate, monitoring activity and making regular reports in the interests of ensuring Roman security. Giving an account of Galba's operations in the north-western Alps during the winter of 57–56 BC, Caesar describes how one of the reports revealed that, in the very town Galba was settling down to winter in, Octodurus (Martigny), where he had taken over one part of the town for winter quarters and allocated the other to the local Gauls, the Gallic sector was suddenly found to be deserted and the heights above the town to have been occupied by armed Gauls. The warning conveyed by the *exploratores* was scarcely in time to allow a Roman reaction but Galba managed eventually to extricate himself. The situation could have turned out quite differently if he had not received the information; what lies behind the episode is the implied fact of a flow of intelligence generated by regular patrolling (*Gallic War* III 2.1ff.).

In a more important case illustrating the effects of a flow of intelligence, this time in the Civil War of 49–48 BC, Caesar shows how an assessment made by Pompey was corrected by intelligence gathered by his *exploratores*. At Asparagium in Illyricum, Caesar had failed to make Pompey face him on the battlefield and so left the area to make a fast thrust towards Dyrrhachium. Pompey had been watching it and initially interpreted the movement as a reaction to inadequate supplies. But he had to change his interpretation when his *exploratores* provided information that allowed him to recognize that there was a quite different reason for the apparent withdrawal. This case is a good one for demonstrating how later information can modify an earlier line of thought in important respects and so allow a commander to keep in close contact with the intentions of an enemy (*Civil War* III 41.4).

The flow of intelligence into a campaign or battle headquarters is not limited to material before a battle – it is a continuous process that follows right through to well after an action has been completed. This can be shown for example from the many indications that it was a standard procedure to assess information about the effects of a battle on the local area afterwards and for the assessment to form part of reports back to higher authorities. In the famous aftermath of the victory of Mons Graupius in AD 84, *exploratores* reconnoitred in detail for traces of the destroyed British force and found nothing: their information was negative and allowed full credit for the victory to be taken (Tacitus *Agricola* 38.2). It is interesting to see a similar operation in train even after a massive Roman defeat: Ammianus describes the remnants of Valens' force besieged in Adrianople by the Goths in 378: one night the Goths disappeared but to check that their withdrawal was a genuine one, *exploratores* were sent out for a reconnaissance before the gates were opened. In view of the defeat and various attempts at treachery, the reliability of these *exploratores* is given some emphasis. What can be seen here is an attempt made to re-establish the flow of intelligence; it reflects credit on the surviving commanders in the town (XXXI 16.2).

From some of the historians' accounts, inferences can be drawn about how much intelligence was generated by a flow of information from *exploratores*. In one such case, Tacitus describes a raid from Vetera (Xanten) by Germanicus against the Marsi in AD 14. While preparations for the raid were being completed, his *exploratores* reported that the Marsi were celebrating a festival, the particular night for it had been identified and the feasting was *sollemnes epulae*, sanctified by their religion. Further, in order to reach the Marsi at the right moment, now that the whole tribe was gathered together, the route that could be followed by Germanicus had already been surveyed – and it was not the obvious shorter route that was used but a longer, less likely one and unguarded (*Annals* I 50.3). From Tacitus' narrative, two points emerge: one, that the longer route taken by Germanicus to this festival certainly entailed much more than just a quick sweep by intelligence-collecting agencies: implicit in the account is a process of intelligence collection over an extended period – the Marsi must have been under observation for some time, because the information brought back to Germanicus was so detailed; the second is a more general one, which supports remarks made earlier about the assessment of intelligence following an action in the field: Tacitus' ultimate source here is the report on the details of the campaign sent back as a dispatch (*relatio*) to the Senate. That report contained the results of discussion and analysis of the raid, including the contribution of intelligence to its success.

Apart from the routine techniques adopted in the collection of tactical intelligence for which *exploratores* were used, there is evidence for some unexpected types of activity that should be examined in an analysis of their duties. One of these concerns the ability of *exploratores* to insinuate themselves through siege lines to take information and instructions to the besieged, and conversely to bring them out. Ammianus' detailed account of the siege of Amida in 359 shows that Ursicinus, his commander-in-chief, made numerous attempts to get *exploratores* into the town but failed because the siege was so closely conducted by the Persians (XIX 3.3). Clearly then, their work included training in the security of movement which many operational situations apart from sieges would have demanded in practice. The undercover nature of some of the normal operations of *exploratores* is noted in two attacks by Ammianus on the notorious Gaudentius, who was a Constantius-man on Julian's staff from the early days of the Caesar in Gaul and was used 'for probing into his actions' (*ad explorandos eius actus*) (XVII 9.7; XXI 7.2). Such an expression can only mean that Gaudentius was working clandestinely, fulfilling one of the roles *exploratores* were trained for. It should be pointed out that no evidence is extant about the training of *exploratores* but there is one piece in Dio's account of Trajan's operations in Armenia and Parthia in 115 which throws some light on this topic. While actually on campaign, Trajan had scouts (*proskopoi*) bring in fabricated information, as a means of practising rapid responses on the part of the troops (and no doubt of their officers) to information received and of course to keep them alert (Dio LXVIII 23.2). From this it may be legitimate to infer that manoeuvres and training periods in peacetime included such intelligence-related exercises.

Tacitus gives two examples of intelligence staff actively creating situations in which totally misleading information would be picked up by the opposition and would be damaging to their morale. Both refer to the Civil War of 69. In the first, Vitellius' *exploratores* were thought to be involved in spreading among the Othonian opposition the rumour that the Vitellians' challenge had collapsed following a (mythical) desertion of Vitellius by his army – the situation this fabrication created was one of temporary confusion all over the Cremona area (*Histories* II 42). The second has close operational similarities: the Flavian side, a few months later, found that an excellent way of spreading alarm with Vitellius was to get hold of captured *exploratores*, give them a conducted tour of the Flavian dispositions and send them back to Vitellius, where of course the material they reported struck at morale, a good piece of psychological warfare sanctioned by antiquity and actually recommended as a practice in one of the handbooks (*Histories* III 54; cf. Herodotus VII 146; Polybius XV 5.4–7; Onasander *Art of Generalship* 10.9). These last cases illustrate an unconventional *modus operandi* in very close proximity to the enemy, a point not particularly remarked on elsewhere in our sources.

The literary references to *exploratores* thus show that the term was used for bodies of troops acting in enemy territory in a more or less overt role; they may have employed skills in camouflage, movement and in using contacts but these were more secondary than anything else. There are a number of passages describing men operating in a similar manner where they are not specifically referred to as *exploratores* but where use of the verb *explorare* or its cognates, or the activities described, nevertheless indicate that we are dealing with the same sort of troops. A few examples are cited below, although others may be adduced (e.g. Sallust *Jugurthine War* 46.6; *Catiline* 60.1).

North-east Spain posed for Caesar some very difficult campaign problems during the early part of the Civil War. In order to force the issue he had to cut off Afranius and Petreius from movement and access to food supplies: at Octogesa it appeared that control by either side of a wild and rugged area nearby would ensure success. Caesar naturally had to know about ways into this crucial area and a party of soldiers under L. Decidius Saxa carried out the investigation and reported back; and Petreius himself was doing exactly the same with some cavalry. Clearly both these opposing groups were acting in the reconnaissance-of-terrain role of *exploratores* (*Civil War* I 66.3–4; 68.1).

Precisely parallel is the examination carried out by Curio of Castra Cornelia just across a tidal swamp from Utica in Africa. Here using his cavalry in the same way, he accompanied them himself and was able to see how good the site was for an encampment; and in addition, he was able to look down on to the activities of his opponents in and around their camp, which abutted on to the town walls, all less than 2 km as the crow flew from Curio's viewpoint (*Civil War* II 24.2; 25.1). In both cases, Caesar's use of the word *explorare* supports such an interpretation. A more self-explanatory use occurs in the account he gives of moves made by the Pompeian Metellus Scipio and the Caesarian Domitius Calvinus in Thessaly before Pharsalus in 48 BC: Calvinus faked a withdrawal from a position on the Haliacmon and set up a big ambush not far away into which he hoped Scipio would fall but a preliminary cavalry reconnaissance in force to trace the movements of Calvinus sprang the ambush early; Scipio thus avoided having to undertake any serious fighting. In this case, the cavalry was acting as *exploratores* would and at the same time doing it in sufficient strength to be able to defend itself (*Civil War* III 38.2). Hirtius' use of *explorare* fits the pattern we are discussing in exactly the same way. This time, however, it is in a revealing case of failure by cavalry to clear an area before moving into it at speed and so falling into a carefully laid ambush. At one point in the campaign against the Bellovaci in 51 BC, the Remi formed part of Caesar's allied cavalry force and lost a lot of men and a leading magistrate by rushing after a decoy and being caught out. Hirtius notes that hard lessons were learned – that outriders had to be positioned after a much more careful clearing of the area ahead and that pursuits had to be undertaken with more care and restraint (*Gallic War* VIII 12.7).

Tacitus uses similar expressions in contexts where it is clear that *exploratores* were the agency involved. In a speech to his soldiers in AD 69 outside the walls of Cremona, Tacitus has Antonius Primus say that in no circumstances should they attempt to enter the town before a full reconnaissance has been made and certainly not in the dark of night, even if the gates were wide open. Any such reconnaissance would probably have to be carried out by *exploratores*, since it appears that Antonius viewed the situation inside the town as so dangerous that even night-time operations using *speculatores* could be unreliable (*Histories* III 20). Two others concern the unfortunate and incompetent Dillius Vocula on the Rhine during the revolt of Civilis in 69–70. In the first, Tacitus analyses why Vocula failed adequately to defend the legionary camp at Gelduba (Gellep) and attributes it to his not having identified the activities of Civilis' forces immediately beforehand – a duty that would naturally have involved *exploratores* (*Histories* IV 34.1). In the second, a few months later, Vocula was lulled into a false sense of security by duplicity on the part of his Gallic troops; he allowed two of his auxiliary officers, Classicus and Tutor, to go ahead to reconnoitre the situation around Vetera (Xanten). Under this operational pretext they used the freedom that reconnaissance allows to establish contacts with the opposition; it led to Vocula's murder and another set of Roman losses in the region. While this case illustrates a role for *exploratores*, it also makes clear that from the first century AD onwards, *auxilia* formed the recruitment group from which were drawn the campaign *exploratores*, as the epigraphic evidence confirms for those on fixed stations (*Histories* IV 57.1; cf. 55.1).

A closely parallel case in Ammianus' account of Julian's Persian expedition in 363 shows the commander of the rearguard, Victor, in charge of a party which had done a reconnaissance along the route from the site of Maiazomalcha on the Euphrates, under siege by Julian, to the walls of Ctesiphon on the Tigris, the next big objective in his advance. That reconnaissance again indicates the duties of *exploratores*, though this time under the command of a very senior man (a *comes*, count), presumably to counter the possibility of any mistake being made (XXIV 4.13, cf. 31). Worth noting are the number of times in fourth-century intelligence contexts that such very senior officers take part directly in the collection process, for both strategic and tactical purposes, though to what extent this practice represents a departure from previous operating procedures is unclear. It may be no more than an illustration of Ammianus' use of this level of officer as one of his sources. Autopsy as a part of intelligence collection carried out by such senior men is discussed further below (pp. 60ff.).

In many of these cases it is of course quite possible that the historians are following standard literary practice in avoiding the use of specific technical vocabulary, merely suggesting it by means of the relevant verb. A more extreme example, where *exploratores* were undoubtedly the agency involved, can be seen in Tacitus' account of the activities of the inadequate L. Paetus in Armenia in 62. Paetus' intelligence on the Parthian threat to him was negligible and when eventually he made some attempt to face Vologaeses' invasion near the *castellum* of Arsamosata, he sent out a reconnaissance party made up of a centurion and a few soldiers to check on the enemy's forces (*visendis hostium copiis*). It did not return. It is very unlikely that the group was anything other than a normal routine detachment of *exploratores* under their centurion, regardless of the formulation here adopted by Tacitus (*Annals* XV 10.4). There is an equally circumlocutory expression used by Ammianus in the course of his account of an operation carried out by the *magister equitum* Arbitio in 355, in the frontier area of Raetia round Lake Brigantia (Bodensee). His *qui adventus barbarorum nuntiarent*, 'the men who were to report the barbarians' arrival', means no more than *exploratores* in the context: Arbitio had failed to wait for their specific information in circumstances that he knew were particularly dangerous and had marched his troops into an Alaman ambush where he took heavy casualties. A lack of basic tactical intelligence had led an experienced commander into trouble (XV 4.7).

As already stated, historians writing in Greek used the word *kataskopos* and its cognates more broadly than *explorator* was used in Latin but it is evident that in the majority of instances it is the *exploratores* whom they are describing.

Arrian, Hadrian's governor of Cappadocia in 135, describes his own *kataskopoi* in circumstances where his force is moving towards a battlefield, carrying out duties which match exactly those assigned by Latin authors to *exploratores* – the *kataskopoi* must move to higher ground to gain a view over enemy dispositions, so that a Roman force can be drawn up in the most effective way as it moves into the battleground situation (*Deployment* 11). Implicit of course is the communication which renders that effectiveness possible. The Dio passage mentioned earlier which describes Trajan's *proskopoi* in the Parthian campaign of 115 provides a practical illustration of the correspondence with *exploratores*. Here these soldiers were used, occasionally in quiet moments, to bring in made-up information so that his army and its systems could practise their response to emergency situations. Quite apart from the training aspect involved, what is being described is standard *explorator* activity, based on patrolling, probing and reporting (Dio LXVIII 23.2).

Polybius' use of the words in Roman contexts is somewhat unspecific and thus serves only as a guide. Hannibal's crossing of the Rhône in 218 BC required a check on where the Romans were landing further downstream and in what numbers, before he could begin the complicated task. For the purpose a body of 500 mounted Numidians were sent off *kataskepsomenoi* ('to reconnoitre'), in what is clearly an overt *explorator*-style action (III 44.3). They returned much later in the day from their *kataskope* ('reconnaissance') in disarray, having run into and been forced away by an aggressive, if smaller, Roman force sent out by P. Scipio the Elder for the same ends, *katopteusantes*, which also means 'reconnoitring' – i.e. also acting as *exploratores* (III 45.1, 3). The latter word, incidentally, is also used to describe the mutual reconnaissance in force carried out by Hannibal and Scipio themselves with all their cavalry forces in the country west of the Ticino in Cisalpine Gaul; this took place after initial reports from foragers had indicated how physically close both sides now were (III 65.1–3).

Among later writers, Plutarch, for instance, is evidently referring to the operations of *exploratores* in noting that cavalry sent out *epi kataskopen* ('for a reconnaissance') discovered and reported to Crassus in northern Parthia that a very large and aggressive force was coming up: this was the force that delivered the great defeat over the Romans at Carrhae (Harran) in 53 BC (*Crassus* 23.2). Zosimus, in a rare flash of technical detail, reports that the defenders of Siscia in Pannonia (Sisak) in the civil war of 351 had organized patrols of *kataskopoi* working in the surrounding countryside and one of them brought in the news that the usurper Magnentius had crossed the River Sava. The men who provided the advance warning needed by the defence were clearly *exploratores* (II 48.1).

In the preceding cases, the direct equation of *kataskopoi* with the Latin *exploratores* seems quite evident. There can be less certainty about such groups as the selected cavalry (*epilektoi hippeis*) who accompanied Titus in 70 in two separate reconnaissances around the defences of Jerusalem. One took place as he arrived there before the siege began in earnest and involved a general assessment of the site and gaining a general impression (*periskepsomenos*) of the response to the appearance of Roman forces. Earlier information had suggested that the general populace was kept from negotiations only by threats of violence from 'rebels and terrorists' but Titus was attacked as he passed one of the gates and had to fight his way out (*Jewish War* V 2.1–2/52ff.). In a brief resumptive conclusion to this episode Josephus actually uses the term *kataskopos* to describe Titus' scouting activity (V 2.2/61). The second reconnaissance was a more detailed one and took place a short time later. It was focused particularly on finding weak points in the defensive works. Josephus covers Titus' action in the word *kateskepteto* (V 6.2/258). Thus while Titus himself was quite clearly carrying out what in Latin would be described as *explorationes*, the selected cavalry with him in both situations can be no more than hurriedly collected soldiers used mainly as defence for their commander and not acting as *exploratores* in their own right. They were therefore rather different from Arrian's *kataskopoi hippeis* ('scouting cavalry'), who operate in two wings ahead of a force on the march and under their own commander and who can perhaps be identified as a formally constituted body of mounted *exploratores* (*Deployment* 1).

### *Spies:* Speculatores

The literary sources (mainly Caesar and Ammianus) distinguish a further group of soldiers engaged in intelligence-gathering, whom they call *speculatores*. These usually appear to be covert in their operations and, to assist their covertness, to be much less numerous in the field than *exploratores*. They were thus picked spies rather than scouts. There seems to have been no substantial difference in the usage of the term *speculator* between Caesar writing in the first century BC and Ammianus writing in the late fourth century AD. Unfortunately, it would appear from epigraphic, papyrological and even some literary texts that in the Principate, at least from the first century AD onwards, the term *speculatores* referred in addition to two specific groups and ranks of the Roman army; that these groups were entirely distinct from each other; and that neither of them had any special involvement in military intelligence or espionage (in the same way, for example, that in the British army a Grenadier no longer specializes in the use of grenades). The different usages are to be carefully distinguished by reference to context and the source involved – for instance, Tacitus, in contrast to his own normal practice and that of historians in general, almost always uses the word in its technical rather than its basic meaning to refer to the two ranks of army officer. The relationship of the basic to the technical meaning will be considered later in our study (pp. 150ff.). In this section, however, we are concerned solely with the functions attributed to *speculatores* as undercover operatives or spies.

Ammianus provides two indications about the way *speculatores* operated, from which some insight into earlier practice can perhaps be gained. In 365, the intending usurper Procopius is depicted as slinking into Constantinople to collect and disseminate hostile rumours about the emperor Valens, looking utterly nondescript, 'just like a highly skilled spy' (*ritu sollertissimi cuiusdam speculatoris*)

(XXVI 6.4–6). In an episode during the opening stages of the Persian invasion of 359, Ammianus himself and his commander Ursicinus captured a Roman deserter, originally from Gaul, who turned out to have been working as a *speculator* for the Persians in the Roman frontier zone and who on interrogation admitted to having sent back frequent and accurate reports (XVIII 6.16). If the Persians maintained *speculatores* as moles on Roman territory, the converse was also certainly true, though our most positive evidence comes from the early sixth century – Procopius mentions that it had always been government policy to do so (*Wars* I 21.11–12; *Secret History* 30.12ff.). These passages all suggest that maintenance of a cover of indistinctiveness was essential for success: they also suggest that some period out of touch with their own side and working on their own was part of the game (cf. e.g. Livy XXII 33.1). If we accept these as criteria for the operations of *speculatores*, then those mentioned in the *Spanish War* fit them quite well – a spy from Cn. Pompeius the Younger's locally recruited legion was picked out and killed by Caesar's troops (*Spanish War* 13.3); and shortly after this incident, four *speculatores*, three of them slaves and another who turned out to be a soldier from the same legion, were uncovered and executed (*Spanish War* 20.5). In a civil war context, such indistinctive covers could not have been too difficult to keep up: what happened in these cases of exposure doubtless represents no more than the tip of the iceberg.

One of the best-known methods of exploiting the cover of indistinctiveness (to the point of its being a commonplace) would have been to use people in the guise of deserters or refugees to penetrate the installations of the opposition. According to the author of the *African War*, Metellus Scipio tried it in 46 BC by sending two well-disposed Gaetulians amid numbers of real deserters into Caesar's camp at Ruspina (Monastir) in an attempt to discover his precautions against elephant-charges. They freely admitted their role to Caesar and were in due course granted refugee status after revealing information about Scipio's intentions (*African War* 35.2–5).

No doubt a variety of other covers also existed but an obvious one was that of negotiation involving men actually known to the enemy. We have already seen (pp. 17f.) how Caesar makes capital out of his failed negotiations with Ariovistus in 58 BC to illustrate the chief's unreliability and arbitrariness; but one of the two men whom he sent as envoys and who were exposed as spies, was well known to Ariovistus and so to Caesar's way of thinking stood a good chance of success when he was instructed to find out what kinds of things Ariovistus was saying (and of course not only to the negotiators) (*Gallic War* I 47.6). The case of the Pinarius who was detected taking notes during a military meeting addressed by Octavian around 40 BC, and was therefore regarded as being a *speculator* in disguise is hardly different in this area (Suetonius *Augustus* 27.3).

In a number of cases, it would seem that, even though they operated in greater secrecy and therefore had greater scope for close action, *speculatores* were used to gather material very similar to that usually collected by *exploratores*.

In the account of events in AD 354 in the long-running Isaurian insurgency, Ammianus mentions that the Roman leadership based on Seleucia was warned beforehand of a dangerous incursion through reliable *speculator* reports and was able to make an appropriate response: it seems that normal intelligence methods would not work in such circumstances so it was necessary to use covert agents (XIV 2.15). The *speculatores* who reported back to Valens at Nice during his march to Adrianople in mid-378 fit this pattern exactly. They were operating covertly close to the Goths who were freely marauding over much of the area from Rhodope in the west to Adrianople in the east, since Roman authority over the countryside had completely collapsed. Naturally conditions in the area were such that only *speculatores* could operate if any form of intelligence was to be gathered. The success of Valens' *magister peditum* Sebastianus in his unconventional guerrilla counter-raid to retrieve booty underlines this view (XXXI 11.2).

Tacitus' only example of the word *speculator* being used in the covert operations sense is closely parallel: just after crossing the Weser in AD 16, Germanicus received information through a deserter about an impending assault under cover of night by Arminius and in a determined attempt not to be caught unprepared, sent out *speculatores* to confirm it and to identify exactly where all this was happening. They heard the noises of horses and a large disordered mob and their report enabled tough Roman defensive precautions to be taken (*Annals* II 12.1). In a rather wider context than Tacitus', Ammianus describes a case of covert *speculator* operations across the Persian frontier in the waiting period of 361, when Constantius II sat at Edessa in increasing anxiety over both the expected Persian attack from the East and, behind him in the West, the proclamation of Julian as Augustus. In this case, because of Persian security, reports sent back by the *speculatores* out in the field and the stories of refugees and deserters were so conflicting that no positive Roman response was possible (XXI 13.4). In both these series of incidents, it is clear that the required intelligence could only be gathered by individuals operating with a low profile and as indistinctively as possible. A final case, which to a degree illustrates the difference between *speculatores* and *exploratores*, is found in Caesar's campaign of 57 BC in north-east Gaul: one night the Belgae were discovered to have moved away from their encampment near the River Aisne not far from Reims, a move immediately passed back to Caesar by his *speculatores*. Roman reaction centred around fear of a trap, so at daylight the whole area was closely checked by *exploratores* before pursuit of the Belgic column began. Here there is an implicit contrast between night and restricted intelligence work and daytime, when more open checking could be carried out. Covert information was here confirmed later by overt means (*Gallic War* II 11.2–3). In this connection, however, it should be noted that Vegetius' recommendation is for *exploratores* to work at night if at all possible (*Epitome of Military Science* III 6).

The situation regarding the kinds of work done by *speculatores* is, however, by no means as clear-cut as this survey suggests, since there are several passages of evidence about them which tend to blur the edges. In some, there appears to be no reason why the word *speculatores* should be used when it is clearly possible, if not likely, that *exploratores* would be carrying out the duties being described. For instance, in 54 BC, in the incidents that followed Q. Cicero's successful defence of his position, the Nervii raised the siege and turned *en masse* to face Caesar, who with his limited numbers was forced to fortify a site across a wide valley cut by a small river but in full view. In this predicament, it was clear that ways out of the valley that were not controlled by the Nervii had to be found. *Speculatores*, according to Caesar, were sent out to carry out an urgent reconnaissance. However, the verb he uses here is *explorat*, which in the context of our present discussion suggests that he means *exploratores* should have been the men used for this kind of task. It is of course quite possible that *speculatores* were required to perform a normal *explorator* duty and that their different functions were simply overlapped on this occasion, because any reconnaissance work in such tense conditions could only have been carried out in circumstances of tight secrecy by very small and inconspicuous groups: hence the use of *speculatores*. A more likely resolution, we think, is that *explorat* is here used simply for reasons of euphony, to avoid the verbal jingle *speculatoribus . . . speculat* but in so doing Caesar dilutes much of the exact technical sense of the word (*Gallic War* V 49.8; cf. V 50.3 and Livy XXI 53.11).

A comparable example, which occurs in a passage where Caesar describes the complex manoeuvrings outside Dyrrhachium against Pompey in 48 BC, is still more difficult to explain, because here the *speculatores* who identified the fact that a number of cohorts of Pompey's troops were moving behind cover and making for an empty fortification are mentioned on two occasions; and their information was corroborated by look-outs, which tends to emphasize that it really was actual *speculatores* who are intended here. The relatively simple information that was conveyed in their report seems to be exactly the same kind as would be expected from *exploratores* in similar circumstances. In view of Caesar's generally careful explanations and accurate technical definitions elsewhere in this area, we may be obliged to accept an explanation suggesting that in such dangerous conditions, where tight security was paramount, as in the previous Belgic example, *speculatores* could be the only agency operating (*Civil War* III 66.1; 67.1).

Two further cases from the *Spanish War* describe the collection of information by *speculatores* but it would be unwise to put too much weight on the precision of this source. In the first, where events preceding the fighting round Munda in 45 BC are described, Caesar had been on the point of moving on when he was told by *speculatores* that Cn. Pompeius the Younger had been standing-to since the third watch; it is conceivable therefore that *speculatores* were being used to operate in night-time conditions (*Spanish War* 28.1). In the second, which deals with the naval and land pursuit of Pompeius after his defeat, *speculatores* were the reported agency who traced the naturally defended place he had managed to reach; they had been sent on far ahead for the purpose by the pursuit troops. Here, the *speculatores* may well have had to use covert means to find the place (*Spanish War* 38.1). A third example in the immediate context describes Pompeius sending out a Lusitanian *speculator* presumably to find out where the pursuers were; he was seen moving and in this way revealed the whole situation to the Caesarians (*Spanish War* 38.3; but note that textual difficulties abound at this point in the manuscripts and render the story obscure in its details). The same caveat from earlier in this paragraph about the *Spanish War* applies to a case from Sallust, in which *speculatores* are characterized by the adjective *citi*, 'fast-moving': this could only refer to overt, visible and active intelligence collection at a simple low level – they must be what other writers would call *exploratores* (*Jugurthine War* 101.1).

On a number of occasions the operation of *speculatores*, even though they may not be referred to as such, is signalled by the use of the verb *speculari* and similar words. In the early stages of the Gallic War, some attempt was made by Caesar to negotiate with Ariovistus, as mentioned above. In view of the dangers to his own officials if they were sent, he made use of two Romanized Gauls who knew Ariovistus personally well enough for the purpose. However, in a face-saving or propagandist response to their arrival, Ariovistus accused them of coming for spying purposes (*speculandi causa*) and arrested them. Here the intelligence emphasis is on the plausible exterior appearance of *speculatores*, their small numbers and their ability to penetrate under a cover to get their information (*Gallic War* I 47.6). We may compare a passage alluded to earlier in the anonymous *African War*, where the dangers of the plausible exterior of refugees allowing them access to information are made clear. Metellus Scipio, wanting to know what some changes in Caesar's defensive activity implied, sent the two Gaetulians across to Caesar as part of the stream of refugees to acquire background information on Caesar's preparations to counter elephant warfare. When they revealed the plot to Caesar, they stated they were acting as *speculatores* for this purpose (*African War* 35.2ff.). In the case of Ammianus' story of his own and Ursicinus' movement to Samosata to ensure the dismantling of the pontoon bridges at Zeugma and Capersana in an effort to hold the Persian invasion of AD 359 on the line of the Euphrates, what indicated that these two places were the Persian objectives were *certae speculationes* of the change in the Persian line of march, only possible at that stage by covert means of observation (XVIII 8.1). Much of the same covert probing must underlie the checking done by Aequitius that showed him that the brunt of the revolt of Procopius in 365 was being taken by the Asiatic provinces and allowed him to take positive action to recover the European provinces (XXVI 10.4). In another episode, *speculationes* were responsible for the successes of the *magister equitum* Iovinus in eastern Gaul very early in 366. Ammianus notes on two occasions here the thorough and reliable information provided by the men in question and their contribution to the prosecution of the campaign. Alamanni had crossed the frontier and followed normal German practice in splitting up to plunder. Romans generally found such splittings-up very hard to deal with but during this winter campaign

Iovinus' well-directed and unobtrusive intelligence searching allowed him to find each of the three groups, follow them up and put them out of action without delay (XXVII 2.2–4). The account makes very clear the relationship between Iovinus' quick successes and his use of his intelligence resources throughout. What exactly is meant, however, by Ammianus' term *speculationes* is not clear: was this a situation in which normal *exploratores* could not operate and thus covert action was the only way? Or, since the commander himself was personally and closely involved (see p. 63 below), does it suggest the unconventional aspects of what were in effect anti-guerrilla operations? It is worth mentioning a burlesque of a military situation in a Roman novel: Apuleius has the brigands who plundered Milo's house and took Lucius the ass away with them to carry their takings leave behind a member of their band in disguise to watch, *ad speculandum*, for the response of the civic authorities in organizing a pursuit (*Golden Ass* III 28). Again, in all these cases the same criteria persist.

Finally, there are the cases where in authors writing in Greek *kataskopoi* are described as carrying out covert intelligence operations and therefore acting as *speculatores*. Polybius' version of Scipio Africanus' negotiations with the Numidian king Syphax in the winter of 204/3 BC contains an unequivocal example, which closely matches the definition of *speculatores* as covert, indistinctive and opportunist. The talks were deliberately protracted to allow groups of experienced men, in disguise as attendants of the negotiators, the chance to look over the layout and construction of the Numidians' camp and later to contribute to a plan for attacking it at night (XIV 1.13; 3.7; cf. Livy's version, XXX 4.1–3).

One of the concerns of *speculatores* noted earlier was to be able to penetrate enemy operations or territory on a long-term basis, using the cover of indistinctiveness. There is good supporting material for this in the anonymous *On Strategy*, where it is observed that *kataskopoi* will find markets good places in which to pick up information, because traders in all shapes and sizes can be found there and so it is easy to pass as one; and again where *kataskopoi* on operations are recommended to live quietly among the lower elements in society so as to avoid detection (42.7, 11).

Useful as a guide to definition here are the two references in the Caesarian corpus to reconnaissance vessels. In the first, the ships are called *speculatoria navigia*: these are used for coastal reconnaissance in hostile waters (Caesar, however, caused them to be used in an entirely non-reconnaissance role by filling them with troops for a naval engagement against the Venelli in 55 BC). No further information survives (*Gallic War* IV 26.4; but cf. Livy XXII 19.5). The second reference calls the fast ship that took instructions from Caesar at Ruspina to his lieutenants in Sicily a *catascopus* (note in passing that he expects the vessel to make the return trip in less than two days!) (*African War* 26.3–4). This word looks like soldiers' slang for the more formal term used above; if this is right, it furnishes some idea of the covert nature of the operations that the vessels were intended for, the speed of their movement and in the context, the close correspondence of *speculator* with *kataskopos*. Polybius too notes that in the course of Cn. Scipio's operations on the Spanish coast in 217 BC, two fast Massiliot vessels were used for reconnaissance purposes some 15 km ahead of his main fleet, round the mouth of the Ebro (*kataskepsomenas* and *epi ten kataskopen*, III 95.6, 8). The account suggests they escaped notice, since when Hasdrubal's lookouts reported the sighting of the larger fleet, only then were the Carthaginians galvanized into action (III 96.1).

*Autopsy*

Autopsy is the next category to be examined. Personal observation by a commander or a senior officer and the ability to make use of the results of the observation represent an ideal, since they allow all possibility of error from intermediaries or subordinates to be eliminated. Given the fact that such errors can and do exist, autopsy may save a commander from compounding them, though the other major advantage from a commander's point of view is that of speed, speed in being able to assess quickly the need for certain kinds of action in response to the problem confronting him. A good example of this is the autopsy carried out on the spur of the moment by M. Porcius Cato (later the Censor) to deflect a potentially disastrous situation in Greece in 191 BC. Plutarch, evidently relying on Cato's own account in a speech or in his *Origins*, records that, as an ex-consul acting as legate to the current consul M. Acilius Glabrio, Cato led a flanking attack on the army of Antiochus III of Syria which was blocking the main pass at Thermopylae. The guide who was directing his forces by the Callidromos pass, a prisoner of war, lost his way (deliberately?) and Cato, to prevent panic spreading through his army, went up on the mountain himself with one companion to find the path and mark out the route before returning to lead his forces through to a successful assault (Plutarch *Cato the Elder* 13). Autopsy of course accords well with the precept enunciated by Vegetius that a commander should be as fully briefed as possible at all times about the nature of the problems facing him, if he is to be the ideal commander (*Epitome of Military Science* III 6).

Strangely enough, Caesar does not make much of his own autopsy. Perhaps he felt that his senior officers were sufficiently experienced to be able to deal with their problems themselves; but worth noting in this context is the remarkable vignette of his working methods provided incidentally by the author of the *African War* (and implicitly denying the close personal involvement autopsy entails): he shows that by remaining in his headquarters divorced from the minutiae of camp organization and administration, Caesar was able to maintain the ordered connection between receiving intelligence, planning and acting on it in spite of the pressure of imminent battle (*African War* 31.4). Usually however, Caesar restricts himself to occasional comments about his noticing something. Outside Gergovia in 52 BC, for example, he noticed that a hill recently occupied by the Gauls had been abandoned: his reaction was to check his observation against information from refugees/deserters and so to confirm earlier information about this particular feature gathered from *exploratores* who had previously reconnoitred it, as we noted above. Moreover, autopsy here led directly to the questioning of the deserters and on to the discovery that the Gauls were worried about the loss of yet more high ground to the Romans; and this was what lay behind their movement off this height and concentration of men on an adjacent one in order to ensure continued control of access to one part of the *oppidum*, the native town (*Gallic War* VII 44). He tells us he carried out a personal inspection of the site of Alesia later in 52 BC but makes no direct connection between it and the actions that follow (*Gallic War* VII 68.3). His personal examination of the site of Thysdra in North Africa decided him to avoid a siege of the place because of the lack of a water-supply. As so often, one suspects that other factors may well have been in play here (e.g. the opposition was too well protected for Caesar to risk his small numbers of men) but whatever the real reason, autopsy contributed to that decision (*African War* 76.2). Similarly with the site and dispositions of his opponents at Hadrumetum (Sousse) at the very end of 47 BC. Here his personal examination immediately after the landing gave him the opportunity to realize that with the untried troops at his disposal it would be unsafe to stay in the area or make any attempt to seize the well-defended town. Autopsy provided the background to the decision to move on, one based on a personal acquaintance with the problem (*African War* 3). It should be noted, however, that these incidents and the senior-officer autopsy exercise conducted outside Octogesa which we referred to earlier are all part only of complex intelligence-gathering and guessing exercises; in the case of the Octogesa situation, what preceded it was the capture of a number of soldiers who revealed that Afranius and Petreius were planning a night move; and Petreius himself too next morning was out with cavalry support to reconnoitre (*Civil War* I 66.1, 3–4). Clearly eye-witness evaluation here represents a closer and more pointed investigation as a preliminary to a tactical action.

Germanicus' campaigns in Germany in AD 15 provide an occasion for a report on a senior man's autopsy. Reliable and experienced, A. Caecina was sent out on what was clearly a reconnaissance in force when Germanicus was contemplating a move to the scene where Varus' disaster had occurred in the Teutoburg forest a few years before. Caecina's orders were for a semi-independent operation designed to probe with the troops under his command for Germans in the forests along the proposed route as well as to clear the old Roman routes of the region: but what was initially an autopsy in force ran into serious opposition on the way back, perhaps with the intention on Caecina's part to draw off the Germans from Germanicus (Tacitus *Annals* I 61.1; 63.3ff.). More specific, though permeated with panegyric, are Tacitus' emphatic remarks on the leadership qualities of Agricola in Scotland, where Agricola himself made a practice of examining and choosing camp-sites and himself took a leading part in reconnoitring estuaries and forests ahead of his main force (*Agricola* 20.2; 25.1). On the surface of it these practices suggest an unnecessary exposure to personal risk on the part of a commander but perhaps more importantly, show the desire of the 'ideal leader' for close acquaintance with features that might condition his response to a military emergency, of which there was a distinct possibility in the conditions of very hostile opposition to the Romans that Tacitus describes. In any case, the difficult relations Agricola appears to have enjoyed with his senior oficers may have contributed to his need to demonstrate those qualities. All the same, Agricola's personal involvement in the operations of the navy reveals an important part of his thinking: the navy was not being used only for the essential strategic reconnaissance work but also in a close tactical support role, which allowed movement ahead to secure landing-places and harbours, land men and ensure regular supply and yet still be protected by the army when at these places (*Agricola* 25.1).

Tacitus credits Ostorius Scapula in AD 50 with a notable success based on the general's own visual examination of the strengths and defects in an unknown fortified site in the territory of the Ordovices. The British chieftain Caratacus had established his defences with some tactical talent, but it is clear that probing by the expert eye revealed flaws. Pressure from Ostorius' troops forced the attack, even though at the beginning the commander was reluctant (*Annals* XII 35). Autopsy here played a major role, as it very clearly did at one point during Corbulo's operations in Armenia in 58. Tacitus notes that Corbulo carried out a detailed personal inspection of the defences of Volandum, a fortress controlling the roads to Artaxata. This took place immediately before the place was subjected to a two-day assault using a diversified approach based on observed weak spots in the defences (*Annals* XIII 39).[2] In Josephus' book on the Jewish War, once again a certain panegyric element pervades, but through it can be seen Titus' careful and thorough approach using autopsy. During the move on Jerusalem in 70, Josephus shows Titus going forward with 600 selected horse to examine the physical details of the site of Jerusalem, after which the full preparations for its enclosure went ahead. This act of autopsy was itself a follow-up on rumoured information received about factional strife within the city, as its second aim was to establish what Jewish attitudes were before the attack began (*Jewish War* V 2.1–2/52ff.). A similar reconnaissance in force was made by Titus during the siege itself, in an effort to detect a point on the defences weak enough to allow an assault to be tried (*Jewish War* V 6.2/258). Such personal involvement, applied here to the search for intelligence, seems to have been a feature of Titus', since it is also referred to in favourable terms by Tacitus in his description of the advance on the city in early 70 (*Histories* V 1.2).

All these cases of autopsy would probably not rate a mention in the literary sources unless it could be demonstrated that there was a direct connection between intelligence gained by its use and signal success. The important ingredient in the success occasioned by the personal involvement emerges from several cases, the most spectacular of which is the story of Diocletian's Caesar Galerius during a campaign in Armenia in 297 or 298. He took on the role of a *speculator* in the company of one or two others and went out to the Persian king's encampment himself. As a direct result of his careful examination, a spectacular victory was won, resulting in the capture of Narses' wives, children, sisters, high-ranking nobility and large quantities of booty (Eutropius IX 25.1; Festus *Breviary* 25; Ammianus XVI 10.3; cf. Synesius *On Kingship* 17). Parallel but on a much smaller scale, is the account in Ammianus of an autopsy by the *magister equitum* Iovinus, carried out in eastern Gaul early in 366 in the wake of earlier careful intelligence work, while he was operating in pursuit of three large predatory groups of Alamanni. In this incident, he is shown working down a heavily forested valley to catch sight of the raiders in relaxed mood, washing, drinking, dyeing their hair red. Iovinus' immediate attack meant their dissolution as a fighting force (XXVII 2.2–3).

As a converse to what has just been said, there appear to be very few cases recorded of autopsy failing to achieve anything. Ammianus' long account of the siege of Aquileia in 361 contains one, however. Bored stiff by the long uneventful siege, a selected group of soldiers walked round the built-up area of the town outside the walls carefully checking to see by what means a break-in could be effected. It appears that this group came up with nothing new, and in fact the effect was that the conduct of the siege began to lose its coherence and sense of purpose. It also appears that this group was not composed specifically of intelligence personnel and thus was unable to wait patiently for scraps of information that would allow a successful action to be planned (XXI 12.14).

The Romans' invasion of Mesopotamia in 363 afforded Julian several opportunities for direct viewing of problem areas, an activity that fits in well with Ammianus' portrayal of him as a highly energetic individual. One does, however, get the impression that much of this energy on the expedition was in fact unnecessary and dangerous. Ammianus reports Julian doing a desert sweep in an area across the Euphrates from Dura in person accompanied by the historian but its military purpose is obscure (XXIII 5.7). It is made clear that as an act of general policy Julian expended a fair amount of energy on personally joining scouting troops ahead of the main force – once the army left the Roman frontier Julian was to be seen actively involved in clearing the way forward with what are clearly the *procursatores* on a number of occasions, and examining in person the obstacles and difficulties both on foot and mounted (e.g. XXIV 1.13). Here autopsy by the commander is a means of sorting out the problems on the spot with minimum delay and so advancing the expedition.

While in many ways such personal checking is useful, it does of course expose the leadership to extreme danger. One of the most notorious examples of this was the personal reconnaissance of a hill facing Hannibal's camp near Venusia by the two consuls of 208 BC, M. Claudius Marcellus and T. Quinctius Crispinus. They were accompanied by only 220 cavalry. Spotted by a look-out, they were ambushed by Numidian skirmishers and their escort put to flight. Marcellus was killed immediately; Crispinus escaped but died of his wounds a few days later. In a single minor skirmish Rome had lost both its supreme commanders and the attempted siege subsequently failed (Polybius X 32; Livy XXVII 26–7;

Valerius Maximus I 6.9; Plutarch *Marcellus* 29; Appian *Hannibalic War* 50). Polybius, himself an experienced general, severely censures the rashness of Marcellus, who is blamed for the reconnaissance, while Plutarch, more rhetorically, says that he died the death of a skirmisher (*prodromos*) or a scout (*kataskopos*), not that of a general. But the desire to do things for himself was characteristic of the man and in other circumstances one of his strengths: in 222 BC, as consul for the first time, he had killed the king of the Insubrian Gauls in single combat and so became the third and last man in Roman history (including the city's legendary founder Romulus) to achieve the supreme military honour of dedicating the *spolia opima*, the 'splendid spoils'. At the time of his death he had won three triumphs and was holding his fifth consulship (*Acta Triumphalia* = *CIL* I pp. 458–9; Plutarch *Marcellus* 7–8; cf. *comparison* 1.2; 3.3–4; *Romulus* 16.7–8).

The future emperor Titus encountered a very dangerous situation during his aforementioned first reconnaissance of Jerusalem, when a Jewish force suddenly emerged from the walls and managed to cut him off from the main body of his support cavalry: he had to fight his way out (Josephus *Jewish War* V 2.1–2/52ff.). Several of the instances of personal inspection by Julian were accompanied by as much care and attention to security as could be used in the circumstances (as emerges from analysis of Ammianus' vocabulary in the immediate contexts). But it should be observed that there were a number of incidents where Julian had some very narrow shaves and in the end his need to see what was happening at the very front of his line of march up the Tigris valley led directly to his death (XXIV 1.13; 2.9; 4.3; 5.3; 5.6; XXV 3.2ff.). The previously mentioned ambush that nearly cost Valentinian his life at Solicinium in Germany is a similar case in point (XXVII 10.10f.).

Autopsy, then, is shown by our evidence to be extremely useful as a method of shortcutting more regular methods of acquiring information. Its riskiness for senior men, however, could well outweigh those advantages, since our sources generally report in a negative way on the many dangerous activities that some commanders turned to, even though the commander in question may have been accompanied by an appropriate body of troops to protect him. It is interesting to see that in very few cases (that of Valentinian at Solicinium being an honourable exception) do the sources provide any information about confirmation from other agencies in cases where autopsy is discussed: the commander's view seems sufficient and is in itself a confirmation of earlier intelligence work.

*Ingenious methods*

During the earlier discussion of strategic intelligence, it was noted that there are some conditions where the lack of intelligence in the field could be seen as significant. In tactical contexts, the situation can be rather different because the need for information can be more immediate. In order to overcome lack of intelligence in some tactical circumstances, one finds ingenious methods used to elicit responses from the enemy that allow certain questions to be answered.

In 57 BC, for instance, Caesar had little knowledge of how good the Belgae were on the battlefield or even how high their morale was. So by a graded series of cavalry skirmishes he was able to probe these two areas and come to the realization that the Roman side was not at a material disadvantage in spite of much inferior numbers. There probably was only one way of finding out how good an enemy was once on the battlefield but Caesar's method of divining it was sophisticated for its controlled gradualness (*Gallic War* II 8.1–2). The same graduated probing can be seen working in his attempts to find out if Pompey at Pharsalus had a preliminary plan or even the will to face Caesar in battle. Again there, Pompey's response to the use of gradually more provocative movements by Caesar's force showed what to expect (*Civil War* III 84.1–2). In both these cases the direct approach was a substitute for adequate intelligence which could not be obtained in good time.

Far different in sophistication but designed to find out quickly what size of force was approaching is Julius Africanus' report of the technique used by bandits in Gaul and Mauretania, one undoubtedly adapted from Roman army practice – that of placing one's ear on a length of wood pressed to the ground; in appropriate terrain, it reveals the noise of hooves at a substantial distance and acts as a guide to the numbers of the opposition. A piece of Wild West lore but superficially credible at least (*Cesti* II 12).

One of the more unusual entries under this rubric would be the famous 'mushroom message' delivered to Trajan during the First Dacian War. The Buri, a Dacian tribe, sent Trajan a message to the effect that he should withdraw from Dacia and restore peaceful relations. Their message to him was inscribed on the smooth top of a very large mushroom, in Latin. The scene was clearly vivid and unusual enough to become part of the frieze on Trajan's Column (scene ix) (see Plate 3), but it plays a role in intelligence also: the warning to withdraw indicated that Decebalus' allies had in no way reached a stage where they were willing to accommodate Roman demands or accept a peace (Dio LXVIII 8.1).

The mushroom message is an illustration of written communication in an environment where there was no access to paper. It calls to mind Pliny the Elder's remark about how an *explorator* might send a report back to his superior officers by incising the text on freshly stripped bark (*Natural History* XVI 35, cf. Loeb edition *ad loc.*); as the bark started to dry, the incisions would have opened up, probably oxidized and darkened, and so the message would have become legible. It may have been more normal, however, for such reports to have been written in ink on prepared wooden tablets, like, perhaps, the tablet describing the 'nasty little Britons' (*Brittunculi*) found at Vindolanda just south of Hadrian's Wall (*Tab. Vindol. II* 164) (see pp. 171–2 and Plate 5).

*Signalling*

Much has been attributed in the past to the effectiveness of Roman signalling systems as modes for the transmission of information over varying distances, no doubt under the influence in some measure of Aeschylus' *Agamemnon*, where Clytaemnestra describes the impressive chain of beacons bringing the news of the fall of Troy to Argos (281–311). In the literary record, Polybius is in part responsible. He discusses at some length his own quite sophisticated system, which involved the use of torches held in different positions to denote letters of the alphabet, apparently a kind of fire-based semaphore arrangement (X 43–7). Caesar and Appian describe the use of fire and smoke as signalling devices (Caesar *Gallic War* II 33.3; *Civil War* III 65.2; Appian *Spanish Wars* 90; cf. Frontinus *Stratagems* II 5.16), and much later, Vegetius notes how they should be used (*Epitome of Military Science* III 5). These few passages represent the total literary evidence for our period.

Archaeology has also been invoked in support of the thesis. On the line of the frontier in Britain, on the Raetian and German *limes*, in Palestine's desert and in Tripolitania, as well as on some seaboards (e.g. the Yorkshire coast), numerous watch-towers have been traced and linked to systems of communication; the towers with protruding torches depicted on Trajan's and Marcus Aurelius' columns have been similarly integrated, as well as their squared piles of logs and the straw-ricks.

Recent scholarship, however, has undermined the position. It has been pointed out, first, that climatic conditions can affect signalling by fire or smoke and render it unreliable; the dampness and wind experienced in much of northern or central Europe and on the drier sections of the empire's frontiers wind and airborne sand can all affect visibility. Second, numbers of the watch-towers evidently do not communicate directly with each other and any nearby base camp; nor are all apparently contiguous installations contemporaneous. Third, many of the supposed 'signal-towers' along the coast of Yorkshire seem now to be *burgi*, established to defend small isolated communities. Fourth, the piles of logs of the Columns need be no more significant than nicely squared-off stacks of drying firewood needed for cooking food and warming the men on duty in the *burgi*. Finally, the protruding beams appear to be big torches, not for signalling but for illuminating the scene in the event of a night incident and the straw-ricks are the same kind of thing. As for the literary passages we allude to, most refer to single or isolated occasions where a predetermined signal is made in order to pass on information of a simple 'yes/no/here' type; in no way can they be used as a basis to prove the existence of an elaborate system of signalling. Polybius' system in itself seems workable, if only in a tightly restricted space, such as a city wall or its immediate environs in a single tactical engagement. It would not work on a bigger scale without the investment of considerable numbers of men, of training and expertise and probably of financial resources to maintain them.

The simple 'yes/no/here' form of signal communication is a useful one and was certainly employed on the battlefield. Ammianus describes how, whilst being pursued by a group of Persian horsemen near Nisibis in AD 359, he came across his own companions dismounted and resting. 'Fully stretching out my arm,' he says, 'and sweeping aloft the tips of my cloak, I indicated the presence of the enemy by the usual signal' (*porrecto extentius brachio et summitatibus sagi contortis elatius, adesse hostes signo solito demonstrabam*) (XVIII 6.13). On a fixed frontier the same sort of predetermined signal was better than nothing. That this is so has been amply demonstrated by the fact of intervisibility of some watch-towers ahead of the frontier and the frontier forts, in areas where they have been identified in sufficient numbers to be part of a recognizable system. In particular, the watch-towers on the Antonine Wall complex, north of it along Gask Ridge and on the Dacian *limes*, are proof enough, but the system can be seen best on Hadrian's Wall, where enough is preserved and identified to show its sophistication.[3]

The sceptical approach we have adopted here suggests that for the communication of information from one frontier installation to others and for communications to centres of command, Roman practice was to use runners or mounted couriers taking the information with them by word of mouth or in written form.

## Non-Roman sources

Important in the field as the Roman sources were, it is clear that an enormous amount of information was obtained from the non-Roman ones in all periods. On its own, however, intelligence based solely on material which is derived from enemy sources, whether they be willing or not, carries with it a risk of incompleteness, inaccuracy and bias or, on occasion, it may be deliberately misleading. Consequently, the evidence suggests that, wherever possible, systems of confirmation were adopted which ensured some chance of cross-checking information – thus we find Roman material confirmed by non-Roman, or, as second-best, non-Roman confirmed by non-Roman. The ideal is to use as wide a spread of information as possible, since it ensures that the information required is derived from as many angles and viewpoints as possible, and the chances of something of importance being missed are substantially reduced.

### Prisoners of war and captured civilians

Prisoners of war and captured civilians are particularly useful as sources of intelligence, the former even more so than the latter for the obvious reason that, as participants in a campaign, they have more precise indications of their side's intentions. We use the word indications advisedly, since most of those captured in the majority of incidents were low-level soldiers who would not have had access to the range of intentions and plans formulated by their senior officers; thus the information they were likely to possess could only serve as indications. Vegetius lays some emphasis on the value of capturing enemy intelligence-gatherers: because they have some idea of their commander's intentions, this very fact becomes a serious liability in the event of capture (*Epitome of Military Science* III 6; cf. Onasander *Art of Generalship* 10.9; Ammianus XVI 11.9; 12.19).

A brief caution first. If a writer uses in this context the words *consilia hostium* ('the enemy's plans') or similar in describing the intelligence gained from a capture, then he is either describing an incident of almost unbelievable good luck (it does happen – luck plays a role in intelligence), or else he is overstating the case. Such an example will not be found in Caesar but in the Caesarian corpus the expression is found in the *African War*, admittedly in a passage where it is implied that the information gained by Caesar from captures at Ruspina (Monastir) was confirmed by deserters from his opponent Labienus: it covered the view that was being publicly expressed by Labienus that Caesar's troops were tired from their sea-crossing from Italy, were inexperienced and had low morale and so could be easily wiped out; his own forces on the other hand were very numerous, reliable, contained a hard core of experienced veterans and were supported by King Juba's royal troops in large numbers. In fact that information, which covered also resources and battle strengths, is so detailed and complex that it must have been derived from senior people or even from written material in their possession, and certainly not simply from captures and deserters (*African War* 19.1–3). Hirtius too uses the words *consilia hostium* about the beginnings of the campaign against the Bellovaci in 51 BC – but here, while much of the basic information must have been gained from the civilian spies who had been captured, the substantial detail he goes on to give can only have come from conflation with later discoveries, all drawn together at the point of writing. This can be gathered from the detailed evaluation of the information at Caesar's headquarters that follows: Hirtius says that Caesar regarded the plans drawn up by the Bellovaci as sound, well-based and quite different from the usual slap-happy Gallic planning methods (*Gallic War* VIII 7.1–4; 8.1).

Captured prisoners of war are one of the main sources for gaining detailed and specialized topographical intelligence as well as information on 'going' – the state of the way ahead for a force. There is much evidence for this, ranging from the basic and unequivocal to the detailed and complex. Examples of both can be seen in the context of Caesar's landings in Britain in 54 BC. In the first category is the simple and rapid identification by prisoners of the position taken up on high ground by the Britons – they had abandoned the coast and moved inland and so had allowed the Romans to seize and fortify a camp-site (*Gallic War* V 9.1); in the second category falls the kind of information about the route north which contained the fact that the Britons had arranged special defences of sharpened stakes both on the banks of the Thames and under the water – peculiarly nasty for troops and horses trying to force a crossing (*Gallic War* V 18.4). This information came from prisoners and was confirmed by deserters and thus did not involve committing Roman manpower to discover it. Very similar, in Julian's campaign in eastern Gaul in 357, were two separate incidents involving the capture of some scouting troops of the Alamanni. The first showed where the Rhine could be easily crossed (somewhere north-east of Tres Tabernae (Saverne), to judge from the sequel) and allowed a sharp little destructive raid by a detachment of Roman troops on Alamanni living on the river banks and islands, which caused them to leave and move back into Germany (Ammianus XVI 11.9). The second, just before the battle of Strasbourg, more seriously indicated another place where the Rhine was low enough at the height of summer to allow large numbers of invaders to ford it. It was a piece of intelligence with important tactical and strategic consequences which was given immediacy and depth by the capture of a further individual shortly afterwards who revealed that crossings by the Alamanni had been going on for three days and nights; a brief calculation would have shown it as a formidable opposition (XVI 12.19). Here, then, is a good example of what began as topographical intelligence being reinforced and refined by subsequent material. After the battle of Strasbourg, as part of the thorough settlement of both banks of the Rhine in 357 and 358, Julian spent time in free Germany raiding or putting pressure on Germanic chieftains in other ways. On one occasion in the Mainz area, a local young German was captured and induced to act as guide; but he turned out to be completely unsatisfactory because the force was led along tracks which had been deliberately obstructed and were thus very dangerous; progress was accordingly very slow and the subsequent response by the Romans at their destination was correspondingly violent towards the inhabitants (Ammianus XVII 10.5–6).

Much information about an enemy can be gained only from prisoners of war. Some of it, since it concerns matters that are not quantifiable (morale, for instance), is of enormous value. It may be simple, basic, factual material but it will also include background explanation – for example, in Caesar's campaign against the Nervii in 57 BC, prisoners brought in revealed an amazing amount of crucial detail and its background: the tribe was just across the Sambre waiting for the Romans; they were also waiting for support from neighbouring tribes who were already on the way and the women and unfit were safe behind marshes close by, inaccessible to the Romans – a considerable amount of information about conditions that would have significant effects on the coming battle. *Exploratores* could have discovered the surface facts but would not have been able to penetrate the reasons behind them (*Gallic War* II 16.1–4). The year before, Caesar had been puzzled when after a long, hard-fought engagement near Mulhouse against Ariovistus, the chief had stopped the battle and withdrawn to his camp: it was only captured prisoners who were able to tell Caesar that the womenfolk had established through divination that the Helvetii could not win before the new moon and that this was the background to the withdrawal. Intelligence of this sort is entirely non-military but has a strong bearing on the conduct of military operations because it affects performance; it was undoubtedly stored in Caesar's mind for exploitation in the future (*Gallic War* I 50.4).

The early stages of an enemy's problems with morale are sooner and more easily detected through prisoners than through deserters, who tend to desert only when conditions on their side are deteriorating; however, individuals such as deserting slaves (who stand to benefit substantially) will have equally valuable information (e.g. *Spanish War* 27.2, amid many other similar examples in this work that mention slaves passing on information). Thus, in 52 BC, Caesar was able to press the siege of Avaricum (Bourges), having learnt from captives that Vercingetorix' forces outside the town were operating on inadequate supplies, and thereby deducing that he was likely to do something drastic in an effort to disengage himself from a difficult situation (*Gallic War* VII 18.1). Later, at Alesia, prisoners, with confirmatory information from deserters, showed how the dispositions inside the stronghold, the pressures for more support outside and the harsh food-rationing reflected the problems now facing Vercingetorix, and directly contributed to Caesar's own increase in the tempo of the siege (*Gallic War* VII 72.1).

The importance of questioning captured troops about enemy morale following an operation can be seen easily in some passages in Caesar and Tacitus. They show once again that detailed debriefing after an operation was a standard procedure, which no doubt contributed to improvements in Roman techniques off and on the battlefield. In 57 BC, during the Nervian campaign, Caesar discovered after the event from prisoners of war that Gallic and Belgic *dediticii* in his entourage (tribesmen who had formally surrendered themselves to Roman authority) were communicating with the opposition at night about the Roman marching order into Nervian territory; the column consisted of individual legions separated by baggage transport and would naturally arrive at its destination piecemeal and not as a unified force. This was a situation that could be exploited in an attack (*Gallic War* II 17.2). Similarly Tacitus, in describing Germanicus' operations in Germany in AD 16, mentions that when he was ravaging his way through the territory of the Marsi, the tribesmen were in general too afraid to face him, or if they did, it was in terror. This information was derived specifically from prisoners and it showed the effectiveness of the harsh policy he had been adopting (*Annals* II 25.2). Again, with Agricola in AD 83, the Caledonians were severely shaken by the sight of a full Roman battle fleet sweeping up the east coast of Scotland: prisoners later described the reaction, which was of course one the Romans intended to create (*Agricola* 25.2). A close parallel, Caesar's information about the alarmed reaction of the Britons at the sight of his fleet approaching the south-eastern coast of Britain, was gained after the landings from captured prisoners (*Gallic War* V 8.6). This kind of *post eventum* intelligence did not have any immediate tactical benefit but it was important in the context of giving shape and depth to other intelligence brought in and provided background against which new material could be assessed.

Prisoners have other uses. In circumstances where all normal intelligence work has ceased to operate because of an emergency, some flow of information can be maintained by capturing enemy soldiers. Frontinus tells of the elder Cato in just such a position in Spain, ordering an attack on an enemy post in order to take a prisoner, who talked under torture (it is possible, however, that this incident is a mistaken reference to the Thermopylae incident described in the previous section (p. 60) (*Stratagems* I 2.5). Witness also both Caesar and Q. Cicero in 54 BC in north-east Gaul after three tribes with their allies had destroyed fifteen cohorts and their two senior commanders and were bidding fair to wipe out Cicero's force (*Gallic War* V 48.2; 52.4). Here the intelligence that was relevant could be obtained only from captures, however risky the process might have been. Risk is inevitable in many similar circumstances but it is compounded when prisoners alone provide the basis for action.

The fact that in a prisoner's initial information there can be much more that needs investigation is not often remarked on in our source material. Caesar is the only writer who gives sufficient detail to illustrate how failure to probe further, not only into prisoners' information but also into a variety of other related intelligence material, is a feature that can lead to disaster: a very clear case emerges from his account of the events that led up to the defeat of his general Curio in Africa in 49 BC. The section on Curio as a whole is a classic exposition of the role of various aspects of intelligence, perhaps because Caesar may have based his account on a detailed subsequent report on the short campaign submitted by someone like Caninius Rebilus, a surviving senior participant (*Civil War* II 23–44). The incidents in question form part of a context of over-confidence on the part of Curio (*spes* and other words for high expectations and optimism appear frequently, e.g. *Civil War* II 37.1; 38.2; 39.3, 5; 40.3), and thus of the forcing of intelligence evidence to fit his preconceptions about what was happening. King Juba of Numidia was known to be moving to support the hard-pressed Attius Varus in Utica when Curio arrived in Africa and a number of successful preliminary engagements had raised Curio's confidence. Initially he had responded appropriately to intelligence about the king's movements and had taken a reasonable line when confronted by problems of morale amongst his own men, brought about by appeals from a lieutenant of Varus to past service and experiences shared by the Roman troops on both sides. But errors of judgement began to creep in: he was given a report about Juba's closeness to Utica but had refused to believe it at first because he had had several successes already and in any case it seemed so unlikely that Juba would contemplate hostile activity after hearing of Caesar's successes in Spain (*Civil War* II 37.1–2). But he did react to strengthen his own position close to Utica at Castra Cornelia when news followed from *certi auctores*, reliable sources, indicating that the king's movement was actually happening. A further intelligence block developed when deserters or refugees from the town appeared with information that Juba's advance had been delayed by trouble at Leptis, and that only the king's lieutenant Saburra was coming on to Utica with a small force. This Curio believed (*temere*, rashly), and sent off cavalry for a night raid on Saburra on the River Bagradas (*Civil War* II 38.1–2). Prisoners picked up during this successful but minor operation were asked no more than who was in command of the force. Their response indicated that Saburra was – but at this point Curio appears to have stopped asking questions and told his troops that this proved that Juba himself was not in the area and that the scope of the raid could be extended. Caesar notes that no further probing took place (*reliqua . . . quaerere praetermittit, Civil War* II 39.2). In every one of these incidents, little further checking had taken place and action had been initiated on the basis of very circumscribed information and selective evaluation. Curio's failure to confirm this intelligence and indeed to follow up any of the indicators in the kind of information he was receiving is harshly criticized by Caesar.

Tactical intelligence derived from chance captures of enemy soldiers occasionally allows a quick and positive course of action to be taken where circumstances are so confused that how to proceed may be obscure. Hirtius details one such action during the campaign against the Bellovaci in 51 BC. On this occasion the Bellovaci had withdrawn during the night and early morning behind a screen of fire and smoke to a new position of some natural strength. The skill of this covering device is remarked on, as is the fact that there was a very strong possibility of a series of ambushes set up behind the screen to deter any Roman follow-up. The ambushes that did occur were sprung on foraging parties but the existence of a much bigger series of ambushes was not discovered until a capture revealed that they were based near stocks of food and fodder towards which the Romans were bound to have to move. Hirtius shows that cavalry now sent to probe near this place were briefed beforehand about Bellovacan intentions and were therefore ready for what happened: individual parties of the cavalry were attacked piecemeal, but, together with fast-moving auxiliary support, were able to resist, and then, as a more regular battle developed, to destroy the Gauls as they were emerging from their ambush positions. The probing carried out by the cavalry following up the prisoner's information, and their use of the intelligence in the field, form a fine example of the continuous use of intelligence on a localized situation (*Gallic War* VIII 17.1–19.1).

The case just discussed demonstrates the value of a rapid response to information extracted from prisoners in the field and it has similarities with the incident in which Minucius Basilus almost succeeded in capturing Ambiorix in eastern Gaul in 53 BC, after the seizure of local men working in the fields had given him the chance to find out exactly where the Gallic leader was (*Gallic War* VI 30.1). Tacitus gives an interesting case where a random capture of some local townspeople outside Cremona in late AD 69 happened to reveal to Antonius Primus the imminent arrival of Vitellius' men following a longer-than-usual day's march. In circumstances where conditions over the whole area were confused and where there was near-mutiny among Antonius' troops, it is clear that little intelligence work of a normal kind (which would have revealed it) had been possible; but this important piece of information quickly brought order back to the ranks and allowed a purposeful deployment to face the Vitellians (*Histories* III 21.1).

There is a very good example of how useful and opportune intelligence gained from a capture can be in Caesar's account of his drive to confront

Afranius and Petreius in northern Spain in 49 BC and bring them to battle: in the area around Octogesa (Mequinenza) this was difficult to achieve, since Afranius and Petreius were not only avoiding battle but also moving to control a new strategic area, which would affect Caesar's mobility in the Ebro valley; in the face of Caesar's daring but hard pushing to get his troops into a strategically stronger position, they had decided to make a silent move during the night. But a water-party which had strayed too far from the Pompeian camp was picked up in the middle of the night by Caesarian cavalry patrols and revealed this information; once Caesar possessed it, he was able to take steps to prevent any such movement merely by giving signals for a night march from his side. The critical timing of the information gained from the capture was important in preventing a march being stolen. This passage is also incidentally valuable for being one of the very few that show patrols operating all night in areas where an enemy was active (*Civil War* I 66.1).

There is a marginally relevant episode in Velleius about intelligence derived from a prisoner – but from a prisoner of the Parthians, captured in the Carrhae débâcle of 53 BC. In 35 BC this man was able to warn M. Antonius, by information to be passed back from outpost sentries, that if he did not want to incur further high casualties on the march back from Armenia, he should avoid a certain route. The source of such information here was an unlikely one, taking great risks to pass on his message, but one whose value was immense, if unexpected, in conditions where it is clear that Antonius was in deep trouble. One wonders how the accuracy of such a message could be assessed or verified (Velleius Paterculus II 82.2).

### Deserters and refugees

The capture of prisoners of war and the seizure of civilians in these contexts necessarily imply the use of pressure in varying degrees to gain the needed information from the victims, with the attendant problems of distortion that can come with material acquired in this way. However, one class of informant that does not require forcible means of capture or handling is the deserter or refugee, who comes across from the other side voluntarily. In the case of deserters, their information is usually freely given in order to establish their credentials more quickly and also because on the side they have left there have been troubles or disputes which have affected them. Two illustrative cases referred to by Ammianus spring immediately to mind here: the case of the ex-*apparitor* Antoninus defecting to Persia (XVIII 5.1–3; pp. 14f. above) and that of the aborted Persian raid on the great annual market held at Apatna on the Khabur in 354, where fear of a punishment drove Persian troops to desert to the Roman frontier garrison and buy their way in by revealing the presence of a raiding force in the area and a great deal of explanatory background information (XIV 3.4). The refugee tends to have less specific military knowledge but can in many cases possess most valuable general background information. It is worth noting that deserters and refugees in our evidence have two roles: they bring information with them on the majority of occasions, but on many others they have the secondary role of returning whence they came to acquire more direct information.

As deserters often take with them sensitive information which is helpful to the opposition and damaging to the side they are deserting, it is interesting to look at the response to the issue of a commander in the field. For example, Caesar inevitably is critical of desertion when it takes place from his own side. While he blames such desertions on faults within the individuals concerned, he is in fact showing resentment at the adventitious element in the acquisition of good intelligence where benefit accrues to the enemy. Nowhere, of course, is there such moral condemnation of deserters to his own side. The two Marsic centurions and their men who defected to Attius Varus from Curio in North Africa in 49 BC took with them the information that there was a crisis of morale among the Caesarian troops. Caesar makes a distinct effort to trivialize the value of their information but the fact cannot be avoided that Curio was not operating as successfully or efficiently as was expected of him; and his defeat and death not long after this incident strongly suggest that the Marsic centurions were right (*Civil War* II 27.1–2; 29.1–2). But more instructive still is Caesar's reaction to the desertions of his two trusted Allobrogan allies in the Illyrian campaign of late 49/early 48 BC: the injured tone is supported by the length and detail of the incident. After being detected in fiddling funds and booty due to be distributed to auxiliary cavalry, and being the objects of strong protest from their fellow-countrymen, they allegedly attempted to murder one of Caesar's senior officers (this was discovered only after the war had ended) and 'borrowed' large sums of money ostensibly to pay off official debts; then they went over to the Pompeians with extremely important information on the incomplete state of Caesar's fortifications, shortcomings in the general running of the campaign, details of distances between guard posts and the timing of guard duties, and much more of crucial value to Pompey. Pompey made instant and very effective use of this intelligence, as is shown by the subsequent attacks on the uncompleted fortifications and the severe problems Caesar had in countering them, so understated in the words *magnum nostris . . . incommodum*, 'a great inconvenience to my men' (*Civil War* III 61.3; 63.5). Chance and good luck in intelligence collection are clearly seen in the episode: deserters cannot be planned for, and indeed one at least of the technical handbooks observes that desertion is an unpleasant fact of life that cannot be avoided (Onasander *Art of Generalship* 10.24). In a sequel to the problems the act of desertion caused, however, luck was on Caesar's side. A number of the Allobroges who had deserted to Pompey encountered *exploratores* operating from Domitius Calvinus' camp at Heracleia (Monastiri) in northern Greece ; and, either because they were stereotype Gauls and therefore prone to showing off, or because they knew their colleagues from the Gallic War days, they fell into conversation with the *exploratores* and talked about Caesar's and Pompey's movements. Domitius had not been able to receive any of Caesar's dispatches to him for some time and did not know where Caesar was, nor was he aware of how close Pompey was. The immediate result of all this information was that Domitius was able to avoid a potentially disastrous encounter with Pompey by a margin of a few hours and very shortly to join Caesar. The chance and luck elements in this episode Caesar again recognizes and remarks on (*hostium beneficio*, 'through the kindness of the enemy') (*Civil War* III 79.6–7).

Deserters and refugees provide information of a type which cannot be identified from the Roman agencies alone, which in their turn cannot penetrate every area where military activity might be taking place, nor reach every place where a strike can with advantage be undertaken. A short initial illustration of this point, from Sallust, is the valuable information about problems within the loose group of Numidian allies surrounding Jugurtha that was brought in by deserters to Caecilius Metellus in 109 BC during the Jugurthine War. They showed that all was not well, following an assassination plot and the execution of a noted supporter. None of this material could have been discovered by any other means, even less so if it were to have any operational value; and so its result was a decision by Metellus to increase the pressure of the war. It also suggested by way of feedback that the pressures so far applied were having some marked effects (*Jugurthine War* 73.1). In North Africa in 45 BC, Caesar's able opponent Attius Varus can be seen seizing on a piece of information originating from a deserter from Leptis, in order to make a sudden attack on inadequately defended Caesarian shipping in and around the harbour – he now knew that no naval defences were present to stop him from exploiting the situation. This intelligence could not have been acquired very quickly without Varus' own men having to become involved over a period of time and at considerable risk before they became familiar enough with the situation for the information to flow back (*African War* 62.4–5). Similarly, when Metellus Scipio attempted unsuccessfully to penetrate Caesar's camp at Ruspina using two Gaetulian 'deserters', he was trying to find out precise details of the anti-elephant precautions Caesar was developing around his camp. That information could only be gained by close inspection of the actual ground, impossible from any distance; yet it was important to get it, since Scipio's elephants could be tactically ineffective and a liability unless he knew how to overcome the obstacles (*African War* 35.2–4). Much later, in the aftermath of the battles at Singara in AD 343/4, deserters from the Persian side brought detailed information about the Persian response to the mixed successes of those events: King Sapor was shocked at the level of his military and civilian casualties, as well as the loss of his son. While Libanius wrote up the story in the usual panegyric terms required for such a topic,[4] his remark on the way deserters present themselves and their information must be seen as a *locus classicus*: 'It is not my speech, composed to gratify, which proves this, but their [sc. the Persians'] deserters who surrendered themselves and clearly announced the news. We must accept their word: for they do not delight in false tales of their difficulties' (*Orations* LIX 119, tr. Dodgeon and Lieu).

The food supply is a particularly sensitive area where information from deserters can be very welcome. Caesar gives a notable illustration of the value of this kind of intelligence: in April 48 BC, during the complicated manoeuvrings that took place round Dyrrhachium, Caesar was critically short of food for his men and fodder for the animals. He alludes to his own side's willingness to eat the bark off the trees rather than let Pompey get away; but to raise morale on his side, he used the information from Pompeian deserters that their own side was in a much worse state, so much so that Pompey's pack animals could no longer be fed and had had to be allowed to die (*Civil War* III 49.2). Further, Hirtius points out in a parallel incident, the siege of Uxellodunum in 51 BC, that information from deserters indicating that the place had plenty of food for its defenders led directly to Caesar having to give thought to planning the interdiction of the water supply (*Gallic War* VIII 40.1).

In just such a supplies context, it was deserters from Labienus who revealed the laying of a substantial ambush for Caesar's men as they collected supplies from underground storehouses during operations round Hadrumetum (Sousse) in 47/46 BC. With that information in his hands, Caesar was able to turn the situation to his advantage by not precipitating action for several days, until carelessness had begun to set in among the ambushers (*African War* 65.3–66.1). Food supplies in the North African theatre of the Civil War were a particular problem to Caesar and careful exploitation of this kind of situation was vital in the interests of survival (e.g. *African War* 67.1–2). Immediately after the above episode, Caesar was able to seize the town of Zeta, having been given the crucial information from a deserter that Scipio, who was blocking any movement towards the town, had sent two whole legions off to collect food: this gave Caesar a chance to make his move quickly at a much lower level of risk (*African War* 68.1–2). Parallel situations of course exist in all periods.

Reports from deserters and refugees from across the borders could naturally have been expected to be a regular feature of the frontier intelligence system but there is surprisingly little evidence for it; the topic surfaces only occasionally in the literary sources. For instance, in describing the poor quality of the response made by the local Roman leadership and its ineptitude in putting down the disaffection in Frisia in AD 29, where losses seem to have been large, Tacitus makes the suggestive point that it was German deserters who later (*mox*) brought in the information that 1,300 Romans had been cut off and had died in two separate last-ditch stands some distance away from the frontier. The actual circumstances in which this intelligence was obtained from deserters are unfortunately not indicated (*Annals* IV 73).

The examples we have noted so far deal with the collection of information which could be used in a direct or an indirect way. Much more direct use, however, was evidently made of a number of deserters or refugees in capacities where the information they possessed allowed them to be turned against their former loyalties. This is particularly clear in incidents where they acted as guides for the Romans or provided very detailed topographical and 'going' intelligence.

The procedure was of course particularly important in the absence of reliable maps, or to supplement what maps there were, and is underlined in some of the manuals (e.g. Onasander *Art of Generalship* 10.15; see pp. 112ff.).

Sallust records the value of deserters in this area in three widely differing contexts: two deal with the useful combination of indistinctiveness with an intimate knowledge of a region as qualities helpful for tracing the movements and composition of Jugurtha's forces in 109 and 107 BC; the third describes indications made to Metellus Celer in 63 BC about a route taken by Catilina in mountainous terrain near Faesulae (Fiesole), information which enabled Celer to block it and so force Catilina to turn back to confront the consul Antonius (*Jugurthine War* 54.2; 100.3; *Catiline* 57.3). In 57 BC Caesar was using prisoners as guides into and through Nervian territory (north-east of Amiens) before the big confrontation on the Sambre (*Gallic War* II 16.1). Just before the battle of Strasbourg in AD 357, the capture of a German infantry scout provided Julian with information about the crossing place and, perhaps more important, the length of time the Germans had been crossing the Rhine, which enabled some assessment of numbers to be made. This man, once captured, was much more co-operative than a mere prisoner and turned with a will to his new role as deserter (Ammianus XVI 12.19–21). Local knowledge and experience of this type could be of considerable further advantage once the Romans were operating in enemy territory. Late in the campaigning season of 357, during Julian's operations across the Main after Strasbourg, a deserter made it quite clear that progress into the deep forests of the area would be very dangerous because of large numbers of Alamanni hiding in specially constructed ditches from which ambushes could easily be launched. In this way Julian was able to avoid having to extricate himself from a potentially most difficult situation (XVII 1.8). Ammianus attributes a lucky break in Constantius II's projected invasion of Upper Germany in 354 to a similar deserter, whose willingness was helped along by a suitable financial inducement. Bridging the river by pontoon had already proved impossible because of the strength of the opposition. But now, seeing that the Rhine would be running very high at this time of the year (early spring), the specific information on where the river could be crossed unobserved by enemy watchers and away from the obvious crossing places known to both sides was of immense value. A number of reasons are advanced for the abandonment of the attempt to cross the river (a suspected security leak from the Roman side, unfavourable auspices or sacrifices on the Alaman), all of which suggest that Constantius' headquarters was sensitively attuned to a shift in intelligence emphasis which showed a change in Alamannic willingness to fight. The invasion thus became a mere demonstration of force but it had produced the desired result of negotiations and so conserved Roman manpower (XIV 10.6–9).

There is an episode in the campaigning in 70 against the Batavian tribes led by Civilis which illustrates perhaps as well as any the close connection between a deserter, his knowledge of the terrain and military dispositions. The conditions in which these engagements were fought were unusually unpleasant and created by ingenious tactical thinking. Civilis had had time to build a weir out into the Rhine at Vetera (Xanten), which diverted water from the river into flat marshy terrain to make its natural swampiness worse, blur the natural pathways through the area and make it impossible for the pursuing Romans to fight in any ordered way. Petilius Cerialis had to fight here in a confused battle, but during it he was lucky to be approached by a deserter who promised to point out a way through the marsh and behind the Batavians. It was precisely this that created the conditions for a tactical victory, since the immediate exploitation of that intelligence led to cavalry being dispatched for the purpose; Cerialis lived up to his reputation for taking risks by being vigorous and positive about going into action. Tacitus makes it clear that the victory would have been much more difficult to achieve without the intelligence (*Histories* V 18). Similarly, Ammianus underlines the precision of timing and location that deserters could bring, when describing a rapid raid under Valentinian's direct control in the area of Aquae Mattiacae (Wiesbaden) to snatch the Alaman chief Macrianus in 372: these informants revealed that the king and entourage were not expecting any hostile action against them and were thus open to such a raid. The information was quickly followed up. A pontoon bridge across the Rhine was quietly assembled and Valentinian's *magister peditum*, Severus, moved at once to Aquae Mattiacae where he found a slave-trading market in progress; the dealers were killed and the slaves seized to avoid any leak reaching Macrianus. The *magister equitum*, Theodosius, and the cavalry swept the route almost to Macrianus' encampment and the whole exercise was led by local guides familiar with the routes of the area. In spite of careful planning and execution, however, it failed at the last moment through Roman indiscipline, not through failure of the well-integrated intelligence work, which used a variety of sources for clearly defined purposes (XXIX 4.2ff.).

More use can be made out of 'turned' deserters than merely the gaining of information and guidance, however. Because of the fact that their information is fresh, current and therefore of immediate value to a commander, and because the decision to receive them is in his hands, they tend to have rapid and early access to him; if it suits his plans, they can then be briefed immediately for a specific role and sent back to their erstwhile colleagues to act as moles. For the individuals concerned, it is an extremely dangerous activity, but for the commander carrying out the operation there is little to be lost if it is unsuccessful and much to be gained if successful. As has been noted earlier, Metellus Scipio tried this at Ruspina in North Africa against Caesar, sending two Gaetulians ostensibly as deserters but in fact as *speculatores* – it backfired for Scipio when they revealed to Caesar what their role was to be (*African War* 35.2–4). A refinement, the deserter's part as an *agent provocateur*, or perhaps better, a spreader of disinformation, is particularly clear in the sub-campaign against the Venelli in 56 BC, during the troubles with the Veneti, when Sabinus selected a Gaul to act as a deserter and divulge all sorts of misleading information about the dire psychological and physical straits Sabinus' men were experiencing as a result of successful pressure from the Veneti earlier. With sharp insight, Caesar indicates that the Venelli heard only what they wanted to hear and rashly acted on it (*Gallic War* III 18.1–6). The practical manuals compiled by Onasander and Vegetius both address the problem, given the absolute inevitability of leaks through deserters. They insist on very tight security of information about intentions and destinations, short- or long-term, which must not be communicated to junior ranks before the very last moment, thus imposing in effect the 'need-to-know' principle. Although both authors lay emphasis on the ways to stop leakages, the widespread prevalence of intelligence gathered from deserters in all our evidence illustrates that any such barriers were not really effective (Onasander *Art of Generalship* 10.22–4; Vegetius *Epitome of Military Science* III 6).

In none of these cases do our sources make it clear whether any suitable confirmation of intelligence derived from the deserters and refugees was obtained. The possibility in all cases existed, except in the Cerialis–Civilis incident, where the force dispatched in response to the unconfirmed intelligence was probably adequate to defend itself in the conditions if things went wrong. A more serious lack of confirmation is hinted at in a passage in Ammianus, unfortunately lacunose, where the historian covers what is arguably the centre point of Julian's Persian expedition in 363. The expedition's transport ships had come down the Euphrates, helping the Roman invasion to move quickly and effectively. At Ctesiphon on the Tigris, Julian ordered nearly all of them to be burnt in preparation for the more arduous march up the Tigris valley. His orders, coupled with misunderstandings over the route north and the associated use of suspect Persian deserters as local guides, meant that the event itself was replete with confusion, as is the account of it. But through it all there runs Ammianus' suggestion that undue trust was being placed on their unchecked information (XXIV 7.3–5). A clear case, though, of non-confirmation, precisely because it was unconfirmable, occurs in Josephus' account of the siege of Jotapata in 67, where a deserter from the town gave Vespasian information about the small size of the defence and their supply situation – but this only happened 47 days after the Romans had initiated large-scale siege works. The capture of the town in these conditions was inevitable, and Vespasian must already have had a fairly good guess as to what the situation inside really was: the probability on balance that this intelligence was right meant that the final assault could begin almost immediately (*Jewish War* III 7.33/316–22).

Occasions where other sources confirmed the information derived from deserters and refugees are, however, frequently noted in our evidence and confirmation must therefore have been a standard procedure in all periods. It is certainly given some prominence in Vegetius' textbook: the recommendation is that a commander should collate information acquired from a variety of local sources and thus establish the truth about the area he is moving into. After describing the combination of carrot-and-stick pressures to ensure that accurate guiding is in fact provided, Vegetius warns about accepting at face value the information that is divulged, suggesting that only experienced and trained staff carry out the investigations to avoid the possibility of error creeping in (*Epitome of Military Science* III 6; cf. Onasander *Art of Generalship* 10.15). Thus while Caesar was making preparations to seal Vercingetorix into Alesia, the real situation regarding supplies as the basis for Vercingetorix' dispositions was made known to Caesar by deserters and was confirmed by captured prisoners: here the two sources were quite separate, one being more willing, the other unwilling, and the coincidence of their information made the intelligence derived from it much more likely to be reliable (*Gallic War* VII 72.1). There is no difference in concept between this incident with its fixed site and a campaign incident in AD 16 in Germany when Germanicus was operating just across the Weser. The large force with Arminius was revealed by a deserter to be preparing a mass night assault; this information the Romans regarded as likely to be right and particularly since fires had now became visible. Then his information was fully confirmed by the report of *speculatores* sent ahead to check detail (Tacitus *Annals* II 12). In four passages in Ammianus, all dealing with the eastern frontier and all from 359–61, emphasis is placed on the process of confirmation. The evidence from Roman sources, i.e. *exploratores* and *speculatores*, was measured against that from non-Romans (Persian deserters and refugees), and in two cases the checks confirmed the reliability of the reports, that very active preparations for invasion were in progress (XVIII 6.8; XX 4.1), while in the other two cases, checks failed to provide adequate confirmation, since conflicting information was coming in which indicated that no forward planning could realistically be implemented (XXI 7.7; 13.4). In all these cases from Ammianus, while the intelligence being sought was of immediate tactical significance and related solely to whether invasion had started or not, there was a longer-term strategic response dependent on it, which Ammianus makes quite clear in the context, and which incidentally further illustrates the close connection between strategic and tactical intelligence.

Confirmation from the type of source represented by deserters and refugees can often be rather general in that it may lack specific detail, but it will provide additional depth to the knowledge that a commander may already have. A good case in point comes from Josephus. Particularly during the winter of 67/8, deserters and refugees kept Vespasian informed about the growth of irregulars and brigandage, and of more organized terrorism, as aspects of bitter Jewish faction-fighting all over Judaea as well as in Jerusalem itself. Vespasian undoubtedly already possessed this information, but the flow of reports was helpful in developing a more effective response to the political and military undercurrents (*Jewish War* IV 7.3/410). Better still, deserters and refugees may provide exact confirmatory detail for generally held information. An instance is noted, again by Josephus, when he describes his own slipping into Jotapata in 67; the fact of his arrival there was transmitted by a deserter to Vespasian, which, in Josephus' eyes at least, gave Vespasian the information required for him to invest a major effort to capture the place, and with it Josephus himself as a leading member of the Jewish hierarchy (*Jewish War* III 7.3/143).

Apart from one or two remarks by other historians about the use of the enemy's deserters or prisoners for the purpose of checking on security within the Roman army on campaign, we hear very little on the topic until the sixth century, when such information starts to appear regularly. Caesar refers to leaks through Gallic and Belgic *dediticii* to the Nervii about his order of march, and to the discovery of the existence of the leaks from prisoners (*Gallic War* II 17.2, discussed above, p. 70); he is evidently aware that at low levels such leaks are very difficult to stop – witness the remark made in the context of the campaign against Indutiomarus and the Treveri in 54 BC about Labienus' emphatic precautions to keep his troops inside his camp and to set sentries over them, in order to prevent any whisper about his fresh cavalry reinforcements from reaching the Treveri outside and to ensure the greatest possible surprise in the following day's attack (*Gallic War* V 58.1; cf. Onasander *Art of Generalship* 10.22–4; Vegetius *Epitome of Military Science* III 6). Ammianus refers only twice to security leaks, but gives no indication of how the leaks were traced back (prisoners, perhaps, or deserters/refugees, whose information was being analysed in post-campaign briefings?): in early 354, when Constantius II had assembled a force at Rauracum (Kaiseraugst) to invade Alaman territory, he had used an Alaman deserter to point out a good place to cross the river; but the plan to divert enemy attention elsewhere fell through when the Alaman leaders decided to enter negotiations. Their change of heart could only be attributed to a leak of information, as some thought (*ut quidam existimabant*), originating from German officers serving in senior capacities in the Roman army, though Ammianus does mention that other possible explanations were canvassed (XIV 10.7–9). A second case appears to have had some influence on the Strasbourg campaign of 357: here, a deserter from the élite *Scutarii* divulged to the Alamanni that Julian's total available force numbered only 13,000 men. The outcome of this revelation was that several German tribes now decided to group together for a substantial invasion of Gaul and to confront the Romans in the field (XVI 12.2–3). Ammianus' other case had much more serious implications. Very early in 378 Gratian was far advanced with preparations to set out for Thrace to assist Valens in the great Gothic crisis, when one of his guard who was an Alaman went on leave back to his tribe the Lentienses, bordering on Raetia. This man's willingness to talk freely (*in loquendo effusior*) revealed to them the extent of Roman troop movements and encouraged them to abandon the peace treaty of 354 and to launch a serious attempt at invasion across the frozen upper Rhine. The emergency forced Gratian to react with a tough little campaign, but it also contributed to delays in his move to join Valens in the East (XXXI 10.3, 20).

*Local inhabitants*

Slightly different from deserters and refugees as sources of intelligence are the local inhabitants of an area. They tend to be mentioned in the sources when their information is useful and willingly given, because we encounter very few, if any, cases of the locals being unhelpful. In the latter circumstances, they are probably lumped together with enemy combatants and suffer the consequences. Undoubtedly, in most cases, one suspects, information is willingly given (even to both sides, though nowhere is it stated in our evidence) in order to get the combatants out of the area as quickly and painlessly as possible. But even so, that information is often extremely valuable. The locals of course would not necessarily have had detailed information or have known about future plans, but they spoke the same language as the Romans' opponents and so had access to at least basic facts. Vegetius' manual is emphatic that such individuals, if they are being used as guides, should be as experienced and knowledgeable as is possible in the circumstances; their information should be taken separately and then collated in confirmation. Low-level locals should be avoided, since they might claim to know all sorts of things but in fact be utterly ignorant (*Epitome of Military Science* III 6). In practice, this knowledge of local conditions could be particularly helpful – for instance, in 50 BC when C. Fabius was operating against Dumnacus in the area between Cenabum (Orléans) and Lemonum (Poitiers), he had to act to cut off a large Gallic force from crossing the Loire as the chief withdrew northwards from Lemonum. The local inhabitants gave Fabius sufficiently detailed information about the geography of the area for him to be able to realize that Dumnacus would have to make for a particular bridge if he was to escape the Romans. Fabius' deduction allowed him to plan a line of pursuit that would permit him to catch up and harass the Gauls severely, and to seize the bridge before they could reach it. A victory was made possible as a direct result of that information (Hirtius *Gallic War* VIII 27.3). There is a close parallel in the case of the assistance given to Caesar by Diviciacus in 58 BC over the route to follow in order to encounter Ariovistus – though the march was longer, it was through more open country, safer and quicker (*Gallic War* I 41.4). On the other hand, little different from rumour, at least in the initial stages, were the facts about his opponents' forces brought to Caesar at the very end of 47 BC while in Sicily awaiting the opportunity to move across to Africa – these alarmist stories were brought over by local inhabitants, but the final figures as they appear in the *African War* could have been reached only by extensive comparisons and analysis of the stories; the stories themselves could have been no more than indicative (*African War* 1.3–4).

Since locals are often caught in the middle in civil war contexts, their helpfulness is emphasized for political, self-justificatory ends: Caesar's arrival at Brundisium (Brindisi) in 49 BC is a case in point, because here the locals on the roofs of their houses signalled him about Pompey's preparations for immediate departure across the Adriatic. This was not really news to Caesar, but the detail is inserted in the story to support the remark made in the context about Pompey's hard-line treatment of the local population. The inhabitants of Brundisium did, however, guide Caesar's men around the sealed-off streets and fearsome barricades and traps that had been constructed to delay the Caesarians' entry into the town at the moment of withdrawal by Pompey's rearguard (*Civil War* I 27–8). One may well suspect that the incident when M. Antonius was warned by some local Greeks of Pompey's imminent arrival outside Lissus (Lesh) on the Epirote coast (in spite of Pompey's elaborate security precautions – no cooking fires, no men allowed outside camp) falls into the same category, though here the news did have some real value in preventing him from having to face the great general unexpectedly (*Civil War* III 30.4–7).

Interestingly, it was a single piece of information provided by locals which took a load off Caesar's mind on the supply side in 46 BC, also during the African campaign. Supplies during this part of the Civil War were always a serious problem, but the position changed on the discovery that large stocks of food were routinely stored in underground storehouses for safety reasons, the area being subject to raids from desert tribes and Numidians, quite apart from civil war armies (*African War* 65.1–2). This case is one of the very few where the food supply and intelligence are specifically linked (it was an informer (*index*) who pointed out the local storage practice); but it should be pointed out that judging from the large number of references to food supplies in all the main authors and some of the inscriptions, the finding and maintenance of adequate resources of food and fodder must have formed a most important part of the intelligence function.

### Fama *and* Rumor

All the sources of intelligence that have been discussed so far are quantifiable and can be assigned to specific named agencies. Beyond these, however, lie the much vaguer and less quantifiable forms, *fama* and *rumor*, terms for which a modern translation might be 'unsourced material'. These elusive sources appear in military contexts mainly in Caesar and Ammianus, where it seems that they are regarded in the eyes of headquarters men as sources of information which are difficult to rate for reliability, but must be taken into account if every source is to be considered sensitively and with responsiveness. To a degree, such a view may come about because an oral method of passing information was as strongly relied on as a written one, and to this extent *fama* and *rumor* are accorded more serious attention than would otherwise be the case. One has only to recall Virgil's striking and famous depiction of the way *fama* works to understand how seriously such material could be taken (*Aeneid* IV 173ff.). Ammianus refers to *Fama* as a kind of living creature in three passages, which while not as colourful or lengthy as Virgil's are still poetic in presentation. The first mention of *Fama* portrays it bringing news somehow to the head-quarters of the usurper Silvanus in Cologne to the effect that Constantius had reacted to his elevation by sending an agent there, the *magister equitum* Ursicinus (and his retinue, which contained Ammianus himself): 'Rumour had revealed us . . . as she flew ahead on some aerial pathway' (*nos . . . aeria via quadam antevolans prodiderat Fama*). The reflection on the speed of *fama* can be no more than a vivid depiction of circumstances in which some form of reaction from the emperor must have been expected and indeed would have been inevitable: but it is an exaggeration of the facts, since Ursicinus had no real difficulty in rapidly becoming an intimate of Silvanus (XV 5.24ff.). The second mention has *Fama* 'fly swiftly ahead through the paths of the sky' (*per aerios tramites praepetem volitare*) and take with it important military information to the Persians. That information concerned the replacement of Ursicinus by Sabinianus, which would mean a period of adjustment while the new man learned the details of the situation and implemented new instructions (and this no doubt lies at the base of Ammianus' depiction of Sabinianus as inactive and ineffectual). In this case it seems that Ammianus exploits the unquantifiability of *fama* to indicate that the Persians had as good an intelligence network operating on the Roman side of the frontier as the Romans had on the Persian and that the sources of the intelligence were not attributable to traceable agencies (XVIII 6.3; cf. also XV 5.24). In his third representation of *Fama*, 'which, they say, wonderfully exaggerates the evidence for facts with a thousand tongues' (*quae mille (ut aiunt) linguis rerum mire exaggerat fidem*), he actually gives the amplified and exaggerated material to show how ridiculous and distorted it was. All the same, there is an underlying sense of the fact that Julian was able to exploit its strength: the *praefectus praetorio per Italiam* Taurus felt it was advisable to abandon his post, accompanied by his colleague *per Illyricum* Florentius, when confronted with the 'information' on Julian's advance into their areas of responsibility in 361 (XXI 9.3–4). Both examples exhibit receptiveness to unquantified material, and both may show that efficient military establishments make use of all available information in the development of their intelligence. All this may amount to a sense of awareness, no more, of what the immediate local population, military and civilian, might be thinking and talking about informally, even to the extent where it could be called informed public opinion: some facts may well underlie what is said.

The less high-flown account of Valens' escape from being trapped in a suburb of Chalcedon during the revolt of Procopius in 365 (because he had reacted immediately to a rumour that had reached him shortly before), is in fact rather more important in the present context. Here Ammianus shows that *rumor* is not merely camp-gossip that reached the emperor's ears but much more like a 'leak', picked up through contact with the locals in the know but not specifically sourced, or even necessarily informed guessing (XXVI 8.3). In Isauria, though, *rumores* as an early-warning system for insurgent incursions cannot be much more than the so-called 'bush-telegraph' (a modern term which attempts to explain the often astounding speed and spread of rumour or information that can take place among some less sophisticated societies where there can be no question of messages passed by any means apart from word of mouth); clearly the military establishment in the region had ways of making use of it (XIV 2.9). Earlier we remarked on the way *speculatores* were used in the conditions in which the fighting in Isauria took place. That situation, taken together with the use here made of *rumores*, makes it clear how difficult the low-grade war was on this internal *limes* and so how sensitive to intelligence this headquarters had to be.

Less like the leaks and more like assessments of merely local sources of intelligence are Ammianus' *rumores* dealing with the expected Persian invasion of 359 (XVIII 4.2, 7, where they are called *densi*, 'very numerous'). In both cases, the intelligence content was reinforced by the fact that the *rumores* were confirmed as accurate by other means: in the case of the first, it is by *nuntii certi*, 'positive messengers', who must therefore be organs of the normal intelligence-collecting agencies or using reports emanating from them; and in the second, the *rumores* are themselves characterized as *certi*, positive or definite. In areas where sources were so unidentifiable and so much was at stake, confirmation was indispensable.

The most pertinent of Caesar's uses of *fama* and *rumor* as exemplifying sources of intelligence are to be found in the *Civil War*. He indicates in one passage that the speed of his crossing from Brundisium forestalled any use being made of *fama* by M. Bibulus on Corcyra to ready troops and rowers for action to prevent Caesar landing in Epirus. Here *fama* was an element that would precede fuller details but that nevertheless would need to be assessed for whatever value was in it: it forms part of the intelligence-collection process, because its existence would have caused Bibulus to go on to the alert (*Civil War* III 7.2; cf. also III 80.7). A further example shows the same principle at work in a wider context than the purely tactical, where the extinction of *rumor* was seen as an element taken into account in military planning. In Spain in 49 BC, the successful building of a bridge over the Sicoris (River Segre) gave Caesar access to food and a better area for manoeuvre with his troops; it also meant that he could take a higher diplomatic profile towards the local tribes. A combination of all these factors led to the end of *rumores* about Pompey's imminent arrival with reinforcements from Mauretania (*Civil War* I 60.5). There is no doubt that Caesar is critical of the use by his opponents of (unconfirmed) *rumores* as an element in their planning. Events showed them up in this case as delusory. Androsthenes, '*praetor*' of Thessaly, is similarly criticized in an ironic remark for relying on *fama* he had received about Caesar's setbacks at Dyrrhachium and so opting for Pompey's side (*Civil War* III 80.2–3).

Equally pointed remarks are made about the delusory optimism in the content of reports sent back to Rome by Afranius and Petreius about Caesar's setbacks in Spain – such serious *rumor*-exaggerated setbacks, that they were thinking in terms of the war being nearly over and were being congratulated for their achievement (*Civil War* I 53.1). Similarly, such propagandist (and optimistic) *rumores* were current in Rome in 51 BC about setbacks Caesar was experiencing in Gaul at the hands of the Bellovaci; Caelius Rufus passed them on in a letter to Cicero in Cilicia. The claim was that Caesar had apparently lost a large number of cavalry, had had a legion mauled and was himself cut off and in deep trouble (Cicero *Letters to his Friends* VIII 1.4). Hirtius' version of the same incidents is altogether cooler and less excited (*Gallic War* VIII 12.1–5). In these contexts *rumor* and *fama* were very much elements of propaganda and should have been treated at the least with caution, but the fact is that they influenced the climate in which military decisions were taken.

Caesar's view of *fama* and *rumor* is nicely summed up in a telling sentence, 'usually, because of its novel content, rumour outstrips the facts' (*plerumque in novitate fama rem antecedit*), which gives the reason for his policy of avoiding a response to the unconfirmed element in them (*Civil War* III 36.1); other commanders, naturally, suffer from this fault. The opening sentence of the second book of the *Gallic War* makes this policy clear in practice: Labienus confirmed in written dispatches the rumours that Caesar had been receiving about the whole Belgic confederacy and its developing hostility to Rome.

*Rumor* and *fama* expectedly affect troop morale, and in this way have to be taken into account as part of the intelligence and planning process. Not only in the Caesarian view above is this so, but it can also be seen operating in Tacitus. A good example, again in a civil war context, can be seen when Antonius Primus did not discourage (and may indeed have prompted) the rumour that had spread on his side on the evening of the second battle of Cremona in 69, to the effect that Mucianus had arrived with reinforcements. That rumour was quite without foundation, but was useful for ensuring good fighting from his troops (*Histories* III 25; cf. also III 43). But here we are reaching the fringes of intelligence work.

Thus short-term tactical intelligence required the Romans to exploit as many types of source as they could and in a variety of ways. Ineffective tactical intelligence showed up either in serious difficulties on the battlefield or in defeat. Three almost random examples culled from Livy make the point sharply: XXI 25.9 (218 BC), in his haste to relieve Mutina (Modena) in Cisalpine Gaul, L. Manlius Vulso moved through wooded country *inexplorato* and ran into serious opposition; XXII 4.4 (217 BC), C. Flaminius approached Lake Trasimene *inexplorato*; and XXVII 26.6 (208 BC), a Roman force moving from Tarentum to Locri *inexplorato* was severely dealt with by the Carthaginians close to Petelia. There are plenty of others.

# 4

# GROPING TOWARDS EMPIRE
## The Republic

The political and military structures of the Roman Republic were not conducive to the development of any standing intelligence organization. Both City and provincial magistrates were replaced annually, and even the development of promagistracies normally extended office for one or two years at most. Republican magistrates were not assisted by any permanent civil service, and relied on personal friends and relations and on an administrative staff who were drawn by individual magistrates from panels (*decuriae*) at Rome.[1] Armies also were impermanent, legionary and allied troops being levied annually. Individual units did come to remain in existence over a period of several years as Roman armies campaigned further and further afield and men could not easily return to Italy at the end of each season, but no unit achieved true standing status until the reforms of Augustus. Permanence resided only in the popular assemblies (*comitia*) at Rome, and in the Senate, which laid claim to the realm of foreign policy as its own domain, and directed and was the ultimate recipient of strategic intelligence. But the Senate itself had no permanent officials or standing committees, its executive officers being those same magistrates whose annual election was seen as a principal safeguard of the constitution. Consequently, the acquisition and processing of strategic intelligence was usually an *ad hoc* affair, done as the situation demanded.

## GEOGRAPHICAL WRITING

Some general information about the areas beyond Roman control was available from the writings of traders and travellers (such as the fourth-century BC explorer Pytheas of Massilia), which were transmitted in the works of Timaeus, Poseidonius, Diodorus Siculus, Strabo and others. The barest fragments of such knowledge survive for us to read. So, the account of Pytheas' travels to Britain and the Northern Ocean beyond can still be glimpsed in Strabo, Pliny and a few other writers,[2] and the two journeys of Eudoxus of Cyzicus to India at the end of the second century were recorded by Poseidonius and quoted from him by Strabo (*Geography* II 3.4/98–100). Diodorus tells of the visits of the merchant Iambulus to an island, perhaps Ceylon, which he reached via Ethiopia and where he recorded the nature and habits of the natives (Diodorus II 55–60), and of Egyptian traders sailing south to the land of the Ichthyophagi (Diodorus III 18.3). Strabo quotes Persian sources on the island at the mouth of the Red Sea, and Augustus' tutor Athenodorus of Tarsus on his visit to Petra, where he found both Roman and foreign traders (*Geography* XVI 4.20–1/779).

But this sort of source had its limitations. For instance, Strabo says that he knows of no one who has travelled along the northern coast of Germany beyond the limit of Roman expansion on the Elbe to the mouth of the Caspian (*Geography* VII 2.4/294). Nor was such information as was available necessarily very reliable. Iambulus evidently recorded that the islanders with whom he lived had cleft tongues with which they could simultaneously hold two conversations (Diodorus II 56.5–6); and Caesar, apparently following the third-century geographer Eratosthenes, regales us with the story that in the Hercynian forest in Germany there exists a kind of goat with jointless limbs which is incapable of standing up once it has fallen and which sleeps leaning against a tree; it can be caught by uprooting a tree but leaving it standing so that, when the goat leans against it, both will fall over together, thus leaving the animal helpless (Caesar *Gallic War* VI 27; cf. 24.2). Indeed, the Roman world seems to have been well aware of the shortcomings of travellers' tales. Plautus produced a parody of them in one of his plays (*Trinummus* 931–45), whilst Polybius indicates his lack of faith in traders' explanations of the current flowing out of the Black Sea (Polybius IV 39.11). It is clear that the sort of information recorded by such writers was often centuries old, usually non-military in nature, limited in extent and sometimes simply false. As such, it must mostly have been of little or no use from the point of view of either tactical or strategic intelligence.

Of greater value was the specific commissioning of writers to find out and record geographical information, although this was comparatively rare and was done by individual commanders, not by the Senate, and not always for military purposes. Scipio Aemilianus sent both the historian Polybius and Stoic philosopher Panaetius, each with a number of ships, to explore the coast of Africa during the Third Punic War but, as has already been noted (p. 30), this was apparently done out of scientific curiosity (Pliny *Natural History* V 9–10; *Index Stoicorum Herculanensis*).[3] Such curiosity was not, however, necessarily incompatible with the collection of militarily useful information. This can be seen from the surviving fragments of the history of Pompey's eastern campaigns in 66–64 BC, written by Theophanes of Mytilene who was asked by Pompey to accompany him for that specific purpose: the fragments show that Theophanes recorded information on peoples and rivers and attempted to calculate the size of Armenia (Theophanes of Mytilene *FGrHist* II B no. 188 F 3–7). Theophanes or another member of the expedition may also have been the ultimate source of the information on drinking water and the distances between towns taken from Varro by the Elder Pliny (*Natural History* VI 51–2). The history of the eastern campaigns of M. Antonius in 36 BC was also written with much geographical detail by one of his junior officers, Q. Dellius (Peter II pp. 53–4).

## *COMMENTARII*

Alongside the publication of this sort of information obtained in the course of an expedition by accompanying scholars or subordinates, we find from the end of the second century commanders themselves, who had always kept notes and produced dispatches for the Senate on campaign, writing up such notes for publication either as part of an autobiography or as military memoirs (*commentarii*). The earliest such works of which fragments survive are the auto-biographies of M. Aemilius Scaurus, consul in 115 BC, and P. Rutilius Rufus, consul in 105 BC, and the *commentarii* of Q. Lutatius Catulus who wrote his own account of his consulship in 101 BC and his campaign against the Cimbri (Peter I² pp. 185 (Scaurus), 189–90 (Rufus), 190–4 (Catulus)). Later, Catulus' subordi-nate in that campaign, L. Cornelius Sulla, the future dictator, produced an unfinished autobiography in twenty-two volumes which described his campaigns in Africa, Italy, Greece and Asia (Peter I² pp. 195–204). Later still, Julius Caesar wrote the only *commentarii* to survive in full, his account of the Gallic and Civil Wars.[4] All of these may have (and Caesar certainly) incor-porated geographical and ethnographical information which could be of general military value; it is clear from the pages of Strabo and Diodorus that the written and verbal reports produced by the campaigns of Pompey, Caesar, M. Antonius and others were major sources of general geographical knowledge (e.g. Strabo *Geography* XI 4.1–8/501–3; 14.10–11/530 from Theophanes; Diodorus III 38.2–3; V 21.1–22.1; Strabo *Geography* IV 2.3–5.5/191–201; VII 1.2–5/290–2 from Caesar; Strabo *Geography* XI 6.3/523 from Dellius). Strabo makes explicit comment on the importance of military expansion in producing such information (*Geography* I 2.1/14).[5]

On the other hand, this sort of writing was published mainly for personal political motives and its primary function was to cast its leading figure in an attractive light rather than to inform. Any strategic information which was imparted would rapidly become out of date, as would eventually the geographical and ethnographical material. Nevertheless, it could have provided background both for individual commanders and for the Senate as a whole, and have been generally influential in the formation of opinions and attitudes – this was undoubtedly the aim of Caesar's *Commentarii*. Some of it, like the information on drinking water and distances between towns in Armenia in Varro, may also have been of value for more detailed planning.

## ROMAN CLIENTS

For information about specific current situations in areas beyond Roman control, the Senate relied to a large extent on the client states and allies which Rome accumulated in the middle and late Republic as the empire expanded. The interest of such states lay in keeping their protector informed about potential threats to themselves.

Hannibal's activities in Spain in the 220s BC, presaging the Second Punic War, were reported to Rome by her ally Saguntum (Polybius III 15.1–2). During the war itself Rome's commander in Spain, Scipio, informed the Senate of Hasdrubal's departure for Italy in 208 (Zonaras IX 8), but it was Rome's allies the Massiliots who confirmed that he had indeed crossed the Pyrenees and was raising troops in Gaul (Livy XXVII 36.1–2). Massilia (Marseille) was the greatest trading city of the north-western Mediterranean, and was evidently regarded as one of the best-informed. Strabo repeats a story from Polybius that a Scipio – it is not clear which one – attempted to gain information about Britain from the Massiliots, albeit unsuccessfully (*Geography* IV 2.1/190). They were still acting as Rome's eyes and ears in the area half a century after the Second Punic War when they reported Ligurian incursions in 154 (Polybius XXXIII 8.1–2).

In Greece and the East also, fear and jealousy led states to keep the rising power in the West well-informed about the ambitions of Macedon and Syria. When Philip V of Macedon made use of Illyrian shipwrights to construct a fleet in the winter of 217–216, the news was passed on to Rome by the Illyrian king Scerdilaidas (Polybius V 109–10). Later, in 203 (unless the story is a Roman fabrication), envoys from allied Greek cities brought information that Philip had sent 4,000 troops to Africa to aid the Carthaginians (Livy XXX 26.2–3), and in 201 Attalus of Pergamum and the Rhodians sent envoys to report the rumour of Philip's alliance with Antiochus III of Syria (Polybius XVI 24.3; Livy XXXI 2.1; Appian *Macedonian Wars* 4.2). In 197 envoys from the allied cities, accompanied by three Roman senators sent by the Roman commander in Greece, T. Quinctius Flamininus, arrived in Rome to explain to the Senate the geography of the area and that if Philip held Demetrias in Thessaly, Chalcis in Euboea and Corinth in Achaea – the 'Fetters of Greece' – Greece could not be free (Livy XXXII 37.2–4). And when, after several years of quiescence in the aftermath of Cynoscephalae, Philip began in 186–185 to interfere in Thrace, it was Eumenes II, the son of Attalus of Pergamon, who let the Romans know about it (Polybius XXII 6.1).

Antiochus too constantly found his plans betrayed to Rome by informers. In 195 his intrigues with Hannibal were revealed by Carthaginian opponents to leading Romans with whom they had a guest-friendship (Livy XXXIII 45.6). In 192 Eumenes' brother Attalus arrived in Rome to confirm rumours that Antiochus had crossed the Hellespont and that the Aetolians were ready to join him (Livy XXXV 23.10–11) and in 190 the city of Colophon proved to be such a thorn in his side by relaying information on all his activities to Rome that he laid siege to the city, a move immediately communicated by the citizens to the Roman praetor at Samos (Livy XXXVII 26.5–9).

When Perseus succeeded Philip V in 179 and proved to be just as ambitious, he also discovered that his enemies were only too ready to keep Rome informed. After a senatorial commission sent to Aetolia and Macedonia in 174 to investigate the situation had reported that Perseus was preparing for war (Livy XLII

2.2), Rome was kept abreast of developments by embassies from the Aetolians and the Thessalians in 173. Eumenes then came to Rome in person in the same year to deliver a detailed account of Perseus' preparations, and his brother Attalus brought further information in 172. He also revealed that Perseus had executed Arthetaurus, an Illyrian, for communicating his plans to Rome, and two Theban leaders, Eversa and Callicritus, for threatening to do the same (Livy XLII 5.1; 6.3; 11.1–13.12, esp. 13.6–7). The people of Issa further reported that Genthius, the king of the Illyrians, was in league with Macedon and had sent spies to Rome to gain information (Livy XLII 26.2–3).

There were, however, some drawbacks in the use of clients as sources of information. For instance, the Numidian king Masinissa was able to exploit Rome's reliance on the reports of her allies to his own advantage, facilitating Numidian encroachment on Carthaginian territory by nurturing Rome's fear of her old enemy. So in 174 he contradicted Carthaginian statements to a Roman delegation that Perseus had sent an embassy to them, claiming rather that Carthage had sent an embassy to Macedonia (Livy XLI 22.1–3). In 172 his son Gulussa was on hand in Rome to attempt to rebut Carthaginian claims of Numidian aggression (Livy XLII 23–4), and in 171 he was in Rome again to persuade the Senate that the large fleet being built by the Carthaginians, ostensibly to help Rome against Perseus, was in fact intended to make them independent (Livy XLIII 3.5–7).

On many occasions the states which supplied information were at the same time pleading for Roman aid. The Senate did not always respond to such appeals, nor did it necessarily take much notice of the information supplied. In 231 the Senate had sent an embassy to the Carthaginian commander in Spain, Hamilcar Barca, to 'spy out' the situation (*epi kataskopei*), but had apparently decided that no direct action need be taken (Dio XII frag. 48). Nevertheless, it seems likely that the alliance with Saguntum was subsequently made to keep Rome informed. Saguntum sent several warnings about Carthaginian activity without eliciting a response, and it was not until Hannibal succeeded his father in the Spanish command that the Senate finally sent another embassy to Spain to investigate before going on to Carthage to protest (Polybius III 15).

## SENATORIAL EMBASSIES

The most usual response to the arrival of strategic information from an ally was the dispatch of a senatorial embassy to confirm and supplement it. It was partly Rome's pre-eminence in the Mediterranean which made this possible, and such embassies no doubt often served as a diplomatic warning and deterrent to potential aggressors. But it is clear that their investigative function was equally important.

In 208 BC, when the ever–reliable Massilia informed Rome of the arrival of Hasdrubal in Gaul, two envoys were immediately sent out. They reported back that they had sent men along with the Massiliot leaders to enquire amongst the Gallic chieftains with whom the latter had connections: they had discovered that Hasdrubal was intending to cross the Alps as soon as possible (Livy XXVII 36.3–4). Thus, even in time of war, the dispatch of individual senators to see for themselves was regarded as an appropriate method of getting a clearer picture of the situation for the Senate as a whole. But as with Saguntum, most such missions were sent out before the outbreak of hostilities and were diplomatic in character. In 196–195 the envoys who had been sent to settle the affairs of Greece and to investigate the intentions of Antiochus reported that he had crossed into Europe and was going to start a war in Greece, that the Aetolians would join him, and that Nabis of Sparta was also a threat (Livy XXXIII 44.5–9). Significantly, after the Senate had debated the matter, it decided to leave the question of what to do to the commander on the spot, T. Quinctius Flamininus (Livy XXXIII 45.1–3). In 190 Scipio Africanus sent Ti. Sempronius Gracchus to Pella to discover Philip's intentions before attacking Antiochus (Livy XXXVII 7.8–14). Then in 186–185 reports of Philip's activities led to the dispatch of three envoys to receive complaints against him (Polybius XXII 6.5–6; 11.1; cf. Livy XXXIX 24.13ff.). In 172, after charges had been brought by Eumenes against Perseus, the report of the ambassadors sent to investigate his intentions led to a declaration of war (Livy XLII 17.1–18.2), and a further embassy was sent to Asia, Crete and Rhodes to ascertain which states would support Rome (Livy XLII 19.7–8; 26.7–9). The embassy sent to Perseus himself to demand reparations and renounce the treaty of friendship with him returned with tales of continued preparations for war throughout Macedonia (Livy XLII 25.1–2).

Best-known of all is Cato's embassy to Carthage in 153 which was invited by the Carthaginians themselves because of the continuing inroads by Masinissa of Numidia. But the ambassadors went beyond mere arbitration and inspected the city and the surrounding territory, noted the stockpiling of arms and ship-timber, and concluded that the resurgence of Carthage after the Second Punic War had reached a stage where she was once again a threat to Rome and had to be destroyed. Cato dramatically made his point in the Senate by letting some Libyan figs drop out of his toga and announcing that they had been grown only three days' sail from Rome (Livy *Epitome* XLVII; Pliny *Natural History* XV 74–6; Plutarch *Cato the Elder* 26–7; Appian *Libyan Wars* 69). When Masinissa's son Gulussa, seizing his opportunity, subsequently reported that recruitment and shipbuilding were under way at Carthage, Scipio Nasica advocated the sending of yet another embassy 'to investigate' (*exploratum*) (Livy *Epitome* XLVIII).

It is clear that the Senate rarely acted solely on the information passed by its clients and allies, and that it usually required confirmation to be made by some of its own number, even when, as with the envoys sent to investigate Hasdrubal's crossing into southern France, their task was more military than diplomatic. But this approach to intelligence-gathering was not without problems of its own. Clients and allies would tell Rome what it suited them to, as we have seen in the case of Masinissa, so that it was only prudent for the Senate to send representatives to see for themselves; but it could then be at the mercy of the prejudices and interests of the men whom it chose to send, as seems to have been the case with Cato's campaign to have Carthage destroyed. Furthermore, this sort of intense diplomatic activity could, on occasion, open the way to bribery and corruption, as Rome found out to her cost in the five years leading up to the outbreak of war with Masinissa's grandson Jugurtha (Sallust *Jugurthine War* 13–16, 20–35), and it was perhaps to check this sort of bribery that the *Lex Gabinia*, forbidding loans to foreign envoys staying in Rome, was passed in 67 (Cicero *Letters to Atticus* V 21.12; VI 2.7).

Diplomacy was thus far from ideal as a tool for keeping the Senate informed of overseas events, especially given the limitations of geographical knowledge, which was only gradually improved by the expansion of the empire. The ignorance of most senators in the middle Republic even of areas long in contact with the Roman world is amply demonstrated by Flamininus' finding it necessary to have the significance of the 'Fetters of Greece' explained. The Senate's isolation in terms of intelligence from most of Rome's military activity from the third century onwards is reflected in the demand of L. Aemilius Paullus in 169 that a senatorial fact-finding mission should go to investigate the condition of Roman forces in Macedonia in advance of his taking up the command (Livy XLIV 18.1–5). The mission returned with a sorry tale of an under-strength army in danger, an ineffective fleet and an unreliable ally in Eumenes II of Pergamum (Livy XLIV 20). The Senate's isolation also allowed M. Aemilius Lepidus, governor of Hither Spain in 136, to justify his continuation of the Numantine War by claiming that the Senate, which had sent instructions to cease hostilities, was ignorant of the true situation (Appian *Spanish Wars* 80–1).

In view of the reliance on clients and diplomacy, and of the apparently low level of awareness about the details of conditions overseas, it is perhaps not surprising that we hear nothing about any Roman secret intelligence service under the Republic. Indeed, strategic spying is most often spoken of as being performed by ambassadors amongst both Romans and non-Romans. So we are told that in 203 M. Valerius Laevinus declared Carthaginian ambassadors to be spies (*speculatores*) (Livy XXX 23.5), that envoys from the city of Issa denounced others from Illyria as acting for Perseus in 172 (Livy XLII 26.3), and that envoys sent by Mithridates of Pontus to Pompey in 66 were claimed to have been spying (Dio XXXVI 45.5). The use of undercover agents was well known to the Greek world and we do hear, for instance, of a Carthaginian spy at large in Rome for two years before he was caught in 217; his hands were cut off and he was then released, which grimly suggests that he may have been a Roman citizen in the pay of the enemy (Livy XXII 33.1). But although the Romans certainly employed spies in disguise to infiltrate enemy lines and obtain tactical information (e.g. Polybius XIV 1.13; Appian *Spanish Wars* 43; Plutarch *Sertorius* 3.2), there is no evidence that they actually maintained their own spies overseas at this period. It may be that any such secret operations never reached the ears of historians, but it is perhaps more likely that the Senate with its annually changing executive never developed this sort of activity, especially since it will have acquired more and more alternative sources of information as the empire grew in power and influence.

## ROMAN COLONIES AND TRADERS

Apart from the increasing number of client and allied states which Rome accumulated, another source of information was undoubtedly the Roman towns and colonies founded in frontier areas, often for military and strategic reasons. This is rarely made explicit in our sources, but Cicero, at least, does so when he speaks of the colony of Narbo in southern France as a 'watch-tower and bastion of the Roman people' (*specula populi Romani ac propugnaculum*) against the Gallic tribes (*On behalf of Fonteius* 5/13). Such towns and colonies could be expected to keep Rome informed about an area in exactly the same way as clients and allies were, but perhaps even more reliably.

A growing source of information, which certainly ensured that individual senators at least became far better informed about areas which were already under Roman control or subject to strong Roman influence, was the large number of Roman and Italian traders to be found around the Mediterranean from the later second century onwards.[6] Mithridates is said to have had 80,000 of them slaughtered in Asia on one day in 88 (Valerius Maximus IX 2.4, Ext.3; Memnon *FGrHist* III B no. 434 F 22.9/31.4; cf. Plutarch *Sulla* 24.4), and in 69 Cicero could speak (no doubt with some exaggeration) of Gaul's being full of Roman traders (*On behalf of Fonteius* 5/11). Roman knights who were trading in Numidia were amongst those who wrote to influential friends in Rome in 109–108 urging the appointment of Marius to the command in the Jugurthine War, which had been sparked off in part by the massacre of Italian merchants in Cirta two years before (Sallust *Jugurthine War* 65.4; 73.3; cf. 26). And in his speech *On Pompey's Command*, delivered in 67, Cicero refers to daily reports from Roman knights (i.e. leading traders and businessmen) on the state of Asia, Bithynia and Cappadocia (*On Pompey's Command* 2/4–5). We know that such businessmen (*publicani*) maintained their own couriers (*tabellarii*) (e.g. Cicero *Letters to Atticus* V 15.3; *Letters to his Friends* VIII 7.1).

## PROVINCIAL GOVERNORS

But from an overall strategic point of view, the most important development of the last two centuries of the Republic was the direct administration of more and more standing provinces by senatorial governors and their staffs, who became a source of information about the empire both during and after their periods of service. Beginning with Sardinia, Corsica and Sicily in 227, Rome acquired the two Spanish provinces in 197, Macedonia and Africa in 146, Asia in 129, Transalpine Gaul in 121, Cilicia *c.*102, Cisalpine Gaul under Sulla, Cyrene and Bithynia in 74, Crete in 67 and Syria in 64–63. The governors of these provinces were responsible for apprising themselves of the state of the territories which they controlled and of any internal and external threats which might face them. Some governors – those who were more energetic or ambitious – were particularly diligent in carrying out these tasks. The fragments of Cato's *Origins* betray a knowledge of the Spanish peninsula which suggests personal investigation during his governorship of 195 BC and which was no doubt drawn upon many times in the senatorial debates of the next half-century (Peter I² pp. 83, 91, fragg. 93; 110). We are told that Ser. Sulpicius Galba, governor of Hither Spain in 151 BC, was able to deduce that an attack by the Lusitani was imminent by noting that they had carried out the unusual ritual sacrifice of a horse and a man (Livy *Epitome* XLIX). Another governor of Hither Spain, P. Crassus, visited the 'Tin Islands' in the mid-90s (Strabo *Geography* III 5.11/176).

Roman commanders in the field were normally given a free hand during a campaign, as has been recognized by recent work on the relationship between the Senate and its generals.[7] However, it was usual for them, at least at the end of a campaigning season, to send dispatches, to Rome. On the basis of these, the Senate could decide to recall the commander and his army and possibly award a triumph, replace him with another commander, or extend his command and perhaps send reinforcements. Our sources only occasionally make specific reference to such dispatches, and rarely in any detail. We are, however, told about C. Terentius Varro's dispatch after Cannae in 216 (Livy XXII 56.1–3) and of the one sent by the Scipio brothers from Spain in the following year reporting their successes but demanding money, clothing and food for the troops and equipment for the fleet (Livy XXIII 48.4). There are even fewer such references relating to the period after 167 for which we cease to have the full text of Livy, although we do hear of the complaints of Pompey, again from Spain, in 75 that he has received insufficient support for his campaign against Sertorius (Sallust *Histories* II 98). Even less do we hear details either of the sort of intelligence gathered or of the strategic information passed on by governors to Rome, although there can be little doubt that their dispatches were the most important basis for senatorial decisions about the provinces and the areas beyond them.

## CAESAR IN GAUL

Only in the very late Republic is a significant amount of light thrown upon all aspects of strategic intelligence, first by Caesar's *Commentarii* on the Gallic War and then by the letters of Cicero, especially those written during his governorship of Cilicia in 51–50.[8]

The *Commentarii* on the Gallic War give an indication of how much control over senatorial as well as public opinion a Republican commander could have by controlling the flow of information to Rome, since it is reasonable to suppose that the published books and Caesar's dispatches to the Senate were of the same tenor. Just as Cato was able to frighten the Senate into seeking the destruction of Carthage and Ser. Sulpicius Galba to justify his ruthless massacre of the

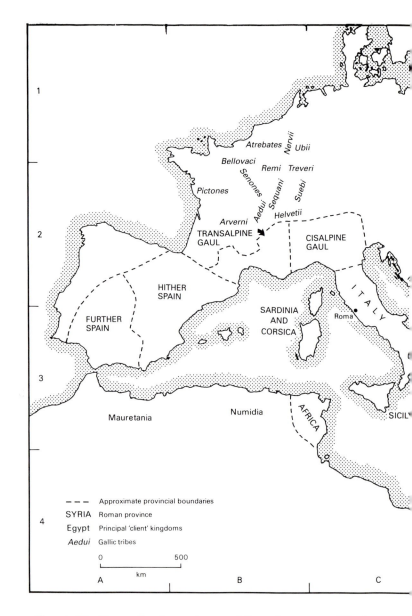

*Figure 1* The Roman Empire on the eve of Caesar's conquest of Gaul

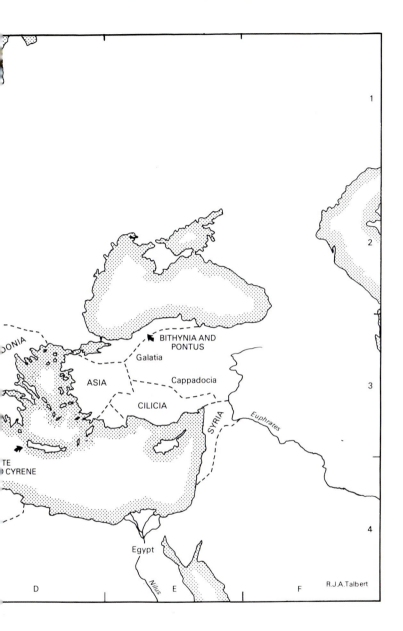

1

2

DONIA

BITHYNIA AND
PONTUS

Galatia

ASIA

Cappadocia

3

CILICIA

SYRIA

Euphrates

TE
CYRENE

4

Egypt

Nilus

D                              E                              F          R.J.A.Talbert

97

Lusitani, Caesar was able to use his dispatches and the *Commentarii* to justify his conquest of the whole of Gaul by emphasizing the threat from the migrating Helvetii, the Germans and the hostile Gallic tribes. It is perhaps significant that Caesar is said to have sent his dispatches to the Senate in a more sophisticated form than hitherto employed (Suetonius *Caesar* 56.6).

The *Gallic War* also shows just how much the commander on the spot was responsible for acquiring his own intelligence. When Caesar conquered Gaul he was soon going very much into the unknown. Cicero proclaims in his oration *On the Consular Provinces* (13/33), delivered during Caesar's third season in 56, that he had been campaigning in regions and against tribes about which no report written or verbal had previously reached the Roman people. No doubt there was an element of exaggeration here but it is interesting to find Cicero writing two years later to his brother Quintus, one of Caesar's legates, that he has no idea where or how far away the Nervii are situated (*Letters to his Brother Quintus* III 6(8).2). Cicero at this time was a senior consular who had several friends as well as his brother serving in Gaul and who regularly corresponded with them and with Caesar himself.

Only the most generalized knowledge of the interior of Gaul and the Germans beyond was available before the conquest. Much of this was based on the writings of the geographer Poseidonius, who had at least visited southern Gaul (Strabo *Geography* IV 4.5/198), had collected information on its people[9] and was possibly the source for at least some of the ethnographical detail supplied by Caesar. Little of it will have been of direct military value to Caesar. In common with the rest of the Senate, his knowledge of the internal politics of Gaul will have come via the usual medium of diplomatic contact.

The Sequani were already known to Rome and their king, Catamantaloedes, had been named 'friend of the Roman people' (*populi Romani amicus*) (*Gallic War* I 3.4). Diviciacus of the Aedui had come to Rome in about 61 to complain of the alliance of the Sequani with the Arverni and the Germanic Suebi from across the Rhine against his own people (*Gallic War* I 31.9; VI 12.5; cf. Cicero *On Divination* I 41/90); Caesar himself had as consul in 59 obtained the title of 'friend of the Roman people' for Ariovistus of the Suebi (*Gallic War* I 35.2; cf. 40.3; 42.3; 43.5; Plutarch *Caesar* 19.1; Appian *Gallic Wars* 16; Dio XXXVIII 34.3). It was undoubtedly through these contacts that the Senate learned of the intrigues in 61 of Orgetorix of the Helvetii. Orgetorix had offered to aid Casticus the son of Catamantaloedes and Dumnorix the brother of Diviciacus to seize the kingship of their respective tribes in return for co-operation in his own bid for the kingship of the Helvetii and in their migration westward from Switzerland (*Gallic War* I 2–4). When the Helvetii finally made a move in 58, Caesar was able to seize upon it as a pretext to raise troops and take military action, making use of popular fear of this tribe who in 107 had killed a Roman consul and forced a Roman army under the yoke (*Gallic War* I 5–8, esp. 7.3).

Once Caesar reached Gaul, however, he will very quickly have had to draw his own conclusions about the sort of people with whom he was dealing – eager to fight but easily demoralized (*Gallic War* IV 5.1–3), divided (*Gallic War* VI 11.2–5) and reckless (*Gallic War* VII 42.2). He will also have had to use such diplomatic contacts as he already had and as many others as he could make in order to provide himself with up-to-date information as he pushed deeper and deeper into unknown territory. As early as his second season in 57 he was able to direct the Senones and other northern tribes to pass on information about the Belgae (*Gallic War* II 2.3–4), and guest-friends kept him informed about the intrigues of Dumnorix among the Aedui in 54 (*Gallic War* V 6.2). The Remi proved to be particularly diligent in performing this sort of service, even ensuring that Labienus was informed about Caesar's defeat of the Nervii in 54 (*Gallic War* V 53.1); among other services, they also revealed to Caesar the preparations of the Bellovaci in 51 (Hirtius *Gallic War* VIII 6.2). Caesar's legates kept themselves informed in exactly the same way when operating independently. So, for instance, Caninius Rebilus heard of a Gallic concentration in the territory of the Pictones in 51 from a local chieftain, Duratius, who had found himself under siege at Lemonum (Poitiers) (Hirtius *Gallic War* VIII 26.1–2).

The use of such clients and allies emerges as one of Caesar's principal sources of strategic intelligence in Gaul, but just as the Roman Senate had always needed to confirm this sort of information by the dispatch of investigative embassies, so Caesar needed to confirm and supplement the information which he received. This was not always easy. As we noted in chapter 2 (pp. 17f.), two ambassadors sent by Caesar to Ariovistus in 58, one of them a Gallic speaker, the other a guest-friend of Ariovistus, were immediately arrested as spies (*speculatores*) (*Gallic War* I 47). And in order to confirm the report of the Remi on the hostile intentions of the Bellovaci in 51 Caesar had to snatch local prisoners who had themselves stayed behind to spy on him. It was from them that he was able to discover which tribes had joined the Bellovaci and where; that the principal leader of the uprising in the area was Correus of the Bellovaci; that Commius of the Atrebates, Caesar's former friend, had gone to seek German help; and that the Gauls would try to offer battle before Caesar had brought up reinforcements, but that if they failed to do so they would sit fast and resort to guerrilla warfare (Hirtius *Gallic War* VIII 7).

The most important passage in Caesar for the understanding of his approach to the collection of strategic intelligence is his description of the first expedition to Britain in 55 (*Gallic War* IV 20–36). Caesar tells us that although the Gauls had repeatedly received military assistance from Britain, they knew nothing about its tribes or geography (*Gallic War* IV 20.1–2). This was not far from the truth, as is strikingly confirmed by an incident which he narrates. He had sent Commius, king of the Atrebates in Gaul, to visit Britain ahead of the expedition because of his supposed influence in the island and in the hope that he might persuade the Britons to surrender. Despite the ambassadors from Britain who had returned to the island with him, he was immediately arrested on landing in Kent (*Gallic War* IV 21.7; 27.2–3). Commius may indeed have had influence amongst the British Atrebates and their allies, but later coin evidence suggests that they had settled in the area of Berkshire and Hampshire over 150 km to the west.

In view of the general ignorance about Britain, Caesar summoned merchants who traded with Britain and interrogated them. The scope of this interrogation has already been described (p. 13). He asked all the appropriate questions: the size of the island, the number and strength of the tribes in it, their mode of fighting, their customs, what harbours there were. But he was apparently unable to elicit the information he required (*Gallic War* IV 20.4).

There were two pieces of information in particular which he might have obtained in this manner but did not. The first was the existence of a harbour large enough to take a fleet at Richborough, successfully used by Claudius a century later but entirely missed by Caesar. The second was that the full moon produced a particularly high tide on the Kentish coast; in combination with a violent storm, this was to wreck Caesar's fleet on the fourth day after his landing (*Gallic War* IV 29). The traders interrogated by Caesar were perhaps unaware of the harbour at Richborough since they themselves would not need to make use of an anchorage capable of sheltering an entire fleet and Richborough is not directly opposite Caesar's invasion base of Boulogne (Portus Itius). But they should have known about the monthly spring tide, and their silence has been attributed to a reluctance to see their trade disrupted by a successful invasion. But it may be that Caesar, a man from the virtually tideless Mediterranean, simply did not think to ask about such matters, and his informants, summoned into the formidable presence of the proconsul, were only too glad to escape the interrogation as quickly as possible.

At any rate, having obtained no information of value from the traders, Caesar decided to send off the tribune C. Volusenus on a five-day reconnaissance with a single ship. He evidently picked the wrong man: Volusenus spent five days cruising along the south coast of Britain without actually landing, and making only a visual reconaissance which formed the subject of his report. Caesar's comment on this is heavy with sarcasm, that Volusenus learned 'as much as was possible for a man who did not dare to leave his ship and entrust himself to the natives' (*Gallic War* IV 21).

After the failure of this half-hearted attempt to rectify his total lack of appropriate intelligence, and despite the lateness of the season, Caesar nevertheless continued with the invasion, having decided that 'it would be of great use to him if only he could visit the island, inspect the nature of its population, and get to know its topography, harbours and approaches' (*Gallic War* IV 20.1–2). And so he sailed across the Channel with his invasion fleet, only to be faced by the White Cliffs of Dover and a defending army. Whilst waiting for his fleet to concentrate offshore, he briefed his commanders at sea with Volusenus' report. He then weighed anchor and groped his way eastward along the coast until he found a suitable beach on which to land, probably near Deal, where he eventually forced a landing and defeated the British defenders. The Britons soon sued for peace, but three days later Caesar's fleet was destroyed, the supply of hostages dried up (from which Caesar correctly deduced that an attack was imminent, *Gallic War* IV 31.1), and the Seventh Legion, out foraging, was nearly cut to pieces and had to learn very quickly how to deal with the novel threat of chariots. After rescuing the legion and a few days later defeating the Britons again and receiving hostages, he and his army sailed back to Gaul.

The whole expedition illustrates how difficult it could be for a Roman commander to find out what he needed to know about previously unexplored territory. In such a situation, the quality of a commander's tactical intelligence became even more important, and here too Roman generals usually had to rely on the good offices of their allies, which normally meant the local peoples who had already come to terms or been subdued. In the early and middle Republic, it was usual for each legion to include 300 Roman cavalry. This cavalry consisted of the wealthiest of the citizenry, quite literally the Roman knights (*equites*), including senators and their families, who could afford to maintain a horse. This sort of cavalry was not always particularly effective as a fighting force, and its last appearance in our sources is in a rout from Tridentum (Trento) in Cisalpine Gaul at the hands of the Cimbri in 102 (Valerius Maximus V 8.4; Frontinus *Stratagems* IV 1.13; Anonymous *On Famous Men* 72.10). Thereafter, the legions may not normally have had a cavalry arm until the imperial period, and Roman cavalry is certainly absent from the pages of Caesar (cf. *Gallic War* I 42; contra *CIL* I (ed. 2) 593.89–91).[10] But in fact, Rome had always relied heavily on her allies to provide the cavalry arm. This meant Latins and Italians at first, although these too are last heard of in the war against the Numidian king Jugurtha from 111 to 105 (Sallust *Jugurthine War* 95.1), and by the first century BC Rome was employing mainly Numidians, Gauls and Germans.

Inevitably, on the few occasions when the origins of *exploratores* are made clear, it emerges that they are drawn from the ranks of allied cavalry. For instance, T. Quinctius Flamininus is specifically stated to have included Aetolians amongst his *kataskopoi* in the campaign against Philip V of Macedon which led up to the battle of Cynoscephalae in 197 'because of their experience of the terrain' (*dia ten empeirian ton topon*) (Polybius XVIII 19.9). Caesar, having only Gallic and German cavalry at his disposal, had no choice but to make use of these for scouting, although this is rarely made explicit. He does tell us, however, that in 53 he used Ubian scouts when operating across the Rhine against the Suebi. Both of these were Germanic tribes inhabiting opposing banks of the Rhine (*Gallic War* VI 29.1). These cases illustrate one of the main advantages of the use of allies as scouts in all periods, namely that they would often have knowledge of the people, territory and even language of the enemy in question. Caesar undoubtedly made use of the Gallic tribes in the same way as he did the German, and we have already seen his abortive attempt to employ Commius of the Gallic Atrebates to make contact with his tribal cousins in Britain. Since the Gallic and German cavalry contingents are unlikely to have been organized on a regular basis, and since different tribes are likely to have provided scouts in different areas, like the Aetolians in Thessaly and the Ubii across the Rhine, we should presume that *exploratores* units were normally put together *ad hoc*. This does not preclude either their being specially selected and trained, or their being employed in this specialist function over an extended period of time. The examples cited in chapters 2 and 3 suggest that they will have reported direct to the commander who appointed them (see pp. 22f., 42ff.).

The availability of allies for the collection of tactical intelligence was one of the factors which enabled commanders to proceed even when their sources of strategic intelligence had dried up. Relying on a combination of these and the Roman army's ability to fight its way out of most forms of trouble, a Roman general would usually opt to press on regardless, especially if he was a Caesar.

## CICERO IN CILICIA

Caesar's *Commentarii* illuminate the approaches to strategic intelligence-gathering available to an active Roman commander in the field. The letters of Cicero from Cilicia in 51–50, some two years after the disaster which destroyed Crassus' army at Carrhae, throw an even clearer and more direct light on how an ordinary governor might cope with anticipating the threats to his own province, and how much the Senate back in Rome would know about and be able or willing to respond to such threats.

The Cilician letters confirm the impression given by Caesar that most of their strategic information came to Roman governors from clients and allies and that it was otherwise on the whole difficult to obtain. They show Cicero arriving in his province, in a state of ignorance. Having entered on 31 July 51, he told Atticus on about 14 August that there was no news of the Parthians threatening the province, but that travellers reported that Roman cavalry had been cut up in Syria (*Letters to Atticus* V 16). On 31 August, a month after entering the province, he was not even sure of the whereabouts of all his forces and complained to his predecessor, Ap. Claudius Pulcher, that he could not trace three of the province's cohorts (*Letters to his Friends* III 6.5). Then on 3 September, Cicero received the first hard news about the military situation from envoys of Antiochus, king of Commagene, who told him that Pacorus, the son of the king of Parthia, had advanced to the Euphrates and was crossing it, and that now there were rumours that Artavasdes of Armenia was about to invade Cappadocia (*Letters to his Friends* XV 3.1; cf. 4.3; *Letters to Atticus* V 18.1; 20.2). By 18 September, in his first dispatch to the Senate, Cicero was able to report that he had originally had his doubts about Antiochus' information but that it had been confirmed by the more trustworthy Tarcondimotus, ruler of the area of the Amanus mountains, and also by the Arab leader Iamblichus who had informed him that the Parthians were at Tyba, close to the border between Syria and Cilicia, and had stirred up a revolt in Syria (*Letters to his Friends* XV 1; cf. *Letters to Atticus* V 18.1). Having received this information, Cicero marched towards Cappadocia, encamping at Cibystra, so as to intimidate King Artavasdes of Armenia and at the same time be able to make use of the advice (*consilium*) of King Deiotarus of Galatia. From Cibystra, he sent ahead a detachment of cavalry into Cilicia proper with orders to advance towards the border with Syria, so as to give early warning of developments in the latter province. But daily messages from Syria, and presumably also from his own cavalry, informed him that Parthians and Arabs had approached Antioch and that his cavalry and praetorian cohort had intercepted a body of their cavalry. He therefore decided to advance to the Amanus region with his whole army on 21 or 22 September. This was communicated to the Senate in his second dispatch and recounted in much more detail to M. Cato in a private letter written in late December (*Letters to his Friends* XV 2; 4). Nevertheless, in a private letter written to Appius Claudius Pulcher on 8 October, Cicero claimed that the 'Parthians' were only Arabs in Parthian dress and that he had been told of their withdrawal (presumably by his own troops) (*Letters to his Friends* III 8.10). He may, however, have been concerned to play down the threat for fear that the Senate would send out a special commander to take control (cf. *Letters to his Friends* VIII 10). Having reached the Amanus range, Cicero began on 12 October to reduce the area which was in revolt, and invested the city of Pindenissus which fell on 17 December (*Letters to his Friends* XV 4.8–10; *Letters to Atticus* V 20.1–5). By then he had heard, contrary to his belief that the Parthian attack on Syria was a sham and had evaporated, that the proquaestor and acting governor of Syria, C. Cassius Longinus, had been obliged to repulse the Parthians from Antioch, and that Pacorus was still in Syria. Furthermore, Deiotarus of Galatia, whose son was to marry the daughter of Artavasdes of Armenia, apparently understood from the latter that Orodes the king of Parthia would himself cross the Euphrates in the following summer, and passed on this information to Cicero (*Letters to Atticus* V 21.2; cf. VI 1.14; 2.6). Hostilities did break out again, prompting the legates and the quaestor of the new governor of Syria, M. Bibulus, to appeal to Cicero for help (*Letters to Atticus* VI 3.2; 4.1; 5.3), but by 18 July Cicero had been convinced by the generally expressed certainty (*hominum non dubio sermone*) that the Parthians had evacuated Syria, leading him to withdraw all the garrisons he had posted, including one at Apamea, which was perhaps a city of that name on the Euphrates. Cicero's attitude may have been influenced by his bad relations with Bibulus, who, he complains, had warned the propraetor of Asia, Q. Minucius Thermus, about the Parthians, but had deliberately told him nothing (*Letters to his Friends* II 17.3, 6; cf. *Letter to Atticus* VI 5.3). The idea that the Parthians had gone was also, no doubt, congenial to him. Sallustius, however, the new proquaestor of Syria, knew better and chided Cicero for this soon after his governorship of Cilicia had come to an end (*Letters to his Friends* II 17.1 and 3).

The Cilician letters, taken in sequence, give us a much more accurate impression of a provincial governor's sources of information, and of how much or how little he might know at any one time, than that provided by any historian or even by Caesar's *Commentarii*, which were written with hindsight and produced to show their author in the best possible light. Cicero begins his governorship in the dark, dependent on rumours brought by travellers and out of touch even with his own forces. Only after a month does he have the first report of what is happening on the eastern borders of his province, from a client prince whom he does not entirely trust. Quite rightly, he feels the need for confirmation from other sources, but this means that he has to wait for further reports from client princes whom he is more ready to believe. The dispatches and letters in fact reveal not only the variety of sources used by Cicero to confirm the facts about the threat to Cilicia, but also the way in which he makes a graded assessment of their reliability. But it is only after he has completed this process, some six weeks into his governorship, that he finally tries to set up his own source of information by sending his cavalry to the eastern end of his province. Their reports are then supplemented by information from Syria, presumably from the beleaguered acting governor, C. Cassius Longinus. Nevertheless, Cicero is sceptical of their analysis of the threat, and apparently prefers to believe rumours that the invaders are not real Parthians and that they have withdrawn. He subsequently learns that the Parthians are still in Syria and, again from a client prince, that they are intending a major invasion in the following summer, but yet again he prefers to listen to rumours that the Parthians have left Syria, and even withdraws garrisons, misguidedly, as it appears.

The shocking picture which emerges is of an *ad hoc* approach, greatly at the mercy of the political leanings of native princes, personal relations with other Roman officials and rumour, and with no standing system of intelligence collection. The affair again illustrates one of the problems which beset all intelligence-gathering, that a commander will often believe what he wants to believe (see p. 32). Cicero, of course, was not a great general, as even he admitted (*Letters to Atticus* V 20.3), but the difference between his approach and that of Caesar in Gaul can be expressed more in terms of character and ambition than of method or sophistication, especially when one considers that Caesar was continually on active campaign and in the front line in Gaul, whilst Cicero was merely preparing to counter a possible attack from an enemy still in a neighbouring province. It might, in any case, be argued that Cicero had found out more about the Parthian threat to Cilicia during his governorship than Caesar had managed to find out about Britain before his first expedition.

Cicero's letters are equally valuable in illustrating the type and level of strategic information reaching Rome from the provinces. Until the Senate received an official dispatch from one of its governors, it had to rely for its information about a province on rumour, on letters sent privately to individual members or their friends, or on reports sent by neighbouring client princes. So, Cicero writes to Lentulus Spinther in 55 that a rumour of Spinther's victories against bandits in Cilicia has reached Rome and that his official dispatch is eagerly awaited (*Letters to his Friends* I 8.7); and in 51 Caelius writes from Rome to Cicero in Cilicia that there are frequent rumours brought by travellers about Caesar in Gaul which say that he has lost his cavalry, that the Seventh Legion has been badly mauled and that Caesar himself has been cut off by the Bellovaci (*Letters to his Friends* VIII 1.4).

Private letters from friends and relatives trading or serving in the provinces must have ensured that some individual senators were rather better informed than the Senate as a body. The role of traders has already been mentioned in this context, and to them must be added the growing number of men serving overseas either with the army or on the provincial governors' staffs. Sallust and Plutarch mention such men as joining in the clamour from Numidia for the election of Marius as consul for 107 and for his appointment to the command against Jugurtha (Sallust *Jugurthine War* 65.4; Plutarch *Marius* 7.4). Cicero expected letters to be sent by his protégé C. Trebatius from Britain in late July 54 (*Letters to his Friends* VII 8.2), and in April 53 he asked him for news of the war in Gaul (*Letters to his Friends* VII 18.1). In addition, he obtained news of the second expedition to Britain from his brother Quintus, who took part in it and reported on the geography, inhabitants and military situation (*Letters to his Brother Quintus* II 16.4; III 1.10, 13; *Letters to Atticus* IV 16.7; 18.5), and also from Caesar himself, both of whom referred to the absence of booty in the island (*Letters to Atticus* IV 16.7; 18.5; *Letters to his Brother Quintus* III 1.25).

Cicero himself sent several private letters from Cilicia reporting in detail on the situation he faced. On about 14 August 51 he wrote to Atticus that he had had reports that Roman cavalry had been cut up in Syria (*Letters to Atticus* V 16.4) and on about 3 September to Cato that he had been given a lot of information on Parthian troop dispositions, the composition of their forces, and their leadership, as well as the possibility of Armenian involvement, by Antiochus of Commagene, but that he would refrain from sending an official dispatch on this to the Senate (*Letters to his Friends* XV 3.2). On 14 November he wrote to Caelius about the war with the Parthians, his march to Mount Amanus and his siege of Pindenissus, but indicated that he would only send an official dispatch once he had taken the town (*Letters to his Friends* II 10). He then let Atticus know of its capture on 19 December (*Letters to Atticus* V 20), ahead of his official dispatch (*Letters to his Friends* III 9.4; cf. II 7.3), and at about the same time sent a full report of his activities in Cilicia and of the Parthian situation to M. Porcius Cato (*Letters to his Friends* XV 4). It is clear that Cicero's correspondents often knew more, and earlier, about the situation in Cilicia during his governorship than the consuls and the other chief officers of the state, just as Cicero probably knew more, about events in Britain and Gaul in the mid-50s. An extreme example of how an individual might be privileged with important information of significance for the Senate as a whole is described by Cicero, who tells how in early April 43, in the admittedly abnormal conditions of a civil war, he was in the Senate when he was handed what was apparently a private letter from Lentulus Spinther about the situation in the East, and felt obliged to read it out immediately (*Letters to M. Brutus* 2 (II 2).3).

It is important to recognize that this sort of private communication was a normal part of the process by which the Senate as a whole acquired intelligence since its recipients were either senators themselves, like Cicero or Cato, or men like Atticus with connections and influence amongst the senatorial class. The

Republican Senate derived the authority (*auctoritas*) by which it had, amongst other responsibilities, the sole direction of foreign affairs, from the collective authority of its individual members which depended on birth, patronage and accomplishments. It acted as the advisory council (*consilium*) to its executive officers, for whom its decisions (*senatus consulta*) were not binding but carried enormous weight, and its essential nature is reflected in its debating procedure by which the presiding officer, usually a consul, asked the opinions first of the consuls designate, and then of the rest of the members in descending order of seniority, beginning with the ex-consuls.[11] Intelligence that had been passed to individuals, like actual experience gained in the provinces, became part of the collective knowledge and wisdom of the Senate and could be presented before it by the individuals concerned with all the weight of their respective authority. This was undoubtedly one reason why Caesar chose to write to Cicero, a senior consular of outstanding personal authority, from Britain and Gaul, and probably why Spinther wrote to him in 43.

But Cicero's Cilician letters also show that dispatches from client princes and provincial governors continued to be the Senate's most important source of information. In his letter of 3 September 51, Cicero wrote to Cato that Antiochus of Commagene had informed both him and the Senate of Pacorus' crossing of the Euphrates. Because of this, and because he expected a dispatch to be sent also by the new governor of Syria, M. Bibulus, he himself would not bother to send in his own dispatch (*Letters to his Friends* XV 3.2; cf. 9.3). Then, on 17 November, Caelius wrote from Rome that Deiotarus had sent information that the Parthians had invaded Syria through Commagene; because Cicero had not written, it was only this dispatch which persuaded the Senate that a similar one from C. Cassius Longinus, which had arrived shortly before, could be believed and that Cassius was not claiming a mere Arab raid as a Parthian incursion. Caelius therefore urged Cicero to be careful in his dispatch to give as full an assessment as possible (*Letters to his Friends* VIII 10.1–2). When another dispatch from Cassius was read out in the Senate on 5 December reporting his repulse of Parthian forces, Cicero's alarmist dispatch which arrived on the same day was (according to Cicero) given more credence (*Letters to Atticus* V 21.2).

What emerges from this is, first, that a senator as experienced as Cicero felt no pressing need to send in his own report on the situation in the East because he thought that the reports of others would give the Senate the information it needed. A similar slackness is reflected in his remark to Appius Claudius Pulcher in a letter of late January 50 that he had only sent off his dispatch to the Senate about his own campaign in Cilicia at the very end of the season and that this had resulted in its being further delayed by bad weather (*Letters to his Friends* III 9.4; cf. II 7.3). Second, Cicero's failure to send a dispatch about the Parthians had led the Senate to doubt the gravity of the situation reported by C. Cassius, a junior senator who had been left in charge of Syria without relief or reinforcement for two years after the defeat of Crassus and was suspected of attempting to frighten the Senate into action. It was presumably mistaken information in private letters, perhaps from Cicero himself as in his letter to Pulcher of 8 October 51 (*Letters to his Friends* III 8.10), that the 'Parthians' were really Arabs which caused this doubt. Similarly, when Cassius' later front-line dispatch was contradicted by Cicero's apprehensions from the rear, it was supposedly the elder statesman's account which was believed. Third, we see information from the client princes being supplied to the Senate as well as to the provincial governors and being accepted by both as of primary importance, especially in confirmation of other reports.

Overall, the letters present a picture of the Senate receiving a reasonable quantity of information, but only intermittently and at the whim of its clients and governors, and easily led astray by the slackness or imperfect knowledge of its informants, the prejudices of its individual members, who could relay privately transmitted information, and its combined prejudices about its different sources of information. The Senate's difficulties were further compounded by the slowness of communications in the ancient world, a problem which grew in line with the growth of the empire itself. In 168 it took 12 days for the dispatches of L. Aemilius Paullus announcing the victory over Macedon at Pydna to reach the Senate, although a rumour had supposedly reached Rome on the third day after the battle (Livy XLV 1). But in 54 BC various letters from Quintus Cicero and Caesar in Britain to Marcus Cicero in Rome took 33, 27, 27 and 29 days respectively (*Letters to his Brother Quintus* III 1.13, 17, 25; *Letters to Atticus* IV 18.5), whilst in 51 a letter from Atticus in Rome took 47 days to reach Cicero in Cilicia (*Letters to Atticus* V 19.1) and Cicero's dispatches to the Senate sent from the same place took some 74 days to arrive in Rome (*Letters to his Friends* XV 1.2; 2.3; *Letters to Atticus* V 19.1; 21.2). With this sort of delay, it would often have been difficult for the Senate to react effectively to the information which it received, even when it wanted to.

## THE LIMITATIONS OF REPUBLICAN INTELLIGENCE

Cicero's letters suggest that the Senate in Rome could only ever receive a confused, incomplete and out-of-date impression of the situation in its provinces and an even less clear understanding of what was happening beyond, about which even the governors on the spot had difficulties in obtaining information. This is a perspective obscured by our historical sources, which necessarily use hindsight to impose order on the chaos, but it is a perspective which there is no reason to doubt or see as abnormal. It also allows us to understand why Republican commanders and provincial governors were allowed so much freedom of action; certainly there is no sign of senatorial interference either in Caesar's campaigns in Gaul or in Cicero's governorship of Cilicia once they had reached their provinces. And, when taken in conjunction with the Senate's function as an advisory body which relied on the combined knowledge and experience of its members and an annually changing series of executive officers, it makes clear why the senatorial archives, the slack administration of which is criticized by Cicero (*On Laws* III 20/46), never became the basis of any centralized intelligence agency.

The result was that on the peripheries of the Roman world Rome's generals, if they were sufficiently ambitious, might find themselves plunging into the unknown. Ultimately, it was only the efficiency and fighting superiority of the Roman military machine which made this possible: while a Caesar might get away with invading Britain in complete ignorance of what he might face, equally a Crassus might allow himself to be led blindly into disaster.

It is thus no exaggeration to say that the Romans groped their way to empire. Strabo, in writing the introduction to his *Geography* a few decades after the fall of the Republic, discusses the importance of geographical knowledge in military affairs. After a survey of ancient history, he moves on to more recent events:

> Leaving ancient times aside, I think that the recent campaign against the Parthians is sufficient evidence for my thesis, and similarly the campaign against the Germans and Celts, in which the barbarians fought a guerrilla war in marshes and impenetrable forests and deserts, making what was nearby a long slog for the ignorant Romans (*tois agnoousi*), and keeping secret from them the roads and the sources of food and other necessities.
>
> (*Geography* I 1.17/10)

It was ignorance, not knowledge of the world which she tried to conquer that was most characteristic of Republican Rome.

*Plate 1* The northern frontier: Hadrian's Wall at Walltown Crags (*photo N.B. Rankov*)

Plate 2  The eastern frontier: a view across the Euphrates from Dura Europos (*photo Richard Stoneman*)

*Plate 3* Trajan's Column (scene ix): the mushroom message. A man fallen from a mule grasps at what appears to be a large mushroom attached to his saddle; this is perhaps the incident referred to in Dio LXVIII 8.1 (see p. 65)

*(photo German Archaeological Institute, Rome)*

*Plate* 4 Segment II of the *Peutinger Table*, a copy of a fourth-century map of the world showing routes, rivers, natural features and towns, and also marking distances between stages. This segment depicts Germany; part of Gaul, the Alps and Liguria in northern Italy and, at the bottom, part of North Africa (see p. 115) *(photo Österreichische Nationalbibliothek, Vienna)*

*Plate 5* A wooden writing-tablet of the late first/early second century AD found at Vindolanda, just south of Hadrian's Wall. It contains what may be an intelligence report from the field describing British cavalry and their method of fighting (*Tab. Vindol. II* 164; see pp. 171–2)

*Plate 6* Trajan's Column (scene xxxvii): two *exploratores* gesture to the emperor Trajan to follow them during a campaign of the First Dacian War against the Roxolani *(photo German Archaeological Institute, Rome)*

*Plate* 7 Memorial of Tiberius Claudius Maximus, who, as a junior officer of *exploratores*, captured the body of the Dacian king Decebalus whose suicide is shown on the relief panel. Found at Philippi in Macedonia (*AE* 1969/70.583; see p. 190)
(*photo Prof. M.P. Speidel*)

*Plate* 8 Trajan's Column (scene cxlv): the death of Decebalus. The rider just failing to prevent the suicide can now be identified as the *explorator* Tiberius Claudius Maximus (see Plate 7) (*photo German Archaeological Institute, Rome*)

*Plate 9* Altar dedication of the *Exploratio Halic(ensis)* dated to the reign of Severus Alexander (AD 222–35). Found at the Feldbergkastell in Germany (*CIL* XIII 7495 = *ILS* 9185; see p. 192) (*Saalburg Museum; photo N.J.E. Austin*)

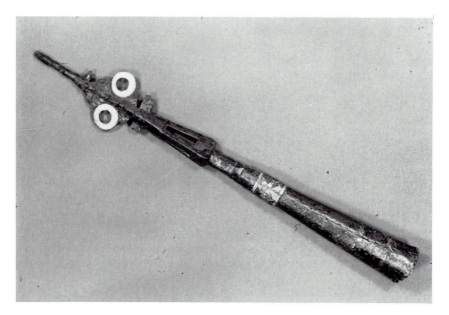

*Plate 10* A *beneficiarius*-lance found alongside a group of *beneficiarius*-inscriptions in the sacred enclosure at Osterburken on the Upper German frontier (see p. 200) (*photo Landesdenkmalamt Baden-Württemberg*)

*Plate 11* The insignia and command of the *dux Britanniarum* (Duke of the Britains), as listed in the *Notitia Dignitatum*, an administrative document of the early fifth century preserved in a number of fifteenth- and sixteenth-century copies (*Not.Dig.Occ.* XL). The Duke has under his command the prefect of a *numerus exploratorum* based at Lavatris (Bowes) (*photo The Bodleian Library, Oxford, MS. Canon. Misc. 378, fols 164v–165r*)

# 5

# THE VIEW FROM ROME
## The emperor's perspective

With the defeat of Julius Caesar's lieutenant M. Antonius by his great-nephew Octavian at Actium in 31 BC, Rome emerged from a century of civil turmoil with what was in effect a new form of government, dominated by one man. Four years later Octavian was granted the title Augustus and began to develop the arrangement by which he and eventually his successors would continue to exercise sole rule within the framework of the old Republican system.

Although the Senate survived and continued to function as a body, its capacity to make independent decisions was circumscribed by the will of the *princeps* ('first citizen' or 'emperor'). It was particularly true in the military sphere where Augustus took control of a 'province' covering the most important military territories and commanded at first twenty of the twenty-six legions of the empire. These legions became permanent and were developed as the core of a standing army some 250,000 men strong. Eventually, each legion had its own senatorial commander who was technically a deputy of the emperor – *legatus Augusti* – and they were organized into a number of army groups under the command of provincial governors, who were also deputizing for the emperor as *legati Augusti pro praetore* (a title akin to the English 'viceroy'). These men were mostly senior ex-consuls of considerable experience, and amongst the most important men in the empire. Their posts were, of course, entirely in the gift of the emperor.

## THE EMPEROR AND HIS *CONSILIUM*

By the end of Augustus' reign only a single legion, in Africa, remained in the hands of a proconsular governor appointed by the Senate, and in AD 39 Gaius Caligula took even that away (Tacitus *Histories* IV 48; Dio LIX 20.7). Thus military decision-making passed entirely from the Senate to the emperor. In the making of both military and other decisions the emperor nevertheless followed in the tradition of the Roman Republican magistrates and consulted with an advisory council. The Roman Senate had originated as the advisory council first to the kings of Rome and then to the consuls, and might still be consulted, at least formally. But Augustus also set up a new preparatory committee of advisers which became known as the *consilium principis*. At first this was a group of senators rotated at six-monthly intervals and consisting of the consuls, a representative of each of the other magistracies and fifteen senators chosen by lot (Suetonius *Augustus* 35.3; Dio LIII 21.4). The *consilium* would discuss important issues and decide on motions to be put before the Senate, but in addition Augustus had a parallel private committee of his own friends (the *amici principis*), chosen by himself, and we may guess that it was in this committee that the decisions which really mattered were taken before presentation to the *consilium*. The latter was reorganized in AD 13 to comprise, in addition to Augustus himself and his heirs Tiberius, Germanicus and Drusus, the consuls and consuls-designate and twenty other permanent members annually elected, but also as many extra members as the emperor desired to discuss an issue. The decisions of the *consilium* now acquired for a short time the force of decrees of the Senate (Dio LVI 28.2–3). But on his accession in the following year, Tiberius made further changes, with the twenty permanent members being nominated by the Senate but not rotated, so that the *consilium* ceased to be a committee representative of the Senate which was intended to prepare business for the larger body. It was now simply an advisory body consisting of important men appointed by the Senate and of friends chosen by the emperor. Indeed, after the reign of Tiberius we hear no more of senatorial appointees and the *consilium* apparently came to consist of such of the *amici principis* as the emperor chose to summon to any particular session, exactly like Augustus' private committee.[1]

In accordance with Republican tradition, the emperor would normally be expected to take consultation with his advisers before making any decision, but equally in accordance with tradition, he was not bound to take any advice offered. Nevertheless, the *consilium* became, in effect, the ruling body of the empire, and the taking of important military decisions came to be the task of the emperor and his committee of friends.

It is perhaps unsurprising that we hear little of the actual workings of this *consilium*, but an unexpected insight into its operation is provided by the early second-century satirist Juvenal. In his Fourth Satire he describes the emergency convening of the *consilium* to discuss what to do with a huge fish which has been presented to the emperor Domitian. Amongst the *amici* summoned are the two Prefects of the Praetorian Guard, Crispinus and Cornelius Fuscus, the distinguished soldier Rubrius Gallus and several other senior ex-consuls. They are called together 'as though he [Domitian] were about to speak of the Chatti or the savage Sugambri, and as though from scattered parts of the globe an anxious letter had come on headlong wing' (Juvenal *Satires* IV 147–9). Each member gives his opinion in turn on what to do with the fish. Clearly, it was possible for Juvenal to envisage the *consilium* urgently discussing a frontier crisis – and, to be sure, the reign of Domitian had had more than its fair share of such crises in Germany and on the Danube, prompting personal appearances by the emperor himself on the frontiers concerned.

In reaching both urgent and non-urgent military decisions the *consilium* had two considerable advantages over the Republican Senate. First, it was able to establish and follow consistent policies with a long-term view in mind, unlike the Republican Senate which had been subject to fluctuations of policy as the result of its internal power-struggles and annually changing magistrates. In contrast, the *consilium* tended to have at its core long-serving *amici principis* who often retained their membership from one reign to the next. This in itself gave imperial policy a considerable degree of stability and continuity, and since the supreme position of the emperor meant that the final decision always rested with him, there tended to be consistency at least within a single reign (though equally it could on occasion mean surprising reversals from one reign to another). Thus really long-term planning at last became possible for the empire.

Second, there can be no doubt that the emperor and his *consilium* would on the whole be better informed about the military situation on the peripheries of the empire than a Republican Senate could hope to be. This was because by the early years of the first century AD the empire had begun to cease expanding.

## THE END OF ROMAN EXPANSION AND THE DEFINITION OF THE EMPIRE

Early in his reign Augustus had sanctioned adventurous expeditions into new territory up the Nile and into Arabia. Elsewhere he came to a diplomatic settlement with Parthia which made the Euphrates a mutual boundary between the two empires, and fought wars of consolidation in Africa and Spain. By the time his own position in Rome had been consolidated in the years following the second political settlement in 23 BC, Augustus' military ambitions had become focused entirely on the North, involving an advance into Germany across the Rhine and Danube. The advance continued without check for a quarter of a century until the Illyrian revolt of AD 6. Within days of the end of a three-year war conducted by Augustus' stepson and heir Tiberius to subdue the Illyrians, news arrived from Germany that the army commander there, P. Quinctilius Varus, had lost his life and three legions in an ambush. Augustus, now over seventy years old, decided to abandon both Germany and a 250-year tradition of Roman expansionism, and Tiberius concurred.[2]

Tiberius' successors, especially those with little or no military experience, continued to feel the need from time to time to conduct aggressive wars of conquest. The expansionist ethos lived on, but after AD 9 the empire began to develop an outer crust of rivers and roads lined with forts, or other, less linear, systems of fortification, to protect and control the territory it already held (see pp. 173ff.). The process was slow and piecemeal and continued for over a century. Its best-known manifestation is Hadrian's Wall, but that represents only one of the forms taken by Roman frontier installations and was itself always part of a system much more complicated than a simple wall 'to divide Romans from barbarians' (SHA *Hadrian* 11.2). In fact, nowhere in the empire was the

Roman frontier a simple line on the ground. Almost everywhere it was defined both by a military presence, disposed in a variety of ways depending on local geographical and other factors, and a diplomatic relationship with the peoples beyond the military frontier which could range from total political dependency of the territory on Rome – a true 'client' or even 'buffer' state – to total independence with the acceptance of an (often hostile) status quo.[3]

Nevertheless, however difficult it is to say precisely where the empire ended and non-Roman territory began, the gradual ossification of the military line allowed a body of general knowledge to build up about what lay at least immediately beyond, the result of past and perhaps more recent campaigning but also of diplomatic and trade contact. Tacitus' *Germania*, a geographical and ethnographical description of Free Germany, written at the end of the first century AD, could not have been produced at the beginning of Augustus' reign. Relatively static frontiers allowed a similar background knowledge to be acquired about all the frontiers of the empire, and should have enabled the imperial *consilia* to form much more precise mental maps of the Roman world and what lay beyond than could have been possible for any Republican senator.[4] By the second century, the increased strength and density of the military installations around the empire which marked the visible frontier line – leading the orator Aelius Aristides to say before Antoninus Pius in AD 147 that the emperors 'did not neglect to build walls (for Rome) but placed them round the empire, not the city' (*Roman Oration* 80; cf. Appian *Preface* 7) – can only have made those mental maps clearer and more focused. By then, Rome's outlook, following upon the withdrawal from Trajan's acquisitions in Parthia by his successor Hadrian, had become defensive and literally entrenched. There is a certain smugness and complacency in Aristides' showpiece oration before his emperor which envisages a Roman world safe and secure behind the walls of its armies and ruled from its capital, distant from any threat, by an emperor whose 'servants and legates, far inferior to him but far superior to those whom they control, perform all their tasks quietly without trouble or disturbance' (*Roman Oration* 89).

But if the concentration of power and the ossification of the empire allowed the new decision-makers at Rome to develop a much clearer concept than their senatorial predecessors of the empire which they controlled, their immediate sources of information remained much the same as before and had the same types of limitations.

## ROMAN MAPPING AND ITINERARIES

Mental maps of the world, of course, owe a great deal to the actual maps which are available (and vice versa). It is clear that for the educated Roman his view of the physical world was a highly urbanized one, in the sense that it conceived of the town with all its amenities and form of government as forming the centre, with the periphery enclosing other towns of a similar nature. Between the towns ran the roads that linked them, not much obstructed by natural obstacles. At the frontiers, this world came to an end, since beyond them there were no towns that possessed these attributes, no individual geographical features with real names and no population that could enjoy them; a good example of this can be found in Arrian's description of the coastline west from the River Borysthenes, where 'at 60 stades, there is a small island, uninhabited and nameless . . . from there to the mouth of the Danube called *Psilon* ("Bare"), a distance of 1,200 stades, [everything] in between is deserted and nameless' (*Circumnavigation* 20.2–3). Translated on to the ground, this view meant that the only places that mattered were the towns, and that the countryside was really no more than the space between towns, space which might include features like rivers, mountains, forests and marshland. The roads cut through all these features in more or less straight lines, and led directly to the next settlement. Apart from the complex situation that obtained on and across the frontiers of the East, there were no real roads that led beyond the frontiers of the North or South because they had no formal, named places to go to. There were of course routes there for trade or transhumance (e.g. the 'Amber Route', the *pistes* of the Sahara) but in no sense were they roads. The inhabitants of these regions (loosely termed *barbaricum*) were at a lower level of development than those on the Roman side of the frontiers, and were self-evidently inferior at the level of Ammianus' *bestiae*, animals (XVI 5.17; XXXI 8.9; 15.2; cf. Libanius *Oration* XV 26), and to be treated as such. The Roman mind, working with such perceptions of physical and human geography, was probably trammelled into circular patterns of thinking that actually made it difficult to apprehend what lay beyond the frontiers and indeed to see any need to do so. Naturally, this would have been the educated view, the one held by the policy formulator, by the person with rank but not necessarily much experience of the frontier regions; the individual on the spot, in touch with the permeability of the frontiers, would probably think differently.[5]

As Roman expansion approached its zenith at the end of the Republic and beginning of the Principate, the boundless military ambition of Julius Caesar and of Augustus produced for the first time at Rome – despite a long Greek tradition – maps which aimed to cover the entire world. The maps commissioned by Julius Caesar (*Geographi Latini Minores*, ed. A. Riese, 21–3) and by Augustus' lieutenant M. Agrippa (Pliny *Natural History* III 16–17 etc.) were perhaps of some use for strategic purposes, as no doubt were the measurements taken for the latter's map which were written up in literary form as *commentarii*. It has, indeed, been argued that the miscalculation in the overall size of the world made by these *commentarii* not only reflected but even encouraged a belief in Augustus of the feasibility of world conquest,[6] but their main purpose would appear to have been propagandist. Perhaps as a result of the preparation of the world maps, the second of which was displayed on a wall of the Portico of Agrippa in Rome after his death, maps in general seem to have become more generally available by the Augustan period (cf. Vitruvius *On Architecture* VIII 2.6; Propertius *Elegies* IV 3.35–40; Tibullus *Elegies* I 6.19–20; 10.29ff.; Ovid

*Heroides* I 31ff.), and this in turn implies a more developed awareness at Rome of the size and nature of the world.

Rome, however, had a tradition of map-making somewhat different from that of the geographical world maps which seem never to have been much used for practical purposes. For relatively small areas, land-survey maps (*formae*) had long been produced to record the laying out of colonies and allotment of land within their territories. This was done by first dividing up the land into areas, usually 20 *actus* square (an *actus* is 120 Roman feet), which were known as 'centuries' (*centuriae*); the whole process was thus known as centuriation. It was carried out with relatively sophisticated equipment by land surveyors known as *mensores* and *agrimensores*. The *formae* they produced depicted topographical features such as cities, roads, rivers, mountains and trees, and the earliest recorded map of this kind, of public land in Campania, was set up in Rome by the praetor P. Cornelius Lentulus in 165 BC (Granius Licinianus XXVIII pp. 9–10, ed. Flemisch). Such *formae* are represented in the manuscripts of a collection of treatises on surveying of the first century AD, known as the *Corpus Agrimensorum* (although the maps themselves may have originated somewhat later than the texts). Other surviving examples include stone maps representing the land-division around the colony of Arausio (Orange) in southern France, the so-called Orange Cadasters. The survey maps made by the *agrimensores* were usually produced in bronze, one copy being kept locally and the other deposited in the public record-office (*tabularium*) in Rome (Hyginus Gromaticus *Constitutio Limitum*, in the *Corpus Agrimensorum*, ed. C. Thulin, i, 165 lines 10ff.).

Roman army units had their own *mensores*, who are well attested epigraphically and otherwise.[7] One such man who served in the Praetorian Guard is designated a 'map-maker and engraver' (*[ch]orographiar(io) [ite]m caelatori*) (*AE* 1947.61), implying that he too worked on bronze. Their principal duties would have included the laying out of both temporary and permanent camps, the surveying of roads, and making other measurements. Balbus, a leading civilian *agrimensor*, apparently specially chosen by the emperor Trajan to accompany him on one of his invasions of Dacia, describes how he was required to lay out military roads and to calculate the width of rivers for the construction of bridges and the heights of mountains to be captured (*Die Schriften der römischen Feldmesser*, eds F. Blume, H. Lachmann and A. Rudorff, i, 92–3). It was presumably military *mensores* who produced two maps mentioned by Pliny the Elder which were the result of military expeditions in the reign of Nero. We are told that 'topographical depictions' (*situs depicti*) were sent back from one of the campaigns of Domitius Corbulo in Armenia, probably in AD 57–8 (Pliny *Natural History* VI 40), and later that a 'map of Ethiopia' (*Aethiopiae forma*) showing the location of palm groves, was produced by a detachment of Praetorians sent up the Nile in anticipation of a possible campaign into Ethiopia (Pliny *Natural History* XII 18–19); Seneca, however, claims that the latter expedition had a purely scientific purpose and mentions two centurions sent to explore the source of the Nile (*Natural Researches* VI 8.3–4). Despite the probable use of *mensores* to produce these maps, it may be a mistake to assume, as has usually been done, that they were more or less large versions of survey-type maps.

For general purposes the Roman army, and Romans in general, seem to have been accustomed to make use rather of simplified road-maps, in the form of illustrated strips, or even just of bare lists of road stations, the *itineraria*, on which the illustrated versions were based: the roads go undeviating from place to place, the geographical features are represented, but almost as ornaments not affecting the course of the roads. Vegetius, who wrote a military treatise at the end of the fourth century, advises the use of itineraries by generals so that they may know the distance and quality of the roads between places, and also the location of short-cuts, halts, mountains and rivers. He suggests that, for preference, the itineraries used should be 'not just in note but also in picture form' (*non tantum adnotata sed etiam picta*) (Vegetius *Epitome of Military Science* III 6).

Examples of such road maps survive in the *Peutinger Table* (see Plate 4), which is a copy of a fourth-century road-map of the whole Roman world, itself based on earlier sources going back to the first century AD, and on a painted shield-cover of the third century AD found in the excavation of the city of Dura Europos on the Euphrates (the Augustan poet Ovid twice makes reference to this practice of decorating shields with maps: *Metamorphoses* V 188–9; XIII 110).

It is possible that the maps of Corbulo and of Nero's Praetorians were more like one of these road-maps than either the world maps of Caesar and Agrippa or the land surveys of the *agrimensores*. There would hardly have been time to do extensive surveying over a whole region whilst on campaign or on a first expedition into the unknown, and both groups of *mensores* were accompanying forces which would have been advancing in a linear manner. In the circumstances, something like a strip-map is the most likely result, and as much is implied for the map of Ethiopia by the fact that Pliny can quote from it the figure of 996 *milia passuum* between Syene and Meroe (i.e. up the Nile) (*Natural History* XII 19; cf. VI 184).

*Itineraria* in list form also survive, giving halts along various routes and the distances between them. The most comprehensive collection is the so-called *Antonine Itinerary*, originally compiled in the second or third century AD for an Antonine emperor; but a route for a fourth-century Christian pilgrimage from Bordeaux to Jerusalem, the *Itinerarium Burdigalense*, provides similar information. Such lists were evidently in common use since they could be employed to decorate various objects such as a group of silver goblets from Vicarello in North Italy, each bearing an itinerary from Gades (Cadiz) in Spain to Rome, and three bronze souvenir vessels found respectively in Wiltshire (the 'Rudge Cup'), Amiens (the 'Amiens Patera') and northern Spain (the 'Hildburgh Fragment'). A passage of St Ambrose even implies that written itineraries (or perhaps the painted variety such as were used to decorate shields) were provided to soldiers travelling on official business (St Ambrose *On Psalm CXVIII*, sermon 5.2 = Migne, *Patrologia Latina* XV, 1251).

Whilst itineraries of both types were clearly readily available for Roman-administered territory, similar information may have been harder to come by for territory beyond the frontiers. However, even if the maps of Corbulo and Nero's Praetorians were not themselves *itineraria picta*, it is evident that the latter expedition at least kept a record of distances covered, and it is highly likely that both in fact produced itineraries. Earlier, about AD 25, a geographical writer Isidore (or Dionysius) from Charax near the mouth of the Tigris had produced a work of which a probable fragment, known by the name of *Parthian Stations* (*Stathmoi Parthikoi*), still survives. This gives places on the route between Zeugma on the Euphrates and Alexandria (Kandahar) (*Geographi Graeci Minores*, ed. C. Müller, i, 244ff.). Pliny the Elder, who tells us of this work and calls the author Dionysius, says that he was dispatched to the East by Augustus in advance of an expedition against the Parthians and Arabs which was to be carried out by the emperor's grandson and heir Gaius Caesar. Augustus apparently sent Isidore/Dionysius to produce a full account of the area (*ad commentanda omnia*) (Pliny *Natural History* VI 141; cf. Athenaeus *Philosophers at Dinner* III 46/93d–94b). A century later, the only surviving sentence from Trajan's memoirs of his Dacian expeditions bears a close resemblance to an itinerary: 'From there we went on to Berzobis, then to Aizi' (*Inde Berzobim, deinde Aizi processimus*) (Priscian VI 13), which suggests that itineraries were kept as his army marched. Thus, for some areas at least, military campaigns and militarily motivated expeditions of exploration provided information which would be of value for future Roman armies passing the same way.

We can, moreover, deduce that itineraries, if not fully surveyed maps, of areas from time to time abandoned by the Romans were kept locally for the use of commanders who might one day have to campaign there. For instance, in AD 16 Germanicus was able to send his deputy A. Caecina to reconnoitre along old Roman routes into Free Germany (Tacitus *Annals* I 61; 63), and anyone familiar with the remains in Scotland both of Roman permanent forts and of the temporary marching-camps which mark the passage of successive campaigns cannot fail to have been struck by the way in which the Antonine forts and Severan marching-camps tend to be situated actually on top of the Flavian sites or in close proximity to them, despite the intervening half-century period of abandonment.[8]

There were also equivalents of the land itineraries for use at sea. They gave distances between harbours and anchorages along various coastlines and were known as *periploi* ('circumnavigations'). They were, in fact, part of a Greek tradition older than the land itineraries, which seem to have been more or less a Roman invention resulting from their own road-building activities, since the surviving *periploi* of the Principate are all written in Greek. These include a fragment of a *Periplous Euxeinou Pontou* (*Circumnavigation of the Black Sea*), produced by Menippus of Pergamum in the late first century BC, a *Periplous Erythraiou Pontou* (*Circumnavigation of the Red Sea*) by an unknown author of the late first century AD, another *Periplous Euxeinou Pontou* by the Hadrianic Senator Flavius

Arrianus (Arrian), which was noted in chapter 1, and fragments of a *Stadiasmus Maris Magni* (*Distance List of the Mediterranean*) of the late third century.[9]

It can be seen that despite the maps of Julius Caesar and Agrippa and the much more advanced world maps exploring orthogonal projection produced by Marinus of Tyre in the early second century AD and Ptolemy of Alexandria about 150 (both of them, significantly, published in Greek), the maps with which Romans were most familiar were the various types of itinerary, especially in military contexts. Thus, although the emperor and his *consilium* would have been able to conceive of the empire in a way resembling our own, it would have been much more natural for them to think in terms of roads – the great military roads built by the Roman army – and distances along them and along coastlines. This was an entirely suitable mode of thinking for the direction of troop-movements within the empire or the selection of invasion routes, but much less so for the assessment of the limits of territory to be annexed or the predetermination of new frontier lines.

The information about distances, halts, rivers and so on provided in itineraries could be used almost indefinitely (it can be shown that the *Antonine Itinerary* and *Peutinger Table* relied heavily on earlier works);[10] it must be very likely that Trajan, for instance, made use of earlier itineraries, including perhaps that of Isidore of Charax, when planning his Parthian campaign. Lucius Verus and Septimius Severus presumably did the same for their own Parthian expeditions some thirty-five and eighty-five years later respectively, and since Trajan certainly kept an itinerary of his Dacian campaign, there may even have been a Trajanic itinerary for them to use.

That itineraries were indeed used by emperors and regarded as essential for their military planning is strongly implied not just by their appearance in the reports to Augustus by Isidore of Charax and to Nero from his Ethiopian expedition, but also by the aforementioned *Periplous Euxeinou Pontou* (*Circumnavigation of the Black Sea*) of Arrian, who governed Cappadocia from about 131 to 137. Arrian addressed this work to the emperor as a literary supplement to his official dispatches in Latin (6.2; 10.1). He describes his own tour of inspection of the province's defences along the Black Sea coast from Trapezus to Dioscurias/Sebastopolis (1–11) and adds, apparently not at first hand, a description of the sea journey from Byzantium to Trapezus (12–16). Arrian then states that in view of the recent death, in 131/2, of King Cotys of the Cimmerian Bosporus (Crimea), he has provided a description of the journey round the coast to the Bosporus as an aid to Hadrian in his consideration of how to react (17). He begins from Dioscurias at the eastern end of the Cappadocian coastline and continues round to the Bosporus and then onward to Byzantium (18–25). As with the Byzantium–Trapezus section, the narrative in the latter part is bare and without personal detail, although enlivened by literary allusions, and, in contrast to the first part of the work, is clearly taken from one or more earlier writers.

Although the *Periplous* appears to be a literary piece and was probably intended for general as well as imperial readership, and although anything of practical importance should have been included in the Latin dispatch on which it is partly based, it nevertheless implies that the emperor could be expected to consult precisely this sort of information when taking political decisions on foreign affairs. Amongst literary sources of information available to the emperor, therefore, the itineraries (including the illustrated variety) and their sea equivalents, the *periploi*, were probably the most useful and important.

## GEOGRAPHICAL WORKS AND *COMMENTARII*

The same campaigns and expeditions which produced maps and itineraries often produced more detailed geographical information in literary form, as the histories of the campaigns of Pompey and Antony in the East by Theophanes of Miletus and Q. Dellius respectively had done under the Republic. The geographical work of Isidore of Charax, apparently a product of Gaius Caesar's eastern expedition, has already been mentioned. King Juba of Mauretania, who accompanied Gaius on the same expedition, dedicated a work on Arabia to him (Juba *FGrHist* III A no. 275 F 1–3): in his section on Arabia, Pliny the Elder claims to be following Juba and, apparently, the military records of the campaign (*arma Romana sequi placet nobis*) (*Natural History* VI 141). C. Licinius Mucianus, the emperor Vespasian's chief lieutenant, wrote a geographical work in the 70s AD which evidently drew in part on his experiences in the East under Corbulo (Peter II, pp.101–7). And in the 80s Domitian sent the schoolteacher Demetrius of Tarsus to inspect the islands around Britain at the time of Agricola's campaigns in the North and he presumably submitted a report on what he saw (Plutarch *On the Decline of Oracles* 2; 18 [=*Moralia* 410a; 419e–420a]; cf. *RIB* 662–3).

Possibly also of military value were the memoirs (*commentarii*) written by commanders about their own campaigns in the tradition of Caesar and earlier generals. Augustus himself produced an autobiography in thirteen books which described his military experiences up to 26 BC including those in Illyricum and Spain, and his deputy M. Agrippa followed suit; later C. Suetonius Paullinus wrote about his campaigns in Mauretania in AD 41 and perhaps also about those in Britain from 58 to 61; Cn. Domitius Corbulo wrote about his campaigns in the East from 55 to 66; the emperor Vespasian about his Jewish campaigns from 66 to 71; and Trajan wrote up his conquest of Dacia over the period 101 to 106 (Peter II pp. 54–64 (Augustus), 64–5 (Agrippa), 101 (Paullinus), 99–101 (Corbulo), 108 (Vespasian), 117 (Trajan)). Tacitus' biography of his father-in-law Agricola shows some characteristics of the *commentarii* and certainly relied in part on new information about Britain brought back by Agricola from his campaigns in the north of England and Scotland from 77 to 83. As under the Republic, *commentarii* regularly contained geographical, ethnographical and military information derived from the notes kept by Roman generals as the basis for their reports to Rome.[11]

Such reports, even if not written up and published as *commentarii* were, of course, available to the emperor and his *consilium* from every part of the empire. Although it is unlikely that the general public would have had access

to these, it would appear that Pliny the Elder, who was himself a senior equestrian official, was able to read reports of earlier campaigns at least. He tells us
that Aelius Gallus, Augustus' second Prefect of Egypt from *c.*27 to 25 BC, was
the first Roman general to invade Arabia and gives us a detailed description
of the country, adding that Gallus 'reported other things which he had found
out' (*cetera explorata retulit*) (*Natural History* VI 161). A few pages later he gives
a similar description of part of Ethiopia invaded by Gallus' successor C. Petronius
(*Natural History* VI 181–2), and notes that the measurements of earlier Greek
travellers in this area had now been corrected by Nero's expedition (*Neronis
exploratores*) (*Natural History* VI 184–6), that is, the Praetorian detachment already
mentioned. Pliny also makes reference to 'twenty-three islands known to Roman
arms' (*XXIII inde insulae Romanis armis cognitae*) off the coast of the Cimbric
promontory in northern Germany, presumably discovered during the
campaigns of the elder Drusus in 12 BC when a Roman fleet seems to have
sailed round Jutland into the Baltic (*Natural History* IV 97; cf. II 167, and Augustus
*Res Gestae* 26.4; Strabo *Geography* VII 1.3/290–1; Tacitus *Germania* 34; Dio LIV
32–3). Since Pliny does not ascribe this information to any published work, it
is reasonable to assume that he was able to read the official reports of the expeditions in some archive in Rome. This may have been the senatorial archive,
the *tabularium*, since Tiberius at least insisted that provincial governors should
follow the Republican custom of sending their reports to the Senate (Suetonius
*Tiberius* 32.1), and we have already seen that the *tabularium* received a copy
of each survey map made by the *agrimensores*.[12] But Tiberius' insistence
on Republican precedent was not necessarily followed either by his stepfather
or by his successors, and it is at least as likely that these reports were kept in
the files (*scrinia*) of the secretary in charge of imperial correspondence, known
as the *ab epistulis*, of whom we shall say more later. If so, Pliny would have had
to rely on his good relations with the emperor Vespasian to gain access.

At any rate, we can be sure that the residual, albeit intermittent, expansion
of the first and early second centuries AD did allow the emperor at least some
knowledge of those areas beyond Roman control or influence. Furthermore,
under the Republic, such knowledge had often come through the patronage and
out of the curiosity or vanity of individual commanders like Scipio Aemilianus
or Pompey who wanted to leave their own achievements recorded for posterity,
but now the emperor himself could send out men like Isidore of Charax or
a detachment of soldiers like Nero's Praetorians for purposes of state.
Unfortunately, although we can certainly assume that geographical reports and
dispatches were read by the emperor when they first arrived in Rome, and it
is clear that they were subsequently available to be read by others with
permission, as they were by Pliny the Elder and other writers who made use
of them, we cannot be absolutely certain that they were used for strategic ends
by later emperors. Indeed, with the exception of itinerary-type material, the
older the information contained in a geography or in *commentarii*, the less valuable
it would have become for military purposes.

Geographical reports or memoirs, if they were consulted, might provide guidance (compare Tacitus' remarks on the Forth–Clyde line as a potential frontier for Britain in *Agricola* 23), but would in any case have to be moderated and subordinated to the recommendations of the men currently on the spot. And when it came to actual campaigning, the limitations of literary sources would have been even more apparent. Even if Septimius Severus did, as seems likely, make use of earlier reports and itineraries in his invasion of Parthia, after his capture of Ctesiphon in 198, his campaign foundered, as we saw in chapter 2 (p. 38), through 'ignorance of the country and inability to obtain supplies' (*to men agnosiai ton chorion to d'aporiai ton epitedeion*) (Dio LXXV 9.4).

## DIPLOMACY AND CLIENTS

A rather more immediate source of information for the emperor and the *consilium* was, as it had been for the Senate under the Republic, diplomatic activity both with foreign powers and with Rome's own client kingdoms – categories which in practice as well as in political propaganda tended to overlap and shade into each other. Some embassies went to the nearest provincial governor but many travelled direct to Rome and were dealt with by the emperor in person, usually in the Senate but sometimes in the *consilium*. The level and types of foreign diplomacy handled directly by an emperor are illustrated in a well-known passage of Augustus' record of his own achievements, the *Res Gestae*:

> Embassies from Indian kings, not previously seen in the presence of any Roman commander, were often sent to me. The Bastarnae, Scythians and kings of the Sarmatians from both sides of the Don, the king of the Albanians, the king of the Hiberi and the king of the Medes all sought our friendship with their envoys. These kings fled to me as suppliants: Tiridates of the Parthians and afterwards Phrates son of king Phrates, Artavasdes of the Medes, Artaxares of the Adiabeni, Dumnobellaunus and Tincommius of the Britons, Maelo of the Sugambri, and ...rus of the Marcomanni and Suebi. The king of the Parthians, Phrates son of Orodes, sent all his sons and grandsons to me in Italy, not because he had been subdued in war but because he sought our friendship by handing over his own children as pledges of good faith. Very many other nations experienced the trustworthiness of the Roman people while I was emperor, who had never before exchanged embassies or treaties of friendship with the Roman people. The nations of the Parthians and Medes, having sent the leading men of those nations as ambassadors, requested and received kings appointed by me: the Parthians received Vonones, son of King Phrates and grandson of Orodes, and the Medes received Ariobarzanes, son of King Artavasdes, grandson of King Ariobarzanes.
>
> (*Res Gestae* 31–3)

The information to be gained from diplomatic contacts was, as we have noted before, slanted in the interests of those who sent the embassies, which were not necessarily those of Rome. But if due allowance could be made, or if the information could be cross-checked from a Roman source or against the counter-claims of an opposing embassy from another party, it could still be of immense value to an emperor.

Some envoys merely brought information as an act of goodwill to Rome or in fulfilment of the obligations of a client. We know from Pliny the Elder that Claudius received an embassy from Ceylon, apparently prompted by the visit of a freedman of a Roman tax-collector for the Red Sea area who had been blown off course whilst operating on behalf of his master. The Ceylonese learned from the freedman about the Roman Empire and so sent four envoys who provided Claudius with a geographical description of the island and its position, wealth and political structure; they also confirmed Roman merchants' accounts of the Chinese with whom they also traded (*Natural History* VI 84–91).

No doubt of rather more immediate concern to an emperor were urgent messages of the sort passed on to Trajan by Pliny's nephew and adoptive son, Pliny the Younger, who served as imperial legate of Bithynia about AD 110. These had been sent by Ti. Iulius Sauromates, king of the Cimmerian Bosporus (Crimea), a major supplier of cereals to the empire. Pliny relates in a letter to Trajan that the imperial freedman Lycormas has written to ask him to detain an embassy on its way to Rome from the Bosporus. None has yet arrived but a messenger has come from Sauromates with a letter for the emperor, and Pliny has sent both letters on to Trajan. In a second letter, Pliny says that news has now arrived from Sauromates which the emperor ought to know as soon as possible and that he has sent the courier on by the public post; and in a third he tells the emperor that he has now sent on an ambassador who has arrived from the Bosporus (*Letters* X 63; 64; 67).

Unfortunately, it is impossible to determine from Pliny's letters whether the information being forwarded is political or military. Some scholars have suggested that it was concerned with the threat to the region from the Alani with which Arrian and Hadrian were concerned twenty years later; but it seems more likely, in view of the involvement of an imperial freedman who ought to be a deputy of the procurator of Bithynia in charge of imperial finance in the region, that it concerned a dispute between the king and Lycormas over Roman subsidies to the Bosporus (cf. Lucian *Alexander* 57; see pp. 147f.).

More often, embassies to Rome came with requests to the emperor either to sort out an internal problem of the client state involved or to seek assistance against a third party; in both cases it is clear that politically significant information would have been provided, even if our sources do not always provide the details. So we can fairly assume, for instance, that the counter-claims of the Parthian pretender Tiridates and King Phrates IV presented to Octavian in Syria in 30 BC, and repeated again after he had become Augustus, in Rome in 23 BC (Dio LI 18.2–3; LIII 33.1–2; cf. Justin XLII 5.6–9), allowed the emperor to formulate a fairly complete understanding of the contemporary situation in Parthia and so plan the diplomatic settlement of 20 BC. Similarly, when King Maroboduus of the Marcomanni appealed for help to Tiberius in AD 17, after he had been attacked by the Cherusci and Langobardi under the leadership of Arminius, the destroyer of Quintilius Varus and his three legions eight years before (Tacitus *Annals* II 46; cf. 63), he would obviously have revealed a great deal about the turmoil going on in Germany beyond the Rhine and Danube. So would the appeals of Vannius, set up over Maroboduus' kingdom in AD 19 by Tiberius' son Drusus, when he in turn had to ask help of Claudius in AD 50 against an internal revolt which was being aided by the Hermunduri and against a threatened attack by the Lugii (*Annals* XII 29–30). It is ironic that, nearly half a century later in AD 91/2, it was the Lugii who had to appeal to Domitian for help against the Suebi (Dio LXVII 5.2).

We also have more explicit testimony to the acquisition of political information from embassies. The Jewish historian Josephus describes the debate before Augustus in 8/7 BC between Syllaeus, chief minister of Obadas III, the late king of the Nabataean Arabs, the historian Nicolaus of Damascus, who was the representative of King Herod of Judaea, and the envoys of the reigning Nabataean king Aretas, who had denounced Syllaeus and were backing Nicolaus. Syllaeus had accused Herod of making war on Arabia, and in the midst of all the charges and counter-charges being made, Augustus had to interrupt the squabbling parties to establish from Nicolaus whether Herod had indeed invaded Arabia, as Syllaeus had claimed. When Nicolaus admitted this but then made a spirited defence of Herod's actions, claiming that Syllaeus had been harbouring brigands and had hugely exaggerated the number of Arabs killed, Augustus was able to put this to Syllaeus. He made no satisfactory answer and was further condemned by reports of brigandage from the cities and the Roman governors of the region. On the basis of this, the emperor decided to put Syllaeus to death and to ignore the charges which he had brought against Herod. But he also confirmed Aretas on the Nabataean throne despite his having succeeded Obadas without permission, evidently intending him to be a counterweight to the ambitions of Herod (Josephus *Jewish Antiquities* XVI 10.8–9/335–55; cf. 9.1–4/271–99).

Less dramatically, Tacitus tells us about the Parthian envoys introduced into the Senate by Claudius in AD 49 who reported on the tyranny and unpopularity of their king Gotarzes. The latter had seized the throne two years before, after the murder of Vardanes, and the envoys were asking for the return of their prince Meherdates, who was then a hostage in Rome, in order to challenge Gotarzes' rule (*Annals* XII 10–11; cf. XI 8–10). Fourteen years later, the Parthian king Vologaeses I sent envoys with a letter to Nero in which he agreed to allow Nero to crown Tigranes as king of Armenia even though the Roman army of L. Caesennius Paetus, governor of Cappadocia, had been forced by Vologaeses to withdraw from the country. Tacitus tells us that this last piece of information contradicted Paetus' own dispatch and that Nero had to question the centurion who had accompanied the envoys in order to establish that what the envoys said was true (*Annals* XV 24–5). A second Vologaeses of Parthia, according to Dio, sent envoys to Hadrian to lay charges against Parthasmanes of Iberia, who had apparently encouraged attacks by the Alani on both Roman and Parthian territory in the Caucasus region (Dio LXIX 15.1–2).

This sort of information was intermittent and had to be treated with caution. The Parthians, of course, only told Rome what it suited them to, but so in varying degrees did those kings who were in practice subordinate to Rome, like Herod, and even they could be untrustworthy. In AD 17 Tiberius had to depose Archelaus of Cappadocia on suspicion of disloyalty (Tacitus *Annals* II 42; Suetonius *Tiberius* 37.4; Dio LVII 17.3ff.), and in 72 Antiochus of Commagene suffered the same fate at the hands of Vespasian (Josephus *Jewish War* VII 7.1–3/219–43). Nevertheless, such information could be and often was checked against other sources. The practice of opposing embassies, as in the case of Herod and the Nabataeans, provided a check in itself, especially when the different parties were subjected to cross-examination by an emperor like Augustus. It was essential for the client to choose a man as skilful as Nicolaus as ambassador in such instances. But the reports of the provincials and of provincial governors were also available, and it was these which drove the last nail into Syllaeus' coffin. Similarly, Vologaeses' letter to Nero was checked against the dispatch of Caesennius Paetus, but this time it was the governor who was concealing the truth and so Nero had to question the centurion accompanying the embassy.

## THE EMPEROR AND HIS GOVERNORS

Nevertheless, the most important source of information that came to Rome was from the provincial governors, even more so than under the Republic. Like the client princes, Republican governors had been able to tell the Senate what it suited them to tell, and we have seen how Julius Caesar was able to exploit senatorial ignorance of the regions and peoples with which he was dealing in order to concoct a justification for his continued conquest of Gaul. Under the Principate the situation had altered. The changes in the Roman political structure meant that there was far less incentive for governors to falsify the situation since the erstwhile reward of political power in Rome was no longer available to them; they also meant that the dangers of misleading the emperor, or ignoring his instructions (*mandata*), whether one was militarily successful or not, tended to be rather greater than those of misleading or ignoring the instructions of a Republican Senate, where the potential penalty could be avoided by success or political influence or flagrant bribery. Governors would still tend to put their own actions in the best possible light, but those actions were now more circumscribed than ever before. Caesennius Paetus was lucky to escape with dismissal from his post and no more after his débâcle in Armenia and the attempt to cover it up; only his kinship by marriage with the emperor Vespasian prevented the total eclipse of his career. The path to honours and advancement for the army commanders of the Principate lay in carrying out the wishes of the emperor, and that meant, in part, keeping him informed.

Our best evidence for the volume and level of correspondence between governor and emperor comes from the tenth book of the letters of the younger Pliny. It contains correspondence which passed back and forth between him as imperial legate of Bithynia and Pontus and the emperor Trajan around the years 109–11. The letters give the impression that a governor would consult the emperor regularly, even on relatively trivial matters, and that the emperor would reply personally. This may be misleading, however, especially in military affairs. Pliny himself was an imperial legate sent out in place of the usual proconsul representing the Senate, in order to deal with the malpractice and corruption which had become rife in the province (*Letters* X 117). He was evidently given an extraordinary grant of consular power in order to underline his special status (*CIL* V 5262 = *ILS* 2927), and he even makes reference to the emperor's having specifically granted him the right of consultation (*Letters* X 31.1). This does not mean that other governors did not have this right or did not use it,[13] but Pliny's special position may have resulted in his tending to refer matters to Trajan rather more than he would usually have done – as is perhaps indicated by the occasional outbursts of impatience in Trajan's replies (e.g. *Letters* X 40.3; 117). It is also suggested by the fact that in the first four months of his governorship Pliny sent fifteen queries to Trajan, in the next eight months only twelve, and in the next four months only four. Thus the frequency of his consultation decreases considerably as he gains experience of the province and confidence in himself and his understanding of the emperor's wishes.[14] This was perhaps true of all imperial governors as they sought to comply with the emperor's *mandata*, issued to them when they left for their provinces, but Pliny's special commission and his pernickety nature, which is illustrated so well in his letters, are likely to have prompted more initial consultations than was usual.

Moreover, Pliny was dealing with matters which could wait for an imperial response: municipal corruption, legal problems, civic and individual privileges, and the like. Bithynia and Pontus was not a frontier province and military problems were minor. Military problems on the frontiers, however, might allow for consultation but often they would not, especially when there was active campaigning going on. The vast size of the empire by the end of the reign of Augustus and the relative slowness of communications by modern standards are of considerable significance here. The usual speed of a courier making use of the imperial posting system (*vehiculatio*) set up by Augustus seems to have been about 75 km per day overland on average, to judge by the various journeys making use of it which have been recorded. This accords fairly closely with the speeds given by Cicero for letters between Britain and Rome and Cilicia and Rome. Recorded speeds do, however, go up to 200 *milia passuum* (300 km) per day in an emergency, like the dash by Tiberius from Rome to the Rhine in 9 BC to be at the bedside of his dying brother Drusus (Valerius Maximus V 5.3;

Pliny *Natural History* VII 84), whilst the eagle-bearer of legion *IV Macedonica* travelled the 185 km between Mainz and Cologne in twelve hours in the midwinter of AD 69 to inform Vitellius, the governor of Lower Germany, that the Upper German legions had revolted against the new emperor Galba (Tacitus *Histories* I 56). The sixth-century historian Procopius implies that 200 *milia passuum* per day had become normal for messengers before his day (*Secret History* 30.1–7), but it is clear from his description that he is looking back to the *cursus publicus*, as it was by then known, at its most developed with frequent well-manned and supplied relay-stations for changes of horses. Since his purpose is to lament the way in which the current emperor, Justinian, has allowed it to run down, we should suspect that Procopius has permitted himself a certain amount of exaggeration about its earlier efficiency. At any rate, it is clear that 300 km per day was well above normal for the Principate and that even the most urgent messages, unless they could be carried by sea and met with favourable winds, tended to travel rather slower. Even at 300 km per day, the closest frontiers in Raetia and Noricum could communicate with Rome in three or four days as an absolute minimum; the German and Pannonian provinces were five or six days away, Dacia and Lower Moesia seven or eight, as perhaps was the North African frontier; the frontiers of Britain were nine or ten days away, and the eastern frontier two weeks. But more realistic figures are likely to have been perhaps twice or rather four times these, and it would, of course, have taken at least double these times for the frontiers to receive a reply.[15]

## THE PROBLEMS OF CENTRALIZED CONTROL

It will be apparent that, despite the improvement in the quantity and the quality of information available at Rome in the early Principate, the capital's isolation from the frontiers continued to restrict the scope of the decision-making which was possible from there. Fergus Millar, picking up the concept of András Alföldi that there was a 'moral barrier on the Rhine and Danube' which caused the Romans to abandon their normal moral standards in dealing with 'barbarians' outside the empire, concluded that the frontiers also constituted an information barrier.[16] Whether this conclusion can be justified in absolute terms will be considered in chapter 7. But once we recognize that the emperor and his *consilium*, while they sat in Rome, were severely limited in what they could know and therefore what they could decide, it follows that we must adjust our idea of the extent of their control over what was happening on Rome's frontiers.

For instance, there is still widespread acceptance of the suggestion, first made by Ronald Syme in 1934, that Augustus' aim in his great expansionist drive to the North from the second decade BC onwards was to establish a frontier line based on the Elbe and Danube Rivers.[17] Brunt, however, has pointed out that 'modern maps make this plausible enough, but they were not at Augustus' disposal'. We have already noted how the form of map most familiar in the

Roman world would have inhibited such planning but the formulation of such a plan at this period would have been impossible for more reasons than this.

First of all, the very concept of a frontier line defined by a river with a road running along it is anachronistic for the period before the Varian disaster. It was in fact that disaster which created the first such defensive frontier by default, since it occasioned the withdrawal of Roman forces to the left bank of the Rhine in its aftermath. Before then, the forts and fortresses along the river had been situated so as to serve as bases for advance into Germany. Even after AD 9, although more forts were gradually built at intervals along the river, the legions remained concentrated mainly in attacking groups in two-legion fortresses at Vetera, Cologne and Mainz, with two other legions elsewhere, probably based separately. Only over a period of time were these concentrations broken up in order to distribute the legions more evenly along the river frontier. The Cologne fortress was only abandoned and its legions separated towards the end of Tiberius' reign at the earliest; Vetera, which covered a major invasion route along the River Lippe, retained two legions until AD 70; and Mainz, covering the other main invasion route through the Wetterau, kept both its legions until 92.[18] The whole Rhine frontier continued to be consolidated and redrawn up until the mid-second century, with a road and later a palisade cutting off the large re-entrant angle between the Rhine south of Remagen and Danube west of Eining.

But even if Augustus had had the model of a fixed, defensible frontier line available to him before he decided to invade Germany, it would still have been impossible for him to know where to locate it. It is significant that the account of Germany given by Augustus' contemporary Strabo (*Geography* VII 1/289–92) is framed entirely in terms of the recent campaigns of Augustus' generals. Strabo specifically says that the tribes of Germany have become known as a result of their making war against the Romans and adds that they would have been better known had Augustus allowed his commanders to cross the Elbe (*Geography* VII 1.4/291). Roman ignorance of Germany between the Rhine and the Elbe before this is confirmed by the geographical limitations of Julius Caesar's account of the Germans, which is confined to the tribes of the area immediately beyond the Rhine: compare his fabulous account of the Hercynian forest derived from Eratosthenes (*Gallic War* VI 25–8; see above p. 88). This had been written only thirty years before Augustus' invasion and there had been no penetration of central Germany in the interim. And Velleius Paterculus, who had accompanied his hero Tiberius into Germany as far as the Elbe in AD 4–5, was able to speak, admittedly in a spirit of adulation, of 'the conquest of tribes who were unknown, almost down to their names' (II 105–6).

Central Germany, therefore, was unknown territory when Augustus began his campaigns. His instructions to his generals not to engage in warfare across the Elbe were intended, according to Strabo, to avoid inciting the tribes there to aid the resistance of those on the left bank (there is no hint of a prohibition on their subsequent conquest). But these instructions can only have been

formulated on the advice of Augustus' stepson Drusus, who attempted unsuccessfully to cross the river in 9 BC (Dio LV 1.3), or of his niece's husband,
L. Domitius Ahenobarbus, who actually did so (if our sources are not referring
merely to the Elbe's tributary, the Saal) between 6 and 1 BC (Tacitus *Annals* IV
44.3; Dio LV 10a.2). And even after these campaigns, Augustus did not have
the information necessary to select a frontier line. Both Strabo and Velleius can
tell us (quite correctly) the distance traversed by Augustus' armies between the
Rhine and the Elbe – 3,000 stades (about 560 km) according to Strabo (*Geography*
VII 1.4/292), 400 *milia passuum* (about 600 km) according to Velleius (II 106.2)
– but neither gives the distance from the North Sea along the Elbe to the
Danube, which should have been known and would have been worth mentioning
if Augustus had indeed intended the Elbe to be a frontier. This would be the
case even if 'frontier' is taken in the sense of a line of military communication
rather than an out-and-out defensive system, which is how Syme chose to refor-
mulate his thesis in his later years.[19]

The most commonly advanced alternative hypothesis was put forward
by Peter Brunt, who suggested that the expansionist urgings of the Augustan
poets and the public display of Agrippa's map reflected a craving in Augustus
for world conquest – 'empire without end' (*imperium sine fine*) as Virgil's Jupiter
prophesies to his Aeneas (*Aeneid* I 279). Brunt argues that the underestimates
of the size of the world which appear in Agrippa's map made such a scheme
appear feasible, especially in the aftermath of Caesar's eight-year conquest of
the whole of Gaul.[20]

There is, however, a third possibility: that Augustus had no clear idea of how
far he would advance, like many other generals before him, including Caesar;
that he sought expansion of the empire because Roman commanders had been
doing the same without pause for over two hundred years; and that it was
conquest pure and simple, and the glory which it brought, which as much as
anything justified both his pre-eminence in the State and his continued control
of the army. It can be no accident that the pursuit of conquest was so prominent
a feature of poetry written in the early part of his reign, as Brunt recognized, or
that his effort was carefully concentrated on a single area of central Europe
between the Rhine and the Danube once the territory on the other fringes
of the empire had been made secure either by limited military activity or by
diplomacy. The timing of the big push into Germany is also significant: it began
in earnest only in 15 BC, after Augustus' own political position at Rome had
finally been stabilized. Disturbances in reaction to his second constitutional
settlement of 23 BC rumbled on until 19 BC, and his final political victory was
eventually symbolized by the celebration of the Secular Games in 17 BC, which
were intended to usher in a new age. The renewed subjection of peoples
outside the empire was carried out mostly by generals who were members of the
new imperial family – Drusus and Tiberius, who were Augustus' stepsons, and
L. Domitius Ahenobarbus (the grandfather of Nero) and P. Quinctilius Varus,
both of whom were married to his nieces. It makes the same sort of military

sense as Pompey's conquest of Asia in the 60s BC or Caesar's conquest of Gaul in the following decade. Both of the latter could be claimed with some plausibility as essential to the security of the empire; both went far beyond the demands of such security: neither the Caucasus nor the British kingdoms posed any threat to the empire; and the ultimate aims of both were political even more than military. So it was with Augustus and Germany. His final military objectives need not have been any more focused than were Pompey's or Caesar's, and in any case they depended upon the situations which faced his generals as they advanced. Augustus' great advantage over his predecessors, however, was that the security of his own political position allowed him to carry on the advance, through his deputies, as long as he had the will to do so. The destruction of Varus crushed that will where Germany was concerned, until it resurfaced in his adoptive grandson, Gaius Caligula, thirty years later.

## ROME AND BRITAIN: A TEST CASE

The recurrence of Roman expansionism after Augustus can and usually should be seen in a similar light. It can be argued that it was often motivated by the need for a new emperor to establish himself in the eyes of the Senate and the People, and sometimes also by his vanity. Often, too, geographical ignorance and the emperor's inability to predict the difficulties or personally to direct the subjugation of an area from Rome conspired to ensure that conquest was carried out without any fixed plan or limitation. A good test case is provided by the conquest of Britain, a province for which we have a wealth of literary, epigraphic and archaeological evidence, and where we can be sure that for much of the time Roman forces were advancing into previously unknown territory.

Caesar had put Britain on Rome's shopping-list of future acquisitions – as Tacitus says, he had 'pointed it out rather than handed it down to those who came after' (*Agricola* 13.1) – and Augustus had evidently made noises in that direction early in his career in 34, 27 and 26 BC (Dio XLIX 38.2; LIII 22.5; 25.2; cf. [Tibullus] *Elegies* III 7 = IV 1. 147–50; Vergil *Georgics* III 25; Propertius *Elegies* II 27.5–6; Horace *Odes* I 21.13–16; 35.29–30; III 5.1–4; IV 14.47–8). But interest in the island then lay dormant for three-quarters of a century until the militarily inexperienced Gaius Caligula was supposedly roused to think of invasion by the flight in AD 39 of an exiled British princeling, Adminius (Suetonius *Caligula* 44.2). Situated on the very edge of the known world (cf. Dio LX 19.2), Britain offered an exotic and glamorous path to glory, as it had done for Caesar and Augustus. As had been known since Caesar's visits, its lowland hills and settled tribes afforded few of the dangers of the forests of Germany. The truth behind the subsequent fiasco surrounding the invasion attempt which appears in our sources, both hostile to Gaius, may be unattainable (Suetonius *Caligula* 46; Dio LIX 25.1–3) but it can hardly be doubted that the failed attempt pointed the way for Gaius' more stable but even more inexperienced and politically insecure uncle, Claudius, only four years later.

The flight of another British exile, Verica, may have provided the pretext (Suetonius *Claudius* 17; Dio LX 19.1), but Claudius' prime motivation is clear in the story of the invasion. The initial campaign was directed wholly at defeating the leading tribe in the south-east of England, the Catuvellauni, and capturing their capital of Camulodunum (Colchester). Claudius would have known from earlier diplomatic contacts and from the exiles Adminius, a son of the Catuvellaunian king Cunobelinus, and Verica, whose own kingdom of the Atrebates had been taken over by the Catuvellauni, that this tribe had in the century since Caesar's expeditions carved a small empire out of their neighbours' territory. Claudius' commander, Aulus Plautius, would have known from the same sources where he was going and how to get there. Having defeated the Catuvellaunian leaders Caratacus and Togodumnus, fought a battle at a river (the Medway?) and forced a crossing of the Thames, Plautius called a halt and, as previously arranged, summoned Claudius himself. Claudius then travelled to Britain, bringing with him a large entourage of senior senators, detachments of the Praetorian Guard and even elephants. On his arrival, he joined his forces at the Thames, crossed over and defeated the Catuvellauni once again, and then watched the capture of Camulodunum. And so, having spent sixteen days in Britain, Claudius went home to celebrate his triumph (Suetonius *Claudius* 17; Dio LX 19–23).

As Suetonius says, since Claudius 'wanted the glory of a legitimate triumph, he chose Britain as the most likely source' (*Claudius* 17.1). The holding up of the campaign solely to allow Claudius to be in at the kill and so qualify for the longed-for reward of a triumph, which his brother Germanicus had once enjoyed and which he took in the archaic manner ascending the steps of the Capitol on his knees (Dio LX 23.1), is a clear confirmation of the overriding importance of this motive. Claudius had outdone Julius Caesar – his army was still in Britain – and had achieved what Augustus had only contemplated.

The extent of Claudius' interest in Britain *per se* is reflected in the length of his stay. This means that soon after Claudius' return to Rome the invasion of Britain would to a large extent have served its purpose: it is hardly surprising that Nero subsequently considered abandoning the province (Suetonius *Nero* 18). In the light of this, it is unlikely that Claudius' instructions to Plautius would have been specific: Dio gives them simply as 'to subdue the remaining areas' (LX 21.5).

By the end of Plautius' governorship, the kingdom of the Catuvellauni was firmly garrisoned by a new fortress of legion *XX* at Camulodunum and Roman forces had advanced toward the south-west, the north-west and the north, extending the province as far as the Fosse Way line which ran diagonally across the country from the Trent to the Severn. The precise nature and purpose of this line is a source of scholarly controversy oddly reminiscent of that which surrounds the Elbe under Augustus. The Fosse Way has been interpreted as either a line of consolidation in anticipation of a further advance into Wales or the intended frontier of the new province. The latter interpretation has been based on the extent of the system of military installations along this road, which has been seen as too dense to be temporary, and on Tacitus' statement that in AD 48 Plautius' successor, Ostorius Scapula, 'prepared to hold the whole area this side of the Rivers Trent and Severn' (*Annals* XII 31). The problem is, of course, that a linear frontier, like the Rhine or Elbe, could be used in both ways. And, as with Augustus and the Elbe, it is not necessary to insist that Plautius had absolutely fixed ideas one way or the other. In view of Claudius' attitude to Britain, it is reasonable to suppose that Plautius was looking for the most economical boundary for the province, and even that he hoped that it would be the Fosse. But given the complete lack of Roman contact with any area of Britain beyond the south-east, the viability of such a frontier could only be determined by experience, and it is unfair to Plautius to imagine that he would not be aware of this. Since Plautius is known to have had considerable influence with Claudius – he was able to save his nephew Plautius Lateranus, one of the many lovers of Claudius' wife Messallina, from death in AD 48 (Tacitus *Annals* XI 36) – it is almost certain that he would subsequently have been summoned to the *consilium* to offer advice on Britain. We know what Claudius decided: Ostorius Scapula was allowed to react to the new situation which arose soon after his arrival in Britain as he saw fit, and the result was the subjugation of Wales. He was operating in territory well beyond the knowledge even of Plautius and it is hard to see how any direction can have come from Rome beyond the simple approval of his reports.

There followed a period of consolidation in Wales and then in England in the aftermath of the Boudiccan revolt of AD 60/1. As we have seen, when Nero succeeded his stepfather Claudius in 54, he even thought of giving up the province altogether, and it is certain that his intentions for it did not go beyond making secure what had already been subdued. His first appointee as governor, Q. Veranius, a soldier with hill-fighting experience in Asia Minor, died in harness in 57 after attacking the Silures once again and declaring in his will that he would have needed only another two years to subdue the province (Tacitus *Annals* XIV 29).

The accession of Vespasian after the Year of the Four Emperors in 69 saw a change to a more vigorous frontier policy. Vespasian, of course, had a particular interest in Britain: he had commanded a legion (*II Augusta*) during Claudius' invasion, as probably had his brother, T. Flavius Sabinus, and his son and successor Titus had served as tribune of a legion in Britain in about 60. But in fact Vespasian's reign saw equally vigorous measures taken in dealing with the problem of the German and eastern frontiers, in both cases involving the annexation of new territory in order to provide a more secure defence. And just as the advance of Scapula into Wales was necessitated by a military threat, so the advance north into Brigantian territory was a response to a potential threat which had recently become actual with the expulsion of the pro-Roman Queen Cartimandua by her estranged husband Venutius (Statius *Silvae* V ii 142–9; Tacitus *Histories* III 45; cf. *Annals* XII 40).

Vespasian's choice was Q. Petilius Cerialis, a close kinsman by marriage (perhaps his son-in-law), who had served in Britain on the fringes of Brigantian territory as legate of *IX Hispana* in AD 60, when he had been ambushed by the forces of Boudicca and had lost 2,000 men (Tacitus *Annals* XIV 32; cf. 38). The elevation of Vespasian to the throne saved his career. He arrived in 71 and picked up where Venutius had left off in a bloody campaign to subdue the Brigantes (Tacitus *Agricola* 17.1). He was succeeded in 73/4 by Sex. Iulius Frontinus, later the most distinguished senator of his age, whose task seems to have been to complete the unfinished subjugation of the Silures in South Wales (Tacitus *Agricola* 17.2).

Frontinus' successor, who arrived either in 77 or 78, seems to have been especially carefully chosen – Cn. Iulius Agricola, a Britain specialist, who had served with distinction as military tribune under Suetonius Paullinus at the time of the Boudiccan revolt and as legate of *XX Valeria Victrix* in Brigantia under Petilius Cerialis (Tacitus *Agricola* 5; 8). He is in fact the only senator known to have served all of his military appointments in one province, and because he happened to marry his daughter to the historian Tacitus, who has provided us with his biography, we are able to follow his governorship in revealing detail.

Agricola's actions at the beginning of his governorship suggest that he was in a hurry. The Ordovices in North Wales had destroyed a Roman cavalry unit before his arrival, and to their surprise and that of his own army, he concentrated his forces, already dispersed to their winter quarters, and ravaged North Wales before carrying straight on to capture Anglesey (Tacitus *Agricola* 18). Such haste implies that, like Cerialis and Frontinus, Agricola had been given a specific job to do and that he wanted as much time as possible to carry it out. The subsequent history of his campaigns suggests that his assigned task from the emperor was to complete the military conquest of Britain, and to terminate the province wherever he thought best.

The next campaigning season was taken up with reoccupying and garrisoning the territory overrun by Cerialis with which Agricola had, of course, become familiar as legate of legion *XX Valeria Victrix*. Then in the following year, which was either the last year of Vespasian's reign, 79, or the first year of Titus' reign, 80, he advanced against new tribes as far as the River Tay (Tacitus *Agricola* 22.1). Since Titus had been closely associated with his father throughout the latter's reign and was sufficiently distinguished militarily not to need to order further conquest on his own account, it is unlikely that this advance marks a change of imperial policy, even if it did coincide with the new reign; rather, it represents the continued execution of the general instructions given to Agricola before he left Rome. Tacitus' narrative certainly reads as if this was simply the next stage of what was originally intended.

In contrast, when recording the consolidation during the fourth campaign of what had been gained in the previous year, Tacitus seems to imply that a halt was contemplated: 'if the courage of the armies and the glory of Rome had allowed, a frontier would have been found within Britain itself; for the Clyde and the Forth, which run far inland on the tides of the two seas, are separated by a narrow stretch of land: this was at that time fortified with garrisons and the whole area to the south made fast, the enemy being removed as it were to another island' (Tacitus *Agricola* 23).

Here we have another, very clear, example of a line of consolidation which was subsequently used as a baseline for further advance. But whose was the decision to make that advance? Those who date the commencement of Agricola's governorship to 77, and therefore the move forward beyond the Forth–Clyde line in Agricola's sixth campaign to 82, have tended to see the resumption of the advance as a consequence of the accession of Domitian in September 81. As Titus' younger brother and the less favoured son of Vespasian, Domitian had largely been kept out of the administration of the empire and, like Claudius, he now sought military credibility, personally directing a campaign against the Chatti in Germany as early as 83. Thus, the abandonment of the Forth–Clyde line has been seen as the result of an imperial command to carry on with the conquest of the whole island. Tacitus, however, provides evidence which shows this interpretation to be highly unlikely. According to him, the resistance met with in the sixth campaign caused 'cowards claiming to be prudent to advise a retreat south of the Forth and a withdrawal in preference to being driven out' (Tacitus *Agricola* 25.3). Whatever the circumstances, such advice, coming presumably from Agricola's legionary commanders, could not have been given if it were contrary to the explicit instructions of the emperor. Tacitus, therefore, implies that the advance was made on the responsibility of Agricola himself, although it is clear that Domitian would have given approval.

Militarily, only Agricola and his subordinates were in a position to judge the situation since they were moving into territory unknown to the Romans until Agricola's own third campaign when he had gone beyond the Forth to the Tay, and Tacitus' account shows that they were not unanimous in their assessment. Agricola's inclinations are shown both by the course of action he took in Scotland and by his evident regret that he had been unable to include Ireland in the conquest (Tacitus *Agricola* 24.3). On the other hand, the strength of his subordinates' hostility to this advance may be reflected in the decision taken to abandon Scotland in 87. This was done only a few years after Agricola's departure from Britain, apparently while conquest was still under way and more had been planned, to judge by the unfinished state of the legionary fortress at Inchtuthil and the hoard of over 875,000 nails, clearly intended for further building, found buried in a pit under the fortress workshop. It is quite clear that the decision to withdraw was taken not in Britain but by Domitian in Rome, in the face of the contemporary disasters on the Danube, to which one of Britain's legions, *II Adiutrix*, had moved permanently by 92 (*CIL* X 135 = *ILS* 2719).

Britain in the first century AD is an extreme example of the problems inherent in controlling the Roman Empire from its centre. Not only was it one of Rome's most distant provinces, but the situations and the peoples being dealt with were constantly changing, and governors were frequently forced to deal with territories about which they themselves had only limited information, and the emperor and his *consilium* none but what the governors supplied. In these circumstances, imperial instructions were determined almost entirely by the judgements of the current legate of the province or by the overriding needs of the empire as a whole. The case of Britain reveals that there was little or no room for the emperor to judge and give directions upon the local situation himself.

Elsewhere, once frontier systems had been established and become permanent, a general knowledge of the area immediately beyond the military line became available to the emperor in Rome through the channels already considered: maps and itineraries, written accounts of campaigns and expeditions, diplomatic contacts, dispatches from the provincial governors, and senatorial and equestrian officers of high rank who had recently served in the provinces and could be called into the *consilium*. The limitations of such knowledge have been discussed above, but it is obvious that much more could be known about an established frontier than about one which was new and constantly shifting, and this would have allowed the emperor to rely less upon what his governors told him and to make some general decisions on the basis of past experience of an area.

A good example of such a decision is that made by Claudius concerning the Lower German frontier at almost exactly the same time as but exactly opposite to the decision which allowed Ostorius Scapula to carry on campaigning into Wales. In 47, the Chauci rebelled: they were a German tribe living along the North Sea coast well beyond the Rhine, and had been the object of campaigning instigated by Gaius Caligula. At the beginning of Claudius' reign they had been subdued, with the recovery of one of the legionary eagles lost with Varus (Suetonius *Claudius* 24.3; Dio LX 8.7). They were now subdued again by the governor of Lower Germany, Cn. Domitius Corbulo, one of Rome's greatest generals, who then began to consolidate the Roman hold on Frisian territory between the mouth of the Rhine and the Chauci, even constructing a fort there (Tacitus *Annals* XI 18–19). In view of Claudius' subsequent reaction, this was clearly done on his own initiative and is itself an indication of how much freedom of action a provincial governor had, or at least thought he had.

It was unfortunate for Corbulo that Claudius probably knew more about Germany and the Germans than about any other frontier of his empire because of his family background. The emperor's father Drusus had begun the conquest of Germany in 12 BC and had died there in an accident in 9 BC, a year after Claudius' birth; his uncle Tiberius had carried on the conquest from 8 to 7 BC and in AD 4 to 5; he himself had been nineteen years old when Varus was killed, and his own brother Germanicus (a name both of them had inherited from their father) had led the reprisals from AD 10 to 16 (though he nearly came to grief on several occasions and had to be restrained by Tiberius from attempting a total reconquest of the area). For the historically minded emperor

– he had written a history of Augustus' reign in forty-one books (Suetonius *Claudius* 41.2) – Germany must have had a deep and terrible fascination. At any rate, according to Tacitus, he feared that Corbulo would arouse a dangerous enemy in the German tribes, and so ordered an end to hostilities and the withdrawal of all Roman garrisons to the left bank of the Rhine (Tacitus *Annals* XI 19; Dio LX 30.4).

Corbulo was furious, but confined himself to the bitter epigrammatic remark that 'Roman generals were lucky men in the good old days' (*beatos quondam duces Romanos*) (Tacitus *Annals* XI 20; Dio LX 30.5). But the free hand granted to the Republican commanders of whom Corbulo was thinking was, as we have seen, largely the result of the ignorance in the Senate about the new territories encountered by its generals. In Britain, Claudius had to give Scapula the same free hand because he was not in a position to form his own judgement of the threat from Wales, and in Germany he stayed Corbulo's hand because he knew all he needed to of the danger across the Rhine. Corbulo was unlucky not so much in his time as in his province.

## EMPERORS ON THE FRONTIERS

Britain and Germany in the mid-first century AD thus represent opposite extremes of the spectrum of military situations which had to be judged from Rome. But in both cases the instructions issued can only have been of the most general and straightforward type: continue, halt or withdraw. This contrasts with the imperial decisions known to have been given to the provinces on civil matters. They could be formulated not just on the basis of a governor's report (which could nevertheless be definitive, as in a query about a point of law, in a way in which the report of a military problem could never be), but also by consideration of supporting documents and written or verbal appeals from the parties involved, and could be based on legal precedents and administrative principles. Furthermore, in such cases the time taken to provide the governor with a comprehensive rescript of the decision was rarely of importance. But if an emperor wished to take over the detailed handling of a military problem, he had no option but to travel in person to the frontier concerned.

Many emperors, of course, did so from time to time, if only for short periods and for the purpose of showing their faces to the armies which kept them secure on their thrones. But in the century and a half after the death of Augustus, Roman emperors only rarely took personal command of campaigns on the frontiers. Tiberius, Nero, Vespasian, Titus, Hadrian and Antoninus Pius never took the field against external enemies after they had ascended the throne. Gaius Caligula presided personally over what came to be regarded as fiascos in Germany and then on the Channel coast in an abortive invasion of Britain (Tacitus *Agricola* 13.2; *Germania* 37.4; Suetonius *Caligula* 43–7; Dio LIX 21.1–3; 25.1–3). Claudius joined his forces in Britain for sixteen days in AD 43 (Suetonius *Claudius* 17.1–2; Dio LX 23.1). But the first emperor after Augustus to lead a campaign in earnest was Domitian in Germany in 83, although this too was later derided as a farce (Suetonius *Domitian* 6.1; Frontinus *Stratagems* I 1.8; 3.10; II 3.23; 11.7; cf. Dio LXVII 4.1). He campaigned again on the Danube in 85–6 without taking executive command, and in 89 was back on the Rhine to deal with the revolt of Saturninus and negotiate with the Chatti (Statius *Silvae* III iii 168) and then on the Danube again, campaigning and arranging terms with the Semnones, Marcomanni and Quadi (Dio LXVII 5.3; 7.1). He also made peace with the Dacian king Decebalus and provided him with subsidies and technical assistance (Dio LXVII 7.2–4).

More aggressively, Trajan led his invasions of Dacia in 101–2 and 105–6 in person (Dio LXVIII 6–14) and wrote *commentarii* on the campaigns (Peter II p. 117, Trajan frag. 1). He later spent the last four years of his life, from 113 to 117, campaigning against the Parthians in the East and expanding the empire to its fullest extension (Dio LXVIII 17–33). Hadrian did not himself campaign as emperor, but he undertook tours of inspection throughout the empire and made some rearrangements to the frontier defences, most notably Hadrian's Wall, the construction of which was a direct result of his visit to Britain in 122 (*RIB* 1051; SHA *Hadrian* 11.2).

But Hadrian was unique amongst emperors in making such tours. Not only did the earlier emperors tend to leave any fighting to their subordinates, but they did not on the whole seem to have felt the need to expand their first-hand knowledge of the empire and its frontiers beyond what they had acquired earlier in their careers. And while some – Tiberius, Vespasian, Titus, Trajan, Hadrian – had previous experience of individual frontiers, others – Gaius, Claudius, Nero, Domitian and perhaps Antoninus Pius – had none at all.

## THE ABSENCE OF A CENTRALIZED MILITARY INTELLIGENCE AGENCY

Despite the limitations of the sources of information already identified and the consequent limitations on the emperor's control over the frontiers, the surprising fact is that no attempt appears to have been made to create a centralized military intelligence organization or to create any system which would have allowed the setting-up of an intelligence cycle operating through Rome. Furthermore, there are strong indications that this was quite deliberate.

One minor indication is that relatively little use was made of an obvious source of information about conditions beyond the frontiers, namely the refugee princes who, from time to time, fled to Rome. Such princes were usually well treated and retired to comfortable homes. What is striking is that, as noted in chapter 2 (pp. 24f.), these homes were, more often than not, far away from Rome. It is true that Herod Agrippa and Mithridates of Iberia were detained at the capital under Tiberius, Ptolemy of Mauretania under Gaius, Mithridates VIII of the Bosporus under Claudius and Nero, Antiochus IV of Commagene and his sons under Vespasian, and Abgar IX of Osrhoene under Caracalla. But these were monarchs who perhaps needed to be kept under surveillance. In contrast, Archelaus of Judaea found himself at Vienne under Augustus and his brother Antipas at Lyon under Gaius; Bato the Pannonian and Maroboduus of the Marcomanni were installed close to their own kingdoms at Ravenna by Tiberius, perhaps as a threat to those who expelled them, but Maroboduus' successor, Catualda, was sent to Fréjus; Vonones of Parthia went first to Antioch and then to Cilician Pompeiopolis, but Rhescuporis III of Thrace found himself in Alexandria, as did Ariogaesus of the Quadi under Marcus Aurelius; Rasporaganus of the Roxolani and his son were settled at Pola on the Adriatic in the second century, and Marcus sent an unlucky Armenian satrap to Britain.[21] Security and political factors seem to have been much more important in dealing with such princes than any value which they might have had as sources of information. We have already suggested, however, that after their initial debriefing such value was minimal and decreased with time, as with modern defectors who, once they have told what they know, are given a new identity and spirited away to start a new life in comfortable obscurity.

A much more important indication is that, whereas we are unable to trace any military intelligence agency centred in Rome, it is possible to identify from the first century AD onwards a body based in the capital which acted as an internal security agency throughout the empire. This was the unit of *frumentarii* housed in the Castra Peregrina ('Foreigners' Camp') on the Mons Caelius. These men were in fact legionary soldiers seconded to the staffs of their respective provincial governors to act as couriers between the provincial capitals and Rome. While in Rome, they formed a regularly organized unit, the *numerus frumentariorum*, with its own junior officers and centurions and a commander who was a senior legionary centurion. In recognition of the unusual provenance of his troops, he bore the title of *princeps peregrinorum* ('Chief of the Foreigners') – hence the name of their camp.[22]

The individual *frumentarii* soon acquired a dual loyalty, to the governors' staffs to which they had individually been seconded from the legions, and to their communal unit in Rome. The emperors were able to make use of this for their own special purposes. By the reign of Hadrian we find one such officer who died at Rome commemorated by his colleagues as a '*frumentarius* of the emperor' (*frumentarius Augusti*) (*AE* 1975.60; cf. 1983.29 and *ILS* 9473); another later describes himself as a '*frumentarius* of the emperor stationed at Lyon' (*phroumentaris Augoustos* [sic] *choras Lougdounou*) (*AE* 1927.84 = *IGRR* III 80 = *ILS* 9476).

If we can trust the Historia Augusta, Hadrian made use of these men to spy on his friends 'for he was inquisitive not only about his own household but also about his friends to the point of investigating all their secrets through his *frumentarii*'. We hear that they intercepted a letter from the wife of a senator to her husband which complained about his self-indulgent lifestyle in Rome. When Hadrian chided the man for this, the puzzled senator asked in amazement whether his wife had written to the emperor also (SHA *Hadrian* 11.4–6). The same not entirely reliable source again speaks of their use as spies by the emperors Macrinus and Gallienus (SHA *Macrinus* 12.4–5; *Claudius* 17.1) and as assassins under Commodus and Didius Iulianus (SHA *Commodus* 4.5; *Didius Iulianus* 5.8; *Pescennius Niger* 2.6; cf. *CIL* X 6657 = *ILS* 1387). The plausibility of these stories is confirmed by two early third-century historians: Herodian says that his contemporary Septimius Severus also made use of *frumentarii* as assassins (III 5.4–5), and Cassius Dio attributes the rise of Ulpius Iulianus and Iulianus Nestor to the Praetorian Prefecture under Caracalla to their previous service as *principes peregrinorum*, when they had been 'of great use to him in satisfying his unholy curiosity' (LXXIX 15.1). Dio also seems to characterize as spying the service of M. Oclatinius Adventus as a centurion of the *frumentarii* and *princeps peregrinorum* under Severus; Adventus too reached the heights of the Praetorian Prefecture under Caracalla, and went on to refuse the imperial throne itself but accept the Prefecture of Rome and an ordinary consulship from Macrinus (LXXIX 14.1–4).[23]

By the end of the third century, the *frumentarii* had become as notorious and hated as any modern security agency. Looking back only half a century to their disbanding by Diocletian, Aurelius Victor says that 'they had apparently been set up to investigate and report upon any potential rebellions in the provinces, and by their wicked concoction of accusations and by spreading fear everywhere, particularly in the most remote areas, they caused the most awful disruption to everything' (Aurelius Victor *Caesars* 39.44). They were replaced by the even more sinister *agentes in rebus*.

What we learn from this is that emperors found it perfectly possible to operate an empire-wide intelligence service to ensure their own security, and that it was based on the couriers who brought news – including military information – from the frontiers. The *frumentarii* could just as easily have been employed to collect and process external intelligence, but, in contrast to their security function, a role in military intelligence-gathering and interpretation is never attributed to them. And if our sources allow us to identify these officers as the imperial security service, there is no reason why we should not be able to trace any parallel military intelligence agency which might have existed. Thus, it is safe to assume both that the Roman Empire had the capability of creating such a service, and that the absence of any evidence for it is a true reflection of the situation.

But if we cannot trace the existence of a specific military intelligence-gathering agency based in Rome, we do know of a bureau which could have assumed at least the duty of processing intelligence as part of its more general role. This was the office of the procurator in charge of imperial correspondence, *ab epistulis*.

Our best evidence for the duties of the *ab epistulis* comes, surprisingly, from a poem by Statius addressed to Flavius Abascantius, the freedman *ab epistulis* to Domitian. There is no post with so many duties, says Statius: the *ab epistulis* sends out the emperor's instructions (*mandata*) to officials and deals with the empire at large; he receives messages from the North, from the Euphrates, from the Danube and the Rhine, and from Britain; he makes recommendations for appointments to the centurionate or to the junior military commands open to equestrians; and he is the first to know about the flooding of the Nile or the change of season in Libya (*Silvae* V i 83–100).

Although we do not know to what extent, if any, the *ab epistulis* was involved in the preparation of incoming correspondence for presentation to the emperor or in the composition of the emperor's own letters, it is clear from Statius that he did read the reports which came in from the provinces, and that he was expected to process at least the letters of recommendation which related to military appointments and which would normally come from provincial governors. The case of Marcius Claudius Agrippa who, according to Dio, was dismissed as *ab epistulis* by Caracalla for arranging the appointment of under-age boys to such posts confirms that these were virtually in his gift (LXXVIII 13.3–4).

We are also ignorant of the extent to which copies of imperial correspondence, incoming and outgoing, were filed in some archive and available for consultation, but Suetonius was able to quote several letters of Augustus (e.g. *Augustus* 51; 71; 76; *Tiberius* 21; *Claudius* 4) which he may have come across during his service *ab epistulis* to Hadrian, although it is more likely that he found them in a published collection (cf. Aulus Gellius *Attic Nights* XV 7.3). The latter might nevertheless have been derived from such an archive; we have already seen that Pliny the Elder apparently had access to official dispatches sent back from Corbulo's eastern campaigns (*Natural History* VI 40). Furthermore, an inscription, probably originally from Rome, refers to an archivist (*scriniarius*) of the *ab epistulis*, obviously implying the existence of some sort of archives (*scrinia*) (*CIL* X 527 = *ILS* 1671).

Here, if anywhere, there was the possibility of creating an intelligence file which would have allowed the monitoring and collation of military information coming in from around the empire. Yet, at least until the 160s, the post of *ab epistulis* appears to have been entrusted to men of literary or academic talents, with little or no military experience, and their staff consisted entirely of imperial slaves and freedmen, with no military representation at all. Indeed, until the end of the first century AD, the *ab epistulis* was an imperial freedman himself, like Narcissus, who was met with derision when sent by Claudius to persuade his invasion force to set sail for Britain (Dio LX 19.2–3), or the abovementioned Flavius Abascantius. Even when equestrians began to be appointed, the preference was for men with a literary background. Such a man was Cn. Octavius Titinius Capito who had served, albeit with distinction, only in the first two ranks of the equestrian military career as prefect of a cohort and tribune of a legion before becoming *ab epistulis* to Domitian, Nerva and Trajan in turn (*CIL* VI 798 = *ILS* 1448; *AE* 1934.154). The younger Pliny portrays him as a man of letters, who urges him to write history and hosts literary recitations (*Letters* I 17; V 8; VIII 12). The next known *ab epistulis* is the biographer Suetonius who served Hadrian about 121 (*AE* 1953.73; SHA *Hadrian* 11.3); we know that he had earlier turned down a military tribunate in Britain which the patronage of the younger Pliny had obtained for him (Pliny *Letters* III 8). L. Iulius Vestinus was a learned sophist who had been head of the Museum of Alexandria before becoming in turn, like Suetonius, *a bibliothecis* (head of the imperial libraries), *a studiis* (rhetorical adviser and provider of research assistance to the emperor) and eventually *ab epistulis* to Hadrian about 135 (*CIG* 5900 = *IG* XIV 1085 = *IGRR* I 136). Sex. Caecilius Crescens Volusianus similarly had no military background at all, serving as *advocatus fisci* (treasury advocate) and *procurator vicesimae hereditatis* (secretary in charge of the inheritance tax) before acting as *ab epistulis* at the end of the reign of Antoninus Pius and the beginning of the joint reign of Marcus Aurelius and Lucius Verus (*CIL* VIII 1174 = *ILS* 1451). In short, the known appointments to this post up to this time imply that military expertise was not a requirement, and therefore that the *ab epistulis* was not specifically involved in the assessment of incoming military information, or in the operation of any sort of intelligence cycle. Rather, this seems to have been left entirely to the emperor and his *consilium*, possibly with the aid of the secretary's archives.

This conclusion seems to be confirmed by temporary changes to the post evidently brought about by the military crises of the reign of Marcus Aurelius. In 162 the Chatti attacked Upper Germany and Raetia just across the Alps from Italy when part of the Germany-based army had been sent to the East to campaign against the Parthians (SHA *Marcus* 8.6–7). At the same time and apparently in concert with them, the Marcomanni on the middle Danube threatened the provinces of Noricum, Pannonia and Dacia. The Roman governors in the area were able to hold them off for a time by diplomatic means (SHA *Marcus* 12.13), but in the years after 166 they crossed the Danube, ravaged Pannonia and laid siege to Aquileia at the head of the Adriatic (Dio LXXI 3.1–2; SHA *Marcus* 22.1; cf. Lucian *Alexander* 48; Ammianus XXIX 6.1): it was the first foreign invasion of the Italian peninsula since the defeat of the Cimbri at Vercellae more than two and a half centuries before. As part of a centralized response to the mounting crisis – a rarity for the earlier Principate – the emperor Marcus Aurelius apparently replaced his *ab epistulis* Crescens Volusianus with a man whose career had been almost entirely involved with military affairs.

This was T. Varius Clemens, who had served in the full range of equestrian military commands, as prefect of a cohort, tribune of a legion, prefect of an *ala* and then as prefect of auxiliary cavalry forces taking part in the campaign in Mauretania in 149, before progressing to the prestigious command of one of the rare milliary *alae*, itself a mark of high favour and military competence. On promotion to the procuratorial ranks he served as financial procurator in two civilian provinces before becoming praesidial procurator (i.e. governor) of two frontier provinces in succession, Mauretania Caesariensis and Raetia, both of which contained strong auxiliary forces. Immediately before his promotion to *ab epistulis* he had been financial procurator of Belgica and the Two Germanies, a key post with responsibility for supply of the four legions and auxiliaries stationed in the German provinces (*CIL* III 5211–16, cf. *ILS* 1362; *CIL* III 15205[1]; *CIL* VIII 2728, cf. 18122 = *ILS* 5795; *CIL* XVI 117; 183). The contrast with the careers of Clemens' predecessors could hardly be greater and cannot be co-incidental. It is a reasonable deduction that, with hostile forces threatening Italy from two sides, Marcus chose a man who could both handle the flood of military information now coming in from the German and Danube (as well as the Parthian) frontiers and co-ordinate junior appointments in the respective armies most effectively.

Soon after Clemens' tenure of the post of *ab epistulis* there was another departure from the earlier arrangement when it was split into two posts, one handling correspondence in Latin (*ab epistulis Latinis*), the other correspondence in Greek (*ab epistulis Graecis*). The significance of this is that official dispatches from the provinces, even from the Greek East or a Greek-speaking governor, appear always to have been written in Latin. Hadrian's governor of Cappadocia in the 130s, Arrian, a Greek-speaking native of Bithynia, wrote his *Circumnavigation of the Black Sea* in the form of a letter in Greek addressed to the emperor but the work was intended as a supplement to Arrian's official dispatch which he twice refers to as having been written in Latin (*Circumnavigation* 6.2; 10.1). The effect of dividing the bureau of the *ab epistulis* would be to concentrate official correspondence in the hands of the *ab epistulis Latinis* and relieve him of the burden of all private correspondence, appeals and petitions from the Greek-speaking part of the empire.

The difference in the duties of the two *ab epistulis* is reflected in two of the earliest appointments to these respective posts, still at the time of the military crisis under Marcus. Although we know nothing of the earlier career of C. Calvisius Statianus, who may have been the first *ab epistulis Latinis* after Clemens, the next man known to have held this post was P. Taruttienus Paternus, who accompanied Marcus in this capacity in the campaigns of 169 to 175 in Pannonia. Paternus seems to have been both a jurist and a military man, since he wrote a work *On Military Affairs* (*De Re Militari*) which appears to have been a manual of military law (*Digest* XLIX 16.7; L 6.7). As *ab epistulis* he was sent in 173 to deal with the Cotini who had offered to campaign with Marcus against the Marcommani (Dio LXXI 12.3), and by 179 he was Praetorian Prefect in command of Marcus' second expedition against the Marcomanni (Dio LXXI 33.3). In contrast, we know that to serve as *ab epistulis Graecis* alongside Paternus, Marcus summoned to Pannonia the rhetor and sophist Alexander Peloplaton ('the Mud-Plato') of Seleucia (Philostratus *Lives of the Sophists* II 5/571).

The broader significance of the appointment of men like Clemens and Paternus to act as *ab epistulis* and of the creation of the two bureaux at this time will be considered in chapter 8. Here it will be sufficient to recognize that these sudden changes when Italy came under threat imply, first, that we are right to see the office of the *ab epistulis* as the most appropriate location (outside the *consilium* itself) for the centralized processing of military intelligence; second, that, despite this, during the first two centuries of the Principate such a task was not normally a function of that office; and third, that this function was not already being performed by any other agency in Rome.

It would appear, therefore, that up to the time of the Marcomannic Wars no attempt was made either to counter the limitations of the information available to the emperor in Rome or to set up any organization which would allow him to make greater use of what information was available. This suggests that Rome's rulers accepted a state of (relative) ignorance about what lay beyond the empire, and gives prima-facie support to Millar's view of the frontiers as an 'information barrier' (see p. 125). But Millar comes to this conclusion because he concentrates, as we have in this chapter, on the viewpoint of the emperor, isolated from the frontiers by inadequate or inappropriate maps, by the self-interest of his informants and, usually, by distance. For the emperor, as we have seen, there was indeed a partial information barrier which restricted considerably his control of military affairs. But this does not mean that information could not be and was not obtained from across the frontiers, only that it was not normally obtained for the direct use of the emperor himself. Military intelligence was collected by the Roman Empire, but it was gathered by and for the emperor's governors, who were in position on the frontiers.

# 6

# FACING FACTS
## The governor and his *officium*

The principal frontier provinces of the Roman Empire were Britain (from 213 just Upper Britain), Lower and Upper Germany, Pannonia (from 106 to 214 just Upper Pannonia, thereafter Upper and Lower Pannonia), Moesia (from 86 Upper and Lower Moesia), Dacia (106 to 120, then again from 169/70 as Tres Daciae), Cappadocia (from *c.* 55), Judaea (Syria Palaestina, from *c.* 128) and Syria (from 194 Syria Coele). Each was governed by an ex-consul with the title of *legatus Augusti pro praetore.* He would normally have had some previous military experience as senatorial tribune of a legion at about the age of 20, and then as a legionary commander (*legatus Augusti legionis*) about ten years later. Now in his late thirties or early forties, he would be in charge of between two and four legions and an equivalent number of auxiliary troops. The governors of the most exposed of these provinces, constantly under threat from invasion, and lying adjacent to areas of serious restlessness, and thus needing the fullest level of protection – Britain, Dacia and Syria (two of which were also the most distant from Rome) – had normally already governed one of the other consular provinces and so were the empire's senior and most experienced army commanders.

In addition, a number of frontier provinces were garrisoned by only a single legion with auxiliaries. These provinces were governed by ex-praetors, usually after they had already held a legionary command. Despite their lower rank they bore exactly the same title and insignia as the consular governors, because both groups were technically the deputies of the Emperor as 'proconsul' of the extended province assigned to him, which consisted of the sum of all the imperial provinces. The single-legion praetorian provinces included Lower Britain (from 213), Raetia and Noricum (from *c.* 170), Lower Pannonia (from 106 to 214), Judaea (from 70 to *c.* 128), Syria Phoenice (from 194), Arabia (from 106) and Numidia (from 38).[1] Curiously, from the end of the first century AD both the consular and the praetorian governors were normally referred to simply as *consulares.*

A few of these single-legion provinces had at one time held no legions at all, only a strong auxiliary force. They were the province of Judaea, before the Jewish revolt of AD 66, and the provinces of Raetia and Noricum, before the Marcomannic invasions of the 160s made a stronger garrison necessary. Their governors were not senators but very senior equestrians with the title of *procurator* (originally *praefectus*). Such men would normally have risen through the ranks of the equestrian career: they would therefore probably have served at least three years as prefect of a cohort, three years as equestrian tribune of a legion, three years as prefect of a quingenary *ala* (a 500-man cavalry unit) and, from the late first century AD, perhaps three years as prefect of one of the few milliary (1,000-strong) *alae* in the empire – perhaps 12 years military service in all, or more. Subsequently, they might have acted as financial procurators of a military province with responsibility for army pay and supply before progressing to their governorship.

Almost all frontier governors, consular, praetorian or procuratorial, would therefore have had at least some military experience, even if in peacetime this would have been of a mainly administrative nature. All would also have served sufficient time as senators (at least ten years), or, in the case of procurators, in the emperor's equestrian service (at least fifteen years), to be well versed in imperial politics and general strategy. And, of course, once installed in their provinces, where they would stay on average for three years, they would need to become acquainted with both the state of the provincial defences for which they were responsible and the nature of any threat or potential threat which faced them.

## TOURS OF INSPECTION

It is likely that Roman governors would normally go on a tour of inspection shortly after their arrival in a province. The only direct evidence for this is the *Periplous Euxeinou Pontou* (*Circumnavigation of the Black Sea*) of Arrian, who was consular legate of Cappadocia from AD 131 to 137 (see pp. 4f., 117f.). As previously mentioned, this unusual work appears to be a Greek literary version of a Latin dispatch to the emperor Hadrian (*Circumnavigation* 6.2; 10.1), and was written after Arrian's initial tour of his province in 131. It describes Arrian's itinerary by sea from west to east along the Black Sea coast between Trapezus and Sebastopolis–Dioscurias. Arrian tells of his visit to the garrison at Hyssos, which, apparently, Hadrian himself had inspected on his own tour of the region in 124 (3.1; cf. Dio LXIX 9), and then to the five-cohort garrison of Apsarus whom he paid and whose arms, defences, hospital and granary he inspected. His opinion on these, he says, has already been forwarded to the emperor in his Latin dispatch (6.1–2). At Phasis he inspected the 400 picked (*epilektoi*) troops in garrison there and the defences of the fort, recently rebuilt in brick and supplemented by artillery on the towers – presumably on Hadrian's orders – to protect the anchorage. He also ordered a third ditch to be dug to enclose the harbour area and the natives living outside the fort (9.3–5). Arrian then carried on to the mouth of the Chabus River where he did something about which, he says, his Latin dispatch will inform the emperor (10.1), and he eventually reached the boundary of the province at Sebastopolis–Dioscurias where he paid and inspected the troops and their horses and weapons, hospital and granary (10.3–4).

Arrian next proceeds to describe, in very brief terms, the subject tribes of the coastal hinterland and to list their rulers. The Sanni, who live near Trapezus, are noted as particularly dangerous brigands at odds with the inhabitants of the city and lax in paying their tribute-money to the Roman authorities. Arrian says that he will either ensure that they do pay in the future or he will 'take them out' (*exeloumen autous*) (11.1–2). Seven other tribes and their kings are listed in order (11.2–3). Apparently whilst Arrian was at Sebastopolis–Dioscurias, he heard of the death of Cotys, king of the Cimmerian Bosporus (Crimea), the event which supposedly prompted him to provide Hadrian with the survey of the whole Black Sea coast which follows in case the emperor should decide to do a tour (17.3). This can be dated to AD 131/2 by Cotys' coin issues (cf. *PIR*[2] F219; I 276; 516) and is evidence that Arrian's own tour came early in his governorship, since in 129 or 130 he was still consul in Rome (cf. *PIR*[2] F219 and *CIL* XV 244; 552).

In this work, and presumably also in his Latin dispatch, Arrian clearly intended to impress Hadrian (who of course would have known more than the average emperor might about the region) with his own thoroughness. Nevertheless, there is no hint that Arrian was doing anything out of the ordinary in undertaking such a tour. Certainly we know both from literary sources (e.g. Pliny *Letters* X (to the emperor Trajan); Suetonius *Vespasian* 4.3; *Galba* 9.2; Philostratus *Lives of the Sophists* I 25/534; etc.) and from epigraphic evidence that both imperial and senatorial governors distributed justice to the provincial cities on an assize system,[2] and we would expect those with military responsibility to visit their troops and defences in much the same way. The so-called Vindolanda Tablets provide indirect corroboration of this. One of these wooden tablets bears a letter of AD 105–20 addressed to the commander of *cohors I Tungrorum*, then stationed at Vindolanda (Chesterholm) on the northern Stanegate frontier of Britain. The letter was apparently sent by the commander of the auxiliary unit at Bremetenacum (Ribchester) in Lancashire informing him that the two riders sent from Vindolanda with dispatches for the governor had passed through. The route taken suggests that the governor was not in London, where an official palace had recently been built for him, but somewhere on the Welsh frontier, perhaps at one of the legionary fortresses of Chester or Caerleon (*Tab. Vindol. I* 30, pp. 117–21). Furthermore, it has recently been pointed out by A.R. Birley that two slightly earlier letters from the same archive clearly imply that Flavius Cerealis, the commander of *cohors IX Batavorum*, then in garrison at Vindolanda, will shortly be meeting with Neratius Marcellus, governor of Britain in 103 (*Tab. Vindol. I* 21.9–11; 37.14–15). Birley suggests that this meeting could well have taken place at Vindolanda rather than at provincial headquarters, since this would explain the presence at Vindolanda of a (civilian) groom of the governor (*equisio co(n)s(ularis)*) to whom a letter was sent from London at about this time (*Tab. Vindol. II* 310.22–6 back).[3]

We can take it, therefore, that frontier governors could be expected to make themselves familiar with their own armies and their own frontier installations. Tours of inspection such as those undertaken by Arrian and, it would appear, Neratius Marcellus, would have provided a governor with a broad knowledge of the general situation on the frontier. Although the forts inspected by Arrian did not form what is generally regarded as a conventional linear frontier, it is clear that their function *vis-à-vis* the native tribes of the area, some of them hostile, was similar: not all of Rome's frontiers looked outwards. As we have seen, Arrian took the trouble to find out about these tribes and even to take action in dealing with them. His initial source of information about them would have been both the local inhabitants – it is clear that the citizens of Trapezus reported the hostility shown to them by the Sanni (*Circumnavigation* 11.1) – and, of course, the officers of the garrisons visited, like Flavius Cerealis at Vindolanda.

## DIPLOMACY AND CLIENTS

Local commanders and communities would be able to provide the governor with detailed first-hand information about particular sections of his frontier and so, cumulatively over a tour of inspection, a broader picture also. Beyond these sources, however, the governor's involvement in diplomacy would help further to round out his perception and understanding of the military and political situation with which he had to deal. As we have seen, diplomacy was a prime source of political intelligence for the emperor. The literary sources provide many notices of embassies visiting Rome to treat directly with the emperor (see pp. 120ff.). But there is also evidence for a considerable amount of contact between provincial governors and neighbouring foreign kings which prepared for, followed up or even replaced the usually more spectacular meetings in Rome.

Kings with the closest connections with Rome, those who were most truly her clients, and especially those whose territory was enclosed or surrounded by directly administered Roman territory, naturally came into contact with the nearest governors and often established a relationship with them (not necessarily always particularly friendly). This was especially true of the various tetrarchs and kings of Judaea, about whom we are well informed, mainly by the Jewish historian Josephus. In 24 BC, Herod the Great applied for famine relief to C. Petronius, the Prefect of Egypt (Josephus *Jewish Antiquities* XV 9.1–2/299–316), and between 13 and 8 BC he played an important role in reconciling M. Titius, the legate of Syria, with Archelaus I of Cappadocia (*Jewish Antiquities* XVI 8.6/270). Agrippa I was less diplomatic: he managed to antagonize both L. Pomponius Flaccus, the governor of Syria, in about AD 33 (*Jewish Antiquities* XVIII 6.2–3/150–4), and subsequently also A. Avillius Flaccus, Gaius Caligula's Prefect of Egypt, by an excessively magnificent state visit to Alexandria in AD 38 (Philo *Against Flaccus* 5/25–35). Later, however, he was able to maintain rather better relations with P. Petronius, Gaius' legate of Syria (Josephus *Jewish Antiquities* XIX 6.3/300–11), and in AD 42, during the reign of his close friend Claudius, went out of his way to greet the incoming legate C. Vibius Marsus (*Jewish Antiquities* XIX 8.1/340). Despite this, the two fell out, with Marsus asking Claudius to stop Agrippa's fortification of Jerusalem (*Jewish Antiquities* XIX 7.2/326–7; cf. 8.1/341–2), and Agrippa in turn attempting to persuade Claudius to have Marsus removed (*Jewish Antiquities* XX 1.1/1; cf. XIX 9.2/363).

These instances, and the career of Agrippa in particular, speak of the regular maintenance of close contact between the Jewish princes on one side and the Prefect of Egypt and legate of Syria on the other. What is more, there was evidently scope for the relationship to go beyond the official to a more personal level, with kings and governors apparently meeting each other on roughly equal terms and being able to afford to pursue personal friendships and enmities. Such close ties could have direct value in the wider military and diplomatic spheres, although they could also backfire. Syllaeus, the regent of Arabia Nabataea, who later fell foul of Nicolaus of Damascus before Augustus (p. 122), offered to act as guide for Aelius Gallus, the Prefect of Egypt, during his invasion of Arabia Felix in 25–4 BC. He supposedly led Gallus astray and thus caused the failure of the expedition, but does not seem to have suffered any adverse consequences at the time: our source for the expedition, Strabo, who was a literary protégé of Gallus, may have concocted the story after Syllaeus' fall (Strabo *Geography* XVI 4.22–4/780–2; XVII 1.53/819). Sixty years later, at the very end of the reign of Tiberius, Herod Antipas, the tetrarch of Galilee and Peraea, acted as broker between L. Vitellius, the governor of Syria and Artabanus, king of Parthia, for their meeting on the Euphrates to establish peace between the two empires. Unfortunately for Antipas, his dispatch on the meeting reached Gaius Caligula, who had just acceded to the purple, before that of Vitellius, and precipitated a breach between the king and the governor (Josephus *Jewish Antiquities* XVIII 4.5/104–5). More happily, we are told that Vespasian as commander in the Jewish War made considerable use of the local client kings in his bid for imperial power in AD 69 (Tacitus *Histories* II 81).

It is evident that in the first century AD on the eastern frontier at least, governors made much use of Rome's client princes in their dealings with territories beyond the empire, just as they had done under the late Republic (pp. 89ff.). This was presumably true of other frontiers as well, although interaction may have been at a rather less sophisticated level where the kingdoms had not come under Roman influence until recently. Client kings would seek to make contact with a new governor soon after his arrival or even as he entered his province for the first time: such was the case with Agrippa and Vibius Marsus, as we have seen. Agrippa's son, Agrippa II, similarly courted his relative by marriage Ti. Iulius Alexander as he arrived to take up the Prefecture of Egypt in AD 66 (Josephus *Jewish War* II 15.1/309; cf. *Jewish Antiquities* XIX 5.1/276–7), and earlier, in AD 19, Aretas IV of Nabataea had entertained at a banquet the newly arrived supreme commander in the East, Tiberius' heir Germanicus, together with the new governor of Syria, Cn. Calpurnius Piso (Tacitus *Annals*

II 57.4). The initial tour of duty coupled with the dutiful approaches of client kings would therefore have presented a new governor within a few months of his taking up of office with a much clearer and more detailed overview of the military situation of his province than could possibly have been acquired, even by the emperor, at Rome.

## SUBSIDIES

Surprisingly, a governor's sources of information probably did not include the mechanism of paying subsidies to external powers. Subsidies had always formed part of Roman foreign policy even under the Republic (Caesar *Gallic War* I 43; cf. Livy XXVII 4.7–10; XXXI 9.5) and became regular under the Principate, as Tacitus makes clear with specific reference to Germany (*Germania* 42; cf. 15.2; *Histories* IV 76). C.D. Gordon has pointed out that subsidies could be applied for a variety of purposes.[4] One was to shore up monarchs friendly or at least neutral towards Rome, by providing money either to help keep them on the throne or to meet the expense of warding off external enemies, or both. Such was the purpose of the subsidies evidently given by Tiberius to Maroboduus of the Marcomanni (Tacitus *Annals* II 26; 45–6 esp. 45.3), by Claudius to Italicus of the Cherusci, nephew of the Arminius who had wiped out Varus' legions in AD 9 (Tacitus *Annals* XI 16), and by Domitian to a later Cheruscan prince, Chariomerus (Dio LXVII 5.1). Another aim (although it often amounted to the same thing) was simply to purchase peace from a potential enemy across the frontier, as in the cases of the financial and technical aid given by Domitian to the Dacian king Decebalus (Dio LXVII 6.5; 7.4; LXVIII 6.1), by Trajan to the Roxolani (SHA *Hadrian* 6.8, despite Pliny's claim that the giving of subsidies had been abandoned by that emperor, *Panegyric* 12.2; cf. Dio LXVIII 6.1), and by Hadrian to several kings (Dio LXIX 9.5; SHA *Hadrian* 17.11). On the other hand, subsidies could also be used for subversion, especially on the eastern frontier. The Parthian pretenders Vonones in AD 8 (Tacitus *Annals* II 2.1) and Phrates in AD 35 (*Annals* VI 32) were both financed by the Romans; likewise Antiochus of Commagene under Gaius (Suetonius *Caligula* 16.3) and Tiridates of Armenia under Nero (Tacitus *Annals* XV 25.3; Suetonius *Nero* 13; Dio LXIII 1–7).

While such subsidies would presumably have to be sanctioned by the emperor, the actual mechanism by which the subsidies were delivered is made clear in none of the passages cited. It is, however, unlikely that money or goods were ever shipped direct from Rome. We may be able to catch a glimpse of how such transactions were actually effected in three letters sent by Pliny as extraordinary imperial legate of Bithynia to the emperor Trajan concerning dealings with the king of the Cimmerian Bosporus (Crimea) (see p. 121). In the first of these (Pliny *Letters* X 63), Pliny reports that the imperial freedman Lycormas has written to ask him to detain an embassy on its way to Rome from the Bosporus. Although no envoys have arrived, a messenger has come from the king, Ti. Iulius Sauromates, with a letter for the emperor and Pliny has sent both the letters on to Trajan. In a second letter (X 64), Pliny says that Sauromates has now written to him to say that there is something which the emperor ought to know as soon as possible and that he, Pliny, has forwarded this courier by public post. And in a third (X 67), Pliny tells the emperor that he has sent on an ambassador who has arrived from the Bosporus. The reason for this frenzied diplomatic activity is left obscure to us but there are some pointers to an explanation. Lycormas, as an imperial freedman, was almost certainly a member of the staff of the imperial procurator in charge of the finances of Bithynia, Virdius Gemellinus (cf. X 27–8). His involvement with Sauromates is therefore likely to have been of a financial nature and probably concerned with the annual subsidy paid to the Bosporan kingdom at this time. Lucian, writing in the second half of the second century, speaks of coming across 'some Bosporans, ambassadors from King Eupator, travelling to Bithynia to escort the annual contribution (*epi komidei tes epeteiou syntaxeos*)' (*Alexander* 57). Although this was previously interpreted as referring to tribute paid by the Bosporan kingdom to Rome, it has more recently been recognized as a subsidy going the other way, as indicated by a passage of the fifth-century historian Zosimus who speaks of gifts (*dora*) being sent by Rome to the Bosporans as late as the third century for 'holding back the Scythians who wished to cross over to Asia' (Zosimus I 31.2).[5]

If these interpretations are correct, we have some valuable evidence for how subsidies might be paid. The money was apparently paid out by the imperial procurator in a nearby province, most likely from the local imperial chest or *fiscus* (Bithynia had such a procurator and *fiscus* even when it was, as normally, a senatorial province, because the emperor had estates there, cf. Pliny *Letters* X 58.5). Ambassadors were sent to collect it. In this particular case, Lycormas and Sauromates would appear to have fallen out, presumably over irregularities involving the subsidy, since Lycormas wants to prevent any embassy reaching the emperor before he can intercept it and Sauromates wants his letter to reach Trajan as quickly as possible. It is unclear whether Pliny has been told the content of the king's letter, although his unwillingness to accede to Lycormas' request to hold back the embassy until Lycormas' arrival perhaps suggests that he knew what was going on without wishing to get involved.

If the mechanism for payment suggested by these letters and by the passages of Lucian and Zosimus is typical, then it would appear that subsidies, being a purely financial transaction, would not normally have required the involvement of the governor, only that of the provincial procurator and his staff. What is more, the subsidy was in this case collected rather than delivered, which no doubt had the political advantage of avoiding the impression that Rome was paying tribute at the court of a foreign king. If this too is representative of normal practice, then the policy of subsidization would have had little part to play in the acquisition of intelligence either for the governor or for the emperor.

Pliny may, however, have had some of his own troops stationed in the Bosporan kingdom, since the two Roman auxiliary units attested at the capital Panticapaeum (Kerch) (*IGRR* I 894 = *CIRB* 666; *IGRR* I 895 = *ILS* 8874 = *CIRB* 726; *IGRR* I 896 = ILS 9161 = *CIRB* 691) are now thought to have been drawn from the garrison of Bithynia rather than that of Lower Moesia. The provision of intelligence would certainly have been part of their function, and this would have obviated the need to make use of the subsidy mechanism. The evidence for their presence is, however, very slender, and it is far from clear that it was long-lived (cf. p. 30). On the other hand, we can be relatively sure that there was a permanent Roman military garrison in the region in the form of troops and office staff of the governor of Lower Moesia based at Olbia and at Chersonesos (Sebastopol) and Charax (Aï-Todor) in the neighbouring Crimea from at least the early second until the third century (cf. p. 200).[6]

It was in fact quite rare for the Romans to maintain any sort of garrison or agents amongst the client peoples situated beyond their military frontier line. Other examples include: the ex-praetor Trebellenus Rufus who was appointed regent of the Thracian kingdom in AD 19 (Tacitus *Annals* II 67.4; III 38.4); the detachment of Roman troops mentioned on an inscription as building fortifications at Harmozica in Iberia (modern Georgia) in the reign of Vespasian (*SEG* XX 112); a centurion recorded near the Caspian Gates (*AE* 1951.263), technicians of all kinds (*demiourgous pantoias technes kai eirenikes kai polemikes*) sent to the Dacian king Decebalus (Dio LXVII 7.4) and cavalry sent to assist the Lugii (Dio LXVII 5.2), all under Domitian; and a Roman officer, Publicius Agrippa, acting as chief adviser to Pharasmenes II of Iberia in the 130s (*SEG* XVI 781; SHA *Hadrian* 17.11–12). The very diversity of this list suggests intermittent and *ad hoc* arrangements, rather than any consistent policy in this direction.

## THE GOVERNOR'S *OFFICIUM*

A provincial governor did not, however, have to rely purely on what he could glean for himself through tours along the frontier or the goodwill of clients. There was a most important source of military information available to him which he was able to consult at any time. This source was the governor's headquarters staff, his *officium*. Despite the best efforts of A.H.M. Jones, who long ago tried to 'correct the impression still too commonly given in textbooks that a Roman magistrate struggled single-handed with his official duties without any staff worthy of the name',[7] the very existence of such staffs is barely mentioned by most modern historians. In fact they existed in all frontier provinces, were usually very large, running in some cases to several hundred personnel, and consisted entirely of trained and experienced soldiers, normally legionaries.

These staffs were enlarged versions of the sorts of staff which had been developed for all Roman army units, probably in the reign of Augustus when a standing army of permanent units had finally come into being. The titles of the various grades of military staff-officers (*officiales*) mostly indicate an origin in the titles of earlier, rather different groups of soldiers, which evidently go back to the Republican era. Thus the *corniculariī* who under the Principate stood at the head of every type of military *officium*, including the governor's own staff, apparently derived their name from the *corniculum*, a military decoration known to have been awarded on a number of occasions in the late Republic which took the shape of a horn, probably worn on the helmet (*ILS* 8888; Livy X 44.5; Suetonius *On Grammarians* 9; Anonymous *On Famous Men* III 72.3; cf. Pliny *Natural History* X 124).[8] Other members of the provincial *officium* included *speculatores* who still appear in the pages of Caesar carrying out the function implied by their name, which means 'spies' (see pp. 54ff.) (*Gallic War* II 11.2–3; V 49.8; cf. 50.3; *Civil War* III 66.1; 67.1; [Caesar] *African War* 12.1; 31.4; 37.1; *Spanish War* 13.3; 20.5; 28.1; 38.1). By the first century AD, however, officers with this title no longer appear as spies but either in the service of the emperor as a cavalry section of his Praetorian Guard or as senior staff officers of provincial governors drawn from the legions and operating as messengers (Tacitus *Histories* II 73; cf. Livy XXXI 24.4, but note Tacitus *Annals* II 12) and as public executioners (Seneca *On Benefits* III 25; *On Anger* I 18.4; *Proconsular Acts of Saint Cyprian* 5; *Digest* XLVIII 20.6; cf. *Gospel of St Mark* 6.27; *Acts of the Alexandrine Martyrs* XI A ii 12; Firmicus Maternus *Learning* VIII 26.6; cf. IV 11.4).[9] *Beneficiarii* is a term employed by Caesar for soldiers specifically attached to a particular commander and so freed from ordinary fatigues by his *beneficium* (*Civil War* I 75.2; III 88.5; cf. Festus *On the Meaning of Words* p. 30L s.v. *beneficiari*); under the Principate the term had come to be used for a specific grade of staff officer within each military *officium*, although the younger Pliny also uses it for staff officers in general (Pliny *Letters* X 21.1; cf. *AE* 1972.573; Pliny *Letters* X 27). The existence of the *frumentarii*, who served both as messengers of the military governors of the Principate and as a form of imperial secret police, has already been noted (pp. 136f.). Their name suggests an origin as requisitioning officers charged with the supply of corn (*frumentum*).

The precise mechanism by which the disparate types of officer came to take on a new role as *officiales* is obscure, but we may guess that it was the result of customary personal contact between such men and their commanders. At any rate, the Roman army developed a host of military staffs: in the provinces one for each auxiliary prefect or tribune; several within each legion – one for each tribune, for the camp prefect and for the legate; and of course one for the governor. The more senior the officer, the higher the relative rank of his *officiales*. So the *cornicularius* of a legionary legate ranked higher than the *cornicularius* of a tribune, and the highest ranking staff officers of a province were those of the governor. At their simplest these staffs consisted of a *cornicularius* and some *beneficiarii*, but senior officers had more complex and developed *officia*, and the governor's *officium* eventually became very highly developed indeed. More and more specialist ranks with titles reflecting their actual functions were added over time to the grades developed from the Republican core groups.

By the third century we have epigraphic evidence for there being a centurion in charge of at least some provincial headquarters. He was the *princeps praetorii* ('chief of headquarters') and was evidently supplied with both a deputy (*optio praetorii*) and low-ranking assistants (*adiutores principis praetorii*). Nevertheless, each provincial *officium* was also provided with two or three *corniculani*, who may have headed some *officia* in the absence of a *princeps* or alternatively have been the executive officers in charge even if there were a *princeps*, since a number of inscriptions describe the governor's headquarters staff as the *officium corniculariorum consularis* ('the staff of the governor's *corniculani*'). These, too, had their own assistants (*adiutores*). Next in rank were a similar number of *commentarienses* (judicial recorders) who first appear in the second century, then the *speculatores*, the *beneficiarii consularis* (employed in a variety of different ways; see pp. 153f., 195ff.), the *frumentarii* and the *quaestionarii* (interrogators and torturers). Specialist troops attached to the *officium* included *interpretes* (interpreters) and a *haruspex* (seer). In addition, there was a variety of secretarial staff including *librarii* (archivists), *notarii* (secretaries), *exacti* (recorders) and *exceptores* (short-hand writers).

Although the division of labour in such an *officium* was by no means rigid, and individuals appear to have carried out a variety of overlapping tasks, it seems that the developed staff comprised both general functionaries such as the *corniculani*, *speculatores* and *beneficiarii* and those with more specific duties such as the *commentarienses*, the *speculatores* in their role as executioners, the *frumentarii*, the *quaestionarii*, the *interpretes*, the *haruspex*, and the various types of secretary. It is the senior and more experienced officers who take on the more generalized roles, and what little evidence we have for the career backgrounds of these *officiales* suggests that many would have been transferred to the *officium* after a number of years of service in their legions and then continued their career progression within the *officium* itself, becoming administrative professionals.

Such staffs were not only highly complex in function and structure but also very large. The best evidence for their size comes from two third-century inscriptions found at Lambaesis, capital of Numidia, which were set up by officers of the governor's staff drawn from the local legion *III Augusta*, including 2 *corniculani*, 2 *commentarienses*, 4 *speculatores*, 30 *beneficiarii consularis*, 4 or 5 *quaestionarii* and 1 *haruspex* (*CIL* VIII 2586; *AE* 1917/18.57). However, not only do these lists not include the secretarial grades, amply attested on other inscriptions at Lambaesis, but they probably only represent half the senior staff supplied by the legion. We know from Tacitus that the legionary commander here, who was *de facto* and then, from about 208, *de iure* governor of Numidia, shared his office staff equally with the proconsul of Africa at Carthage (*aequatus inter duos beneficiorum numerus*) (Tacitus *Histories* IV 48; cf. *CIL* VIII 2532 = 18042 = *ILS* 2487; Dio LIX 20.7). Furthermore, the normal complement of *speculatores* in a province appears to be ten for each legion stationed there. A similar inscription from Tarraco (Tarragona), capital of the one-legion province of Hispania Tarraconensis, lists 2 *corniculani*, 2 *commentarienses* and 10 *speculatores* (*CIL* II 4122); another from Aquincum (Budapest), capital of the two-legion province of Lower Pannonia, lists 20 *speculatores* (*CIL* III 3524); and a third from Carnuntum, capital of the three-legion province of Upper Pannonia, lists 3 *corniculani*, 3 *commentarienses* and 30 *speculatores* (*CIL* III 4452).

If the Lambaesis inscriptions do represent only half of an *officium*, then, taken in conjunction with the three ·inscriptions from Tarraco, Aquincum and Carnuntum, they allow a tentative reconstruction of the full complement of senior NCOs of the *officium* of a one-legion province as perhaps 2 *cornicularii*, 2 *commentarienses*, 10 *speculatores*, 60(?) *beneficiarii consularis*, 10(?) *quaestionarii* and an *haruspex*. Such a reconstruction has the advantage of giving a neat correspondence of 1 *speculator* and 1 *quaestionarius* post per cohort of a legion and 1 *beneficiarius* post per century, which would have appealed to the Roman military mind (cf. Tacitus *Annals* I 32).

If our reconstruction is correct, then this group of officers comprises some 84 men, but it of course represents only the core of such an *officium*. To them we must add the *princeps praetorii* (if there was one: one of the Lambaesis inscriptions records the name of a centurion on the side of the stone, who may have been the *princeps*), his deputy and assistants, the *frumentarii* and the secretarial staff. There were certainly several *frumentarii* drawn from each legion. They do not appear on the Lambaesis inscriptions as such, presumably because their role as couriers to Rome and members of the Castra Peregrina made them separate from the main office staff but 5 *ex* (i.e. former) *frumentariis* appear on one of the inscriptions, apparently as candidates for promotion to the rank of *beneficiarius consularis*. Furthermore, the barrack provision for them at the Castra Peregrina is sufficient for about 400 men, or 12 to 13 from each legion in the empire. This might represent about half the total complement if a similar number could be found at their respective provincial capitals at any one time. Secretarial staff are also likely to have been numerous. We have no direct evidence for governors' staffs, but two inscriptions from Lambaesis recording *librarii* of the legion, who were probably attached to the camp prefect, list 22 serving and 28 veteran *librarii* respectively (*CIL* VIII 2560; 2626). The governor ought to have had more, and this does not take into account possibly similar numbers of other secretarial staff. At any rate, as far as it goes, the evidence we have suggests a total staff of between 100 and 150 men.

That figure, however, is for a single-legion province, but the inscriptions already referred to from Aquincum and Carnuntum suggest that the number of *speculatores* at least was proportional to the number of legions in the province – 10 for a single-legion province but 20 for a two-legion province and 30 for a three-legion province. If the principle is extended to the whole *officium*, then there is the possibility of there having been 200 to 300 staff for a two-legion province and 300 to 450 for a three-legion province. And this is to leave out of account the governor's grooms (*stratores*), who were in charge of requisitioning horses for the provincial armies and performed other administrative duties; they were also sufficiently numerous to form a legionary bodyguard for the governor, apparently as many as 200 men strong, with their own officers. There was also the main gubernatorial bodyguard (*singulares*) of both infantry and cavalry troops seconded from the various auxiliary units of the province and numbering between 500 and 1,500 according to the total number of troops in the province.[10]

Most of the evidence relates to the late second or early third century when the military habit of setting up inscriptions was at its strongest, and such figures therefore perhaps reflect the *officium* at its most developed and may be rather too mechanically calculated. Nevertheless, the main point is clear, that by the early third century, and probably as early as the first, military governors were served by a very substantial specialist staff whose size was probably directly proportional to the size of the armies under their command. This is of the greatest significance for the present study.

The significance lies in the information which could be processed and stored by such a staff and which could therefore be available for the use of each successive governor. The *officium* carried out a variety of duties and, indeed, dealt with whatever the governor required of it. For instance, it certainly assisted the governor in one of his most important duties, which was the administration of justice in the province. This is guaranteed by a considerable amount of literary evidence, including the Roman law codes and the more trustworthy of the Christian martyrologies, which reveal individual *officiales* at work in the governor's court: a centurion receiving a written statement from a litigant (*Digest* XLVII 2.73), and a *princeps* even acting as a judge himself in a property case (*P.Oxy.* XIV 1637.9–10); *corniculariī* overseeing the execution of capital sentences and attending martyr trials (Firmicus Maternus *Learning* III 5.26; *Martyrdom of Tarachus* 6 (Greek)); *commentarienses* acting as recorders and jailors in similar circumstances (Firmicus Maternus *Learning* III 5.26; *Martyrdom of Pionius* 21, *Crispina* 1, *Agape* 3, etc.; cf. *SB* XVI 12949.27, *CIL* II 4179 and *Digest* XLVIII 20.6); *speculatores* carrying out executions by the sword (Seneca *On Benefits* III 25; *On Anger* I.18.4; cf. I 16.15; *Proconsular Acts of St Cyprian* 5; Firmicus Maternus *Learning* VIII 26.6; cf. IV 11.4; cf. *Gospel of St Mark* 6.27; *Acts of the Alexandrine Martyrs* XI A ii 12; and *Digest* XLVIII 20.6); *beneficiarii consularis*, *stratores* and *frumentarii* making arrests and assisting at executions (*Proconsular Acts of St Cyprian* 2; St Cyprian *Letters* 81.1; Eusebius *Church History* VI 40.2; *Martyrdom of Fructuosus* 1; 4; St Augustine *Conversation with the Donatists* III 15/27; 17/32; cf. *CIL* III 433; *AE* 1933.256); and *quaestionarii* apparently interrogating and torturing (*CTh* XVI 12.3 (*Sirm.*3), AD 384; St Jerome *On Joel* ii 21/27; Scholiast on Juvenal *Satires* VI 480; cf. St Cyprian *Letters* 66.7).

*Officiales* were also used in more general tasks to do with the administration of their province: *speculatores*, *beneficiarii*, *frumentarii* and *singulares* are all known to have acted as couriers all over the empire (Tacitus *Histories* II 73; cf. Livy XXXI 24 and *CIL* III 1650 add. p. 1021(*speculatores*); SHA *Hadrian* 2.6 (*beneficiarius*); Dio LXXIX 14.1; 34.7; 39.3; SHA *Maximus and Balbinus* 10.3; St Jerome *On Abdias* 18; *CIL* III 2063 = *ILS* 2370; *CIL* III 14191; cf. III 3241; *P.Mich.* VIII 472; 487; 500; 501; IX 562 (*frumentarii*); *P.Oxy.* VII 1022.24–6; LV 3810.14–17; cf. *P.Amh.* II 137.2 (*singulares*)). In Numidia, *beneficiarii* seem to have acted as attendants at the governor's palace (*CIL* VIII 2797; *AE* 1917/18.52; 76); in Asia *frumentarii*, albeit apparently seconded from the Rome unit, acted as a sort of provincial police force (*AE* 1907.35 = *ILS* 9474; *AE* 1964.231; *IGRR* IV 1368;

J. Keil and A. von Premerstein, *Bericht über eine dritte Reise in Lydien und den angren-zenden Gebieten Ioniens, ausgeführt 1911* (Wien 1914), no.9; no.28), whilst in Egypt a *centurio frumentarius* is recorded in charge of the porphyry quarries at Djebel Dokhan (*SB* V 8161.2). Also in Egypt, the Prefect's *princeps* apparently sent out copies of one of his letters to various *strategoi* (*P.Oxy.* XIX 2228.16–21), whilst a whole series of papyri reveals that *beneficiarii* were stationed all along the Nile and acted as local representatives of the governor, collecting taxes (*P.Petaus* 34.7; *SB* VI 9409.3 vii 162; *P.Oxy.* XIV 1651.13; XX 2286.2; XXXVI 2794.4; 2797.2), making arrests (*BGU* II 388 i 10; *P.Oxy.* I 65.1), investigating complaints (*P.Amh.* II 77.27; *Stud.Pal.* XXII 55.1; *P.Lond.* II 342 (p. 173).1; *PSI* VII 807.1; *P.Cair. Isid.* 62.1; 63.1; 139.1; *P.Laur.* III 60 r.1), sitting in arbitration (*P.Oxy.* XVIII 2187 r.8) and forwarding petitions to their master (*P.Amh.* II 80.12; *P.Oxy.* XVII 2130.20–4; XLVI 3304.21–2). One papyrus even gives a rare glimpse of the internal working of the *officium*, with a senior *beneficiarius* of the Prefect of Egypt passing on a petition which he has received for the emperors Valerian and Gallienus to the *kanaliklarios* (*cornicularius?*) of the *officium* (*P.Oxy.* XLVII 3366 B r. ii 25–8; cf. 38).

A provincial governor's *officium* was evidently a hive of activity of all sorts, but the sheer size of the frontier *officia* and the fact that they were drawn almost exclusively from a province's legions are strong indications that their main employment lay beyond that already described and in the military sphere. This is made clear by the stark contrast between these military *officia* and the relatively small civilian staffs afforded to proconsular governors.

Proconsuls normally disposed of only a few auxiliary units or parts of units within their provinces. It is unsurprising, therefore, that with the exception of the proconsul of Africa, who appears to have continued to receive part of the military staff of the legate of legion *III Augusta* from Numidia (see above p. 151), proconsuls seem to have had no military *officiales*.

Instead, they continued the Republican practice of drawing civilian staffs (*apparitores*), many of them ex-slaves from the panels (*decuriae*) which served magistrates at Rome. Such *apparitores* are never recorded in the service of military governors, who were technically not magistrates in their own right but only the emperor's deputies. The exception which proves the rule is the five lictors, the bearers of the governor's rods of office (*fasces*), who were allowed to both praetorian and consular legates (Dio LIII 13.8; LVII 17.7; and *CIL* VI 1546; VIII 7044; 18270; XIII 3162; cf. III 6759; VIII 21069; XIII 593; 1813; *AE* 1967.225). This was one lictor less than the six allowed to proconsuls of praetorian rank and seven less than the twelve allowed to proconsuls of consular rank, and it indicated that their power of command (*imperium*) was delegated. Proconsuls had, in addition to their lictors, secretaries (*scribae*), messengers (*viatores*), heralds (*praecones*) and perhaps other minor *apparitores*, although the epigraphic evidence is not abundant; the vast majority of *apparitores* are attested at Rome where most of them served. At any rate, a proconsul's civilian staff was certainly much less developed and far less numerous than the military staff of a frontier legate, even though the administrative burden of dealing with the petitions and litigation and criminal processes of highly civilized provinces like Africa, Asia or Achaea must have been rather heavier than that in relatively backward military provinces like Britain or Germany or Pannonia. The conclusion to be drawn from this contrast is inescapable: that the *officia* of the military provinces were principally concerned with the administration of the provincial armies and frontiers.

## THE GOVERNOR'S ARCHIVES

The large *officia* were necessary because of the extent and meticulousness of the Roman army bureaucracy. It is common in modern scholarship to deny the efficiency and even the true existence of the Roman bureaucracy, to see it as no more than the accumulation of documents without purpose or end beyond the symbolic, and as a collection of archives to be consulted but rarely and with difficulty. Such a conclusion may be disputed, even for imperial and senatorial archives and other civilian bureaux, but it is demonstrably false of military *officia* which, as we have indicated, administered almost three-quarters of the provinces of the empire and all its armies.

The amount of paperwork generated by the Roman army was vast, and is amply represented by survivals from Britain, Syria, Egypt and elsewhere in the form of wooden writing-tablets, papyri and even inscribed potsherds. At the cohort fort of Vindolanda (Chesterholm), just south of the line of Hadrian's Wall in Britain, archaeologists have now recovered well over 2,000 fragments of wooden tablets, most of them with at least some writing on them, dumped from the fort archives and covering the period from *c.* AD 90 to 115/20. These have to date yielded more than 250 texts of significance (cf. Plate 5). It is likely that there are still more to be found, others which have been lost and many more which were retained at the time of dumping because they contained information which was still 'live'.

This gives some idea of the volume of such documents which could accumulate at a single fort. If one then considers that Britain in the mid-second century was garrisoned by some three legions, each of them ten times the size of the Vindolanda garrison, together with approximately sixty auxiliary units, one begins to appreciate the mountain of paperwork being generated within the army. Moreover, many of the documents which survive must represent originals or file copies of other documents also kept at the governor's headquarters. These include unit-strength reports of various kinds, records of casualties and promotions, notes from the governor assigning new recruits and animals to individual units, and letters to and from the governor.

Several different types of strength report have now been identified – morning reports, monthly summaries, reports made on the last day of the month or year, known as *pridiana* (from *pridie kalendas* (say) *Ianuarias*, 'on the day before the 1st of January'), and other interim and daily reports, some of which, at least, were known simply as *renuntia* ('reports'). Their type and frequency may have varied from unit to unit and from province to province, but in general they provide information such as the unit's name, the date, the unit's current headquarters, the name of its commander and perhaps of his predecessor, its total enrolment, including officers and men, and numbers of those present and absent, sick and wounded, and died or transferred since the last report. There is a strong presumption that copies of at least some of these, perhaps the monthly or annual reports, were forwarded to the provincial governor.

There is at any rate good evidence for the maintenance of much more detailed information even than this about individual army personnel in the governor's archives. For instance, what may be a rough casualty list of the period of the Jewish Revolt of AD 115–17 includes men and centurions of both Egyptian legions *III Cyrenaica* and *XXII Primigenia* (*P.Vindob.* L 2 recto and verso = Fink 34), and is therefore likely to have been compiled for the only officer in Egypt with such a broad command, the Prefect himself. Similarly, a list of auxiliary decurions and centurions of *c.* 243/4 clearly covers two units, an *ala* or *cohors milliaria* (a thousand-strong cavalry or mixed unit) and *cohors III Ituraeorum*. The officers are listed within each unit according to seniority and the document notes both the dates of their promotions and the name of the Prefect of Egypt who issued the orders (*P.Mich.* III 164 = Fink 20). Clearly, the document cannot have come from the archives of a single unit and again it is most likely to have originated in the *officium* of the Prefect of Egypt.

There is indeed reason to believe that a governor would have a record of every individual soldier serving in his province. This is specifically claimed by the second-century historian Appian (*Civil Wars* III 43) and is also implied by the anecdote told in the fourth-century biography of the third-century emperor Severus Alexander who kept summaries of troop strengths and details of soldiers' length of service in his bedroom (SHA *Alexander* 21.6–8); whatever the reliability of the anecdote itself, it must have been at least plausible to its fourth-century audience. A record of transfers on a papyrus of AD 241 from Dura Europos in Syria makes explicit reference to the soldiers involved as being entered on to the roll of *cohors XX Palmyrenorum* from a letter(?) of the governor Attius Rufinus (*ex [epistula] Atti Rufini*) (*P.Dur.* 121 = Fink 29; cf. *P.Oxy.* VII 1022 = Fink 87). The governor's responsibility for commissions, recruitment and transfers is demonstrated by a *pridianum* of *cohors I Augusta Praetoria Lusitanorum Equitata* dated 31 August 156, which notes a centurion commissioned (*factus centurio*) by the Prefect of Egypt Sempronius Liberalis, and nine new recruits approved (*probati*) and two men transferred from legion *II Traiana Fortis* (*accepti ex leg(ione) II Tr(aiana) Fort[i]*) by the same Prefect (*BGU* II 696 = Fink 64, i 19–21, 31–3; ii 13–15); similarly, a morning report of *cohors XX Palmyrenorum* dated 27/8 May 239 lists two recruits approved by a governor of Syria (*P.Dur.* 89 = Fink 50, i 14). We possess a copy of a letter of 103 from a Prefect of Egypt, C. Minicius Italus, which orders enrolments in *cohors III Ituraeorum*: the Prefect attaches a list of the six recruits to be entered with their ages and distinguishing marks, and there can be little doubt that this list was copied from a document kept in the *officium* at Alexandria (*P.Oxy.* VII 1022 = Fink 87). An Oxyrhynchus papyrus of AD 52 likewise shows that governors had responsibility for discharges from military service (*P.Oxy.* I 39). Even if the actual mechanism of recruitment and discharge was in the hands of his subordinates, these documents prove that the governor's formal approval was required for both, and that the orders for enrolment were issued from his *officium*.

Surprisingly, the same appears to have been true even of the horses which were assigned to individual units. A papyrus from Dura Europos consists of individual letters of AD 207–8 from the governor of Syria, the biographer Marius Maximus, glued together to form a roll. They were addressed to the tribune of *cohors XX Palmyrenorum* and ordered the entry on to unit records of horses approved by the governor for assignment to named troops of the cohort (*P.Dur.* 56 = Fink 99). A similar letter survives from a later governor of Syria, Aurelius Aurelianus (*P.Dur.* 58 = Fink 100), and a list of men and horses of AD 251 seems to have been made up from such letters issued by auxiliary prefects, successive military commanders (*duces*) in charge of the frontier section and the provincial procurator, as well as by the provincial governor Atilius Cosminus (*P.Dur.* 97 = Fink 83). By the latter date at least, if not before, not all army horses were being approved by the governor.

These papyri imply that the governor's archives contained entries for every man recruited for his provincial army and for some or all of the horses acquired as well. The individual entries may well have been very short, as for instance 'Marcus Antonius Valens, 22 years old, mark on right side of forehead' (*P.Oxy.* VII 1022 = Fink 87, 21–3) or 'a 4-year-old horse, reddish, masked face, no brand, approved by me (i.e. the governor) for Iulius Bassus trooper of *cohors XX Palmyrenorum* which you (i.e. the tribune) command, at 125 denarii' (*P.Dur.* 56 = Fink 99, 1. (Frag. a).5–7). Nevertheless, the implications are staggering. The Syrian army of the mid-second century consisted of some 30,000 men including about 7,000 cavalry, the British army of 50,000 including 9,000 cavalry. There should therefore have been files at Antioch and London with a corresponding number of entries, which presumably had to be kept up to date as men were recruited, discharged or died, or as new horses were approved and assigned. Even if every soldier survived to serve his full 25-year term, it would require 1,200 recruits per year in Syria and 2,000 in Britain to maintain this establishment; more realistic figures are perhaps half as many again in each province. Although even the larger figures would represent an average of only about 5 and 8 new entries per day respectively, these of course represent only the tip of an administrative iceberg. For each entry details had to be received from the recruiting officer, checked and filed. Once recruitment had been formally approved by the governor, the actual entry would have to be made into files organized by unit and the letters of notification, such as those referred to above, drafted, written out, signed by the governor, copied (like the collection of outgoing letters copied on to a file of the *strategus* of the Panopolite nome in Egypt in AD 298: *P.Panop. Beatty*[1]) or catalogued (cf. *P.Oxy.* XII 1511 = Fink 102, a list of outgoing letters written in five or six different hands) and then dispatched. The basic files of men recruited to each unit would, of course, need to be kept up to date as they were transferred, promoted, discharged or died, each change itself being the result of incoming letters which had to be read, acted upon, catalogued and filed.

But files dealing with personnel were only one portion of the total of military files which had to be kept and handled at provincial headquarters. As we have seen, there were also periodic strength and status reports made by each unit, some of which are likely to have been intended for the governor's use. Monthly reports from more than sixty units in Britain or thirty units in Syria, which had to be checked, collated and filed, together with, one presumes, the preparation of conspectus reports of the state of the army for the governor, would have added further to the administrative burden. And then there was the governor's ordinary correspondence with the commanders under his control: reports on local problems, requests for men, animals, equipment, requests for leave or personal favours such as letters of recommendation or positions or promotions for friends and clients, as well as purely social correspondence. Once again, the volume of such correspondence was directly proportional to the number of units in the province, and each letter had to be filed, catalogued and perhaps answered.

When one also takes into account the non-military correspondence and the host of non-secretarial duties handled by the *officia*, the numbers suggested above for such staffs, both in the purely secretarial and in the administrative grades, begin to make sense, as does the suggested proportionality between the size of the provincial garrison and that of the *officium*.

What must also be stressed is that each of the numerous files which is indicated for the provincial *officia* could be and often was retrieved, consulted and modified. This is clearly implied by the governor's very ability to make detailed documents listing casualties or officers in order of seniority and indicating commissions, enrolments, transfers and discharges. In addition, there is the evidence suggesting that copies of outgoing files were kept and the letters catalogued. But there is also still more direct evidence in the form of docketing of individual documents for filing, and the appearance of countermarks, of annotations and of several different hands on many military documents which have survived. For instance, a stylus-tablet recently excavated at Vindolanda bears on the rim a docket stating 'Ninth Cohort, Cerialis, number 3121' (*Current Archaeology* No. 128 (Vol. XI no. 8, March 1992), p. 344); this suggests that it was meant to be retrievable. The duty rosters of *cohors XX Palmyrenorum* found at Dura Europos contain a variety of marks, some of them certainly added after the original compilation of the document.

These include added indications of assignments enclosed in an angular mark, heavy black dots used as check-marks, the use of the Greek letter *theta* to indicate death (*thanatos*) and words added in a different hand from the main part of the document (Fink 1–4, 8, 34, 38, 63, 73, etc.; see Fink's introduction, pp. 11–17). The expression 'theta-ed' (*thetatus*) derived from the archival annotation seems to have entered soldiers' slang, always replete with euphemisms for death, since the word appears on at least two military documents (*P.Vindob.* L 2 = Fink 34, recto ii. 19; verso ii. 14; *P.Lond.* 2851 = Fink 63, ii 11, known as Hunt's *Pridianum*). But the use of the *theta* for death was also so well known amongst the general population that the first-century poets Persius and Martial were able to make reference to it in their works (Persius *Satires* IV 13; Martial *Epigrams* VII 37.2); it also appears on epitaphs (e.g. *CIL* I 1042; III 4850; 12659; V 3466).[11] Nothing could demonstrate more clearly the extent of popular familiarity with the concept of archives.

The appearance of several hands on one document ranges from minor notations bringing the document up to date, such as 'has not returned' (*non reversus*) placed against a soldier's name in one of the Dura rosters (*P.Dur.* 101 = Fink 2, xii 18), to the cataloguing by five or six separate hands in turn of outgoing letters addressed to unit commanders, possibly from the Prefect of Egypt himself, on the recto side of a papyrus later reused and found at Oxyrhynchus (*P.Oxy.* XII 1511 = Fink 102).

The examples cited are far from unique among military or even purely civilian documents, but they are sufficient to show that military documents could be and were retrieved from the files on a regular basis and without great difficulty. Furthermore, the mechanisms by which this was achieved can still be traced. Documents could be filed under the name of the person whose archive they formed, as apparently with the docketed tablet found at Vindolanda which evidently came from the archive of Flavius Cerialis, who is well attested on other tablets as Prefect of the local Ninth Cohort of Batavians. But they could also be filed by subject, even within the archive of an individual official. Thus copies made from an archive can be headed as being 'from the roll of day-books' (*ek tomou hypomnematismon*) of a particular commander (*CPR* I 18.1) and 'from the roll of census records' (*ek tomou epikriseon*) (*BGU* I 113.1; 265.2; III 780.1; IV 1033.1) or 'from the box of petitions' (*ek teuchous bibleidion*) of the Prefect of Egypt (*BGU* II 525.6; III 970.4).

Rolls were made by glueing together (*kollan*) individual documents or sheets (*kollemata*), and such a roll was known in Greek as a *tomos synkollesimos* (*P.Grenf.* II 41.18). Surviving examples include a roll of eighteen sheets of census declarations of AD 174 from Theresis in Egypt (*P.Brux.* I 1–18) and a roll of letters from Marius Maximus, governor of Syria, assigning horses to the unit at Dura Europos in 207–8 (*P.Dur.* 56 = Fink 99; cf. 97 and 83). Groups of such rolls were kept together in pigeon-holes or boxes (*teuche*), probably also arranged by subject, like the 'box of petitions' already mentioned. Papyrus labels, made either for attachment to individual rolls or for such pigeon-holes or boxes, have survived at Dura Europos. Three of these labels bear personal names, but one has the words 'horse letters' (*epistulae equorum*) written upon it (*P.Dur.* 130 = Fink 116).

Quite apart from such labelling, sheets, rolls and boxes, could all be given numbers to allow citation and cross-referencing, and so facilitate retrieval. For instance, each of the sheets on the roll of census declarations from Theresis is individually numbered, although not consecutively; presumably the numbers indicate order of receipt. That documents were referred to by such numbers is shown by a Hadrianic list of names from Egypt which gives citations for census registrations such as 'box 4, roll 1, sheet 36' (*d teuch(ous), a tom(ou), ko(llematos) lz*) (*P.Ryl.* II 220.69; cf. 78–80); again, a second-century petition of a woman of Ashmunen in Egypt for her son to be recognized as descended from a gymnasial family includes precise references to earlier census documents recording his ancestors, for instance citing 'roll 70, sheet 138' (*tom(ou) o ko(llematos) rle*) (*P.Amh.* II 75.41; cf. 47, 54, 70; also *CPR* I 233.6; *P.Flor.* III 382.93). The evidence for such referencing, unsurprisingly, comes almost entirely from Egypt, but the Vindolanda docket is sufficient to prove that the basic concept was known and used at the other end of the empire, even if its traces have, for the most part, disappeared.

It is clear that Roman filing systems, and especially military filing systems, were more than sophisticated enough for documents to be catalogued, filed, retrieved, added to by glueing on another sheet, annotated with check-marks and alterations, copied, or just made available to a commander or governor as he required. Requests for documents were hardly rare occurrences and copies might need to be made for a variety of purposes: a papyrus found at Oxyrhynchus is a certified copy (*exemplum*) of a letter from C. Minicius Italus, Prefect of Egypt, dated 103, which assigns recruits to the *cohors III Ituraeorum*. At the end of the copy Avidius Arrianus, the *cornicularius* or head of the cohort's headquarters staff, 'certifies that the original is in the cohort's archives' (*scripsi authenticam epistulam in tabulario cohortis esse*) (*P.Oxy.* VII 1022 = Fink 87). The copy was perhaps produced for somebody who needed to prove that one of the recruits named had indeed been assigned to the unit. Documents like the famous *Feriale Duranum* (*P.Dur.* 54 = Fink 117), a third-century calendar of Roman army feast-days, clearly had a practical purpose and would need to be consulted regularly. For it to be possible for soldiers travelling on official journeys to be issued with itinerary maps (St Ambrose *On Psalm CXVIII*, sermon 5.2 = Migne, *Patrologia Latina* XV, 1251; see p. 115), there must have been master copies filed and retrievable at provincial or unit headquarters. Another Oxyrhynchus papyrus records a payment made to a 'searcher in the Prefect's archives' (*hairetes hegemonikes bibliothekes*), so that it appears that in Egypt at least even civilians could ask for documents to be copied from the governor's records (*P.Oxy.* XIV 1654.7; cf. U. Wilcken, *Archiv für Papyrusforschung* vii (1924), 97). The importance placed upon caring for such records and the significance of the governor's own office as the main provincial archive is reflected in a group of papyri which record the misfortune of the superintendents of the archives of the Arsinoite nome who in AD 90 supplied the Prefect of Egypt, Mettius Rufus, with a document which had lost its preamble. Rufus dismissed them for negligence and made them repair and recopy the text from his own records (*P.Ludg. Bat. VI* 14; 15; 17; 24).[12]

## THE CENTRALIZATION OF PROVINCIAL BUREAUCRACY

The emergence of this level of bureaucracy appears to have begun with the early Principate. It seems unlikely that Roman army records or the staffs who handled them were much developed before the time of Augustus. Under the Republic troops were probably levied by local authorities in Italy and then assigned to their legions, along with the City recruits, in Rome itself (Polybius VI 20.1–21.5; cf. P.A. Brunt, *Italian Manpower* (Oxford, 1971), 625ff.). Unit records would have been kept only as long as the unit continued in existence, perhaps a single campaigning season, perhaps up to 16 or 20 years in the very late Republic, but no longer. Relatively small numbers of office staff would be required to look after these documents. Very few of the staff recorded under the Principate derived their titles from Republican grades, and none of the latter seems to have had primarily staff duties (see pp. 149f.). Roman military bookkeeping was probably rudimentary,[13] and it is very likely that the establishment of permanent units by Augustus provided the stimulus for the development of the sort of staffs described above.

Nor would Republican governors have needed particularly large staffs. Their own records – administered by their *apparitores* brought with them from Rome (see pp. 87, 154f.) – are likely to have been slight, probably taking the form of private day-books (*commentarii*) which they took back with them on departure (Cicero *Verrine Orations* II i 119; iii 26; v 54; cf. *CIL* X 7852). Since the praetor's edict which defined the terms of jurisdiction in each province was modified by each governor and handed down to his successor (cf. Cicero *Letters to Atticus* VI 1.15), some documents must have been passed on. But without permanent residences or staff permanently established in the province to provide continuity, it is hard to see how any provincial archive could have been very extensive. Bureaucratic control of a province's military forces would in any case have been difficult when one was dealing with temporary units without permanent bases. Hence Cicero as governor of Cilicia, through the non-cooperation of his predecessor Ap. Claudius Pulcher, could only too easily lose trace of three of his cohorts (see p. 102). The changed nature of provincial government under the Principate, at least in the imperial provinces, made this sort of thing impossible.

Developed military staffs begin to appear in the papyrological and epigraphic record from the first century AD onwards, and reach a zenith of complexity and sophistication by the third century, after which our evidence tends to dry up. Most likely the evolution began right at the beginning of the Principate with Augustus' *legati*, who were not entitled, as nominal deputies, to the use of the *apparitores* from Rome, but all of whom commanded large armies. In such circumstances it would have been an obvious move for them to select literate personnel from amongst their own troops to supply their need. The model would have been the embryonic legionary staffs which were themselves becoming larger and more regularized as particular units were kept in being after the end of the Civil Wars, eventually becoming permanent.

The growth of military staffs and bureaucracy would itself have been fostered by the occupation of winter bases (*hiberna*) over several years as military movement on all but the northern frontier slowed and then came to a halt in the course of Augustus' reign. The Varian disaster in AD 9 led to the beginning of effective ossification of the frontiers, even in the north. The process of ossification, punctuated by fitful bursts of renewed expansion, continued throughout the first century and beyond, and with it came the development of relatively fixed frontiers together with the bureaucratic staffs to administer them.

At the heart of these frontier systems, operated locally by the legionary and auxiliary commanders, lay the provincial governors and their staffs. The centralization of provincial bureaucracy is confirmed by the construction in most of the frontier provinces, from the Flavian period onwards, of governors' palaces which had both residential and administrative accommodation. In the first half of the first century AD, frontier governors had no doubt based themselves at one or more of their legionary fortresses; this may explain how an early British governor's *beneficiarius* came to be buried outside the legionary fortress at Wroxeter (*RIB* 293) and how the traveller Demetrius of Tarsus, mentioned by Plutarch as having accompanied Agricola's campaigns in Scotland in the early 80s, came to make a dedication 'to the gods of the governor's headquarters' (*theois tois tou hegemonikou praitoriou*) at York (Plutarch *On the Decline of Oracles* 2; 18 (= *Moralia* 410a; 419e–420a); *ILS* 8861 = *RIB* 662). But soon after the Roman withdrawal from Scotland about 87 a palace was built for the governor in London. In Lower Germany, by the late first century, a palace had been built for the governor at Cologne on the site of the headquarters of a double legionary camp which had been abandoned towards the end of Tiberius' reign. In Upper Germany there appears to have been a palace situated within the old double legionary fortress at Mainz by the Flavian period. The palace on the Danube island at Aquincum (Budapest) in Lower Pannonia is of early second-century date and that at Carnuntum in Upper Pannonia perhaps somewhat later.[14]

Governors of single-legion provinces appear normally to have based themselves in the residences (*praetoria*) and headquarters buildings (*principia*) of their legionary fortresses. This was certainly the case at the Trajanic camp at Lambaesis in Numidia and at York which became the capital of Lower Britain in 213. An inscription set up to honour one of the earliest governors of Lower Britain by his *beneficiarii* has been found on the site of the legionary *principia* under York Minster (*AE* 1971.218). Such *principia* normally had a whole series of rooms, ranged round the courtyard, which could and did act as administrative offices and archive chambers. The extensive governors' palaces excavated at London, Cologne, Carnuntum and Aquincum were also equipped with a

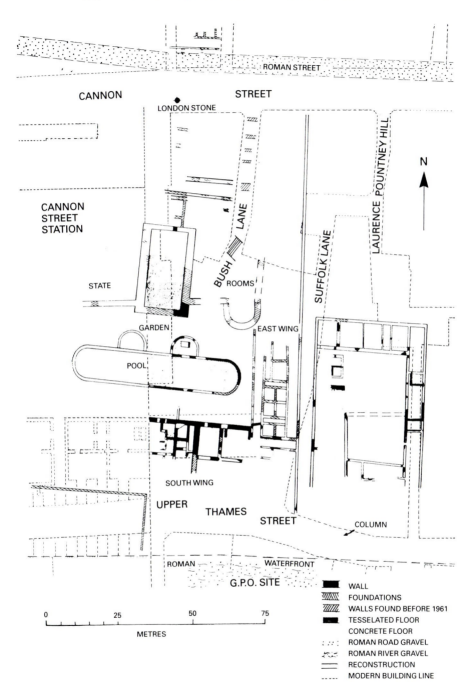

*Figure 2(a)* The governor's palace at London (after P. Marsden)

163

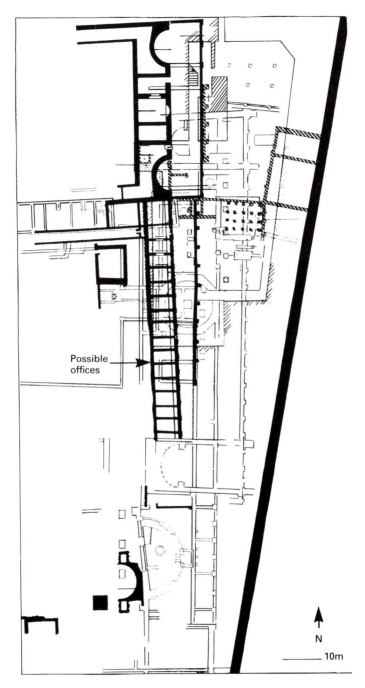

Possible offices

N

10m

*Figure 2(b)* The governor's palace at Cologne (after G. Wolff)

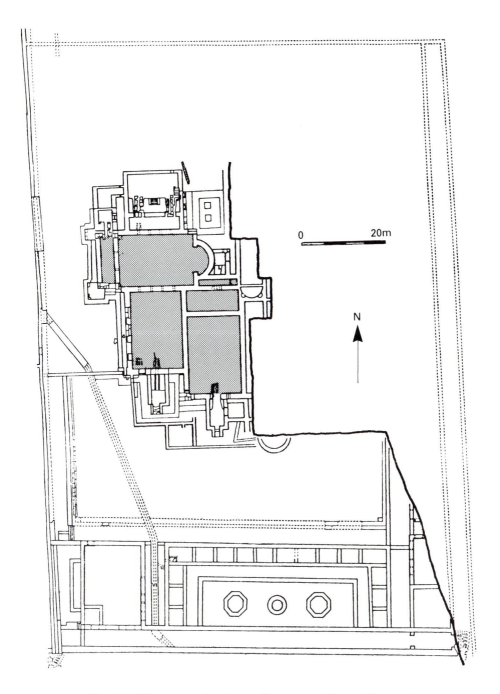

*Figure 2(c)* The governor's palace at Carnuntum (after A. Obermayr)

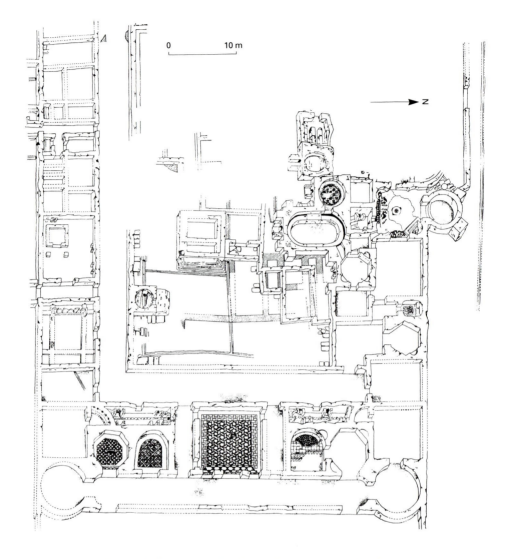

*Figure 2(d)* The governor's palace at Aquincum (after J. Szilágyi)

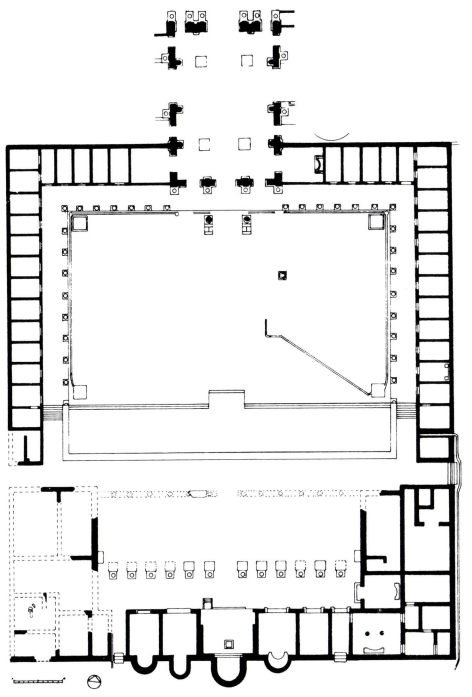

*Figure 2(e)* The *principia* at Lambaesis (after Y. Le Bohec)

large number of relatively small rooms, at least some of which may have served a similar function (see Figs 2(a)–(e)).

The identification of the cities mentioned and others throughout the empire as centres of provincial administration, civil as well as military, is guaranteed not just by the discovery of such buildings but also by finds of inscriptions recording the governors' *officiales*. These finds are concentrated almost exclusively in one major city in each province, the only exceptions being inscriptions of officers such as *frumentarii*, *beneficiarii* and *speculatores* who are specifically attested as having been employed in outposts (*stationes*) or as couriers (see pp. 153f., 195ff.). Even though governors continued to tour their provincial defences and dispense justice on assize, it is clear that after the initial period of conquest and consolidation in each province they settled down to operate from the base of a single capital city where their headquarters staffs and therefore their archives were located.

This arrangement did not preclude at least a portion of the personnel and papers from accompanying a governor when he did move about his province. Amongst the roll of letters assigning horses sent out by Marius Maximus as governor of Syria was at least one dispatched from Antioch, usually regarded on epigraphic and general historical grounds as the provincial capital but also another from Hierapolis (Membij) (*P.Dur.* 56 = Fink 99); it implies that some records travelled round with Marius.

The growth of the centralized provincial bureaucracy was a corollary of the development of static frontiers. The precise mode of this frontier development did of course vary from region to region and period to period. Sometimes it took the form of lines of forts and fortresses laid out along a military road (*limes*), often following a river as on the Rhine and Danube; sometimes forts were situated rather to block or control specific invasion or transhumance routes as in North Africa or on parts of the eastern frontier; sometimes there was a mixture of the two modes as in the developed Hadrian's Wall system in northern Britain; and sometimes forts were deployed to defend a line of communication as in Egypt or keep watch on a potentially hostile native population as in Wales or Judaea or Isauria. The common factor which is of the greatest importance from the intelligence point of view was the relative permanence of the forts and their units. Each fort thus became in itself a centre where local intelligence could be gathered, filed in the unit archive and then passed on to provincial headquarters. This situation was completely different from that which obtained under the much more fluid situation of the Republic.

Furthermore, as time went on and the inhabitants of newly conquered territories gradually became Romanized, recruitment from the territories where a unit had originally been raised was in most cases replaced by local recruitment. This was often from amongst the sons of veterans who had settled down with local women in the villages (*vici*) which tended to grow up outside each permanent fort. By the end of the first century AD most provinces were being garrisoned by legions and *auxilia* drawn from their own natives, people who knew the area and spoke the local languages. And since governors drew their staffs from their own legions, this was equally true of the men at provincial headquarters. It would often mean that the provincial governor would have men at his disposal whose mother tongue was the same as that of peoples across the border, even though dialects might differ.

Sometimes, however, it was necessary to make use of men with special linguistic skills. The epigraphic evidence for men who were specifically employed as interpreters at Carnuntum, Aquincum and Viminacium, the capitals of Upper and Lower Pannonia and Upper Moesia respectively, has been cited in chapter 2 (see pp. 28f.). This evidence, mostly of third-century date, suggests that by that time, if not before, provincial governors were regularly engaged in cross-frontier contacts.

What is striking in all this evidence is that at no stage of Rome's history is there any sign of the creation of specialized military-intelligence staffs either at Rome or in the provinces; compare this with the readily identified agencies concerned as part of their regular duties with internal political intelligence, the *frumentarii* from perhaps the late first century onwards, and after their disbandment by Diocletian, the *agentes in rebus* (see pp. 219ff.). Nevertheless, we have demonstrated in the preceding pages the array of sources of military and strategic information which were available to an incoming governor: the initial tour of inspection, the client princes within and beyond his frontiers, the intelligence in his archives passed on from the frontier forts, and the military personnel on his staff who had years of experience of the province and its army. All this meant that the new governor would very quickly be far better informed about the current state of his province than the emperor or anyone else in Rome.

# 7

# THE WATCH ON THE FRONTIER

## The governor's perspective

While the emperor sat in Rome, his view of the frontiers and what lay beyond was restricted by time, distance and the filter of self-interest amongst his informants. The governor active in his province enjoyed the benefits of local staff, accumulated archives, and the ability to go and see for himself. The contrast is striking. The emperor's sources of knowledge and their limitations have already been considered in chapter 5. In particular, attention has been drawn to the fact that there is no indication of any attempt to set up a military archive or staff in Rome parallel to the provincial staffs we have described. It can be seen that the bureau of the *ab epistulis* did not begin to compare with what any frontier governor had available to him. Since by the third century a significant number of emperors had served as frontier governors prior to their elevation, we must assume that they saw no practical advantage in setting up a specifically military staff in Rome and that this was a conscious omission. It implies a long-sustained perception that only the man on the spot was in a position to handle military information in detail. It also indicates that the control and defence of the frontiers must in practice have been far more devolved to the provincial governors than historians have hitherto been prepared to concede. This is not to say that emperors never attempted to interfere from Rome but when they did so it was usually either for political reasons, as with Claudius and the invasion of Britain, or because of broader, empire-wide strategic considerations, as with Domitian's withdrawal from Scotland. An emperor in Rome was always too far away from the action to attempt detailed control of affairs on the frontier with any hope of success (see pp. 124ff.).

We are now in a position to modify the concept of the frontiers as an 'information barrier'. While this may have been valid for an emperor based in Rome, it was not so for a governor in the frontier zone itself. We have argued that the governor's headquarters provided a nerve-centre into which information could be fed by the frontier forts. But what is the evidence for such a flow of information? What sort of information could the forts have supplied and what could the governor do with it? And how far beyond the immediate frontier zone did the surveillance of the forts extend?

170

## THE GOVERNOR AND HIS FRONTIER

The passage of military intelligence between forts and provincial headquarters is in fact nowhere explicitly attested, but there is no doubt that all sorts of correspondence did move constantly between the two. Reference has already been made to the evidence for the dispatch of letters from the governor assigning troops and horses to various units. The personnel files which these and other documents imply were kept at provincial headquarters can only have been maintained through a constant flow of detailed memorandums from the frontier. Some at least of the regular strength reports made by each unit and preserved on papyrus are likely to have been intended for the governor. Particularly interesting in this context is a papyrus found at Dura Europos in Syria which contains a circular letter sent for information by the governor Marius Maximus to the 'tribunes and prefects and *praepositi* of units'. The circular incorporates a copy of another letter sent by the governor to the provincial procurator ordering him to ensure that a certain Goces, who is the envoy of the Parthian king to the emperors Septimius Severus and Caracalla, is properly entertained at the frontier forts through which he will pass (*P.Dur.* 60 = Fink 98). The dispatch of a circular letter in this way suggests that correspondence between governor and frontier was fairly routine.

As already noted, correspondence was often carried for the governor by members of his staff or bodyguard (p. 153). The letter listing recruits to *cohors III Ituraeorum* from the Prefect of Egypt, for instance, was delivered by Priscus the bodyguard (*per Priscum singul(arem)*) (*P.Oxy.* VII 1022 = Fink 87, cf. *P.Oxy.* LV 3810.14–17 and *P.Amh.* II 137.2)). Unit commanders would send messages by means of their own troopers. So, one of the Dura rosters records men who had now 'returned having formerly been dispatched to the governor's headquarters with letters' (*reversi q(uondam) d(e)p(utati) ad praet(orium) praesidis cum epistul[i]s*) (*P.Dur.* 82 = Fink 47, ii 7). One of the Vindolanda tablets already mentioned is a letter to the fort commander, apparently from the commandant at Ribchester (Bremetenacum), reporting that the two riders which the former had sent with letters for the governor had passed through (*Crispum et E[. . .] ex coh(orte) I Tungrorum, quos cum epistulis ad consularem n(ostrum) miseras, a Bremetennaco . . .*) (*Tab.Vindol.* I 30.3–6). Presumably, couriers would return carrying further correspondence.

Regular written communication between governor and frontier is not therefore in doubt. It would be perverse to deny that dispatches might include reports of any incidents or snippets of military information, although no such dispatch has survived. The sort of information which could have been passed on is perhaps reflected in a now famous tablet from Vindolanda (see Plate 5). The text covers one side of half of a diptych tablet with no other writing upon it and states: 'The Britons are nude. There are very many horsemen; the horsemen do not use swords, nor do the nasty little Britons stop (?) in order to throw their javelins' (*nenu. . . . [.]n. Brittones, nimium multi equites; gladis non utuntur*

171

*equites, nec residunt Brittunculi ut iaculos mittant*) (*Tab. Vindol. II* 164). It has been suggested that the tablet was a scout's dispatch written in the field, or even part of the rough draft of a report written by a unit commander for his successor, but another recipient of such a report might of course have been the governor. Regardless of the actual circumstances of the writing of this document, it is in itself proof that the Roman army could and did take note of intelligence information, put it in writing and then file it; the tablet can hardly have been unique.

The diligence and acumen with which this sort of intelligence was recorded and reported will have varied from unit to unit, depending on the efficiency of their officers and commandants. Nevertheless, whatever was passed on, including purely negative intelligence of quiet on a particular sector, would have gained enormously in significance from the fact that it was being processed through a single headquarters. The likelihood is that the governor would have read all dispatches himself, however cursorily, since personal attention to correspondence seems to have been the norm in Roman administration. Certainly, the letters found at Dura Europos assigning men and horses were all written in the first person as if they came direct from the governor. It is clear from both Egyptian papyri and the Vindolanda tablets that whilst outgoing documents might be written out by secretarial staff it was customary for the official in charge to add the greeting in his own hand (the equivalent of a modern signature). And Millar has persuasively argued that the emperor himself dealt with even the most trivial matters which were put before him (this is one of the principal theses of *The Emperor in the Roman World* (London, 1977)). What was true of the emperor should also have been true of his deputies.

In such circumstances, hints of trouble along the frontier could not have gone unnoticed by an official as senior and experienced as a frontier governor. Incidents which might have seemed isolated to a unit commander could acquire much greater importance when seen as part of the larger picture which the developed frontier system made available to a governor. In other words, one result of the creation of static frontiers and a centralized provincial bureaucracy under the Principate was the *de facto* creation of provincial intelligence cycles (see pp. 8f.) much more regular and efficient than had ever been possible under the Republic. Information picked up on the frontier could be collated, evaluated and interpreted by the governor and his advisers, making use of his professional military staff and his archives; it could then, if necessary, be disseminated back to the frontier by circular letter, together with instructions defining what local commanders needed to watch for or investigate further. The process need not have been developed in any formal way. Rather, it would have been the natural corollary of other developments in the Roman army and provincial administration under the early Principate.

The methods of collecting intelligence have been discussed in detail in chapters 2 and 3. Much could have been picked up casually in the normal course of events. Unrest amongst the local population, reports from traders operating across the frontier, hostile sightings by outposts or routine patrols along the frontier road (*limes*), and minor skirmishes would all have attracted the attention of even the most inexperienced unit commander and required comment in dispatches to the governor. The extent to which such intelligence was sought actively, and over what range, are rather more vexed questions, and the answers will have varied over time and the different types of frontier. They are also bound up with our interpretation of the purpose of Roman frontiers in general.

## FRONTIERS AS BARRIERS: RIVER FRONTIERS

The tendency of scholarship over the last decade has been to play down the role traditionally ascribed to Roman frontiers as defensive barriers and to see their military installations rather as a means of controlling traffic across the frontier or protecting traffic along it. The positioning of these installations has been seen as a matter of bureaucratic convenience, or as part of the creation of a military zone to control interaction with the local population, or even simply as the ossification of the empire's line of advance.[1] There is some truth in all these interpretations, especially since Roman frontiers vary considerably in both form and function. But the reaction against the traditional interpretation has in general gone too far and has led to some peculiar and untenable assertions.

This has been particularly true of the riverine frontiers of the empire. The observation that rivers do not form natural boundaries in themselves but serve to link rather than separate the peoples settled along their banks has caused them to be seen as providing militarily ineffectual frontiers. This notion has gained a considerable vogue in recent work, but it crucially ignores the effect of planting fortifications and a military road along one bank of a river. The manner in which this was accomplished along the Rhine and the Danube makes sense only in terms of military defence since it can be shown to be incompatible either with convenience or ease of cross-frontier control or even of ossification of line of advance. The positioning of forts, almost without exception, along the Roman banks of these rivers, together with the very obvious and therefore deliberate absence of permanent bridges across them, in practice turned them into one element (but only one) of a defensive system. The role which a river fulfils in such a system can in some ways be likened to the ditches around a Roman fort, useless in themselves, but deadly in combination with the defences within them.

Rivers, as has been said, are not insuperable obstacles in themselves, and sometimes they can betray their defenders by freezing over or dropping in level. Both the Rhine and the Danube froze regularly (Ovid *Tristia* III 10.27ff.; *From Pontus* I 2.79–80; IV 7.9–10; 10.32–4; Pliny *Panegyric* 12.3; 82.4–5; Herodian VI 7.6–7; Ammianus XIX 11.4; etc.) and they frequently made a path for invaders: Cotiso and his Dacians caused trouble by crossing the Danube even before it had become a proper frontier in the 30s BC (Florus II 28); the Chatti were prevented from crossing the frozen Rhine in AD 89 by an unexpected thaw (Suetonius

*Domitian* 6.2); the Iazyges living east of the Danube bend were defeated in a battle on the ice in 173/4 (Dio LXXI 7); and the great invasion of Vandals, Suebi and Alani into the German and Gallic provinces on the last day of 406 was probably made possible by the freezing of the Rhine (Orosius VII 38.3–4; 40.3; Prosper Tiro 1230 in *Chronica Minora* i, p. 465, cf. p. 299; Zosimus VI 3.1). But as long as rivers continue to flow reasonably vigorously, they do seriously slow down any attacker and allow the concentration of forces and fire against him.

In fact, no barbarian force of any size could normally cross a river except by a pre-existing bridge or by procuring a significant number of boats. This was true of any river which could not be forded, let alone the great waterways of the Rhine, Danube and Euphrates. To swim one of these equipped to fight was a great feat even for the Batavians, who originated near the mouth of the Rhine and had developed a special technique of swimming alongside their horses. A thousand of these men, probably serving in Hadrian's imperial horse guard, swam the Danube in Pannonia in 118 as an exercise with the emperor watching. Hadrian himself may have written the verse epitaph, preserved on an inscription, which honours one of the swimmers (*CIL* III 3676 with p. 1042 = *ILS* 2558), and Dio says that the exploit terrified the local barbarians (LXIX 9.6).[2] The implication is that the Batavians possessed a unique skill. And even if an armed force did manage to swim or row across a fortified river, it could still expect its landing to be opposed by troops from the two nearest units deployed along the *limes*, to be reinforced in due course by others from further along the line.

But if rivers could cause problems for anything more than a handful of invaders, they were equally an obstacle to patrols crossing from the Roman bank. This would not have been the case had the Romans built bridges from the forts, but there is no good evidence for the maintenance of permanent bridges across any of the major river frontiers before the early part of the fourth century AD, and even then they were few and far between (see p. 236). On the contrary, there is good reason to believe that the Roman Empire was throughout its history very wary of building permanent bridges into hostile territory.

On the German frontier, for instance, under the Principate the only known bridges across the Rhine were situated at Xanten, Neuwied, Koblenz and Mainz. The bridge at Xanten is known from Tacitus (*Annals* I 49; 69) and its piles may have been identified in the nineteenth century. It was built by the imperial prince Germanicus for his reinvasion of Free Germany to restore discipline amongst his mutinous troops in AD 14. But in the following year Germanicus' wife Agrippina had to prevent it from being dismantled by terrified local commanders when rumours spread of an imminent German attack in the wake of Germanicus' less-than-successful expedition. In a story which Tacitus tells us he took from the elder Pliny, he describes how this formidable lady waited at the bridgehead to greet her husband's bedraggled legions as they returned. We do not hear of the bridge again and it is not clear how long it remained in use. The bridges at Neuwied, Koblenz and Mainz all lie upstream of the point where the Rhine ceased to mark the frontier line after the advances made by Vespasian and Domitian in the 70s and 80s. The piles which have been noted at Neuwied are undated. Those at Koblenz have recently been shown by dendro-chronology to have been cut in AD 49, and have therefore been associated with a projected invasion by the governor of Upper Germany, P. Pomponius Secundus, of the territory of the Chatti in retaliation for a raid in that year (Tacitus *Annals* XII 27). Since all the piles date from the same year, it would appear that the bridge was never renewed, and whilst it may have survived until the end of the century, it may equally have been broken within a few months of construction.[3] At Mainz the piles of an early first-century pontoon bridge have been found, which linked the legionary fortress to a possible bridgehead fort at Kastel and to known forts at Wiesbaden and Hofheim. Significantly, they are the only two Roman forts across the Rhine which appear to have been held continuously between Germanicus' recall from Germany in AD 16 and the reoccupation of this part of the right bank under Vespasian, when the Mainz bridge and the fort at Kastel were rebuilt in stone.[4] Nevertheless, after this area of the right bank had been overrun by the great Alamannic invasion of 233, the emperor Severus Alexander had in 234/5 to construct a bridge of boats at Mainz to carry his counter-invasion force (Herodian VI 7.6; cf. *BMC* VI, p. 209, no. 967 and pl. 31). In other words, so far as is known, the permanent bridge at Mainz always led into Roman-held territory. There is thus no evidence for the maintenance of any Roman bridge across the Rhine into barbarian territory between the last mention of the bridge of Germanicus in AD 15 and the construction of Constantine's stone bridge linking Cologne with the new bridge-head fort at Divitia (Deutz) in 310.

Similarly, bridges across the Main, which flows into the Rhine opposite Mainz, can only be traced on the stretch of the river where it did not mark the frontier: going upstream from west to east these have been found at Kostheim, Höchst, Schwanheim, Frankfurt, Bürgel, Hanau and Gross-Krotzenburg. At Gross-Krotzenburg, where there was a frontier fort, the river now ran from south to north and started to mark the frontier line. The bridge there did not cross into non-Roman territory but carried the *limes* road south at the point where the latter ceased to mark the frontier. South of here as far as Miltenberg, where the road again became the frontier, there are no known bridges. Further south still, the bridge over the Jagst at Jagsthausen again carried the *limes* road and did not lead into barbarian territory.[5]

Only on the River Neckar, which marked a section of the Upper German frontier in the late first and the first half of the second century, do we find that, although all the forts are still situated to the west of the river, the *limes* road itself apparently crosses from one bank to the other in places in order to shorten its line.[6] This appears, however, to have been a relatively quiet stretch of the frontier, since in the middle of the second century the emperor Antoninus Pius was able to move the frontier 30 km forward from here, as far as we know without any fighting. And even here there is no evidence of the construction of bridges as opposed to fords.[7]

The situation in the German provinces is paralleled by that along the Danube. The absence of bridges on the Danube and Euphrates before Trajan's time is implied by an anecdote in Ammianus who records that Trajan used to re-inforce his statements with the words 'So may I see Dacia made a province' and 'So may I cross the Danube and Euphrates *on bridges*' ('*sic* pontibus *Histrum et Euphratem superem*') (XXIV 3.9). And indeed, no permanent bridges across the Danube into Dacia (modern Romania) are known archaeologically from before the second century. During and after Trajan's conquest of Dacia in the early years of that century bridges were thrown across the river at Drobeta, Oescus and Transdierna, linking Lower and Upper Moesia with the new province.[8] Further upstream, however, Viminacium, the capital of Upper Moesia and base of legion *VII Claudia*, which faced barbarian territory, had no bridge. Likewise, there are no traces of a bridge at Carnuntum, the capital of Upper Pannonia, despite its being situated at the crossing point of the so-called 'Amber Route', ancient even in the Roman period. As late as 358, when a completely different approach to the defence of the empire had made permanent bridges more acceptable, Constantius II had to throw a pontoon bridge across the Danube somewhere between Singidunum (Belgrade) and Viminacium (Ammianus XVII 12.4–6), and in 375 the emperor Valentinian had to do the same just north of Aquincum (Ammianus XXX 5.13).

The Euphrates was not heavily fortified with military installations, and not fortified at all on its lower reaches, but it nevertheless marked the provincial boundaries of Cappadocia and Syria for part of its course. It too was unbridged. At Samosata and Zeugma, only fords are known, both of them protected by legionary bases. When Nero's general Corbulo needed to cross the river at Zeugma in order to repel a threatened Parthian invasion in AD 62, he had to throw across a pontoon bridge whilst under hostile attack (Tacitus *Annals* XV 9). In 165 Avidius Cassius had to do the same in similar circumstances for L. Verus' invasion of Parthia (Dio LXXI after 3.1[1] = *The Suda* s.v. *zeugma*). Further south, the emperor Julian also had to build a bridge of boats across the river in 363 while *en route* with his army from Hierapolis to Batnae (Ammianus XXIII 2.7).

The negative evidence, both archaeological and literary, is cumulatively de-cisive: it would appear that the Romans deliberately avoided bridging their river frontiers. The implications of this conclusion are of considerable importance for our understanding of Roman frontiers. It shows not only that the Romans *did* regard rivers as being of defensive value in themselves, but that the require-ments of defence outweighed any need to oversee cross-frontier movement or even to exercise direct control of the zone across these rivers, which functions would have been facilitated enormously by permanent bridges.

Our emphasis on defence is borne out by two very strong pieces of literary evidence. The first is Tacitus' tale from the elder Pliny about Agrippina's having to prevent the breaking of the bridge at Xanten in the face of a threatened German invasion: the story assumes a perception of the Rhine as an effective barrier. The second is even more striking. This is the case of Trajan's bridge across the Danube at Drobeta, built by his architect Apollodorus of Damascus, who was also responsible for Trajan's Forum in Rome where his column stood. The bridge was used to carry the emperor's invasion of Dacia during the Second Dacian War of 105/6 (Dio LXVIII 13; Procopius *Buildings* IV 6. 13–15). But despite its fame – it is prominently depicted on Trajan's Column (scenes xcviii–c) – and the grandeur of its construction as described by Dio and confirmed by its remains at Turnu Severin today, it was not long in use. As Dio says, 'the bridge, however, is of no benefit to us now, but its piers stand useless without a roadway, as though they were built for a single purpose of showing that there is nothing that human cleverness cannot do. For Trajan was fearful that if ever the Danube froze hostilities would break out against the Romans on the far bank, and thus built the bridge so that reinforcements could reach them quickly across it. But his successor Hadrian feared on the contrary that the barbarians would overcome the guards and that it would give them an easy crossing into Moesia, and removed the superstructure' (Dio LXVIII 13.5–6). Once again the river is seen as a barrier to invasion, and a bridge, even one leading to Roman-occupied territory, as a potential aid to attackers. It may be noted incidentally that the passage assumes that a frozen river at this point (where the Danube is 1 km across) would be a barrier to the sending of reinforcements, presumably because it would not freeze sufficiently to bear the weight of troops and horses but would make crossing by ferry or boat impossible.

A final indication of Roman nervousness about bridges is that even where permanent bridges were eventually built across river frontiers, they were always provided with a bridgehead fort. This was already true of the bridge at Mainz in the Flavian period, and probably before, which was protected by Castellum Mattiacorum (Kastel); it was also true of Trajan's bridge with its bridgehead fort at Drobeta (Turnu Severin), and it was the norm in the Late Empire, as with Constantine's bridge at Cologne (Divitia–Deutz).

The major rivers, then, were seen by the Romans as barriers to invasion so important that they must not be bridged, even at the cost of hindering their own movement across. This implies that on the river frontiers the Romans had adopted a general principle of dealing with threats only as they manifested themselves on the frontier line, even as the enemy were crossing and landing. It also strongly suggests that patrolling across the frontier was not a primary Roman objective.

The alternatives to crossing a river by bridge were to use either boats or ferries. In contrast to bridges, possible quays and jetties have been identified at several fort sites on the Roman banks of the Rhine, Main and Danube (though much more rarely on the barbarian bank opposite). Some if not all of these structures will have been used by ships of the river fleets, the *classis Germanica*, the *classis Pannonica* and the *classis Moesiaca* (the *classis Syriaca* was a Mediterranean not a riverine fleet). Inscriptions and literary evidence show that these fleets were equipped mostly with liburnians, which appear to have been light two-level twenty-oared vessels as depicted on Trajan's Column (scenes xxxiii–xxxiv, xlvi, lxxix–lxxx, lxxxii, lxxxvi).[9]

The principal role of such vessels was to patrol along the river, just as cavalry patrolled the *limes* road, and they played their part in ensuring that attackers should not cross by boat or even be able to obtain boats for that purpose. The fleets may also have used either these ships or special freight-carriers to supply the forts. A well-known third-century relief from Neumagen on the Moselle shows what is apparently an oared warship (possibly, however, converted to civilian use) carrying wine-barrels, whilst a *pridianum* of AD 105 records the detachment of men from *cohors I Hispanorum veterana*, temporarily posted to Moesia during the Second Dacian War, to serve on grain ships (*naves frumentariae*) (*P.Lond.* 2851 = Fink 63, ii 33). Similarly, either liburnians or specialized transports (*naves actuariae*) could have been used to transport patrols across the rivers. Certainly, it is likely to have been the river fleet which provided this service in view of the need for competent oarsmen to be available at the bidding of a fort commandant.

*Naves actuariae* are attested for a river fleet only during Germanicus' German campaign of AD 16 (Tacitus *Annals* II 6), but even these could have transported only a limited number of troops at a time. Any cross-river patrol intending to operate beyond the immediate vicinity of the river bank directly opposite its home base would have to be mounted, but a cavalryman with his horse takes up the space of five infantrymen. Calculations from figures given by Caesar and Livy suggest that even the largest sea-going transports could only carry about thirty horses with their riders (the equivalent of a cavalry squadron or *turma*) (Caesar *Gallic War* IV 22.4; cf. 35.1, eighteen ships carrying the cavalry attached to two legions, which should come to 600 men at this period; Livy XLIV 28.7 and 14, thirty-five ships carrying 1,000 cavalry; cf. H.D.L. Viereck, *Die römische Flotte* (Herford, 1975), 85–8). This was the number of horses which could have been carried by a converted trireme, manned by sixty rowers, in the fifth and fourth centuries BC (Thucydides VI 43; cf. *IG* II$^2$ 1628.154–5, 161–2, 470, 475, 480; cf. J. Morrison and J. Coates, *The Athenian Trireme* (Cambridge, 1987), 226–8). Elsewhere, however, Livy speaks of transports of up to thirty oars (XXXVIII 38.8), and Cicero of small transports of ten oars (*Letters to Atticus* XVI 3.6), while the Althiburus mosaic from Tunisia, which depicts different types of ship, seems to show a six-oared horse-transport (*hippago*) which would have had room for only a few horses at most. These figures give us at least some idea of the capacity of purpose-built or converted transports. The capacity of a twenty-oared liburnian patrol-ship is likely to have been relatively smaller for its size.

How many ships, if any, a fort might have regularly attached is unknown, although it would make sense for the fleet to be dispersed along the river in order to allow effective policing. In AD 70 the ships of the *classis Germanica* in the region of the so called 'island of the Batavians' (*insula Batavorum*) had to be concentrated after the local forts had been attacked and burned; there appear to have been twenty-four ships distributed amongst approximately ten forts (Tacitus *Histories* IV 15–16). Thus, if a fort had two or three liburnians available on a regular basis, it would have been easy enough, given a decent landing place on the far bank, to send across a patrol of *turma* strength or less. Any more would perhaps have necessitated repeated trips. These could certainly be managed but would begin to be cumbersome, especially where the river was of a significant width and had a strong stream running, as the Rhine and Danube would have had for much of their lengths, even before the construction work of the nineteenth century deepened the channels in places.[10]

At some crossing points raft-ferries drawn along on cables could have replaced ships of the fleet for carrying similar-sized patrols. These, however, would be impracticable where the rivers were really wide and would also have been a potential nuisance to both military and civilian shipping moving up and down. Nor has any good evidence for the existence of such ferries, such as quays opposite each other on either bank, yet been discovered.

In most places, therefore, patrolling across the rivers was probably accomplished with the assistance of the river-fleet. But how much patrolling actually took place and how much could it achieve? There is no doubt that at certain times on certain stretches of frontier the Roman army attempted to maintain a cleared strip on the hostile bank. We know from Tacitus that in AD 59 the Frisii moved in to occupy unoccupied land set aside for military use (*agrosque vacuos et militum usui sepositos*) on the right bank of the Rhine near its mouth (*Annals* XIII 54). The width of this strip is not recorded, nor the extent to which it was patrolled. But it is clear that the infiltration of the Frisii was not countered until after it had taken place, which suggests a certain laxity in surveillance.

Many forts were situated opposite the point where a tributary river valley joined the main stream and so offered a potential invasion route to both Romans and barbarians. A patrol from the Roman side might well have to ride in a more or less straight line away from the main river, and its range for a day's patrolling would then be half a day's ride, say 20–30 km.[11] But the distance from the river would be much reduced if there were a necessity to cover territory to left and right of the crossing point. And since forts on the *limes* could be situated up to 25 km apart, any single patrol group hoping to cover the whole of a fort's sector might not be able to move very far from the river bank at all.

Reconnaissances of more than a day's duration would start to be problematical. Horses could graze off the land if the topography and the season were right,[12] and men could carry several days' rations with them, but the real difficulty was one of security. Roman forces of any significant size, when marching through hostile territory, regularly built themselves turf ramparts with palisades to enclose their tented overnight camps for protection (Polybius VI 27–32; Josephus *Jewish War* III 5.1–4/76–92; Hyginus *On Camp Fortifications*; Vegetius *Epitome of Military Science* III 8; cf. Trajan's Column *passim*). Remains of these temporary camps have been found in Scotland, Wales, Germany and other parts of the empire, the smallest of just over an acre in area still being sufficient to hold an auxiliary cohort, the largest of more than 160 acres being able to accommodate several legions and their auxiliaries. Regular patrolling in force beyond the frontiers ought to have left several series of such camps striking into barbarian territory from all along the linear frontiers, and they should show signs of constant reuse. This does not, however, accord with the patterns of camps so far discovered nor is it how archaeologists have interpreted them. Aerial photography and excavation have suggested sites occupied only on a single occasion by army units and groups moving from one site to another on campaign. This is of course what one should expect if, as has been suggested, patrols consisted of tens rather than hundreds of men. Unless one assumes universally friendly natives prepared to accept regular billeting, such small patrols would find it impracticable to build a fortification and would have to pitch their tents in the open. This would make them extremely vulnerable to attack, especially as mounted troops, who have to protect their horses as well as themselves, cannot be ready to fight as cavalry at a moment's notice in the way that infantry can. Further, reuse of earlier fortifications, in Scotland for instance, which were designed to hold large numbers of men, could turn into a death trap for a small patrol if cornered inside.

All this makes regular deep reconnaissance beyond the river frontiers inherently unlikely. In time of peace it would be uncomfortable and tedious, and it would be an extraordinarily efficient army which would maintain it over more than a few years if there were no signs of hostility. Conversely, if a threat did arise, it would immediately become immensely dangerous and would demand much more substantial patrols, which ought to have left more traces in the form of temporary camps or at least of finds of lost and discarded military equipment.

Some idea of what depth of patrolling might have been thought possible can be gained from the arrangements known to have been made by the emperor Marcus Aurelius during the Marcommanic Wars. After personally conducting operations against the Quadi in AD 172 and Marcomanni in 173, Marcus forbade the latter to attend markets on the right bank of the river in Pannonia and forced them to vacate a strip of land on the left bank. The exclusion zone was to be 15 km wide, although it was later reduced to 7.5 km (38 stades) (Dio LXXI 15; cf. LXXII 3.2). Then in 175, after the Quadi and the Iazyges had been defeated, the latter had to evacuate a strip 15 km across to the east of the Danube Bend (Dio LXXI 16.1). Presumably 15 km represented a couple of hours' ride away from the river, and was as much as Marcus felt it possible for the Roman army to supervise. Even this may have proved difficult since by 179 the Iazyges were merely forbidden to approach the islands in the Danube and were allowed to attend markets on the left bank under Roman supervision (Dio LXXI 19.2; cf. Tacitus *Germania* 41) (see pp. 26f., 209f.).

## FRONTIERS AS BARRIERS: DRY FRONTIERS

Attention has so far been focused on the river frontiers and in particular the Rhine and the Danube. But, although the rivers undoubtedly compounded the difficulties, the arguments for the impracticality of regular long-range patrolling apply equally to many of the dry frontiers of the empire. In the North, linear frontiers were the norm even where they were not based on a river. They consisted of a *limes* road policed from a line of forts running along it and often fronted by a palisade or rampart or stone wall.

One such frontier was the Upper German–Raetian *limes* which cut off the angle between the two great rivers. Vespasian began moves to reoccupy the right bank of the Rhine beyond Mainz in the 70s and then his son Domitian, in the wake of a war against the Chatti in 83, reoccupied the Taunus–Wetterau region and ringed it with a line of forts, fortlets, watch-towers and even palisades. In the later years of his reign and the early years of Trajan, this was extended southwards to the Main, along the river, across the Odenwald and down the Neckar to join up eventually with the new Alb *limes* running to the north of the headwaters of the Danube and down to the river at Eining. Hadrian added a palisade along the whole length, and then his successor Antoninus Pius moved forward the Odenwald–Neckar section about 30 km to a new line of much the same elements with a palisade running dead straight for some 80 km. A rampart and ditch (the Pfahlgraben) was later added to the rear of the palisade, but in Raetia it was replaced in turn by a wicker fence (the Flechtwerkzaun) and then a stone wall (the Teufelsmauer).[13]

Similar lines of forts were laid out in Dacia after the conquest by Trajan. The *limes Porolissensis* in the north-west consisted of forts and fortlets behind a line of watch-towers, and near the forts at Porolissum there were short stretches of both turf and stone ramparts (see Fig. 3). In the south-west two parallel lines of forts are known. One, the *limes Alutanus*, was laid out behind the River Olt, whilst the other, the *limes Transalutanus*, ran along a road some 30 km to the east and was fronted by a continuous earth and timber rampart. The exact relationship of the two is still a matter of debate, but current thinking is that they are roughly contemporary fortified roads of the Trajanic/Hadrianic period protecting routes into the new province of Dacia, although the rampart on the *Transalutanus* does suggest an additional concern with attack from the East.[14]

What these and the river frontiers have in common is precisely their narrow linearity: there are no outposts or multiple lines. Presumably this linearity was valued in part because of its suitability for dealing with what have been termed low-intensity threats. Neither the artificial barriers nor the rivers were in themselves impenetrable, but they would slow up an attack at any single point of the frontier. In the meantime, watch-towers or patrols would be able to signal or send messengers along the *limes* itself to the two nearest forts to either side. These could then send out an initial reaction force, to be reinforced in due

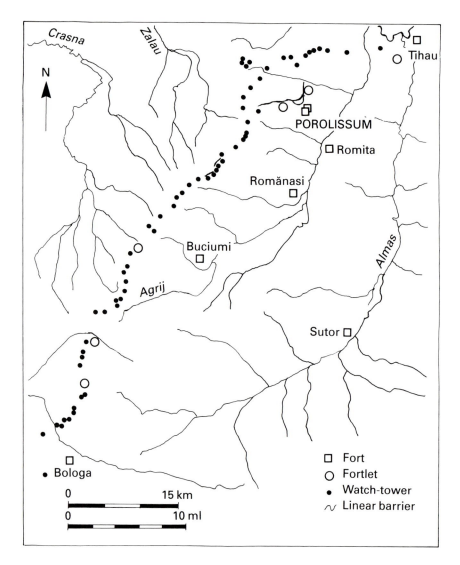

*Figure 3* The *limes Porolissensis*

course from the forts and fortresses further along the line.[15] The underlying principle appears to be one of dealing with any threat as it presents itself, on the frontier line itself. Presumably the system was developed on these particular frontiers and maintained over the first two centuries of the Principate because that was what was found to work. But not all Roman frontiers were organized in this way.

In the East, the system of client kingdoms inherited by Augustus from the late Republican period was maintained but gradually run down until the middle of the second century, as Pontus, Armenia Minor, Commagene, Cappadocia and Arabia became provincial territories. The principal perceived danger in the region came from the Parthians, who might attack by the northern route through Armenia or along the Euphrates and across the Syrian desert. In addition, Sarmatians from the steppe, whom the Romans first encountered on the Lower Danube, from time to time came down through the Caucasus and threatened both the Romans and the Parthians. The provinces were protected by a variety of frontier arrangements dependent on local conditions.

The mountains of Anatolia and the upper reaches of the Euphrates provided a restricted number of east–west invasion routes in the northern part of the region from Colchis and Armenia into the consular province of Cappadocia, and those routes were blocked by troop concentrations housed in permanent forts. The route along the Black Sea coast of Asia Minor was lined with auxiliary units which also kept a watch on the interior, as described by Arrian (see pp. 143f.); these were supplemented by the fleet based at Trapezus (Trabzon). At Satala and Melitene on the Euphrates, single legions controlled the interior routes towards Ancyra (Ankara). The Euphrates invasion route was the responsibility of the consular governor of Syria, where individual legions protected the river-crossings at Samosata and Zeugma.

Where mountain gave way to desert further south, the nature and indeed the purpose of the Roman frontier changed. There was only one potential route for major invasion, namely the caravan road to Damascus, via Rome's independent and powerful ally Palmyra. In the early Principate, it is thought that troops were billeted in the cities of the fertile regions of southern Syria, Judaea (after 128 known as Syria Palaestina) and Arabia, with legions at Raphanaea, Caparcotna, Jerusalem and Bostra respectively. These legions were distributed, as Isaac has recently argued, as much to act as garrisons watching potentially rebellious native populations, especially in Judaea, as to meet any external threat.[16] Only in Arabia were desert nomads like the Saracens liable to pose such a threat, and then it was mainly in the form of raiding rather than full-scale invasion and not particularly serious until the late second century.

The situation in Egypt, ruled by the emperor's Prefect, was not dissimilar. There, one legion plus auxiliaries was stationed in Alexandria in order to keep the peace in a city always divided between its Greek and Jewish population. Initially, two legions more were deployed further up the Nile, but these had been transferred out of the province by the Hadrianic period. Nevertheless, throughout the Principate, a heavy auxiliary garrison was distributed along the river as far as Hiera Sykaminos and perhaps Primis (Qaṣr Ibrîm). These troops were concerned both with internal policing and, in the southern part of the province, with external defensive duties, protecting the thin fertile strip of the Nile valley from the depredations of nomadic tribesmen such as the Blemmyes, Nubians and Trogodytes. A number of fortified roads also ran east of the Nile to the Red Sea, through the mining districts of the Mons Porphyrites and Mons Claudianus.

To the west of Egypt, there was apparently no threat to the province of Cyrene and only a minimal garrison. Beyond Cyrene lay the great senatorial province of Africa, one of the richest and most Romanized in the empire, then the military zone of Numidia, and, from the reign of Claudius, the two procuratorial provinces of Mauretania Caesariensis and Mauretania Tingitana. Here, the frontier zone lay within the broad strip of often mountainous pre-desert separating the fertile coastal area from the Sahara. The pre-desert was crossed by numerous transhumance routes through which desert nomads drove their animals to and from their summer pastures. Roman military installations were gradually moved forward under the Flavians and Trajan, and consolidated into a frontier by Hadrian. Hadrian's system combined forts, watch-towers distributed along roads, and stretches of continuous barrier consisting of walls cut through by causeways and gates. The continuous barriers were not, however, garrisoned and defensible in the same way as Hadrian's Wall in Britain or even his palisade in Upper Germany. Rather, they were only of use to channel transhumant flocks and herds past army posts. This is confirmed by a famous inscription found at Zaraï in Numidia, which lists customs duties chargeable at that point (*CIL* VIII 4508). The military centre of the whole system was the legion *III Augusta*, which by the reign of Hadrian had acquired its final base at Lambaesis. After AD 39, its commander was *de facto* governor of Numidia.

Rome's desert frontiers extended from southern Syria round to the Atlantic coast: physically, they differed considerably from her frontiers in Europe and were directed more towards control than outright defence (though, as we noted earlier, some scholars would claim that this was true of all Roman frontiers). In the North, the frontiers occupied a relatively narrow zone of territory, virtually a line on the ground; by contrast, in the East and on the African continent, there was a somewhat deeper distribution of military posts to block lines of movement into and through Roman territory. In all areas, problems were dealt with in the frontier zone and, until the second century, there were hardly any attempts to set up outposts which could give advance warning of trouble. Throughout the empire, only occasionally are there traces of a Roman military or official presence beyond the main line of installations in the first century and a half of the Principate. Where these appear, they are temporary arrangements, usually in aid of a client king (see pp. 29f., 148f.). There is no evidence in this period for any systematic attempt by the Romans to maintain a watch beyond the frontiers.

# 8

# BRIDGING THE GAP

## Emperors on the frontiers

Not until the Marcomannic Wars are there indications of a more proactive approach to frontier defence. Attacks by various Germanic tribes first on the Rhine and then on the Danube frontiers in the 160s provoked major imperial campaigns to drive out the invaders and then repair the damage caused. It could not yet have been known to the Romans that these invasions were but the first ripples of a tidal wave of pressure from the East which would continue intermittently over the next three centuries and would eventually sweep away the western part of the empire. Nevertheless, in the immediate aftermath of the incursions we begin to see structures put into place on the frontiers which would allow earlier and better warning of any threat which might materialize. The new structures first appeared on the German and the Danube frontiers, as one might expect, but they were soon imitated in other parts of the empire, though by no means all of them.

### OUTPOSTS

We now at last find evidence of three forts situated on the 'barbarian' banks of the two great European rivers, one on the Rhine and two on the Danube respectively. At Divitia (Deutz) opposite Cologne, inscriptions may record the presence of a unit of Britons in the early third century (*CIL* XIII 8492; 8495), although there are no physical remains of either a bridge or a fort before the reign of Constantine. On the Danube, across the river from the fortress of legion *I Adiutrix* at Brigetio, a fort was built at Celamantia (Iža-Leányvár) in the 170s on the site of an earlier temporary fort. There was no known bridge between the two banks, and the fact that the fort was not situated opposite the legionary fortress but a little downstream itself suggests that the two were linked by boat. The permanent garrison of Celamantia, if there was one, is unknown. There also appears to have been a fort across from Aquincum at Transaquincum (Rákospalota) from the reign of Septimius Severus at the latest.[1] What is perhaps most striking about these examples is that, even after the Marcomannic Wars and until the fourth century, they remain the only three permanent outposts as yet identified along a frontier in Europe some 4,000 km long.

*Figure 4* The Roman Empire in AD 214

More outposts can be identified on the eastern frontier from the late second century onward. As a result of the eastern campaigns of Marcus Aurelius' co-emperor L. Verus in AD 163–6, Sohaemus, an ex-consul of royal ancestry from Emesa (Homs), was installed as king of Armenia and backed up by a Roman garrison at Kainepolis (Echmiadzin) which was maintained into the 180s at least (*ILS* 9117; 394; cf. *CIL* III 13627a). At the same period, auxiliary forces were deployed along the Khabur and the central Euphrates to Dura Europos and beyond. The copy of Marius Maximus' circular letter of AD 208 to his unit commanders, arranging hospitality for the Parthian ambassador Goces (see p. 171), names five garrison towns along the Euphrates through which Goces will pass, including Dura itself (*P.Dur.* 60 = Fink 98, 2). As a result of the campaigns of Septimius Severus, Osrhoene and Mesopotamia became provinces in 197. Legionary garrisons were installed probably at Resaina and/or Nisibis, and at Singara on the eastern edge of Mesopotamia. Ammianus specifically states that Singara was occupied to provide advance warning of attack from the East (XX 6.9). Intriguingly, a Latin inscription (now lost) of unknown date was found a further 120 km east of Singara, on the right bank of the Tigris near Mosul, which lay at an important crossing point of the river opposite Nineveh (D.L. Kennedy, *ZPE* 73 (1988), 101–3). The stone is reported as bearing a relief sculpture of an eagle and the words 'the eyes of the legions' (*occuli legionum*), implying the presence of a watching post at the very limit of Rome's reach. The eclipse of the Arsacid Parthians by the Sassanian Persians after 224 made life much more difficult for such outposts and many, including Dura Europos, were destroyed and abandoned in the middle years of the third century before the Diocletianic reorganization. Further south, again under Septimius Severus, auxiliary forces were sent into the Arabian desert to occupy the oases at Azraq and Jawf. A century later, a milestone of the reign of Diocletian speaks of the road running through these as being 'linked by outposts' (*praetensione colligata*) to the provincial capital Bostra (M.P. Speidel, *Historia* xxxvi (1987), 213–21). Isaac has, however, recently argued that the function of this road was more to provide policing against raiding by the nomadic Saracens on areas of Romanized settlement than to provide defence against any major external threat like the frontier arrangements in northern Syria and Mesopotamia.[2] The two functions are not, in fact, incompatible.

Outposts also appear in the African provinces, especially at the oasis sites which are unavoidable for those approaching the fertile area from the desert. Here the problem was, in general, neither tribal raiding nor major invasion, but the control of transhumant nomads to minimize any adverse affect on the fertile area. There is no doubt, however, that the general problems of the empire in the third century, including the internal struggles which led to the disbanding of the Numidian legion *III Augusta* from AD 238 to 253, resulted in an increase in the level of frontier disturbances. In the area of Tripolitania under the command of the legate of the legion *III Augusta*, who also governed Numidia, a small fort was built beyond the main frontier line at Tisavar in the reign of Commodus (*CIL* VIII 11048; 22759 = *AE* 1978.887), and under the African emperor Septimius Severus legionary troops were installed at the oases of Bu Ngem (*IRT* 913–16; *AE* 1976.697–8; 700), Ghériat el-Gharbìa (*AE* 1967.539) and Ghadàmes (*IRT* 909; *AE* 1960.264). Bu Ngem has produced inscribed potsherds (*ostraca*), apparently used for military archives, which make reference to men 'from the watch-towers' (*de speclis*), and an individual serving on outpost as a *proculcator* (cf. Ammianus XXVII 10.10), and another 'with the Garamantes' (*cum Garamantibus*) (R. Rebuffat and R. Marichal, *REL* li (1973), 285). In Mauretania Caesariensis, a fort was built at Medjebel as early as 148–9 (*AE* 1938.51), probably as one of a line of forts stretching westward from the Numidian frontier to the north of the Ouled Naïl mountains. Much further west still but less certainly connected with military surveillance, an isolated inscription was found at Agneb in the region of the Djebel Amour. The inscription was a votive dedication set up in AD 174 in gratitude for a safe return by officers of two auxiliary units; it is far from clear, however, that it indicates the presence of an outpost or even an official military expedition, and a subsidiary inscription on the side of the stone seems to refer either to a lion-hunt or the carving of lions in relief in the local mountains (*CIL* VIII 21567; cf. Y. Le Bohec, *La troisième légion Auguste* (Aix/Paris/Marseille, 1989), 380–1). From the time of Septimius Severus, lines of forts can be identified either side of the Ouled Naïl. And in the far south-eastern corner of Mauretania Tingitana lay an outpost which bore the significant name of Exploratio ad Mercurios (*Antonine Itinerary* 3.2; cf. *Ravenna Cosmography* III 11/163).

## THE DEVELOPMENT OF *EXPLORATORES* UNITS

In many provinces, the precautions demanded by local threats and geographical conditions went beyond simply pushing garrisons out ahead of the main military line. From the later second century onwards, we begin to see the employment of local scouts to operate immediately beyond the frontiers. This can be traced in most parts of the empire, but shows most clearly on the relatively short section of dry frontier in Upper Germany which cuts off the angle between the headwaters of the two great European rivers. There, new units of *exploratores* are recorded from the second century AD.

Unfortunately, they pose a problem of interpretation which cannot be resolved with absolute certainty. Republican *exploratores* and *speculatores* seem to have been drawn from Rome's allies, with individuals or units being seconded for special duties (see pp. 101f.). It is not clear whether they were ever formally constituted, although by the time of the Triumvirate a coin of M. Antonius' does record a *cohors speculatorum* (*BMCRR* II, p. 527, nos 185–6). The same *ad hoc* approach appears to survive into the early Principate. On the few occasions when we have any specific information on the troops carrying out scouting and patrolling duties, they appear to be auxiliaries detailed for the purpose. Classicus and Tutor, for instance, who carried out a reconnaissance around Vetera (Xanten) during the

Batavian revolt of AD 70, were regular auxiliary officers, both of them from Augusta Treverorum (Trier): Classicus was commander of a Treveran cavalry unit (*praefectus alae Treverorum*) and Tutor had been put in charge of the Rhine bank (*ripae Rheni . . . praefectus*) (Tacitus *Histories* IV 55.1; 57.1). This appears to be a case of ordinary allied troops being temporarily assigned to intelligence-gathering, in this case with disastrous results. Another example is given by the papyrus document known as Hunt's *Pridianum*, which is a status report on *cohors I Hispanorum veterana* from the period of the Second Dacian War (AD 105/6) and reveals that while the unit was stationed at Stobi in Macedonia a number of junior officers and men, including twenty-three cavalry and some infantry, were sent 'across the Danube on an expedition' (*trans Danuvium in expeditionem*), and another group of cavalrymen, this time under the command of a centurion, also crossed the river 'to scout' (*exploratum*) (*P.Lond.* 2851 = Fink 63, ii 29–30; 32). We may even have an example of a whole unit temporarily assigned to scouting duties: on a single inscription of the mid-second century from Weissenburg in Raetia, the *cohors IX Batavorum equitata milliaria*, which is very well attested elsewhere as an ordinary auxiliary unit both before and after this date, is designated *expl(oratorum)* (*CIL* III 11918 = *ILS* 9152; cf. *CIL* III 12480).

On the other hand, the men who accompanied Titus on his reconnaissance of Jerusalem in AD 70 are described as 'selected cavalry' (*epilektoi hippeis*), and so presumably formed, at least temporarily, a special élite unit (Josephus *Jewish War* V 2.1/52). A clear example of this approach is provided by the memorial of Ti. Claudius Maximus at Philippi, which records that this man, who had a distinguished career in the cavalry of legion *VII Claudia* in Moesia before transferring as a junior officer (*duplicarius*) to *ala II Pannoniorum*, was specially selected by the emperor Trajan as an *explorator* for the Second Dacian War. The emperor had presumably been impressed by the courage which had gained Maximus decorations in Domitian's Dacian War and was subsequently to win him awards on two further occasions. Maximus was the leader of a squadron of *exploratores* which must have been operating almost recklessly deep behind enemy lines, since he failed, apparently by a matter of seconds, to prevent the Dacian king Decebalus from cutting his own throat at the end of the war. He was able, as the inscription informs us, to take the king's head and deliver it to Trajan at the otherwise unattested Ranisstorum. For this exploit, Maximus was promoted decurion in his own *ala*, which implies that he had remained on its books throughout (*AE* 1969/70.583; cf. M.P. Speidel, *JRS* lx (1970), 142–53; see Plate 7). The incident is illustrated not just on this stone but also on Trajan's Column (scene cxlv; cf. cxlvii; see Plate 8), where the figure which we can now identify as Maximus is surrounded by a splendid body of horsemen, all of them bearing shields with different blazons. If this is not just an artistic device, the designer of the frieze may have intended them to indicate a special force drawn from several units. The same type of temporary secondment was employed to form the units of bodyguards (*singulares*) attached to provincial governors. Men were detached from the province's cavalry forces for a period of approximately three years.[3] The Dura rosters show that they too remained on the books of their original units (see Fink, index p. 552 s.v. *singularis*).

There is in fact no evidence for the existence of standing units of *exploratores* in the Roman army until the early second century AD. It would appear that from the time of the Second Dacian War, if not before, some *ad hoc* units did not return their troops to the home units after service in a particular campaign but were themselves made permanent. This seems to have happened with some provincial guards units which were re-formed as either cavalry *alae* or infantry *numeri* or cohorts, such as the *cohors I Aelia singularium* based at Auzia in Mauretania Caesariensis (*CIL* VIII 9047; 9054; 9055; 9058; 20753), which had been formed out of the infantry guard of the governor of Lower Pannonia which came to Africa in AD 150 as part of an expeditionary force.[4] There is no reason to suppose that after this reconstitution they continued to operate as a bodyguard or were in any way different from other regular auxiliary units of the Roman army. Some *exploratores* units appear to have undergone a similar process.

Michael Speidel has argued that several units of *exploratores* recorded around the empire were originally raised from the German armies as spearhead troops in imperial campaigns of the second and third centuries.[5] An early third-century inscription in Greek records the career of T. Porcius Cornelianus, who passed through several auxiliary commands before becoming *praiphektos exploratoron Germanias* ('commander of the scouts of Germany' (*ILS* 8852), and it seems likely that he commanded just such a specially raised unit in the field. At the end of campaigning, the units were made permanent and became a regular part of the garrison of the province where they had been operating.

Speidel suggests that an early second-century *explorator* from Cologne who was buried at Orăştioara de Sus in Dacia (*AE* 1972.486) had come to the province during Trajan's Dacian Wars as part of a *numerus exploratorum Germanicianorum*, that is, a unit of scouts put together from the Lower German army. This unit appears to be attested at the fort by tile-stamps reading *NGER* or variations thereof (*AE* 1972.487; cf. 1974.548). Several other *numeri exploratorum Germanicianorum* raised from one or other of the two German armies are attested in various places throughout the empire, including Tsanta in Thrace, Burginatium (Neu-Luisendorf) in Lower Germany and Albulae in Mauretania Caesariensis (cf. *CIL* III 14207[10]; XIII 8683; *ILS* 9187). Some have the additional title of *Divitienses*, that is, based at Divitia (Deutz) on the right bank of the Rhine opposite Cologne, although these are not attested there but only at Serdica in Thrace, at Auzia in Mauretania Caesariensis, and at Mainz and Niederbieber in Upper Germany (*CIL* III 7415; VIII 9059; XIII 6814; 7750; 7751). Other similar units may be the *numeri exploratorum Batavorum* recorded at Matilo (Roomburg) in Lower Germany in 205 (*CIL* XIII 8825 = *ILS* 9186) and perhaps at Albulae (*CIL* VIII 21668 = *ILS* 9187a); also the *exploratores Triboci et Boii*, recorded first at Benningen on the Odenwald *limes* of Upper Germany in the first half of the second century

(*CIL* XIII 6448) and then at the corresponding fort at Murrhardt on the Antonine *limes*, to which it will have been transferred when the frontier was moved forward in the 150s (*AE* 1981.692). Such units probably varied considerably in size: the fort at Niederbieber, for instance, where only the *Divitienses* are attested, could house a milliary unit of around 1,000 men, while the *Triboci et Boii* appear to have shared both their forts with a regular cohort. Whether units raised for a specific campaign would retain any specialist scouting function when they became permanent garrison troops may be doubted. The analogy of the *singulares* perhaps suggests that they did not.

There are, however, a number of units known from Upper Germany which have no ethnic title but instead bear adjectival titles of a form ending in -*sis* or -*ses*. These titles are normally interpreted as being derived from the local name of the fort where each was based, as was probably the case with the *Divitienses* before their move to Niederbieber. The units include the *exploratio Halic(ensis)* who occupied a fort at the Feldberg in the reign of Severus Alexander (*CIL* XIII 7495 = *ILS* 9185; cf. *CIL* XIII 11958 and 6763; see Plate 9), the *exploratores Nemaningenses*, recorded in AD 178 on a stone which is likely to have originated either at Stockstadt or at Obernburg am Main (*CIL* XIII 6629; cf. 6642); the *exploratio Triputiensis* at Miltenberg-West (*CIL* XIII 6599) and the *exploratio Seiopensis* at Miltenberg-Ost (*CIL* XIII 6605; cf. XI 3104); the *exploratio Stu. . .* at Walldürn in 232 (*CIL* XIII 6592); and some unnamed *exploratores* at Welzheim-Ost (*CIL* XIII 6526). In addition, the graffito *explo* on a third-century potsherd found in the civilian settlement outside the fort at Zugmantel suggests that there may have been a further unit there (*Saalburg Jahrbuch* v (1913), 81 no. 16 and Taf. XVI. 16; cf. 19). The units on the Feldberg, at Miltenberg-Ost, Walldürn and Welzheim-Ost were all housed in small forts, in the last two cases alongside units of Britons. The others were all brigaded with infantry or mixed *cohortes*. Moreover, an inscription from Falerii in Italy records a man who had served as commander (*praepositus*) of the *exploratio Seiopensis* of a *numerus Aurelianensis*; this can be interpreted as referring to a scouting unit which served at Miltenberg (Seiopa) but was itself detached from an ordinary unit based at Öhringen (Aurelia) (*CIL* XI 3104; cf. XIII 6542; 6543). It is clear from this that we are dealing with very small units indeed, in some cases perhaps consisting of only a few dozen men. This and the unit names suggest that their function would have been small-scale local patrolling, perhaps carried out individually amongst the native communities in the vicinity of the frontier.

The concentration of *exploratores* units is unique to Upper Germany. No other province can show a similar distribution along the full length of its frontier. With the exception of the *exploratores Triboci et Boii*, none of the units need have been in existence before the Chattan invasions of the 160s. The evidence is consistent with our seeing their appearance as part of the long-term reaction to that disaster and the continuing pressure on the area in the late second and early third centuries, which climaxed in the emergence of the Alamannic confederation.[6] Nevertheless, it is possible to see a similar, if less intense, development in Pannonia, the African provinces and northern Britain.

Pannonia was, of course, the other area to have suffered from invasion in the 160s at the hands of the Marcomanni and other Germanic tribes from north of the Danube. *Exploratores* are recorded there in the late second or early third centuries, although units are never named and their organization is unclear. In Upper Pannonia, we have a dedication to the *Genius exploratorum* from Brigetio (*AE* 1944.122 = *RIU* II 424) and from nearby the tombstone of a local who is described simply as an *explorator* (*CIL* III 4276). In Lower Pannonia, we have a dedication by a 'centurion of scouts' (*centurio exploratorum*) from Cirpi (Dunabogdány) on the Danube Bend north of the capital Aquincum (Budapest) (*CIL* III 3648), and a similar dedication which probably came from Aquincum itself since it was found reused, together with milestones removed from very near to the city, at Titel on the River Tisza 50 km north of Belgrade (*CIL* III 3254 = *ILS* 2633); it is thought that these were stones stolen and taken down the Danube to build a palace for Attila the Hun in the middle of the fifth century (cf. Priscus *Byzantine History* 8 *FHG* IV p. 85). And from Lugio (Dunaszekső) we have the memorial set up by an *explorator* for his son (*AE* 1966.303). It may be significant that Brigetio, Aquincum and Lugio all lie at important Danube crossings, two of them protected by forts on the left bank, as we have seen, and opposite points where major routes across barbarian territory reached the river. The construction of watch-towers (*burgi*) and fortlets (*praesidia*) to block the furtive crossings of 'bandits' (*latrunculi*) on the stretch of the Danube south of Aquincum is recorded by a series of inscriptions of AD 185 (*CIL* III 3385; *RIU* V 1127–37).

In the military area controlled by the governor of Numidia, amongst the military archives written on potsherds (*ostraka*) found at the third-century fort at Bu Ngem in Tripolitania (see p. 189), one *ostrakon* mentions a man posted amongst the local tribesmen (*cum Garamantibus*) (*REL* li (1973), 285). In Mauretania Caesariensis, inscriptions of the third century record a unit of *exploratores* which was most certainly named after its home base at Pomaria (Tlemcen), almost at the western end of the province. Unlike the units in Upper Germany or Pannonia, this was organized as a regularly constituted *ala*, officered by *decuriones* and commanded by prefects (*CIL* VIII 9906 (= *ILS* 2634); 9907 (= *ILS* 4492); 9745; 21704). The *ala exploratorum Pomariensium* was in fact unique in the empire, as far as we know, which perhaps indicates that the creation of *exploratores* units was done under local initiative rather than by central directive. The existence of a place by the name of Exploratio ad Mercurios in Mauretania Tingitana has already been noted (p. 189).

The picture in Britain is slightly clearer. The outpost fort of Netherby forward of the western section of Hadrian's Wall is listed in the *Antonine Itinerary* as the 'Camp of the Scouts' (*Castra Exploratorum*) (467.1). In the first decade of the third century, two outpost forts were reoccupied on Dere Street forward of the western section, Risingham and High Rochester, which had probably been abandoned in the 180s in the wake of the withdrawal from the Antonine Wall. Possibly as a result, there had been trouble in the Lowlands of Scotland at the end of the century, and eventually the governor Alfenus Senecio (AD 205/7) had formally asked for an imperial expedition to settle the northern frontier (Herodian III 14.1). Risingham was rebuilt under the direction of the provincial procurator, M. Oclatinius Adventus (*ILS* 2618 = *RIB* 1234), and by 213 was garrisoned by a milliary cohort, a unit of Raetian spearmen (*Raeti gaesati*) and a unit of *exploratores* (*RIB* 1235). High Rochester was probably rebuilt and re-garrisoned at the same time; by the reign of Gordian III (AD 238–44) it was held by a milliary cohort and a *numerus exploratorum Bremeniensium*, clearly named after the fort, which we know to have been called Bremenium (*RIB* 1262; *ILS* 2631 = *RIB* 1270; cf. Ptolemy *Geography* II 3.7/10; *Antonine Itinerary* 464.3; *Ravenna Cosmography* V 31/434). A likely restoration of the fragmentary inscription recording the Risingham unit would give them a similar title, *exploratores Habitancenses*, derived from the attested name of the fort, Habitancum (cf. *RIB* 1225). These units are therefore likely to have been raised specifically for service at these forts, like those in Upper Germany. If they were raised by Oclatinius Adventus, then we can see them as part of the preparations for the expeditions of Septimius Severus and Caracalla from 208 to 211, possibly in reaction to the lack of intelligence which had crippled Severus' last expedition to the East in 197–9 (cf. Dio LXXV 9.4). Adventus may even have been chosen for Britain with this in mind, since he had started his career as a common soldier in the legions, had served as a *speculator* on the staff of a provincial governor, and had then become a *centurio frumentarius* and *princeps peregrinorum*, that is, chief of the imperial couriers who doubled as the internal security service (Dio LXXVIII 14.1; see pp. 136f.).[7]

In other provinces of the empire, a slightly different approach may have been taken to providing specialist scouting capabilities on the frontier, by selecting small numbers of *exploratores* to serve within pre-existing units. One example may be a scout and standard-bearer (*expl(orator) [e]t sig(nifer)*) of an otherwise unknown *ala Gaetula I* commemorated at Quiza in Mauretania Caesariensis (*CIL* VIII 21516), but the stone is difficult to interpret and it is far from certain whether this reading is correct and, if it is, where this unit may have been based. Much better evidence is provided by the duty rosters of *cohors XX Palmyrenorum*, partially preserved on papyri found at Dura Europos in Syria. One roster dating from AD 219 makes reference to 15 *exploratores* out of 721 men recorded (the estimated original total being 1,210) (*P.Dur.* 100 = Fink 1); the other roster of AD 222 refers to 9 *exploratores* out of 651 (estimated original total 1,040) (*P.Dur.* 101 = Fink 2). These men seem to have been on a posting of up to three years or more, rather than holding a rank, like the bodyguards (*singulares*) seconded to serve the provincial governor. This can be deduced from the fact that five of the *exploratores* on the first roster have returned to general duties on the second, and another of them has done so on a third roster of AD 222/8 (*P.Dur.* 102 = Fink 8), as has one from the second. More interesting, given that the first two rosters are approximately 60 per cent preserved, is the small number of men involved in this duty, and that five of the *exploratores* on the first and four on the second were infantry rather than cavalrymen. This suggests that these men do not represent standing patrols but were intended to operate individually, some of them on foot, a model once again best suited to keeping a watch on native communities in the immediate vicinity of the frontier.

The evidence for the use of scouts on the frontiers is, therefore, patchy and shows a variety of approaches. Nevertheless, it does demonstrate that by the late second century and early third century, specialist troops organized in small groups were being used by provincial governors to improve their intelligence-gathering. The initial impulse for this is most likely to have been the problems in the North in the 160s, and the evidence as we have it is certainly consistent with this, but the phenomenon undoubtedly became widespread over the next century.

## THE ROLE OF THE *BENEFICIARII CONSULARIS*[8]

Parallel with the improvements in the collection of intelligence effected through the establishment of outpost forts and the development of scouting forces, members of the governor's *officium* in several provinces began to be organized in a way which may have improved the efficiency of the intelligence cycle as a whole. The mechanism for this improvement was the network of posts (*stationes*) manned by *beneficiarii consularis* (see pp. 150ff.). It can be traced in several frontier provinces in the late second and third centuries AD thanks to the habit of these officers of leaving behind votive inscriptions at the end of their tour of duty at these posts.

The purpose of these *stationes* has never been absolutely clear, but Hirschfeld, associating them with the statement of the second-century Christian writer Tertullian that 'military outposts are distributed throughout all the provinces in order to track down brigands' (*Apologetic* 2.7), saw the *beneficiarii* essentially as a police force, whilst the observation that many of the *stationes* lay at road crossings led von Domaszewski at the beginning of this century to interpret them as intended for the control of traffic, and these are the theories which have generally held sway.[9] But it is far from clear that Tertullian was thinking about *beneficiarii* rather than troops in general, whilst von Domaszewski believed, incorrectly, that all the *stationes* were situated at crossroads and was himself mainly interested in reconstructing the empire's road network. In fact, the distribution pattern is considerably more diverse, and a great many of the *stationes* were situated at the sites of auxiliary forts and legionary fortresses where the functions suggested are much more likely to have been the responsibility of the garrison as a whole.

Nevertheless, police work (though not the pursuit of brigands) was certainly carried out by *beneficiarii* of the governor's office in Egypt alongside centurions, decurions and ordinary soldiers on outpost (*stationarii*). The papyri which record these make it clear that individual *beneficiarii* were assigned to each nome all along the Nile and that, like other officers, they received and investigated complaints about minor crimes. They also acted as liaisons with their master, the Prefect of Egypt, acting as his representatives and forwarding petitions to him.[10] *Beneficiarii consularis* may have performed a similar function on imperial estates in other provinces, since a number of inscriptions derive from these estates, especially in the mining districts of the Danube provinces (the mining of precious metals normally being an imperial monopoly).[11]

It has also been suggested by S.J. de Laet that they were intended to protect the customs posts of the *portorium*, which exacted duties on goods travelling between the various customs districts of the empire.[12] But despite the fact that our knowledge of the *stationes* both of the *portorium* and of the *beneficiarii consularis* is almost entirely derived from epigraphy, the overlap between the distributions of inscriptions is not particularly striking. The few certain coincidences are almost always at major administrative and military centres such as Cologne, Bonn, Mainz and Aquincum, or at major crossroads and centres of population such as Savaria and Siscia where both might be stationed for entirely separate reasons and where there was plenty of protection available without the need for a man to be detached from the governor's own staff.

In fact, whatever the merits of these various suggestions, no single explanation of the function of *beneficiarii consularis* and their *stationes* fits all the recorded cases, and it is probably a mistake to seek one. Nevertheless, close consideration of the dating and overall pattern of the *stationes* in various parts of the empire suggests a possible intelligence function for at least some of them.

First, only a very few *stationes* are attested before the latter part of the second century. The earliest inscription from the sacred precinct recently excavated at Sirmium (Sremska Mitrovica), which contained eighty-four altars dedicated by *beneficiarii consularis* of Lower Pannonia, dates possibly from the reign of Trajan;[13] we know of early *stationes* in Egypt from a letter on papyrus written by a *beneficiarius* of Rammius, Prefect of Egypt between AD 117 and 119, who 'had care of' (*epimelomenos*) the district (*nomos*) of Apollinopolis Heptakomias (*P.Brem.* 5.3–6, cf. *P.Brem.* 6), and from another papyrus of AD 139 which refers to a *beneficiarius* who was set 'over the localities' (*epi ton topon*) of the *nomos* of Arsinoites Heraklidou (*P.Amh.* II 77.27); a *beneficiarius* of Ummidius Quadratus, governor of Lower Moesia around AD 120, made a dedication at Charax (Aï-Todor) in the Crimea (*AE* 1965.152), and another of Statorius Secundus, governor of Cappadocia around 127/8, set up an altar at Cermik in the province (*IGRR* III 110 = *AE* 1968.504); in 150, a *beneficiarius* of Caesernius Statianus, governor of Upper Germany, is recorded at Pontailler-sur-Saône on the road linking Mainz with Lyon (*CIL* XIII 5609). No other *statio* in any province need be dated before the 160s. Thereafter large numbers of inscriptions are attested: in Upper Germany, beginning with an altar from Stockstadt dated to AD 166 (*CIL* XIII 6649); in Lower Germany, beginning with a dedication made at Remagen by a *beneficiarius* of Salvius Iulianus, a governor either in the 150s or around 180 (*CIL* XIII 7791); in Noricum, beginning with one made at Iuvavum (Salzburg) by a *beneficiarius* of the procurator Egnatius Priscus and dated before 171 (*CIL* III 11759); and in the Pannonias, beginning with a stone of 164 found at Mursa

(Osijek) (*AE* 1973.448). The earliest securely dated inscriptions from other frontier provinces are of AD 191, set up at Cataractonium (Catterick) in Britain (*ILS* 3929 = *RIB* 725); of AD 195, set up at Kačanik in Upper Moesia (*CIL* III 8184); and of AD 211–12, set up at Buciumi in Dacia (*CIL* III 7645). Although one needs to apply caution in view of the sporadic nature of epigraphic evidence and the fact that inscriptions become more common in general in the latter part of the second century, it is tempting to deduce from this pattern that the impulse for the spread of *stationes* in the German and Middle Danube provinces came from the Chattan and Marcomannic crises which threatened those provinces in the 160s and 170s, with other frontier provinces developing their own networks in imitation in the succeeding decades. If this is correct, then the purpose of the *stationes* will have been primarily military.

Second, a similarity in the distribution of *stationes* in some of the northern provinces may reflect a similarity of purpose. With only a handful of exceptions out of several hundred examples, the inscriptions which mark the *stationes* in Britain, Lower and Upper Germany, and Upper and Lower Pannonia are confined to the forts of the *limes* itself and to the major military roads linking the provincial capitals with the frontier and with Italy. Other provinces show a different pattern, and there the *stationes* may have served a different purpose.

In Britain, one group of *stationes* is situated on the Leeming Lane/Dere Street road running north from York, headquarters of legion *VI Victrix* and capital of Lower Britain, up to Hadrian's Wall and through into the eastern Lowlands of Scotland; they are attested at the forts of Catterick Bridge, Binchester, Lanchester and Risingham. Two more *stationes* can be traced at the forts of Greta Bridge and Brougham on the road branching off Leeming Lane across the Stainmore Pass towards Carlisle/Stanwix and through the Wall into the western Lowlands via Netherby. There was another at the fort of Vindolanda (Chesterholm) half-way along the Stanegate, the road which runs behind Hadrian's Wall, and one at the fort at Lancaster, exactly half-way between Carlisle and the legionary fortress at Chester. Only two *stationes* are attested in the civilian area of Britain, at Winchester and Dorchester-on-Thames.

In Lower Germany the majority of known *stationes* lay at the military installations on the *limes* road running along the left bank of the Rhine. They are unequivocally attested at the legionary fortress at Xanten (Vetera), at Moers-Asberg, at the legionary fortress at Bonn and at Remagen, although there are possible indications of others at forts all along the river. Two more *stationes* are attested at Billig and Marmagen on one of the main routes between the capital Cologne and the city of Trier in Gallia Belgica. Trier was the seat of the procurator of Gallia Belgica and the Two Germanies, who had responsibility for the supply of the German armies.

There were further *stationes* on the left bank of the Rhine in Upper Germany, even though the river did not mark the frontier for most of the history of the province. One lay on the south bank of the Vinxtbach, the stream which marked the boundary between Lower and Upper Germany and lay opposite the point on the right bank of the Rhine where the second- and third-century *limes* struck eastwards from the river. The other *stationes* on the Rhine lay to the south of the capital, Mainz, in the vicinity of Altrip, at Germersheim, at the legionary fortress of Strasbourg (Argentorate), perhaps at Ehl an der Ill, and at Solothurn, whence the road continued over the Alps into Italy via the Great St Bernard Pass. An early, isolated *statio* lay at Pontailler-sur-Saône, on the road between Mainz and Lyon (Lugdunum), the capital of Gallia Lugdunensis. Another two were situated on the road running north-east from Mainz up the Main valley into the Wetterau frontier region: these were situated at Frankfurt-Praunheim and at the fort of Friedberg. Yet another group lay on the road south-east from Mainz (followed by the line of the modern autobahn), which ran down to the Odenwald and then south along the line of the Domitianic *limes* and the valley of the Neckar, until it turned east along the Suebian Alb *limes* and finally south to the capital of Raetia at Augsburg (Augusta Vindelicum): these *stationes* were situated in the vicinities of Heidelberg and of Neckarburken or Wimpfen, and at Heilbronn-Böckingen, Walheim (?), Bad Cannstatt and Köngen. Possibly the most important group, however, lay on the frontier itself, on the section running south from the eastern end of the Wetterau *limes*, along a short stretch of the River Main, and then along the straight line of the Antonine outer *limes* which joined up with the Suebian Alb frontier of Raetia: *stationes* are attested at the forts of Grosskrotzenburg (where the Main takes over the frontier), Seligenstadt, Stockstadt, Obernburg am Main, Miltenberg (where the Antonine palisade takes over), Osterburken, Jagsthausen and Mainhardt.

In other provinces, this sort of pattern is less clear. Only one *statio* can be traced in Spain, in Tarraconensis at Segisamo (Sasamón) (*CIL* II 2915), the site of an important crossroads on the route linking the capital Tarraco (Tarragona) with the legionary fortress at León. Likewise in Raetia we know of only a single *statio*, in the interior of the province at Brigantium (Bregenz). In Noricum, there appear to be three *stationes* on the road through the south-east corner of the province linking Upper Pannonia with Italy, one at Celeia (Celje) and another on the border with Italy at Atrans (Troiane). Further *stationes* are attested on the border with Raetia, in the region of Boiodurum (Passau) on the *limes*, and at Bedaium on the road linking Augusta Vindelicum and Virunum, the respective capitals of the two provinces. With the exception of a *statio* at Iuvavum (Salzburg), all the others are in the iron-mining district around the capital Virunum.

In the two Pannonian provinces, *stationes* appear on the road linking Carnuntum (Deutsch-Altenburg), the capital of Upper Pannonia, with Emona (Ljubljana) in Italy, at Winden am See (?), Scarbantia (Sopron), Savaria (Szombathely), Poetovio (Ptuj), Celeia (Celje) and Atrans (Troiane), the last two lying in Noricum; at Savaria, the road branches to the south-east leading eventually to Viminacium (Kostolac), the capital of Upper Moesia, with *stationes* attested at Sopianae (Pécs), Mursa (Osijek), Sirmium (Sremska Mitrovica) in Lower Pannonia and at the legionary fortress of Singidunum (Belgrade) just across the border of Upper Moesia; at Poetovio, the first road branches again towards the province of Dalmatia, with *stationes* at Siscia (Sisak), Petrinja and Ad Fines (Topusko) on the border. No *stationes* are known on the *limes* itself in Upper Pannonia, but in Lower Pannonia a governor's groom (*strator consularis*) is recorded at the fort of Arrabona (Györ) (*CIL* III 4365) and *beneficiarii* at Pone Navata (Visegrád), Transaquincum (Rákospalota), Intercisa (Dunaujváros) and Teutoburgium (Dalj), and at Singidunum. Another five possible *stationes* are less easy to fit into a pattern, although one at least, at Tricciana (Ságvár), was situated on what was probably an imperial estate (*CIL* III 13364; cf. *CTh* XI 36.26, AD 379(?)).

Dalmatia, the only consular province in the empire without its own legion, had a governor's staff and hence *stationes* manned by *officiales* borrowed from the legions of the neighbouring Pannonian provinces, Lower Moesia and Dacia. *Stationes* are found on the continuation of the road from Upper Pannonia to the capital Salona (Split): beyond the border post at Topusko they appear at Josipdol, Velike Crkvine, Burnum (Kistanje) and Magnum (Balijina-Glavica). The same road carries on beyond Salona parallel to the coast, with *stationes* at Tilurium (Trilj), Novae (Runović), Ad Turres (Stolac), Narona (Vid) and Doclea (Podgorica). Apart from a *statio* of unknown significance at Raetinium (Golubić near Bihać) and another near the border with Upper Pannonia at Banja Luka, all the others in the province were situated in the lead- and silver-mining districts of Domavia and Municipium S. . . (Pljevlja).

The association with mining is still more striking in Upper Moesia and Dacia. *Stationes* in the former are concentrated around the lead and silver mines of Dardanica and Ulpiana, with others in the vicinity of the borders with Lower Pannonia at Singidunum (Belgrade), Dalmatia at Novopazarska Banja and Prizren, and with Macedonia at Scupi (Skoplje), at the city of Naissus (Niš) (where several of the governor's grooms are also attested), at Hammaeum (Prokuplje) and Combustica (Kladrop). A *speculator* is recorded as serving at the Danube fort and probable fleet base at Aquae (Prahovo) (*AE* 1959.330). In Dacia, *stationes* were to be found in the main gold-mining district at Micia (Vețel), Ampelum (Zlatna) and Alburnus Minor (Roșia Montănă). Otherwise, apart from individual *beneficiarii* recorded at the major city of Sarmizegethusa, all other *stationes* were located in the northern frontier district: at the legionary fortress of Potaissa, on the road running north-west from there to the frontier at Napoca (Cluj), and in the frontier zone itself at Buciumi, Porolissum (Moigrad), Samum (Căşei) and Crăciunel. The link with mining is also attested in the western portion of Lower Moesia in the form of *stationes* at Montana (Mihaiiovgrad) and Almus (Lom) in the local gold-mining district.[14]

Elsewhere, despite the large number of *beneficiarius* inscriptions from the province, their distribution shows no obvious pattern. Most are not even situated on major roads and only a couple, from Mihai Bravu and Noviodunum (Isaccea), were found in the frontier district. The *beneficiarii consularis* of Lower Moesia recorded at Chersonesos (Sebastopol) and Charax

(Aï-Todor) in the Crimea presumably administered Roman interests in this corn-producing region, as well as keeping a watch on the neighbouring Bosporan Kingdom and the Scythians beyond (see pp. 148f.).

Few *stationes* are attested in the eastern portion of the empire, but this must in part be because far fewer military inscriptions in general have been found there. This is demonstrated in particular by the situation in Egypt, where no *stationes* can certainly be identified from inscriptions but at least seven are known from papyrological evidence in administrative districts (*nomoi*) all along the Nile. The documents show that the *beneficiarii* performed administrative police functions alongside centurions, decurions and ordinary soldiers entitled *stationarii*; they also appear to have acted as district liaisons with the governor's headquarters at Alexandria.[15] Five *stationes* are recorded by inscriptions in Cappadocia, all of them in the hinterland with the exception of one at the city of Tyana, and none of them associated with major roads or frontier installations. In Arabia *stationes* are known only at the major cities of Philadelphia (Amman) and Adraha (Deraa); at the latter *beneficiarii* are recorded as being in charge of construction work on the fortifications of the city between AD 259 and 262.

Very few *stationes* are known in the African provinces west of Egypt. In Numidia, the best-attested is at Vazaivi (Aïn Zoui) to the east of the capital Lambaesis, where, uniquely, we find a *beneficiarius* accompanied by shorthand-writers (*exceptores*). Others are known in the El Kantara gap, to the immediate south of which two watch-towers (*burgi speculatorii*) were erected in the reigns of Commodus and Caracalla respectively (*CIL* VIII 2494–5), and at Cuicul (Djemila) near the border with Mauretania Caesariensis. Finally, in the latter province, *stationes* are found just across the border from Cuicul at Satafis (Aïn El-Kebira) and at the outpost fort of El Gahra on the road running along the southern slopes of the Ouled Naïl mountains.

The proper starting-point for the understanding of all these *stationes* is to recognize that in each province they represent the outposting of governor's staff officers sent out from the provincial capital. This was symbolized by the special spear-standards, known in the modern literature as 'Benefiziarierlanzen', which were carried by these officers. They are depicted on many of their inscriptions, and normally consisted of a lance, usually with a bulbous head pierced by round holes or slits and with streamers attached. The shaft is often shown as fitted with lifting handles like other military standards. A few actual examples have survived and been identified, most clearly one found in a sacred precinct full of *beneficiarius*-inscriptions excavated on the Upper German frontier at Osterburken (see Plate 10). In addition, miniature lance-badges, probably orig-inally attached to leather belts or straps, have been found on several military sites in Britain, Germany and Pannonia. Such lances are shown only on inscrip-tions concerned with men attached to provincial headquarters staffs, and more specifically with the three grades whom we know from epigraphic and literary evidence to have carried out duties away from the capitals, namely the *frumen-*

*tarii, beneficiarii consularis* and *speculatores*. There can be little doubt that these spears marked these men out as officials of the governor, operating on his behalf and independently of any other military commander in the province.[16]

Given that governors each had a number of different responsibilities and that these varied in detail according to the nature of their several provinces, it should come as no surprise that the distribution of their outposted *beneficiarii* follows no consistent plan. Nevertheless, the above summary shows that there are some recurring trends. The use of such officers as the representatives of the governor in mining districts (and perhaps on other imperial estates) in the Danube provinces is absolutely clear. Since the financial side of mining operations was in the hands of the emperor's procurators, the duties of the governor's *beneficiarii* here may have been analogous to the police functions exercised by the *beneficiarii* of the Prefect in Egypt. The presence of *stationes* at provincial boundaries is also striking. And in the northern provinces at least, there is a clear association of *beneficiarii* with the major military roads and with the frontier forts.

In the context of these roads, and bearing in mind the possibility that the development of the network in the Rhine and Middle Danube provinces may have been prompted by a military crisis, there is some evidence suggesting that the role of *beneficiarii consularis* in this area involved travel and that they may have been associated with the transmission of messages. The Historia Augusta tells us that when the young Hadrian was on his way to Cologne to inform Trajan that the emperor Nerva was dead and that he had therefore acceded to the imperial throne, the governor of Upper Germany, Servianus, deliberately delayed him at Mainz and sent on his own *beneficiarius* with the news so as to have the honour for himself. The officer was apparently travelling by cart or on horseback, but Hadrian supposedly pressed on with his journey on foot, overtook the man and arrived first (SHA *Hadrian* 2.6). This sort of anecdote in this particular source is unfortunately extremely unreliable, though it must at least have seemed plausible to its fourth-century writer that a member of the governor's staff should have been employed in this way. In the north, apart from the general distribution of *stationes* only along major roads, their preoccupations may be reflected in dedications to the horse goddess, Epona (*CIL* III 4776; 5176; 12679; 14959; *AE* 1933.76; cf. *CIL* XIII 5170), and to the crossroad goddesses, the Quadriviae, Triviae, Biviae (*CIL* XIII 6437; 11816; *AE* 1927.66; cf. *CIL* XIII 5621). Such dedications are not, however, out of the ordinary for the army as a whole. More striking is the restoration by a *beneficiarius consularis* of an altar at Catterick Bridge in Yorkshire which had been dedicated to 'the god who invented roads and paths' (*deo qui vias et semitas commentus est*) (*ILS* 3929 = *RIB* 725).

The importance of roads for the activities of *beneficiarii* is more certainly reflected in the fact that on the rare occasions when we find more than one such officer making a dedication and therefore, presumably, serving together at a *statio*, it is always either at a legionary base (*CIL* XIII 8621 (Vetera/Xanten,

Lower Germany); *AE* 1930.26 (Bonna/Bonn, Lower Germany); *CIL* XIII 11603 (Argentorate/Strasbourg, Upper Germany); *AE* 1964.261 (Singidunum/Belgrade, Upper Moesia); or at a major route node (*CIL* XIII 6628 (Obernburg am Main, Upper Germany); *AE* 1947.30 (Savaria/Szombathely, Upper Pannonia); *CIL* III 10842 (?); 10843; 15181[1] (Siscia/Sisak, Upper Pannonia); M. Mirković in V.A. Maxfield and M.J. Dobson (eds), *Roman Frontier Studies 1989* (Exeter, 1991), 252–4 (15 altars) (Sirmium/Sremska Mitrovica, Lower Pannonia)). Moreover, and most untypically for the Roman army, it would appear that a number of the available positions as *beneficiarius consularis* in each provincial headquarters may have been set aside for men who had previously served as *frumentarii*. An inscription from Lambaesis, the headquarters of the commander of legion *III Augusta*, who was also *de facto* governor of Numidia, lists the members of the legate's *officium* and includes thirty named *beneficiarii consularis*, followed by six *candidati*, that is, men awaiting promotion to *beneficiarius*, and five *ex frum(entariis)* who seem to fall into the same category (*AE* 1917/18.57; cf. *CIL* VIII 2586). The phrase *ex frumentario* ('former *frumentarius*') appears on a number of other inscriptions from around the empire, always describing a man who was currently serving as a *beneficiarius consularis* (*CIL* III 10057 = 3020 (Josipdol, Dalmatia); *Spomenik* 71 (1931), no. 209 (Titova Mitrovica, Upper Moesia); *CIL* VIII 17627 (Vazaivi/Aïn Zoui, Numidia); cf. II 4154 (Tarragona, Hispania Tarraconensis); the phrase also appears on some of the unpublished inscriptions from the *beneficiarius* precinct discovered at Sirmium/Sremska Mitrovica (Lower Pannonia) in 1988). This suggests that service amongst the *frumentarii*, who acted as couriers between the provincial capital and Rome (see pp. 136f.), was seen as a particularly appropriate qualification for *beneficiarii consularis*. Finally, attention may be drawn to the *beneficiarius consularis* who chose to include the *Genius catabul(i) co(n)s(ularis)*, 'the presiding deity of the governor's stables', among the gods to whom he dedicated an altar at Mainz, capital of Upper Germany, in AD 208 (*AE* 1976.502 = 1979.423). It can hardly be doubted that this man had had occasion to make use of these stables in the course of his career.

In view of this, it is possible that the network of *stationes* in the German and Middle Danube provinces, and later in Britain also, was set up alongside and beyond the *vehiculatio* to improve the speed and efficiency of communications. In these regions they are most clearly associated with the roads linking the provincial capitals with the frontiers, with each other and with Italy. As we noted earlier, messages were carried between forts and provincial capitals by riders detached from the unit in question, whilst governors made use of their own *singulares, speculatores* and especially *frumentarii*, travelling by the official posting system (*vehiculatio*), for communication with Rome (p. 153). We may confidently assume that such *officiales* were also used to bear messages to the frontier when riders from the forts were unavailable, as implied by the Historia Augusta's anecdote about Hadrian. One purpose of the *beneficiarius* posts could have been to ensure the provision of mounts and carts and the efficient operation of the system on the key routes.

The *beneficiarii* stationed on the frontiers themselves are potentially even more significant. They were in an ideal position actively to listen for and pick up local gossip and other information coming with arrivals from across the frontiers (cf. pp. 26ff.), as well as to monitor and ensure the transmission of anything of significance which came through local military contacts. Here, we may note in particular the presence of *beneficiarii* both at Divitia (Deutz), opposite Cologne (*CIL* XIII 8494), and at Transaquincum (Rákospalota) opposite Aquincum (Budapest) (*CIL* III 3617); the officer recorded at the latter made a dedication *Genio commercii*, 'to the presiding deity of trade'. Also of interest is the former *beneficiarius consularis* who was appointed commander of a trireme (*trierarcha*) at Brigetio (*CIL* III 4319), opposite which the fort of Celamantia (Iža-Leányvár) was established on the northern bank of the Danube in the reign of Marcus Aurelius. Furthermore, *exploratores* are known to have been stationed in the vicinity of all three of these places, at Divitia, Aquincum and Brigetio. *Beneficiarii consularis* and *exploratores* also coincide at Habitancum (Risingham) in Britain, and at Zugmantel and Feldberg (where miniature lance-badges have been found) Stockstadt/Obernburg and Miltenberg in Upper Germany.

The advantage to the governor of having his own men outposted on the frontiers would lie in their experience of the operation and requirements of provincial headquarters, including the sorts of intelligence which were of value. They could both seek information on their own account and liaise with the local unit commanders, including those in charge of *exploratores*. An additional benefit accrued on the return of such men from their outposting. The inscriptions which are the evidence for the *stationes* were apparently set up in the main to mark the end of a tour of duty, as is sometimes made explicit by phrases such as *emerita, exacta* or *expleta statione*, or *expleto tempore* (*CIL* VIII 17626 = 10718; 17628 = 10717; 17634 = 10723; XIII 11603; *AE* 1974.446).

*Beneficiarii consularis*, who were mostly seasoned legionaries perhaps with twenty or more years' service behind them and at the pinnacle of their careers, could expect to serve more than one such tour at an outpost once a network had been developed. The man stationed at Risingham in Lower Britain refers to its being his 'first posting at Habitancum' (*Habitanci prima sta(tione)*) (*RIB* 1225), and stones from the vicinity of Bonn in Lower Germany (*CIL* XIII 11989), Siscia (Sisak) in Upper Pannonia (*CIL* III 3949) and Samum (Cǎşei) in Dacia (*AE* 1957.329) refer to a second tour (*iterata statione*). Both terms appear on inscriptions found in the *beneficiarius*-enclosure recently excavated at Sirmium (Sremska Mitrovica) in Lower Pannonia (M. Mirković in V.A. Maxfield and M.J. Dobson (eds), *Roman Frontier Studies 1989* (Exeter, 1991), 253). An inscription from Osterburken in Upper Germany even records a third tour (*tertia statio*) (*BRGK* 58 (1977), Nr. 44). A number of individuals have left behind inscriptions at more than one outpost, such as L. Flavius Paternus who served both at Stockstadt (*CIL* XIII 6634) and at Jagsthausen (*CIL* XIII 6556 = 11762), and C. Paulinius Iustus who served at Friedberg (*CIL* XIII 7399; 7400) and at Osterburken (*AE* 1985.685), all in Upper Germany.

We have some evidence for the length of such tours. A large number of the inscriptions bear precise dates, which are normally taken to be those of the end of the tour in question. In Upper Germany the dates are mostly (though not invariably) either the Ides (13th) of January or the Ides (15th) of July, which suggests that those were the usual change-over days for that province. Moreover, the *beneficiarius*-precinct at Osterburken contained one altar dedicated on 15 July 212 and another on 13 January 213. It is therefore a reasonable assumption that the normal tour in that province was of six months' duration, beginning and ending on the days indicated. The evidence for other provinces is less good, and they may have had less regular tour-periods. Noricum, however, may have used the Ides (15th) of May as a change-over date (*CIL* III 5575; 5580 (= *ILS* 4853); 5690; 14361). Some stones from the *beneficiarius*-precinct at Sirmium (Sremska Mitrovica) in Lower Pannonia which bear two names indicate the presence of individual officers over up to four years, but in association with others changed annually or, in some cases, possibly after six months.[17] These men presumably returned to provincial headquarters after their tour of duty; if they did not, we should expect to find inscriptions recording individuals with more than a third posting. We can therefore say that at any one time the governors of Lower Britain, and of the Germanies, and perhaps of other provinces on the northern frontiers, would probably have had access to at least one experienced officer who had recently served at any of the frontier forts about which he might require information. Such men would have been well acquainted with local topography, with the nature of the local native population either side of the frontier, with any recent indications of potential trouble, and also with the current state of efficiency of the local unit and the competence of its officers and commander.

In the final analysis, the state of the evidence for the *stationes* of the *beneficiarii consularis* does not allow us to say anything for certain about their purpose, except perhaps that it varied from province to province and that it reflected the needs of the governor. Even so, there is a prima-facie case for supposing that the network developed in the Germanies and perhaps in the Pannonias in the wake of the Marcomannic Wars, and slightly later in northern Britain, and perhaps some of the individual *stationes* in other of the frontier provinces, may have been connected with the transmission of information, especially between the provincial capitals and the frontier zone. This implies involvement with the collection of military intelligence on the frontier itself, and possibly with its collation once the outposted men had returned to headquarters. The *beneficiarii* could indeed have served this last purpose even if their outposting to the frontiers was for entirely other reasons. At any rate, from the late second century and until at least the latter half of the third, there was in place on the northern frontiers a structure which, together with the placing of the new *exploratores* units, would have allowed a greater sensitivity to cross-frontier military information than had been possible hitherto.

## EMPERORS ON THE FRONTIERS

Finally, alongside the stationing of *exploratores* and *beneficiarii consularis* in the frontier zones, another development of the 160s had a still more important effect on the handling of military intelligence. This was the regular appearance of the emperors themselves on campaign and in areas of military crisis. Emperors had, of course, taken the field against foreign enemies before – Augustus, Caligula, Claudius, Domitian, Trajan – mostly in order to establish a military reputation and consolidate their regimes (see pp. 134f.). Hadrian withdrew from most of Trajan's eastern conquests, and his successor Antoninus Pius remained in Italy throughout his reign. From the time of Marcus, however, imperial campaigns became a norm. This was no longer a matter of the pursuit of military glory, but was dictated by a new level of threat to the empire, which had in truth had relatively little to fear from her neighbours in the previous two centuries.

From the 160s the empire was plagued by simultaneous crises on the Rhine, Danube and Euphrates. The response, directed from the frontier itself, was a much more centralized approach to the defence of the area than had obtained hitherto. In 162, Marcus sent his friend Aufidius Victorinus to deal with the attack by the Chatti (SHA *Marcus* 8.8; cf. W. Eck, *Epigraphische Studien* 14 (Köln, Bonn, 1985), 67–9), and an inscription from Cologne, the capital of Lower Germany, may indicate the presence there of the Praetorian Prefect T. Flavius Constans a few years later, although this has been doubted (*CIL* XIII 12057 = *ILS* 9000). A stronger reaction was required in the East. As a result of a Parthian invasion of Armenia, it was decided that Marcus Aurelius' co-emperor L. Verus should lead an eastern expedition between 162 and 166. Soon after Verus' return, the threat on the Danube, which had hitherto been contained by the diplomatic moves of the frontier governors (SHA *Marcus* 12.13), materialized in the form of an attack by the Marcomanni and Quadi on Pannonia. The response here was all the more vigorous since these tribes presented the first serious threat to the core of the empire since the defeat of the Cimbri in 101 BC, reflected most dramatically in the invasion of Italy which resulted in the sack of Opitergium (Oderzo) and the siege of Aquileia at the head of the Adriatic in AD 170 (Lucian *Alexander* 48; Ammianus XXIX 6.1). Marcus, alongside Verus, was forced to campaign on the Danube frontier from 167 until the latter's death in 169, and by himself thereafter up to 175 and again from 178 until his own death at Sirmium in Pannonia in 180. Throughout this period the emperors appear to have been based mainly at Carnuntum (Deutsch-Altenburg), capital of Upper Pannonia (*AE* 1982.777–8; Marcus Aurelius *Meditations* III heading; SHA *Marcus* 14.6; *Verus* 9.7–8; Eutropius VIII 13.1), or at Sirmium (Sremska Mitrovica) in Lower Pannonia (Philostratus *Lives of the Sophists* II 1/560; Tertullian *Apologetic* 25.5).

It is clear that from the beginning operations were envisaged over a broad front. The emperors themselves took control of the *limes* facing the Marcomanni and Sarmatians, and already in about 166, two new legions, *II Pia* and *III*

*Concors* (both of them later renamed *Italica*), were being raised for service on the Danube (*CIL* VI 1377 = *ILS* 1098; *AE* 1956.123; cf. *CIL* III 1980, with p. 1030 = *ILS* 2287; *AE* 1920.45). These legions are in themselves evidence that a long term strategy had been developed even before the outbreak of hostilities, since new legions were usually raised in anticipation of an extension of the empire, and the Historia Augusta specifically states that Marcus intended to create the new provinces of Marcomannia and Sarmatia (*Marcus* 24.5; 27.10; cf. Dio LXXI 33.4²). In 168, as a long-stop, a new military zone was set up to the north-east of the Julian Alps protecting Italy, the so-called *praetentura Italiae et Alpium*, under the command of the consular Q. Antistius Adventus (*ILS* 8977; cf. SHA *Marcus* 14.6). In the following year, the command of the three Dacian provinces lying to the west of the Great Hungarian Plain was unified under a single governor, Claudius Fronto, and in 170 he also took command of Upper Moesia to the south (*CIL* III 1457 = *ILS* 1097; *CIL* VI 1377 (cf. 31640) = *ILS* 1098).

In order for Marcus and Verus to co-ordinate these commands and to maintain contact with the empire as a whole, it was essential that communications should be as speedy and efficient as possible. It has already been suggested that the network of *beneficiarii consularis* outposted in the German and Danube provinces from the 160s may have been developed to improve local communications, and this may have been the result of a central directive. In 170, while Aquileia was under siege, a *centurio frumentarius* was sent out from the Castra Peregrina in Rome with detachments of the two new legions *II* and *III Italica* to build walls for the Adriatic port and capital of the province of Dalmatia, Salona. This was presumably to protect the sea-borne route between Italy and that province (*CIL* III 1980, with p. 1030 = *ILS* 2287; cf. *CIL* III 6374 = 8655). Two years later Marcus, having issued an edict forbidding cities to construct their own fortifications without imperial permission (*Digest* L 10.6), nevertheless ordered the construction of walls for the city of Philippopolis (Plovdiv) in Thrace (*CIL* III 6121 = 7409 = *ILS* 5337), and Marcus and Commodus did the same for Serdica (Sofia) during their joint reign between 176 and 180 (*IGBulg.* IV 1902). Both cities lay on the principal route linking the eastern and western portions of the empire, whilst Philippopolis was situated at the southern end of the main road running south from Dacia via Oescus. The stables of the posting system along the latter were rebuilt at imperial expense towards the end of Marcus' reign.[18] Similarly, in 202, according to an inscription from Pizos, which lies between Philippopolis and Adrianople (Edirne), the emperors Severus and Caracalla were 'prompted by concern for the road-stations' (*tei proopsei ton stathmon hesthentes*) to support them by ordering the local establishment of trading-settlements (*enporia*) such as Pizos (*IGRR* I 766).

Marcus and Verus could not co-ordinate defence over such a broad area without assistance. In formulating and effecting their strategy, they were aided and advised by a host of experienced military men who now came to the fore. When L. Verus went to the East in 162, he was accompanied by one of the Praetorian Prefects, Furius Victorinus (*CIL* V 648* = VI 1937* = XIV 440*; *IGRR* III 1103 = *ILS* 8846), a former governor of Syria, Pontius Laelianus (*CIL*

VI 1497 + 1549 = *ILS* 1094 + 1100; Fronto *Letters to the Emperor Verus* II 1.19), and the governor of Lower Moesia, M. Iallius Bassus (*CIL* III 6169; XII 2718 + 2719 = *AE* 1961.171). Statius Priscus, suddenly transferred from Britain, was put in charge of the province of Cappadocia (*CIL* VI 1523 = *ILS* 1092; Dio LXXI 3.1[1]; SHA *Marcus* 9.1; *Verus* 7.1), and in 164 Sohaemus, a Roman senator descended from the Arsacid kings of Parthia, was installed as king of Armenia (*BMC* IV, pp. 420ff. nos. 261ff.; Fronto *Letters to the Emperor Verus* II 1.16; Dio LXXI 3.1[1]). Marcus was likewise assisted by a military *consilium* in organizing the defence of the Danube during his campaigns in the North from 168 to 175 and 177 to 180. In 169, for instance, it appears to have included the two Praetorian Prefects, M. Bassaeus Rufus (*CIL* VI 1599 + 31828 = *ILS* 1326; *CIL* IX 2438; Dio LXXI 5.2–3) and M. Macrinius Vindex (*CIL* IX 2438; Dio LXXI 3.5), a recent governor of Lower Pannonia (and Marcus' son-in-law), Claudius Pompeianus (Dio LXXI 3.2; SHA *Pertinax* 2.4; *Caracalla* 3.8), and two former governors of Upper Pannonia, Pontius Laelianus again (*CIL* VI 1497+1549 = *ILS* 1094+1100) and Dasumnius Tullius Tuscus (*CIL* III 4117; XI 3365 = *ILS* 1081).

It is in this context also that we must place the appointment for the first time of military men as imperial secretaries *ab epistulis*. As indicated in chapter 5, the campaign in the East, the breakthrough of the German frontier in 162 and the simultaneous threat of war on the Danube with the Marcomanni appear to have prompted Marcus to replace the rather literary *ab epistulis* Sex. Caecilius Crescens Volusianus with the much more soldierly T. Varius Clemens and subsequently to split this post into a Greek and a Latin branch. The first two holders of the Latin branch, who would have dealt with all official letters, including correspondence with the army commanders, were C. Calvisius Statianus and P. Taruttienus Paternus, who rose to be Prefect of Egypt and Prefect of the Praetorian Guard respectively (*CIL* III 12048; cf. 13573; V 3336 = *ILS* 1453; Dio LXXI 12.3; 28.3–4; 33.3).

The personal direction of the war by Marcus and his *consilium* is also reflected in the choice of officers to carry out special missions to deal with the military crisis. These were often equestrians of proven ability who will have been brought to his attention by his advisers, including the *ab epistulis* whose task it was to issue letters of appointment for junior officers (see p. 138). One such was M. Valerius Maximianus, whose astonishing career as a soldier took him from the ranks of the local nobility of Poetovio (Ptuj) in Upper Pannonia to the consulship and the *de facto* governorship of Numidia. In 170 or 171 he was sent with detachments of men from the Italian and British fleets to bring supplies down the Danube for Marcus' army, and was at the same time given select African and Moorish cavalry with which to scout along the Pannonian bank (*ad curam explorationis Pannoniae*), which must have been infested with invaders. Maximianus was subsequently adlected into the Senate and, after a number of legionary commands, was in 179/80 placed 'in charge of the legionary vexillations wintering at Leugaricio' (*AE* 1956.124). This place can almost certainly be identified from an inscription recording the presence of Maximianus and 855 troops which was cut into a rock high above the River Váh some 130 km north of Brigetio (*CIL* III 13439; cf. Dio LXXI 20.1). At the same time as Maximianus was scouting along the Danube, Marcus' son-in-law Pompeianus was given overall charge of driving the Marcomanni and Quadi out of Italy and Pannonia, and took as his assistant an equestrian procurator commanding troop detachments by the name of P. Helvius Pertinax; he too was later adlected into the Senate and eventually, for a few months in 193, became emperor (Dio LXXI 3.2; SHA *Pertinax* 2.4–5). Similarly, the procurator Vehilius Gratus Iulianus was put in command of troop detachments and assigned to removing the Costoboci from Macedonia and Achaea (*ILS* 1327).

The emperor's reliance upon advisers and assistants who had military competence in effect created, at least for the duration of hostilities, the equivalent of an imperial general staff, and by the same token introduced an additional intelligence mechanism to the threatened frontiers. Incoming reports had to be collated and interpreted, and the emperor's own instructions formulated and drafted by these men; we are told that Marcus in particular never took any action without consulting his advisers (SHA *Marcus* 22.3–4). Moreover, all the intelligence material available to the individual governors in their *officia* would of course be readily available to the emperor and his advisers also. We can see in this the elements of a geographically extensive intelligence cycle centred around the emperor, now based in or near to the war zone, which would be additional to and would subsume those centred on the provincial governors. This development could not prevent the disasters of 170 when Marcus' own offensive on the Middle Danube appears to have met with defeat (Lucian *Alexander* 48), at the same time as the Marcomanni and Quadi broke through the Julian Alps into Italy, when they destroyed Opitergium and besieged Aquileia (Ammianus XXIX 6.1), whilst the Costoboci killed Claudius Fronto, overall governor of the Three Dacias and Upper Moesia, before invading Greece, destroying Eleusis and threatening Athens (*CIL* VI 1377 = *ILS* 1098; Aelius Aristides *Oration XXII* 34.5; Pausanias *Guide to Greece* X 34.5). It will, however, have helped Marcus to reorganize his armies, close the gaps and drive out the invaders.

Marcus' advisers will also have helped him to handle the many envoys and embassies from hostile tribes which came to negotiate with him. Marcus' active role in the campaigning meant that he was often acquainted with the territories and peoples concerned at first hand: the second book of his philosphical work, the *Meditations*, which was composed in 172, bears the heading 'written amongst the Quadi on the Granua', that is on the Hron, a tributary of the Danube which runs southwards through the country of the Cotini and the Quadi just to the west of the Great Hungarian Plain. An anecdote even shows him personally interrogating a prisoner, a young boy so frozen by the cold that he refused to give any information until he was provided with a coat (Dio LXXI 5.1). Such personal experience, together with the accumulated knowledge of his staff, will have made his negotiations particularly effective. Several of the settlements made by him show an understanding of the geographical and political relationships between his enemies over a wide area.

It was, moreover, possible for Marcus as emperor to take a global view and consider the security of the Danube provinces as a whole, and it is clear that he often attempted to play one tribe off against another. For instance, while based at Carnuntum in 171 he provided a subsidy to one tribe to check some of their neighbours who had attacked Dacia, and did the same for the Astingi, who had themselves invaded Dacia, to persuade them to make war on Rome's enemies (Dio LXXI 11.1; 12.1–2; cf. 11.6). Meanwhile, on his own stretch of frontier, he made peace with the Quadi with the hope of detaching them from their Marcomannic allies. They were forbidden to receive Iazyges or Marcomanni into their territory or even allow them to pass through. Moreover, despite their treaty and the indemnities they had been forced to hand over, they themselves were forbidden to attend markets in the Roman provinces for fear that Iazygan or Marcomannic spies would be able to pose as Quadi and obtain military information and supplies (Dio LXXI 11.2–3). Another tribe which Marcus attempted to use against the Marcomanni was the Cotini. This time negotiations were conducted not by Marcus himself but by his *ab epistulis Latinis*, Taruttienus Paternus, who apparently travelled into their territory and was mistreated for his trouble (Dio LXXI 12.3). There are signs that this policy of 'divide and rule' had the desired effect and caused dissension both between the tribes and within them. In 174, Marcus received embassies from both the Marcomanni and the Iazyges, represented by their second king, Banadaspus, who was subsequently imprisoned by his own people for his approach (Dio LXXI 15–16.1).

Marcus was also able to make arrangements which an ordinary governor would probably have felt himself unauthorized to make. The decision to settle some of the barbarians taken into the empire at this time in Italy, at Ravenna, can only have been taken by the emperor; it was also one which Marcus came to regret when these people revolted and seized the city (Dio LXXI 11.5). Similarly, it is unlikely that any governor would have been bold enough to create on his own initiative exclusion zones across the Danube. As noted in the last chapter (p. 180), these had first been imposed on the Marcomanni and subsequently the Quadi after their defeat in 172. The zone was initially 15 km wide, but was reduced to half that distance (38 stades) as a result of the embassy of 174, when market days and places were also specified (Dio LXXI 15). Marcus imposed a 15 km zone and similar terms upon Zanticus, the senior king of the Iazyges, after his defeat in 175, and demanded the surrender of 8,000 cavalry in addition for service in the Roman army; 5,500 of them were immediately shipped off to Britain, which must have been a crippling blow to the tribe (Dio LXXI 16.1–2). The terms were later eased, although markets continued to be restricted and the Iazyges were banned from using boats of their own or landing on the islands of the Danube. They were, however, allowed to cross Dacia with the permission of the governor in order to maintain contact with their cousins the Roxolani (Dio LXXI 18–19). The outbreak of renewed hostilities in the last three years of Marcus' reign resulted in the garrisoning of Marcomannic and Quadic territory, where according to Dio some 20,000 men were stationed in forts (*phrouria*) permanent enough to have bath-houses (LXXI 20.1). One of these may have been at Celamantia (Iža-Leányvár) opposite Brigetio, which has already been mentioned (p. 185), another the as yet untraced camp of Maximianus at Leugaricio in the vicinity of the inscription above the River Váh, and yet another at Mušov, on the River Thaya, a tributary of the Morava, about 130 km north of Carnuntum.[19] After Marcus' death in 180, his son and successor Commodus abandoned all Roman outposts in this area beyond a 7.5 km exclusion zone, although assemblies were limited to specific places once a month under supervision of a Roman centurion (Dio LXXII 2); a similar exclusion zone on the borders of Dacia was imposed on the Buri and other tribes (Dio LXXII 3.2). The restriction on assemblies at least allowed local governors to maintain some sort of surveillance in barbarian territory, although it must have been extremely uncomfortable for the centurions assigned to the task, and neither this arrangement nor the exclusion zone are likely to have been maintained for very long.

Douglas Lee, in a recent work on information-gathering in the Late Empire, argues that there was a major difference in the quantity and quality of the intelligence which could be obtained on the eastern and the northern frontiers. Basing his investigation mainly on Ammianus and Procopius, he suggests that, whilst the eastern frontier was highly permeable to information travelling in both directions with hostages, scholars, pilgrims and merchants, there was far less traffic of any kind in the North. Furthermore, the political centralization of the Persian Empire meant that it was easy for both sides to pick up any hostile intentions by the other well ahead of their translation into action, whereas in the North the Roman Empire was dealing with numerous tribes and kings whose relatively small-scale and localized threats might be much more quickly formulated and executed.[20] There is undoubtedly much truth in these observations for the earlier as for the later period. But we have argued that the quality of Roman intelligence-gathering structures, centred on the provincial governors, must not be underestimated, and that these structures were quite sophisticated by the later second century. The long-term presence of the emperors on a particular frontier lifted Roman intelligence-gathering on to a still higher plane, and the control of cross-frontier relations which Marcus and Verus were able to exercise in the North, albeit at considerable personal cost, must have gone a long way towards offsetting the problems which Lee identifies for this sector of the empire.

The experience of Marcus and Verus was soon to become the norm for Roman emperors. Although it was not yet clear to the Romans, by a process which is still not fully understood, movements of peoples such as the Goths from Scandinavia and eastern Russia, and yet others such as the Huns from still further afield, were starting to affect the tribes settled on Rome's northern frontiers. Caught between these newcomers and the resistance of the empire, they began to form larger coalitions of tribes, such as the Alamanni ('All the People') who first appear in our sources in the early third century. A similar process can be traced in Scotland, partly under pressure of migration from Ireland, which resulted in the formation of the Picts ('The Painted People') by the early fourth century. In Parthia, the death of the Arsacid, Artabanus V, in 224 and the elevation of the first of the Sassanians, the Persian Ardashir, two years later brought with it an aggressive, new stance towards the Roman Empire which culminated in the victories of Sapor I and the capture of the Roman emperor Valerian in 260.

The multiple pressures over several fronts brought with them political as well as military problems. An emperor could not be present in more than one war zone at a time, and a successful defence of a distant frontier by a subordinate might lead to his elevation as a rival emperor. Conversely, an emperor's military failure was likely to bring assassination at the hands of his own troops. Political insecurity was a fact of life in the third century. Septimius Severus came to the throne with the backing of the Danube legions in 193, after the assassination of Marcus' son Commodus and his successors Pertinax and then Didius Iulianus, all within three months. He then spent the next four years eliminating his rivals Clodius Albinus, governor of Britain, and Pescennius Niger, governor of Syria. His political problems in part prompted the subsequent imperial expeditions in those areas, but they also led to two developments of military significance.

One was the reorganization of the three-legion province of Syria, which was by 194 divided into the two-legion province of Syria Coele and the single-legion province of Syria Phoenice (*AE* 1930.141; cf. Dio LV 23.2–3; 24.3). Severus' bid for the throne had been founded upon his own control of three legions as governor of Upper Pannonia, and he was all too well aware of the dangers inherent in such a concentration of armed forces. Epigraphic evidence reveals that his son Caracalla completed the process, dividing the three-legion province of Britain probably in 213 (*contra* Herodian III 8.2), and transferring the legionary fortress of Brigetio from Upper to Lower Pannonia, probably in 214. These changes reduced the political risk but by the same token complicated the co-ordination of any response to an external threat. In other words, they intensified still further the pressure for the emperors to take personal command on these sectors whenever they came under attack.

The other development was more important and marks a turning-point in the history of the empire. Severus' two predecessors had been elevated and then deserted in turn by the Praetorian Guard. These men, recruited according to Dio (confirmed by inscriptions) from Italy, Spain, Macedonia and Noricum (LXXIV 2.4), could no longer be trusted. Having tricked them into surrendering Rome without a fight in 193, Severus disbanded the existing cohorts and replaced them with larger units drawn from his own Danubian legionaries (Dio LXXIV 1.1–2; 2.4–6; Herodian II 13.1–12; SHA *Severus* 6.11). The Guard's ten cohorts may also now have been doubled in strength to an establishment of 1,500 men each.[21] In addition, Severus eventually brought to Rome one of the new legions he had raised for his eastern campaign of 197–9, the *II Parthica*, which inscriptions show to have been housed in its own camp at Albanum twenty kilometres south of the capital. This both boosted the garrison of Rome and gave him a large and loyal striking force of more than 20,000 men with which to meet any threat from his rivals. It also added a further stimulus to the appearance of emperors on the frontiers since this force represented the empire's largest military reserve.

In the 260s, the reserve was further built up by Gallienus in the aftermath of the capture of his father Valerian and the temporary loss of the western portion of the empire to the breakaway Gallic Empire of M. Cassianius Postumus. To supplement the powerful infantry force represented by the Praetorians and the Alban legion, Gallienus created an élite cavalry striking force consisting of units formed from the cream of the provincial cavalry (Zosimus I 40.1–2; 43.2; 52.3–4; Cedrenus I, p. 454 Bekker). They gave the reserve true mobility and paved the way for the central field armies later developed by Constantine and his successors.

On campaign, the imperial field army would have its own scouts and collect its own intelligence to supplement that provided by the provincial governors and their armies. This would have been true even when it was based around the Praetorian Guard and the old imperial horse guard, the *equites singulares Augusti* formed by Trajan, but the availability of a mass of élite cavalry from the later third century will undoubtedly have boosted the potential for long-range reconnaissance. The career inscription in Greek of the general Traianus Mucianus found at Augusta Traiana in Thrace reveals that he commanded *exploratores* in an imperial field army in Mesopotamia in about AD 270 (*IGBulg.* III 2, 1570). Gallienus, moreover, appears to have created for himself something like a junior staff, the *protectores divini lateris* (literally 'imperial body guards'), to supplement the senior officers of his *consilium*. There may indeed have been little distinction between the two groups to begin with, since under Gallienus all senior army commands had finally passed from senators to equestrian officers and the title of *protector* was initially conferred on equestrian legionary commanders and tribunes. By about 290, the title was given to officers of lower rank, former centurions and the like, who were being marked out for promotion.[22] In both cases, the effect will have been to give the emperor a wider pool of military expertise on which to draw. Overall, the reforms of Gallienus can only have improved the intelligence process still further.

The three-quarters of a century following the death of Severus in 211 was a time of military crisis, with repeated invasions and breakthroughs of the frontiers by the Alamanni and later the Goths in the North and the revitalized Persian Empire in the East. It also saw a long line of emperors – some twenty-seven legitimate and a similar number of usurpers – raised to the purple only to succumb to assassination or revolt a few years or even months later. Despite the chaos and the loss of significant portions of frontier territory on the Rhine and in the East, the empire as a whole held, due in great measure to the energy of these same short-lived emperors. As we have seen, the presence of the emperor on the frontier where the threat was greatest had considerable impact on the general efficiency of operations, but also marks an important advance in the handling of intelligence. First of all, it allowed the emperor and his advisers to see the military situation immediately and for themselves, and to use their field armies, made more powerful under Severus and especially under Gallienus, to gain their own tactical intelligence. Second, it allowed them direct access to the intelligence material already available to the frontier governors from unit commanders, the *exploratores* at the forts and the networks of *beneficiarii*, and enabled them to bring their own considerable expertise to bear. Third, it allowed the emperor to take decisive action which could be implemented straight away, and also to conduct negotiations in person and make definitive settlements with the enemy. And finally and most importantly, it allowed the emperor to co-ordinate his response over a wide front in a way in which provincial governors, whose commands had to be limited for political reasons, could not. The overall effect was to superimpose, albeit temporarily, a much larger and more efficient intelligence cycle on the pre-existing cycles which had been set up in the provinces. In this way, the crisis of the late second and third centuries at last brought about the bridging of the gap between the view from Rome and the watch on the frontier.

# 9

# HIERARCHIES OF
# INTELLIGENCE
## The fourth century

The chaos of the third century was a direct product of the pressure on the frontiers, pressure which gave the opportunity for multiple usurpation. The political problem could only be resolved by a series of bold strokes which would reduce the chances of a successful challenge to the legitimate authority. The emperor Diocletian, who came to the throne in 284, recognized this, and appointed his fellow-Illyrian Maximian as Caesar (junior emperor) in 285, and as co-Augustus in 286. More significantly, by 293 he had arranged for the adoption of Galerius and Constantius Chlorus as Caesars in addition, thus creating the so-called Tetrarchy. This was forced on the two Augusti by a period of frantic campaigning on virtually every frontier of the empire.

Diocletian also initiated a programme of rebuilding the frontiers, dilapidated by half a century of raiding and invasion from the outside; the internal problems created by usurpation and civil war had left the army weakened and inefficient. It was now reformed and increased in size, though the scale of the increase is a matter of debate. We can estimate the size of the third-century army at roughly 350,000 men. A hostile contemporary, Lactantius, asserts that Diocletian quadrupled this figure (*On the Deaths of the Persecutors* 7.2–3), which is patent nonsense. The sixth-century historian Agathias offers 645,000, still far too high (V 13), but the figure of 435,266 quoted by his contemporary, John the Lydian, despite its spurious precision, is within the bounds of credibility for a paper figure (*Months* I 27; cf. Zosimus II 15). This army was essentially built up to garrison the refurbished frontiers, but Diocletian of course retained a core of troops who formed a mobile strategic reserve just as his predecessors had done.

In 305 Diocletian and Maximian retired into private life, a unique achievement. The empire was left to their Caesars, now promoted Augusti, who in their turn adopted as Caesars Maximinus Daza and Severus. The arrangements did not last. By 311 Constantius Chlorus' son Constantine was vying for control of the Western Empire along with Maximian's son Maxentius, while Galerius' adopted son Licinius held the East. By 324 Constantine ruled the whole empire as sole Augustus, with his sons Crispus, Constantine II and Constantius II as Caesars. Constantine and his sons were involved in numbers of campaigns, on the Rhine against the Alamanni, on the Danube against the Goths, and significant preparations for a major war against Persia were in train by the time of Constantine's death in 337.

Having survived eighteen years of civil wars, Constantine built up his own strategic reserve into a major field army, as much to safeguard his own position as to prosecute the wars against the barbarian. This process could only be undertaken by reducing the frontier garrisons, as is specifically and critically noted by the fifth-century historian Zosimus (II 34); it set the pattern for future developments that will be discussed later in this chapter.

## CENTRALIZED BUREAUCRACY: THE MASTER OF THE OFFICES AND INTERNAL SECURITY

One result of the military reorganization of the empire brought about by Diocletian and Constantine was a final separation of civil and military command on the one hand, and the beginnings of an increasingly centralized administration on the other. It is certain that during the fourth century the imperial bureaucracy surrounding the emperor or emperors developed rapidly.

There continued to be an imperial secretary *ab epistulis*, although he soon took on the title *magister epistularum* ('Master of the Letters'). As we have seen, in time of crisis military men had sometimes been appointed *ab epistulis*, presumably in order to co-ordinate imperial intelligence, but for the most part these secretaries were scholarly or literary figures. The latter continued to monopolize the post as *magistri epistularum* (see *PLRE* I, s.v. Eugnomonius; Nymphidianus; Eutropius 2; Calliopius 3; and Minervius 2) and by the end of the fourth century their duties appear to have been entirely non-military, including the handling of delegations from the cities of the empire (*legationes civitatum*), referrals to the emperor (*consultationes*) and petitions (*preces*) (*Not. Dig. Or.* XIX 8–9; *Occ.* XVII 12).

Certainly, one of the earlier links of the *ab epistulis* with the military, the responsibility for the issuing of junior commissions (see p. 138), was transferred to the successor of the secretary *a memoria*, known as the *magister memoriae*. It involved the keeping of what was known as the 'lesser register' of appointments (*laterculum minus*) and although it continued to be kept up to date by the staff of the *magister memoriae*, its control subsequently passed to a new and more senior, but equally unmilitary, official first appointed by Constantine, the Quaestor of the Sacred Palace (*quaestor sacri palatii*). It is true that in the Western Empire it was successfully wrested from him before the early fifth century by the army commander-in-chief, the *magister militum praesentalis*, probably in fact by the formidable Count Stilicho who held the latter office under his father-in-law Honorius, but it is remarkable that this central register remained for so long in civilian rather than military hands (*Not. Dig. Or.* XXVIII; XXXI–XXXVIII; XL; *CTh* I 8.1, AD 415; 8.2 (= *CJ* I 30.1) and 3, AD 424).

*Figure 5* The Roman Empire in AD 314

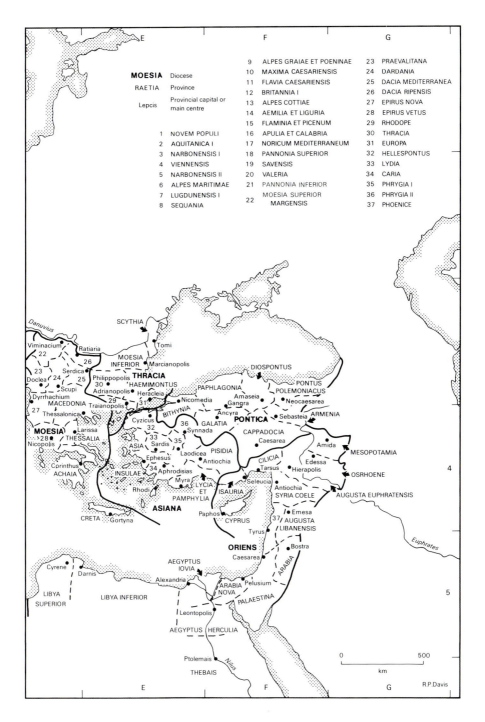

| | |
|---|---|
| **MOESIA** Diocese | |
| RAETIA Province | |
| Lepcis | Provincial capital or main centre |

| | | | |
|---|---|---|---|
| 1 | NOVEM POPULI | 23 | PRAEVALITANA |
| 2 | AQUITANICA I | 24 | DARDANIA |
| 3 | NARBONENSIS I | 25 | DACIA MEDITERRANEA |
| 4 | VIENNENSIS | 26 | DACIA RIPENSIS |
| 5 | NARBONENSIS II | 27 | EPIRUS NOVA |
| 6 | ALPES MARITIMAE | 28 | EPIRUS VETUS |
| 7 | LUGDUNENSIS I | 29 | RHODOPE |
| 8 | SEQUANIA | 30 | THRACIA |
| 9 | ALPES GRAIAE ET POENINAE | 31 | EUROPA |
| 10 | MAXIMA CAESARIENSIS | 32 | HELLESPONTUS |
| 11 | FLAVIA CAESARIENSIS | 33 | LYDIA |
| 12 | BRITANNIA I | 34 | CARIA |
| 13 | ALPES COTTIAE | 35 | PHRYGIA I |
| 14 | AEMILIA ET LIGURIA | 36 | PHRYGIA II |
| 15 | FLAMINIA ET PICENUM | 37 | PHOENICE |
| 16 | APULIA ET CALABRIA | | |
| 17 | NORICUM MEDITERRANEUM | | |
| 18 | PANNONIA SUPERIOR | | |
| 19 | SAVENSIS | | |
| 20 | VALERIA | | |
| 21 | PANNONIA INFERIOR | | |
| 22 | MOESIA SUPERIOR MARGENSIS | | |

R.P.Davis

217

From the reign of Constantine another new official appeared who would undoubtedly have been well informed about the general state of the empire, the Master of the Offices (*magister officiorum*). The post originally carried the relatively lowly military rank of tribune (*tribunus*) (*CTh* XVI 10.1, AD 320; XI 9.1, AD 323) but despite an increasing involvement with the military in the fourth and fifth centuries it seems always to have remained essentially civilian in nature. The *magister officiorum* took over general administrative control of the archives (*scrinia*) of the *magistri epistularum*, *memoriae* and *libellorum*, that is, of the secretariat in charge of imperial correspondence, of imperial comments on requests and of imperial replies to petitions respectively; the *magistri* themselves apparently remained independent of him (*Not. Dig. Or.* XI 13–15; *Occ.* IX 10, 12–13). He similarly had control of the *officium admissionum*, although again not of its *magister*, which organized the audiences of the emperor, and he had personal control of the *scrinium dipositionum*, this time including its low-ranking *magister*, which prepared the emperor's programme of engagements and imperial journeys (*Not. Dig. Or.* XI 16–17; *Occ.* IX 11 and 14). The journeys were prepared by the quartermasters (*mensores*) who are recorded under the direct command of the *magister officiorum* (*Not. Dig. Or.* XI 12; cf. *CJ* XII 40.1 (AD 393) and 2 (AD 398)).

By the middle of the fourth century the *magister officiorum* had the much more senior rank of *comes*, was a member of the emperor's privy council, the *consistorium* (*CIL* VI 1721 = *ILS* 1244, *c.* AD 346; *CTh* VIII 5.8, AD 357; XI 39.5, AD 362), and had special charge of imperial audiences, including the escort and reception of foreign ambassadors (cf. Cassiodorus *Variae* VI 6.4). In 365 it was the *magister officiorum* Ursatius who offended the ambassadors of the Alamanni, who consequently returned home intending to make war (Ammianus XXVI 5.7). In connection with these duties the *magister* had interpreters of every language (*interpretes diversarum gentium*) on his personal staff (*Not. Dig. Or.* XI 52; cf. *Occ.* IX 46).

Despite his being a civilian official, the *magister officiorum* did have duties which encroached on the military sphere. He was, for instance, the commander of the palace guard (*scholae palatinae*) (*Not. Dig. Or.* XI 4–10; *Occ.* IX 4–8), which replaced the Praetorian Guard disbanded by Constantine in 312 (Zosimus II 17.2) and which will have passed into the hands of the *magister* when Constantine finally deprived the Praetorian Prefects of their military command (John the Lydian *Magistracies* II 10 = III 40; III 41). The *magister* had charge of their recruitment (*CJ* XII 33.5, AD 524; I 31.5, AD 527), promotion (*CTh* VII 1.14, AD 394) and discipline (Cassiodorus *Variae* VI 6.1; *CJ* XII 29.1 AD 441), but he did not normally command them in the field. By the end of the fourth century he also controlled the weapons factories (*fabricae*) which supplied the Roman army (*CTh* X 22.3 = *CJ* XI 10.2, AD 390; *Not. Dig. Or.* XI 2, 18–39; John the Lydian *Magistracies* II 10 = III 40), but it was not until the middle of the fifth century that he acquired the duty of annually inspecting the state of the frontiers and frontier troops and reporting on the condition of the forts and the guard-boats on the river frontiers (*Nov. Th.* XXIV 5, AD 443).

Amongst the most important of the *magister's* duties, and of the most significance here, was his control of the public post (*cursus publicus*) and his direct command of its inspectors and principal couriers, the *agentes in rebus*, who were his own personal force. By the reign of Constantius II some of these officers were being employed under the title *praepositi cursus publici* to inspect the passes (*evectiones*) which allowed individuals to make use of the imperial posting system (*CIL* X 7200 = *ILS* 5905; *CTh* VI 29.1, AD 355; 2, AD 357; 6, AD 381; 8, AD 395; 9, AD 412). They soon came to be referred to in this capacity as *curagendarii* or *curiosi* (*CTh* VI 29.1, AD 355). Selected by the *magister* according to seniority, in the fourth century two were sent out annually to each province (*CTh* VI 29.2, AD 357; 4, AD 359; 6, AD 381) and thus gave their commander control over all official traffic within the empire.

The *agentes* themselves were probably set up by Diocletian to replace the corps of couriers, the *frumentarii*, which he had had to disband. Corrupt *frumentarii* had apparently thrown the provinces into turmoil in carrying out their secondary duty of tracking down and reporting potential rebellion (Aurelius Victor *Caesars* 39.44). The number of *agentes* was considerable, probably several hundred, to judge by the number of the *frumentarii* who had been housed in Rome in their camp on the Mons Caelius. Julian temporarily reduced the *agentes* to 17 (Libanius *Orations* II 58) but by AD 430 there were 1,174 (*CTh* VI 27.23). They were organized, as the *frumentarii* had been while they were in Rome, as a military unit, classified like the palace guards units as a *schola* (*Not. Dig. Or.* XI 11; *Occ.* IX 9). Their various recorded ranks suggest a cavalry unit, and indeed they were often known as 'dispatch riders' (*veredarii*) (*CTh* VIII 5.17, AD 364; St Jerome *On Abdias* 18). Another name they had acquired by the early fifth century was *magistriani* – the *magister's* men – marking them out as the special corps of the *magister officiorum* (*IG* XIV 949a (p. 694); cf. *CTh* I 9.1, AD 359), and they were recruited by him with great care (*CTh* VI 27.4, AD 382).

Their duties they inherited from the *frumentarii*. Like them, they carried messages (Libanius *Orations* II 58; XVIII 135; XLVIII 7; LXII 14; see O. Seeck, *RE* I (1893), 778) and made use of the *cursus publicus* to do so (*CTh* VIII 5.9, AD 356; 5.7, AD 360; VI 29.6, AD 381). As has already been mentioned, some were posted to the provinces to serve as inspectors of the post (cf. *CTh* VI 29.2, AD 357; I 9.1, AD 359), and as such they became the 'eyes of the emperor' (*hoi basileos ophthalmoi*) (Libanius *Orations* XVIII 140), just as the *frumentarii* had been and it was their duty to report all they saw to the chief (*princeps*) of the *schola* (*CTh* VI 29.4, AD 359). It is also clear from the pronouncements of Constantius II that, like the *frumentarii*, they were all too eager to use their position to imprison the innocent (*CTh* VI 29.1, AD 355), and Julian complained that they knew only how to snatch and not how to receive (Ammianus XVI 5.11). Symmachus tells of an *agens* bringing false accusations against a senator in 384 (Symmachus *Dispatches* 49), and Libanius and Ammianus both describe *agentes* acting as informers (Libanius *Orations* IV 25; XVIII 135ff.; Ammianus XVI 8.9). In 354 drunken complaints against the emperor that had been made at a dinner party held by the governor of Pannonia Secunda were reported by an *agens* to his fellow-*agens* in charge of the staff of the Praetorian Prefect of Illyricum (Ammianus XV 3.7–9). As the *frumentarii* had been, they too were on occasion employed as imperial assassins (Ammianus XIV 11.23; XXII 3.11).

In the light of their role as an internal security service, it is significant that, from the time of Constantius II, senior *agentes* served as chiefs-of-staff (*principes officii*) to many high-ranking officials including some provincial governors, the deputies of the Praetorian Prefects (*vicarii*), the Praetorian Prefects themselves and the Prefects of the City (*Not. Dig. Or.* XXI–XXVI; *Occ.* XVIII–XXIII; cf. A. H. M. Jones, *The Later Roman Empire 284–602* (Oxford, 1964), 579 with n. 36). They were also attached to senior military officers including most of the frontier commanders (*duces*) in the eastern part of the empire, except those in Illyricum and Thrace (*Not. Dig. Or.* XXVIII; XXXI–XXXII; XXXIV–XXXVIII). It is reasonable to suppose that such appointments were made as a check on the high officials involved. John the Lydian in fact calls the *princeps officii* of the Praetorian Prefect *curiosus* (*Magistracies* II 10 = III 40), and an imperial rescript of 387 to the Prefect of the City reminds him that no official act may be carried out without the counter-signature of the *princeps* (*CTh* VI 28.4).

The *magister officiorum* thus lay at the centre of an ever-growing network of minor officials, a network which has been described in some detail in order to illustrate that the later Roman Empire was capable of centralized information-gathering at a level considerably more sophisticated than the Principate had attained. The *magister officiorum* had access to imperial correspondence and archives, and control of the conduct of foreign embassies; he had considerable involvement with the military, which eventually extended to inspection of the frontiers; in view of all this, it is remarkable and significant that there is no evidence that he ever became the focus of the operation of military intelligence as he did of internal security. Just as there is nothing to suggest that the *frumentarii* were ever employed in espionage beyond the frontiers, neither do we hear, apart from a single occasion, of the skills of the *agentes in rebus* being turned in that direction.

The exception which proves the rule is the mission of the *agens* Clematius into Persia in 355 (see pp. 20f.). Clematius is known to have served as an *agens in rebus* on the staff of Gallus Caesar's *magister officiorum*, Palladius, in Antioch in 354 (Libanius *Letters* 435.9), and had apparently accompanied his master when the latter took over the same position under the Augustus Constantius after Gallus' murder. He appears to have carried an imperial letter from Milan to Antioch in 355 (Libanius *Letters* 405; 407; 411; 430). While in Antioch, he crossed the Euphrates to spy on the movements of the Persians. He did not, however, report to the *magister officiorum* or the emperor, and indeed did not return to Italy from Antioch until much later in the same year (Libanius *Letters* 430; 435; 491); we are specifically informed that he reported to Strategius, the Praetorian Prefect of the East, who was based at Antioch

(Libanius *Letters* 430.7). It would appear that Strategius, who in the following two years attempted to negotiate a peace-treaty with the Persians (Ammianus XVI 9.2–4; 10.21; Themistius *Orations* IV 57b), simply made use of the *agens* while he was available before he carried dispatches back to the emperor.

## THE EMPEROR AND THE *CONSISTORIUM*

In the military sphere, the fourth century saw the development of large, central-ized field armies whose commanders operated throughout areas much wider than the provincial commands of the Principate. Furthermore, in the western portion of the empire at the very end of the fourth century there was a general concentration of military command into the hands of a single officer as a result of the ascendancy of the *magister peditum praesentalis* Stilicho, but the causes and effects were political rather than military. Nevertheless, it does not appear that these developments resulted in the creation of a centralized military intelligence agency any more than did the emergence of the *magister officiorum*.

In order to find any sign of a centralization of military intelligence-gathering, we must look not to the *magister officiorum* but to the emperor himself. While on campaign the emperor seems, as before, to have personally directed intelligence operations on the frontier where he was situated.

In 359 the Caesar Julian sent an unattached tribune (*tribunus vacans*), Hariobaudes, a reliable officer thoroughly acquainted with the local dialects, across the Rhine to negotiate with the previously subdued Alamannic king Hortarius. The intention was that he would then move on to the frontiers of the still hostile kings and use his knowledge of their language to discover what they were plotting (Ammianus XVIII 2.2; see p. 18). In the same year, AD 359, Constantius II sent two tribunes, both accompanied by interpreters, across the Danube to question the Sarmatian Limigantes about their reason for breaking the peace-treaty established the year before (Ammianus XIX 11.5). And in 361 the soldiers of Julian, now joint-emperor, intercepted a letter being carried by a secretary of the Alamannic chieftain Vadomarius to Constantius which revealed that Vadomarius was being employed to keep watch on Julian; the latter consequently issued secret orders to his own secretary (*notarius*) Philagrius to have Vadomarius arrested (Ammianus XXI 3.4–4.6).

The emperor Constantius II is shown at the centre of the intelligence process during operations on the eastern front, also in 361. He was informed at Antioch by messages from his frontier commanders (*duces*) that the Persians had united their forces and were approaching the Tigris led by Sapor himself. This prompted Constantius to collect his own forces, cross the Euphrates and advance to Edessa. There he awaited reports from scouts and deserters, and when these turned out to be contradictory, he ordered the two commanders of his field army (*magistri militum praesentales*), Arbitio and Agilo, to carry on to the Tigris and keep watch for where Sapor would cross. Scouts and deserters continued to bring in conflicting accounts of Persian intentions, which can only reflect a general lack of hard information coming out of Persian headquarters. By contrast, Constantius was at the same time plagued by positive reports (*nuntii certissimi*) that Julian, now in open revolt, had invaded Illyricum from the West. Finally, however, news arrived that Sapor had met with unfavourable auspices and had withdrawn, so allowing Constantius to turn his attention to the domestic problem (Ammianus XXI 13.1–8).

In all these instances, the emperor was principally concerned with his immediate local problems, although, as in 361, he might have to keep an eye on which stretch of the frontier might require his presence next. So, in 351 Constantius II sent the Praetorian Prefect of the East, Flavius Philippus, to the usurper Magnentius 'on the pretext of negotiating a truce and peace but in reality to spy on Magnentius' army and to discover its morale and intended route' (Zosimus II 46.2). And in 366 the emperor Valens sent another high-ranking officer, the *magister equitum* Victor, to discover why the Goths in Dacia had aided the usurper Procopius (Ammianus XXVII 5.1); similarly, in 369, Victor was sent back to the same area, together with the *magister peditum* Arinthaeus, to investigate the effects of sanctions imposed against the Goths and the genuineness of their request for peace (Ammianus XXVII 5.7, 9). There is no suggestion that any particular area of the empire was regarded as being the province of the emperor himself, with other areas being relegated to the care of lower-ranked officials. The East, for example, occupied Constantius' attention a great deal, but when Gallus was appointed Caesar and was based at Antioch, Constantius was committed in the West. Similarly, when Julian was elevated to the purple by his troops, Constantius dealt directly by letter with the Alaman Vadomarius to incite him into frontier raids against Julian (Ammianus XXI 3.4f.); and also in his turn, in 374, Valentinian negotiated in person with the Alaman chief Macrianus, successfully bringing him and his followers into a close and valuable alliance (Ammianus XXX 3.3ff.).

Whether on campaign or monitoring affairs from a distance, emperors also continued to discuss and decide upon military matters in consultation with a body of advisers, now named the *consistorium*, which was the successor of the *consilium* of the Principate. In addition to the purely civilian advisers, the *consistorium* almost certainly included the Praetorian Prefects as before (although they too were mainly civilian officials after 312); it also now included the *comes domesticorum*, who was the commander of the *protectores domestici* who had in part replaced the Praetorians as the imperial guard after their dissolution by Constantine (*CJ* XII 16.1, AD 415); and from the latter part of Constantine's reign, the two commanders of the infantry and cavalry sections of the large, new field armies in attendance upon the emperor, later known as the *magistri militum praesentales* (cf. Ammianus XV 5.8; St Ambrose *Letters* 57.3).

We are fortunate in having a number of detailed accounts of the operation of the *consistorium* in the pages of Ammianus. He tells us that in 355 a meeting of the *consistorium* was held at Milan to discuss accusations of a plot by the infantry commander (*magister peditum*) Silvanus against Constantius II (Ammianus XV 5.5). He also describes the meeting subsequently held when the news arrived that Silvanus had proclaimed himself emperor, which resulted in the decision to dispatch the 'disgraced' cavalry commander (*magister equitum*) Ursicinus to deal with the affair (Ammianus XV 5.17–22).

In 357 Julian was urged by his advisers, led by the Praetorian Prefect Florentius, to fight the Alamanni at Strasbourg (Ammianus XVI 12.14), and two years later the same Florentius and the *magister equitum* Lupicinus hurried to Mainz to a meeting of the *consistorium* which had been summoned to discuss the report on the Alamanni brought back by the tribune Hariobaudes. Both of them argued for a crossing of the Rhine in that vicinity, but this time Julian refused to take their advice for fear of upsetting the local Alamanni who had already been subdued (Ammianus XVIII 2.7). In 363, Julian's *consistorium* advised him to withdraw from the siege of Ctesiphon on the grounds that the city was impregnable and that a relieving force under Sapor was imminent (Ammianus XXIV 7.1).

Two years later Valentinian was informed whilst on his way from Milan to Paris of an attack on the German frontier by the Alamanni and, on the same day, also of the revolt of the usurper Procopius in the East. The news of this revolt came without any details from the military commander (*comes rei militaris*) in Illyricum, Aequitius, who had himself received only the barest account from a tribune in Dacia Mediterranea. The *consistorium* advised Valentinian not to leave Gaul, threatened as it was by the Alamanni, and to allow Aequitius, whom he had raised to *magister militum per Illyricum*, to defend the lower Danube against Procopius (Ammianus XXVI 5.8–13). The same emperor in 374 received a report near Basel from the Praetorian Prefect Probus that the Quadi had devastated Illyricum. He sent the *notarius* (a secretary to the *consistorium*) Paternianus to investigate but was restrained by the *consistorium* from going to deal with the situation in person (Ammianus XXX 3.1–3). It was at a meeting of the *consistorium* at Brigetio in 375, convened to give audience to an embassy from these same Quadi, that Valentinian died in a fit of apoplexy (Ammianus XXX 6).

Most detailed of all is Ammianus' account of the meeting of Valens' *consistorium* held before the battle of Adrianople in 378, where the supporters of the *magister peditum* Sebastianus urged an immediate engagement whilst the *magister equitum* Victor and others recommended that the emperor should await the arrival of his nephew and colleague Gratian with the Gallic army (Ammianus XXXI 12.5–7; cf. 10).

The meetings of the *consistorium* recorded by Ammianus were summoned mostly in reaction to a particular emergency. Those held at Ctesiphon and Adrianople at least were concerned with a rather more general discussion of the military situation. Perhaps not unexpectedly, we do not hear of any regular meetings to discuss foreign or frontier policy, although the requirement made of the eastern *magister officiorum* in 443 to submit an annual report every January on the state of the frontiers in Thrace, Illyricum, the Orient, Pontus, Egypt and Libya is perhaps evidence that they did take place, at least in the fifth century. It is significant, however, that the *Novella* which makes this requirement indicates that the motive behind it is to facilitate the reward and punishment of frontier commanders in the interests of efficiency, rather than to allow any strategic planning (*Nov. Th.* XXIV 5). What is also striking about the meetings recorded by Ammianus is the poor quality of the information which reaches the emperor and on which he and the *consistorium* make their decisions. Ammianus implies, for instance, that Julian and his advisers had no hard information and were merely fearful of the arrival of a Persian relief force at Ctesiphon. The bare news of the revolt of Procopius was reported vaguely (*obscure*) by the tribune Antonius to the senior military officer in Illyricum, Aequitius, who then passed it on to Valentinian in simple terms, we are told, without his having received any further clear account. Probus' report of the devastation of Illyricum was apparently so deficient that a *notarius* had to be dispatched to provide a fuller account.

Valentinian's action in this last case is of interest. The man whom he sent to Illyricum, Paternianus, was a *notarius*, a member of the secretariat of the *consistorium*. By the later fourth century such an official would have been a man of some standing, who even without further promotion could expect to retire with the equestrian rank of *perfectissimus* (*CTh* VI 35.7.1, AD 367). On several occasions we find emperors entrusting missions of considerable importance to their *notarii*. In 357–8 Constantius II sent Spectatus, a senior *notarius* with the rank of tribune, as an envoy alongside the Count Prosper and the philosopher Eustathius, to Sapor in Persia (Libanius *Letters* 513; 331; 333; 352; Ammianus XVII 5.15; 14.1–2), and in 358–9 he sent the similarly ranked Procopius, the future usurper, along with the Count Lucillianus on a second embassy when the first failed. It was on this mission that Procopius sent back the famous scabbard-message which warned the *magister equitum* Ursicinus that a Persian invasion was imminent (Ammianus XVII 14.3; XVIII 6.17–19; see pp. 19f.). Another *notarius*, the infamous former *agens in rebus* Gaudentius, was sent by the same emperor to keep a watch on the Caesar Julian in 358 (Ammianus XVII 9.7), and three years later to organize the defence of Africa against him (Ammianus XXI 7.2). In 365 Valentinian sent the *notarius* Neoterius, along with the staff officer (*protector domesticus*) Masaucio and the guards officer (*scutarius*) Gaudentius (not the former *agens*), to organize the defence of Africa against the usurper Procopius (Ammianus XXVI 5.14). Rather more disastrously, in 369 the *notarius* Syagrius was dispatched to ensure that the local *dux* Arator should speed up the construction of a fort across the Rhine in Alamannic territory near Heidelberg. The protests of the Alamanni were ignored, they attacked, and Syagrius alone survived the ensuing massacre of the construction force and was (temporarily) disgraced (Ammianus XXVIII 2.5–9).

The emperors therefore made use of the secretariat of the *consistorium* on numerous occasions where the task at hand can be assumed to have included elements of intelligence work, although their main function seems to have been political. Their proximity to the emperor ensured that their missions were executed in accordance with his wishes, even when they were nominally under the direction of a senior officer, and there would have been the added bonus of the availability to the *consistorium* of their specialist knowledge of areas and peoples with whom they had dealt on their return. Many *notarii*, who were perhaps a rather select band (Julian reduced their number to four, Libanius *Orations* II 58), achieved high office: Procopius was a *comes* when he was declared emperor and both Neoterius and Syagrius rose to be Praetorian Prefects and consuls.

Despite these quasi-military activities, the *notarii* were of course civil servants, apparently without any military background. The emperors did, however, have military officers attached to themselves, and these could be employed in much the same manner as the *notarii*. These were the officers known as the *protectores (et) domestici*, a sort of bodyguard first formed, as we have seen, in the mid-third century or even earlier (see p. 212). Although Gallienus had appointed relatively senior officers as *protectores*, by the end of the third century they were mostly chosen from ordinary soldiers or centurions; some, however, were directly commissioned civilians of good family. They formed a sort of officer-training corps, and were usually appointed after a number of years of service to the command of a unit. Those attached to the emperor came to be designated *domestici*, probably from the time of Constantine, to distinguish them from the *protectores* regularly attached to the new *magistri militum*.

Like the *notarii*, the *protectores domestici* could be employed to undertake special missions, although perhaps mainly those of lesser importance and of a more military nature. One of the best documented of these officers is Flavius Abinnaeus, who recounted his past career in support of a petition to the emperors Constantius II and Constans in 341, a draft copy of which is still preserved on a papyrus from Egypt. Abinnaeus tells their majesties that as a *ducenarius* (non-commissioned officer) of the *vexillatio Parthusagittariorum* (a unit of Parthian archers), after thirty-three years of army service he was ordered by the former *comes limitis Thebaidos Superioris* (the military commander of the frontier region of the Upper Thebaid in Egypt), Senecio by name, to accompany him in escorting some refugees from the Blemmyes to the imperial court at Constantinople in 337/8. There he was promoted *protector* by being ordered to 'adore the venerable purple', that is, by kissing a portion of the imperial robes, and was sent back to the country of the Blemmyes as escort to the refugees. He spent three years with them, which, if it does not represent the length of the return journey (not excessive for diplomatic travel in the Roman world), may imply that Abinnaeus lived amongst the tribe as imperial representative before returning to court at Hierapolis with recruits from the Thebaid in about 341 (*P.Abinn.* 1).

Reference has already been made to the dispatch by Valentinian of the *protector domesticus* Masaucio in the company of a *notarius* and a guards officer to see to the defence of Africa in 365 (Ammianus XXVI 5.14). Ammianus notes that Masaucio was the son of the former *comes* Cretio who had held Africa against Julian in 361 (cf. Ammianus XXI 7.4; *CTh* VII 1.4, AD 349; 4.3, AD 357), and that Masaucio had grown up there and knew all the places which might be susceptible to attack.

The activities of these *notarii* and *protectores* can often be assumed to encompass intelligence work, but this would usually be incidental to a more general diplomatic or military function. A good instance of this is the scabbard-message sent back by the *notarius* Procopius in 359 warning of an imminent Persian invasion (see pp. 19f.). His ploy looks like an emergency measure rather than a premeditated piece of spying – the use of a scabbard may have been suggested by a stratagem remembered from the handbook of Frontinus (*Stratagems* III 13.5). Moreover, Procopius' lack of military expertise may be reflected in the fact that the message left obscure by which of the two possible routes the Tigris would be crossed, along the Jebel Sinjar or 80 km to the north near Bezabde.

Neither the *notarii* nor the *protectores* amount to any sort of organized intelligence staff, and it is clear that for specific tasks emperors made use of the most appropriate officers to hand, including very senior officers, as the need arose. Furthermore, missions aimed principally at the acquisition of military information for the emperor were always related to the immediate defence of the frontier where the emperor himself was operating, as was the case with Hariobaudes, or to which he was thinking of moving, as with the dispatch of Paternianus to Illyricum. We do not hear of the emperor's involving himself directly in intelligence-gathering on any frontier where he was unlikely to take personal command. It is significant that when Procopius saw from his embassy to Sapor that a Persian invasion was threatened, he sent back the scabbard-message not to the emperor Constantius at Constantinople, but specifically to the regional *magister equitum* Ursicinus at Amida. Ursicinus was in a position to react, Constantius was not.

## THE *MAGISTRI MILITUM* AND THE REGIONAL FIELD ARMIES

The presence of the emperors and their field armies on the most threatened sections of the imperial frontiers continued the practice of Marcus in the late second century which was developed throughout the third. Diocletian's small standing field army, much enlarged by Constantine at the expense of severely reduced frontier forces (*limitanei*), was an extension of what his predecessors had done. The role of these field armies was to move quickly to deal with major incursions into any particular area whilst the local frontier forces held out in heavily fortified towns and forts, delaying the invading barbarians until the field-forces arrived. As we have seen, the emperors became the focus of intelligence-gathering wherever they were situated. They utilized existing local intelligence resources, as when Constantius II was informed at Antioch in 361 by his generals, presumably the frontier *duces*, that Persian forces were approaching the Tigris (Ammianus XXI 7.6), and supplemented them by employing their own staff and senior officers to obtain specific information. The new field armies, moreover, produced a new grade of commander, the *magister militum*, who on occasion operated independently of the emperor. As the field armies multiplied with the creation of additional Caesars and Augusti and with the development in the second half of the fourth century of standing regional field armies, the numbers of *magistri* and of lower-ranking field-army commanders, the *comites rei militaris*, multiplied. With them multiplied the potential foci of intelligence-gathering to supplement that done by the frontier commanders.

To a certain extent, this development was anticipated by the occasional use of Praetorian Prefects as army commanders from the first century onwards, a practice which became frequent in the civil wars of the late third and early fourth centuries. The Prefects had been regular members of the emperor's advisory council, the *consilium* which was the ancestor of the *consistorium*, probably from their first appointment and certainly by the end of the first century AD. There they served in part as military advisers (see Juvenal *Satires* IV 111–12, cf. 144–9). The first Prefect to command an army in the field was the ill-fated Cornelius Fuscus in the crisis of the Dacian invasion of Moesia in 86 (Suetonius *Domitian* 6.1; Dio LXVII 6.6; LXVIII 9.3; Scholiast on Juvenal *Satires* IV 112; Eutropius VII 23.4; Orosius VII 10.4; Jordanes *Gothic Wars* 13/77) and Marcus Aurelius made heavy use of his Prefects as army commanders during the Marcomannic Wars: T. Furius Victorinus in 167 (SHA *Marcus* 14.5; cf. *ILS* 9002), M. Macrinius Vindex in 170 and 172 (Dio LXXI 3.5; Peter the Patrician *FHG* IV p. 186) and Taruttienus Paternus in 178 (Dio LXXI 33.3). Didius Iulianus employed his Prefect Tullius Crispinus in the civil war against Septimius Severus in 193 (SHA *Didius Iulianus* 6.4; 7.4; 7.6), and then in the Tetrarchic period Constantius Chlorus used Asclepiodotus to deal with the usurper Allectus in Britain in 296 (Eutropius IX 22.2; Zonaras XII 31; Orosius VII 25.6), and Maxentius sent Rufius Volusianus against the African usurper L. Domitius Alexander in 311 (Aurelius Victor *Caesars* 40.18; Zosimus II 14) and Pompeianus Ruricius against Constantine himself in 312 (*Latin Panegyrics* IV (X) 25; XII (IX) 8; 10,3).

By the end of the third century, apart from their employment in the field, the Praetorian Prefects had acquired functions which gave them a more general involvement with the army as a whole, including, apparently, rights of jurisdiction and supervision of the military corn-supply (*annona militaris*) (Zosimus II 33.4). Nevertheless, the implication of certain passages of the Historia Augusta (SHA *Avidius Cassius* 5.8 and 12; *The Gordians* 28.2–4) that they had already by the late second century taken far-reaching responsibility for army supply and inspection of the frontiers would appear to be anachronistic for a period when senatorial army commanders and equestrian procurators were still in place in the frontier provinces. The evidence falls well short of allowing us to recognize in the Praetorian Prefects of even the early fourth century anything like army chiefs-of-staff or supreme army commanders, and there is no reason to suppose that they ever had a specific responsibility for intelligence within the imperial *consilium* or *consistorium*.

With the disbanding of the Praetorian Guard after the defeat of Maxentius in 312, the Prefects lost their own regular military command (Aurelius Victor *Caesars* 40.24–5; Zosimus II 17.2). Although they now became civilian officials, they did apparently continue to have oversight of the military corn-supply (Zosimus II 32–3; John the Lydian *Magistracies* II 10 = III 40). Moreover, as deputies of the emperors operating each in his own particular section or Prefecture of the empire, they continued to be involved in its defence. As we have seen, they could advise the emperor on purely military matters, like Florentius before the battle of Strasbourg or after the mission of Hariobaudes to the Alamanni; they passed on military information like Probus' report to Valentinian of the devastation of Illyricum, or even collected it themselves, like Flavius Philippus on his espionage mission to Magnentius or Strategius in sending the *agens in rebus* Clematius to spy on the Persians.

The military jurisdiction previously in the hands of the Prefects passed to the new *magistri militum*, first appointed perhaps towards the end of the reign of Constantine as commanders of the newly enlarged field armies attached to the emperor (Zosimus II 32–3; John the Lydian *Magistracies* II 10 = III 40; cf. Aurelius Victor *Caesars* 41.12). These officers quickly became the leading military figures of the empire. The earliest certain reference is in a constitution of 347 (*CTh* V 6.1) and initially there appear to have been only two of them, an infantry commander, the *magister peditum*, and a cavalry commander, the *magister equitum*, although in practice their roles were not so clearly defined (Zosimus II 33.3; IV 27.2). When Constantine was succeeded by his three sons Constantine II, Constans and Constantius II in 337, each of them appears to have appointed his own pair of *magistri* in charge of separate pairs of field armies, although as early as 347 Sallustius Bonosus may have held a unified post as commander of cavalry and infantry (*magister equitum et peditum*) under Constantius II (*P.Abinn.* 2.11; *CTh* V 6.1; cf. XI 1.1, AD 360). Then, under the sole rule of Constantius II (AD 350–61), we find in addition to the central pair of field armies the creation of regional field armies, initially those attached to Caesars. These were commanded by local *magistri equitum*, who nonetheless led both cavalry and infantry.

The earliest regional *magister* attested is the man who became Ammianus' chief, Ursicinus, commander in the East (*magister equitum per Orientem*) from 349 to 354 and subsequently commander in Gaul (*magister equitum per Gallias*), attached to the Caesar Julian from 355 to 356. By 351 it appears that the count Lucillianus was operating by himself as commander in Illyricum (*magister equitum per Illyricum*) (see A. Demandt, *RE Suppl.* XII (1970), 569–77; *PLRE* I s.v. Ursicinus 2; Lucillianus 3). The complement of one *magister peditum* and one *magister equitum* attached to the emperor (subsequently distinguished as *praesentales*) and three regional *magistri equitum* in addition remained the basic pattern, with variations, until the division of the empire between Valentinian and his brother Valens in 364. Under Valentinian in the West there were the two *praesentales*, a *magister equitum per Illyricum* and another *per Gallias* (the last post disappearing temporarily under Valentinian's son and successor Gratian in 375). Under Valens in the East there were another two *praesentales* (who often operated independently of the emperor) and a *magister equitum per Orientem*, but in 377 he sent a super-numerary *magister peditum* and a supernumerary *magister equitum* to deal with the Gothic invasion in Thrace. In the following year he appointed a further *magister equitum* and *magister peditum*, so that he had in all seven *magistri* in the East at the time of the battle of Adrianople; two of these fell in that disaster (see A. Demandt, *RE Suppl.* XII (1970), 577–605; 702–9). With the development of the regional field armies, a distinction arose between these forces and those still attached to the emperor and his *magistri praesentales*. The regional armies continued to be designated *comitatenses*, companion troops, as the original central field armies had been, but the higher status of the praesental armies was marked by their being entitled *palatini*, palace troops (cf. *CTh* VIII 1.10, AD 365; *Not. Dig. Or.* V–IX; *Occ.* V–VI). The gradual multiplication of *magistri*, each of them representing a further focus of information gathering, must have enhanced signif-icantly the effectiveness of the emperor's intelligence coverage. The Germanic origin of many of the recorded *magistri* and, for instance, the employment in this rank on the eastern front in 363 of Sapor's own brother, Hormisdas, must also have allowed more accurate interpretation of any information obtained (Ammianus XXIV 1.2; 2.4, 11, 20; 5.4).

We happen to be relatively well informed about how the *magistri militum* func-tioned as foci of intelligence-gathering because of the military service of our principal source for the later fourth century, Ammianus Marcellinus. As has already been mentioned, he served as a *protector domesticus* seconded to serve the *magister equitum* Ursicinus, and himself undertook intelligence operations on his chief's behalf on the Persian front. He was one of a small group of officers, including unassigned tribunes (*tribuni vacantes*), *protectores domestici* on secondment from the imperial staff and ordinary *protectores* regularly attached to the *magister*, who together formed Ursicinus' military staff. In 355, when Ammianus ac-companied Ursicinus to Cologne to deal with the rebel Silvanus, there were ten tribunes and *protectores domestici* in the party (Ammianus XV 5.22), which may give some idea of the normal complement of such a staff. A *magister* was not surrounded by senior officials who could act as advisers like those in the emperor's *consistorium*. He will therefore have had to rely on these men who may in practice have formed something like a modern general staff when attached to a *magister militum*.

The *magistri militum* did have their own regular administrative staffs (*officia*), usually made up of non-soldiers like almost all the *officia* attached to senior of-ficials of the Late Empire, military or civilian. In the *Notitia Dignitatum*, which provides most of our information on these *officia*, only those of three of the eastern *magistri*, that is, the first *magister militum praesentalis* and the *magistri militum per Thracias* and *per Illyricum*, consist of soldiers seconded from the units under their command (*Not. Dig. Or.* V 67; VIII 54; IX 49). The reason is unclear, but all three positions were creations of the very late fourth century, close to the date of the final composition of the eastern half of the *Notitia*; these may therefore be temporary arrangements, and indeed we know that by 441 all the eastern *magistri* were served by civilian *officiales* (*Nov. Th.* VII 4, AD 441).

Whether made up of soldiers or non-soldiers, all the magisterial *officia* in the East had the same composition: a judicial section with a *princeps* (chief) and a *commentariensis* (recorder); a financial section with two *numerarii* (accountants), *primiscrinii* (chief clerks) and *scriniarii* (clerks); and clerical staff including *exceptores* (short-hand writers) and other *apparitores* (general staff). The only exception amongst the *officia* listed in the *Notitia* is that of the *magister militum per Orientem* which includes *mensores* (billeting officers) in addition (*Not. Dig. Or.* VII 66). The magisterial *officia* in the West had a judicial section consisting of a *princeps*, a *commentariensis*, an *adiutor* (assistant) and a *regerendarius* (officer in charge of petitions); a financial section consisting of a single *numerarius*; and clerical staff, again consisting of *exceptores* and other *apparitores*. The *magister equitum praesentalis* had an additional *primiscrinius* in the financial section (*Not. Dig. Occ.* VI 89); and the *magister equitum per Gallias* drew his *princeps* from the *officia* of the two praesental *magistri* in alternate years, and two *numerarii*, one from each of their *officia*, each year (*Not. Dig. Occ.* VII 112; 114).

The constitution of these *officia* is in fact very similar to those of the purely civilian officials, and, despite the use of soldiers for a time in some of the eastern *officia*, they show no sign of any section devoted to intelligence-gathering or any other specifically military function, except perhaps for the *mensores* of a single *magister* in the East. Thus, although the presence of clerical staff does indicate that records and documents must have been kept,[1] some of which may have been of use for intelligence purposes, we should infer that these civilian *officia* contributed rather less to the intelligence process than the huge military *officia* of the provincial governors of the Principate. The interpretation of intelligence was most probably left entirely to the *magister* himself together with his staff of *tribuni* and *protectores*.

Ammianus relates an incident which vividly portrays the close attendance of such officers upon their general in a manner reminiscent of the staffs of Napoleon's marshals, who trailed their commanders across the battlefield ready to relay orders or to perform any other task required of them. In 359, as Ursicinus and his staff were pushing on towards the Tigris from Nisibis to deal with the Persian invasion of Mesopotamia, they came across an eight-year-old boy abandoned two miles away from the city. Ursicinus immediately ordered Ammianus to take the boy back to Nisibis, which he did, seating him in front of himself on his horse. Having set the boy down within a half-open postern gate, Ammianus discovered that he was being pursued by a troop of Persian cavalry and galloped off in mortal terror to rejoin his chief (Ammianus XVIII 6.8–13).

These staff officers could also be used to carry out special missions. The *tribuni* and *protectores* sent to fortify the right bank of the Euphrates after the Persians had invaded Mesopotamia in 359 were presumably members of Ursicinus' staff (Ammianus XVIII 7.6), and, of course, Ammianus himself had taken part in a spying expedition into Persia shortly before. After the Nisibis incident, Ursicinus had moved to Amida where his scouts brought him the scabbard-message from Procopius, warning that Sapor himself would soon cross the Tigris (see pp. 19f.). Ursicinus, of course, understood immediately that the message did not sufficiently specify the route to be taken, and Ammianus was therefore sent back down the river with a centurion to cross into Corduene. There his old acquaintance, Iovinianus, a former hostage of the Romans in Syria and possessed of pro-Roman sympathies, was currently Persian satrap. Iovinianus gave Ammianus a single guide and sent him south to a spot from which he could watch for the approach of the main Persian army from a considerable distance (as far as the fiftieth milestone (*ad quinquagesimum lapidem*), some 80 km, he tells us, had his eyes been good enough). On the third day he caught sight of it being led, he says, by Sapor in person accompanied by other kings and leaders, and he was able to assess that it would take them at least three days to cross the Anzaba, a tributary of the Tigris, across the single bridge available. Ammianus then returned to Iovinianus, with whom he stayed for a while (presumably passing this information to him) before hurrying to Roman territory and reporting the news to Ursicinus. Ursicinus in turn sent word to the army commander (*dux*) and the civilian governor (*praeses*) of Mesopotamia to prepare for the invasion by instituting a scorched-earth policy. He also, apparently, sent some of his staff officers to fortify the Euphrates, as has already been mentioned (Ammianus XVIII 6.17–7.6). The secret mission undertaken by Ammianus shows the *magister equitum* actively in charge of the intelligence process. It is, moreover, of considerable interest not just for what it reveals of the complexity of Roman–Persian relations, which is also reflected in the defection of the bilingual Antoninus (see pp. 14f.): it also implies that the Roman authorities in this region had no regular spy-network infiltrated far enough into Persian territory to do this job. Another *magister equitum* recorded as the direct recipient of intelligence is the Count Theodosius, father of the emperor of the same name, who was sent to Africa in 373 to crush the rebel Firmus. We hear of his personally questioning various African officials at Caesarea about Firmus' plans and later learning of his flight through an *explorator* (Ammianus XXIX 5.19; 40).

Alongside the *magistri*, smaller regional groups of the field army were commanded by military counts (*comites rei militaris*), first attested in the mid-fourth century, like the Count Aequitius commanding in Illyricum, who passed on to Valentinian the news of Procopius' revolt in 365 and was then promoted *magister militum* to protect the area against the usurper (Ammianus XXVI 5.3, 10–11). Many of these *comites* had *ad hoc* commands, like the earliest known, Count Gratianus, father of the emperor Valentinian, who was sent to Africa and then Britain by the emperor Constans (Ammianus XXX 7.2), and Count Prosper, who commanded the army of the East in 354–5 as temporary substitute for the *magister equitum* Ursicinus (Ammianus XIV 11.5; XV 13.3), and Count Lucillianus, who was apparently *comes* and then *magister equitum* in Illyricum in 361 (Ammianus XXI 9.5 and 7); the last two, of course, were Constantius' envoys to Persia in 357–9 (Ammianus XVII 5.15; 14.1–3; XVIII 6.17–19). The *Notitia Dignitatum*, however, lists regular *comites* in charge of field armies in Illyricum, Spain and Britain at the end of the fourth century (*Not. Dig. Occ.* VII 40; 118; 153; 199), and others in charge of mixed forces of *comitatenses* and *limitanei* in Tingitania and Africa (*Not. Dig. Occ.* VII 135; 206; XXVI, *comes Tingitaniae*; VII 140; 179; XXV, *comes Africae*). Although we have no explicit evidence, there is no reason to suppose that they operated in any way differently from the slightly more senior regional *magistri* for whom they sometimes deputized. They too, therefore, will have provided further foci for intelligence which they could use themselves or, like Aequitius, transmit to the emperor or his *magistri*.

## THE *DUCES* ON THE FRONTIERS

The emperors and their *magistri* and *comites rei militaris*, however, represent only the upper layers of intelligence-gathering. They operated throughout territories which included several provinces, each with its own border troops and under the military command of a *dux* (the *comites* of Tingitania and Africa performed the role of *duces* in their own provinces, and, confusingly, some *comites*, those of the Saxon Shore in Britain, of Isauria and of Egypt, commanded only *limitanei* and may have been nothing more than promoted *duces* themselves (*Not. Dig. Occ.* XXVIII; *Or.* XXVIII–XXIX). These *duces* evidently gathered their own intelligence, which would, of course, have been available to the emperors and the senior officers of the field armies. The generals on the eastern front in 361 who warned Constantius at Antioch of Sapor's approach towards the Tigris (Ammianus XXI 7.6) presumably included the frontier *duces*, especially those of Mesopotamia and Osrhoene. In the fourth century at least, the *duces* technically came directly under the control of the emperor, as implied by the listings of the eastern portion of the *Notitia Dignitatum*. But the western portion lists them as 'under the disposition of the illustrious praesental Master of the Infantry' (*sub dispositione viri illustris magistri peditum praesentalis*), which is taken to be a development instituted by the all-powerful Count Stilicho at the very end of the fourth century, and laws of the first half of the fifth century indicate that by then the eastern *duces* also had come under the authority of the regional *magistri* (*CTh* VII 17.1, AD 412; *Nov.Th.* IV, AD 438; XXIV, AD 443). That this was the situation in practice for the fourth century is also, as we have seen, confirmed by Ammianus.

In fact, it is clear that both the *duces* and the civilian governors (*praesides*) were expected to co-operate with both military and civilian superior officers as and when necessary, regardless of the technical chain of command. We have already seen how, according to the letters of Libanius, the Praetorian Prefect Strategius sent the *agens in rebus* Clematius across the Euphrates to spy on the Persians in

355 (Libanius *Letters* 430.7). Ammianus is almost certainly referring to Clematius when he says that Strategius (whom he calls by his other name Musonianus) sent 'emissaries who were skilled in deceit and incrimination' – a perfect description of an *agens in rebus*; but he also goes on to tell us that Strategius and Cassianus, the *dux* of Mesopotamia, were separately informed by their own spies (*speculatores*) that Sapor was having trouble with hostile tribesmen at the other end of his empire (XVI 9.2–3). Strategius' use of Clematius, like Ursicinus' use of Ammianus on the same frontier four years later, implies that these senior officials did not normally have available to them specialist agents such as the sixth-century historian Procopius claims to have existed in his day (*Wars* I 21.11–12; *Secret History* 30.12–16). It also indicates that the sort of information which they required could not usually be obtained from other sources. Certainly in the case of Ammianus, and probably in the case of Clematius, this entailed very deep penetration of enemy territory. Nevertheless, it is clear from Ammianus that the local *dux* did have spies of his own operating in the border territories between the empires, and that he and the Praetorian Prefect could on occasion pool their resources. Acting in concert, Strategius and Cassianus sent some low-ranking soldiers (*ignotos milites*) as *agents provocateurs* secretly to subvert the nearest Persian commander, Tamsapor, and induce him to persuade the king to make peace with Constantius. Strategius subsequently reported to the emperor that a peace-treaty was now a possibility, although nothing came of it in the end (Ammianus XVI 9.3–4; 10.21; XVII 5.15; cf. Themistius *Orations* IV 57b). The whole episode shows that it is a mistake to draw too rigid a division between the civilian and military administration of the empire.[2]

The frontier commander was, at any rate, as concerned with the collection of intelligence which affected his own frontier as his predecessors of the Principate. Diocletian's separation of military and civilian powers, completed by Constantine, had transferred to equestrian *duces* the military commands of the late third-century provincial governors, the *praesides*. The latter were themselves equestrians who had replaced the senatorial *legati* in the late third century. These ducal commands usually covered the territory of a single Late Roman province, but sometimes spanned more than one (as for instance in Britain, *Not. Dig. Occ.* XL; see Plate 11). The *duces*, who were usually promoted from amongst the ordinary unit commanders, had responsibility for the control of the frontier armies and river-fleets, and for the construction and maintenance of the frontier installations (*ILS* 762; 770; *CTh* XV 1.13, AD 365; *Nov. Th* XXIV 1, AD 443).

Furthermore, an edict of 412 relating to the construction and maintenance of river-patrol craft by the *duces* (or *dux*) of the Moesian and Scythian provinces makes clear their responsibility for patrolling and reconnaissance along the rivers. In particular, they are to 'choose well-fortified bases for spying out conflicts or an opportunity for expeditions' (*CTh* VII 17.1; cf. Vegetius *Epitome of Military Science* IV 46). The boats used would have been *lusoriae* such as the sleek thirty-oared craft recently excavated at Mainz.[3] They were assisted by civilian staffs very similar in composition to those of the *magistri militum*. Their staffs were therefore very different from those of the provincial governors of the Principate who were their predecessors and whose military archives they may have inherited, although this last assumption is uncertain. At the time of the *Notitia*, in the East the *officia* of the *duces* consisted of a judicial section with a *princeps*, a *commentariensis*, an *adiutor* and an *a libellis* or *subscribendarius* in charge of petitions, and a financial section with *numerarii*, together with the usual clerical *exceptores* and other officials. The Count of Isauria (*comes Isauriae*) in southern Asia Minor, whose command was in practice that of a lower-ranking *dux*, nevertheless had some additional officials, namely a *cornicularius* (senior clerk) and an *ab actis* (archivist) in the judicial section, presumably because of his higher rank (*Not. Dig. Or.* XXIX 11; 15). The Count of Isauria and the *duces* along the Danube frontier appointed their chiefs (*principes*) from within their own *officia*, but the rest received these officers from amongst the *agentes in rebus* of the *magister officiorum*, apparently as a security measure. These *principes* subsequently retired with the honorary rank of *protector* ; the *princeps* of the Count of the Egyptian Frontier (*comes limitis Aegypti*), who was a senior *agens* (*ducenarius*), even retired *cum insignibus*, that is, apparently, with proconsular rank (*Not. Dig. Or.* XXVIII 48; cf. *CTh* VI 28.7, AD 410). In the West the ducal *officia* consisted of a judicial section with a *princeps*, a *commentariensis*, a *cornicularius*, an *adiutor*, a *subadiuva* (junior assistant) and a *regerendarius*, a financial section with one (for *duces*) or two (for *comites*) *numerarii*, and a clerical section with *exceptores*, *singulares* (no longer bodyguards, as under the Principate but now junior secretaries) and others. Probably as a result of the domination of the *magister peditum praesentalis* Stilicho at the end of the fourth century, the *principes*, *commentarienses* and *numerarii* of the western *duces* were drawn from the *officia* of one or both of the praesental *magistri*. The only exceptions were in the ducal *officia* of Belgica Secunda and, as in the East, amongst the Danube provinces, which took their *principes* and apparently other senior *officiales* from within the *officium* itself. These, however, are probably the remnants of the normal situation throughout the empire in the fourth century, before the *magistri officiorum* in the East and the *magistri peditum praesentales* in the West acquired their later importance. The *officia* were evidently quite small, perhaps only forty men strong (cf. *SEG* IX 356 § 2, AD 501; *CJ* I 27.2.20–34, AD 534). A constitution of Anastasius in the early sixth century, however, reveals that the *dux* of Libya had, in addition to his official civilian staff, a personal staff of servants and attendants as well as 27 soldiers seconded from the units under his command, including 15 couriers, 5 doormen and 7 prison guards (*SEG* IX 356 §§ 8; 14, AD 501).

As with those of the *magistri militum*, the ducal *officia* show no sign of any specialization in specifically military tasks such as the processing of intelligence (although the evidence of military couriers in Libya probably reflects the normal arrangements made by the *duces* for their own communications). Once again, however, the composition of their *officia* implies the existence of archives available to these commanders which would have allowed them to co-ordinate reports from their frontier units, albeit without the assistance of an experienced military staff such as the unattached tribunes and *protectores* available to the *magistri*.

## FORTIFICATIONS *IN BARBARICO*

The task of the *duces* in obtaining intelligence will have been made easier by the large-scale refortification programme instituted by Diocletian, which put troops back on the frontiers, in particular in places from which the depredations of the third century had removed them. City walls were constructed and forts rebuilt throughout the German, Pannonian and Moesian provinces. In the East, Circesium at the confluence of the Khabur and the Euphrates was fortified (Ammianus XXIII 5.1), while small, square forts known as *quadriburgia*, which appear in Syria, Arabia, Egypt and Africa, have generally been attributed to this period. The simple presence of forces in forward positions undoubtedly made it easier to maintain surveillance on local threats.

On some portions of the frontier, the collection of intelligence will have been further boosted by the construction of outpost forts, watch-towers and fortified landing places in what was effectively barbarian territory, although this development was often very localized. Under Diocletian, a number of these fortifications were built on the Pannonian frontier from the Danube Bend southwards, as is attested both archaeologically and from literary sources. In 294, 'forts were constructed in Sarmatia opposite Aquincum and Bononia' (*castra facta in Sarmatia contra Acinco et Bononia*) (*Constantinopolitan Consular Lists* s.a. AD 294 in *Chronica Minora* i, p. 230); both of these were situated opposite legionary fortresses and are listed in the *Notitia Dignitatum* as being *in barbarico* (*Occ.* XXXIII 48, Contra Acinco; XXXII 41; 48, Onagrinum). Also likely to have been Diocletianic are two other left-bank fortifications listed in the *Notitia*, Conradcuha and Contra Tautanum (*Occ.* XXXIII 27; 55); Conradcuha may be a corruption of Contra Herculia, which might identify it with a watch-tower found opposite Castra ad Herculem. In addition, a number of fortified landing places of the period have been identified archaeologically at Nógrádveröce at the apex of the Danube Bend, and opposite Cirpi, Lussonium and Lugio; the last of these may be identified with the Contra Florentiam of the *Notitia Dignitatum* (*Occ.* XXXIII 44). The impression given by all this evidence is that the left bank of the Danube in this area was regularly visited by Roman troops and that the Great Hungarian Plain was now more thoroughly under surveillance than before. This impression is strengthened by the existence of an extensive set of earthworks, the Devil's Dyke, running eastward from the Danube Bend, across the Tisza to the mountains of Dacia, before turning south to meet the Danube again in the vicinity of the legionary fortress at Viminacium. Archaeological dating of these earthworks to some time after AD 300 suggests that they may be connected with Diocletianic building across the Danube and that they may therefore mark a diplomatic boundary under Roman guarantee between the Sarmatians of the Plain and the peoples to the north and the east. A similar set of earthworks, known by its Roman name of the Brazda lui Novac du Nord and possibly of Constantinian date, runs eastward from Drobeta (Turnu Severin), some 70 km north of the Danube and parallel with it. This, too, will have delineated some sort of military zone.

Constantine's policy of weakening the frontier forces in order to build up his field army will, if anything, have reduced the intelligence capabilities of the *duces*. Nevertheless, he did establish a few fortified landing places opposite forts on the Rhine and the Danube, namely Whylen across from Kaiseraugst on the Rhine and Daphne across from Transmarisca on the Danube, whilst Celamantia (Iža-Leányvár) opposite Brigetio was rebuilt at this time. Much more striking, however, is Constantine's construction of permanent stone bridges across these rivers for the first time since the destruction of the bridge of Apollodorus. Even so, there were only two on the Rhine, at Cologne and Mainz, and one on the Danube, at Oescus. All of them linked a legionary fortress with the barbarian bank, and all of them were protected by powerful bridgehead forts. The Cologne bridge was built in AD 310 (*Latin Panegyrics* VI (VII) 13) and protected by a new fort at Divitia (Deutz) with external towers and a strong garrison. Construction of the fort is dated by a copy of a lost inscription to AD 312–15 (*CIL* XIII 8502), some years after the bridge, which perhaps suggests that initial confidence later gave way to caution. At Mainz, the bridge led to the site of an earlier fort of Castellum Mattiacorum (Kastel), which may have been rebuilt at this time, to judge by its depiction on a Constantinian lead medallion found at Lyon; the approaches to the bridge may have been subject to surveillance from watch-towers of uncertain date extending eastwards from Kastel towards Wiesbaden. The bridge between Oescus and Sucidava on the Danube, almost 2.5 km in length, was built towards the end of Constantine's reign in AD 328 (Aurelius Victor *Caesars* 41.18; Anonymous *Epitome on the Caesars* 41.13; *CTh* VI 35.5; *Chronicon Paschale* in *Chronica Minora* i, p. 233). Constantine's bridges reflect the strategic thinking behind his expansion of the mobile field army, which shifted the emphasis from reliance on static defence at the frontier line to dynamic reaction and punitive pursuit.

Building was limited in the years after Constantine's death, and it is not until the 360s that another major programme of construction was instituted. Julian's refurbishment of a Trajanic fort deep in what was now Free Germany in AD 358, as recounted by Ammianus, clearly falls within the context of a punitive campaign (XVII 1.11). The outpost must have been very isolated indeed and cannot have been held for long. More important were the constructions of the most aggressive emperor of the fourth century, Valentinian, who actively sought to project Roman power into barbarian territory across the Rhine. New forti-fied landing places were established at Rheinbrohl, Engers, Niederlahnstein, Mannheim-Neckarau and Zullestein. We also hear of Valentinian's troops coming under attack as they attempted to build a fortification deep inside Alamannic territory (Ammianus XXVIII 2.5ff.), and of the construction of similar outposts across the Danube amongst the Quadi (XXIX 6.2).[4]

Perhaps surprisingly, the fourth-century emperors on the whole show a greater willingness to push installations and troops into hostile territory than did their predecessors of the Principate. This is partly a reaction to the higher level of threat which demanded earlier warning, but is also a function of a strategy which is based more and more on aggressive counterstrike. Outposts could provide that earlier warning as well as a springboard for reaction. Ammianus specifically notes the intelligence role of the fortress at Singara, part of the command of the *dux* of Mesopotamia, which, he says, had been built long before his time (in the reign of Septimius Severus, in fact) as a suitable place for obtaining advance warning of sudden hostile attacks; he also notes, however, that it was so exposed and difficult to reinforce that it had been captured by the Persians several times and had become a liability (Ammianus XX 6.9). And in Britain there was a special force known as the *Areani* whose purpose was to 'range over long distances' (*per longa spatia discurrentes*) in order to provide advance warning of trouble threatening amongst the tribes neighbouring the frontier. Significantly, they seem to have operated in the Lowlands of Scotland where there were at least three units of *exploratores* permanently stationed in the third century (*RIB* 1235; 1243–4; 1262; 1270 (= *ILS* 2631); *Antonine Itinerary* 467.1). The generals to whom Ammianus says they reported can only be the successive Dukes of the Britains (*duces Britanniarum*) and perhaps also the Counts of the Saxon Shore (*comites litoris Saxonici*). The Count Theodosius, father of the emperor of that name, 'removed them from their posts' in 368–9 after the massive joint invasion by Picts, Attacotti and Scots in 367, known as the 'barbarian conspiracy' (*barbarica conspiratio*), had resulted in the capture of the Duke of the Britains, Fullofaudes, and the death of the Count of the Saxon Shore, Nectaridus: the *Areani* had supposedly been bribed to tell the barbarians about Roman activity. Ammianus says that the force had been set up long before and he makes it clear that they were already in existence in 343 when the emperor Constans visited Britain (Ammianus XXVIII 3.8; cf. XXVII 8).

Yet another force apparently special to Britain was the twenty-oared scout vessels (*naves exploratoriae*) called *picati* ('covered in pitch'), which patrolled the ocean to intercept and gain advance warning of maritime raiders. Vegetius, writing at the end of the fourth century, says that these ships and their sails and rigging were painted a sea-blue colour, which was also the colour of the crews' uniforms, as a camouflage device (Vegetius *Epitome of Military Science* IV 37). It is most likely that these ships were attached to the command of the officer in charge of the defences of the North Sea and Channel coast, the Count of the Saxon Shore.

## *EXPLORATORES* IN THE *NOTITIA DIGNITATUM*

At first glance, the *Notitia Dignitatum* even seems to provide evidence that some *duces* had scouts (*exploratores*) stationed at some of the forts under their command, but this is misleading. In all, units of *exploratores* are attributed to three *duces* and to one of the *comites* with only *limitanei* under his command. Four units are recorded in close proximity on the south bank of the Danube, at Novae, Taliata and Zmirna, under the *dux* of Moesia Prima, and at Transdierna, under the *dux* of Dacia Ripensis (*Not. Dig. Or.* XLI 34; 35; 37; XLII 29). The units under the *dux* of Moesia Prima are all stationed within the extremely narrow Iron Gates gorge, where the river narrows and flows at its fastest, and where sheer cliffs on both sides make crossings extremely difficult. Only Transdierna lay at a crossing point, opposite the fortress of a vexillation of legion *XIII Gemina* stationed at Dierna (Zernis) on the north bank (*Not. Dig. Or.* XLII 37). Nevertheless, a whole series of Late Roman forts is known in the region[5] and Justinian was to rebuild the forts on the south bank and construct new ones opposite them on the north bank in the sixth century (Procopius *Buildings* IV 6.1–5); like their predecessors, they were probably intended to protect river traffic. It is not at all clear why *exploratores* should be recorded only on this very short stretch of the Danube, spanning two provinces and ducal commands and in positions from which only one of the four units would seem to be capable of patrolling beyond the frontier. Their description in the *Notitia* simply as 'scouting troops' (*milites exploratores*), without a designation of unit-type, probably implies that they were raised relatively late in the fourth century,[6] and their unusual concentration may indicate that they were in fact formed by dividing up a large, single body of scouts. Such a body is most likely to have been attached originally to the field army of a *magister militum*, perhaps the *magister militum per Thracias* first appointed at about the same time, rather than to the frontier forces, whose units by this period were all relatively small. They may then have been transferred to these two ducal commands to deal with a partic- ular crisis in this area. If this is correct, then, with the possible exception of the unit at Transdierna, they are unlikely to have retained their specialist function.

Two further units of *exploratores*, this time designated specifically as units (*numeri*), are listed in the *Notitia* under two separate commands in Britain. One was stationed at Lavatris (Bowes, North Yorkshire) as part of the command of the *dux Britanniarum* (see Plate 11), and the other at the Saxon Shore fort of Portus Adurni (Portchester) as part of the command of the Count of the Saxon Shore, an officer who despite his rank commanded only *limitanei* (*Not. Dig. Occ.* XL 25; XXVIII 21). These are usually regarded as being identical with two of the *numeri* of *exploratores* known to have been in Britain in the third century at Netherby, Risingham and High Rochester (see pp. 193f.). Once again, it is not clear of what special use scouts would be at Portchester, or how they would operate in any way differently from the mixture of *numeri*, *equites* (cavalry units), a cohort and a legion listed at the other forts of the Saxon Shore command along the Channel and North Sea coasts (*Not. Dig. Occ.* XXVIII). These scouts, too, may therefore have lost their specialist function by the fourth century.

The Portchester unit, moreover, seems to have been transferred by the time of the compilation of the western part of the *Notitia* around 420 to the forces listed for the *magister equitum per Gallias* as *pseudo-comitatenses*, the name given to *limitanei* who have been upgraded to join a field army. This has been inferred from the appearance together amongst the *pseudo-comitatenses* of the field army in Gaul of a unit of *Abulci* followed by another of *exploratores* (*Not. Dig. Occ.* VII 109–10), which corresponds to the consecutive listing of a *numerus Abulcorum* at Anderidos (Pevensey) and the *numerus exploratorum* at Portchester in the list of the Count of the Saxon Shore (*Not. Dig. Occ.* XXVIII 20–1). The list of forces which make up the Master's command is part of a general list of field-army units (*distributio numerorum*) within the *Notitia* which is regarded as reflecting the field forces available to the *magister peditum praesentalis*, the supreme commander in the West, at the time of the final compilation of the whole document. The Count's list, however, is usually taken to reflect the state of his command (which probably no longer existed except on paper) some years previously. It is a reasonable assumption therefore that these units in Britain and Gaul are identical and that the two of them were transferred together from the Count's command to that of the Master in Gaul, probably in the early fifth century. And if the Portchester *numerus* had already ceased to be a specialist scout unit in Britain, it is unlikely to have reverted to its ancient role in Gaul.

The *Notitia Dignitatum* (the intractability of which is well represented here and will be familiar to anyone who has tried to use the document) is thus somewhat disappointing when it comes to providing evidence for the existence of regular, specialist scouting forces amongst the frontier troops of the Late Roman army. Indeed, if this reconstruction is correct, it would be unwise to assume that there were any such forces at all, and we should take the ducal *exploratores* referred to by Ammianus to be specially selected individuals rather than members of standing units. Such a practice would, in fact, hark back to the situation of the first and second centuries AD, and probably to the practice of the Republic. Paradoxically, we may be able to guess from the *Notitia* that the Late Roman field armies nevertheless included at least one genuine scouting unit, not the *exploratores* actually listed for Gaul, but a hypothetical unit in Thrace, apparently split up and demoted only a few years after its formation.

## SHARING OF INTELLIGENCE

Even though the *Notitia* is unhelpful, there is still more than enough evidence to show what we should in any case have to assume, that localized intelligence work was the responsibility of and co-ordinated by the frontier commanders, albeit through a variety of agencies according to local conditions, to judge by the British examples. But as we have seen, the frontier commanders were only one of several overlapping groups of foci for military intelligence. As in the later Principate, the emperors themselves pursued their own intelligence whilst on campaign in addition to that available from the frontier commanders. So, from the time of Constantine, did the praesental *magistri militum* when operating independently with their field armies, and these, of course, multiplied with the emperors. The appearance of independent regional field armies under senior *comites* and regional *magistri equitum* in the middle of the fourth century was a significant development, because it created long-term or permanent field-commanders concerned with the defence of specific areas and thus set up in each region a standing focus of intelligence superimposed on a whole group of *duces*. More and more of these commands came into being throughout the fourth century, so that by the end of it most frontier forces had a regional field army to back them up in addition to the praesental armies, which meant that two separate commanders were normally interested in the security of any single territory or stretch of frontier. As with Strategius on the eastern front, the regional Praetorian Prefects, who had come into being around the mid-fourth century, sometimes added another element. The strategic developments of the fourth century thus brought with them as a corollary a much denser coverage of military intelligence.

Furthermore, what evidence we have suggests that these overlapping layers of intelligence worked together and complemented each other. There was undoubtedly some military co-operation along the frontiers between the provincial governors of the Principate. This can be deduced, for instance, from the occasional seconding of headquarters staff from one province to another or the regular transfer of the *IV Flavia* legion from Singidunum (Belgrade) in Upper Moesia to Aquincum (Budapest) in Lower Pannonia whenever *II Adiutrix* went on campaign (both attested epigraphically). But the *legati Augusti pro praetore* of the Principate were the leading men of the empire, responsible only to the emperor himself both in theory and in practice. When they co-operated, they were usually co-operating with their equals. Presumably they did so only circumspectly and with the approval of the emperor, since the latter might rightly be suspicious if the ties between two such commanders were too close, as perhaps they were between Gaetulicus and L. Apronius under Tiberius and Gaius (Tacitus *Annals* VI 30) or the ill-fated Scribonii brothers under Nero (Dio LXIII 17.2–4). This in itself would militate against any very close collaboration between neighbouring governors, whilst aristocratic rivalries might wreck it altogether, as in the case of the dissent between Corbulo and Caesennius Paetus on the eastern frontier, again under Nero (Tacitus *Annals* XV 6–17; Dio LXII 20.4–22.4).

By contrast, the role of the *duces* as it developed in the fourth century was to slow down incursions into their territory. They used their forces, which consisted of small units of low-grade troops, to hold out behind the walls of the forts and towns along the frontiers and main roads running into the provinces, thereby delaying the raiders who wanted the loot and food within them. Their strategy was to survive either until the raiders withdrew of their own accord, or until relief arrived in the form of the nearest field-army units. The development of the regional field armies further increased the efficiency of this strategy in the course of the fourth century.

Clearly, it was both the duty and in the interests of the *duces* to co-operate with the senior officers, *magistri* and *comites*, in charge of the field armies, and also with the Praetorian Prefects who were in charge of their supplies and themselves took an interest in the security of the territories over which they had civil control. This evidently included the sharing of intelligence with them, thus multiplying the efficiency of each. No doubt the presence and demands of such senior authorities served to make the *duces* even more diligent in the collection of information than they would otherwise have been, whilst the *magistri* and *comites* could obtain the essential element of confirmation for their own intelligence. It is perhaps no accident that the most cataclysmic and unexpected invasion of Roman territory in the fourth century was the 'barbarian conspiracy' of 367 which befell the British provinces, defended only by two frontier commanders who were isolated by the Channel from the nearest field army.

That disaster aside, the fourth-century empire had a remarkably good record of anticipating through diplomacy, espionage and military surveillance the timing, nature and direction of the threats to its territory, and this can be seen as a by-product, perhaps unintentional, of the overall strategy which it had evolved and the overlapping hierarchies of intelligence-gathering which this had produced. As a result, amongst the periods of Roman history for which we have good evidence, that covered by Ammianus appears as a high-water mark of Roman strategic intelligence. It is a tragic irony that it was brought to a close by a catastrophic failure in the exploitation of tactical intelligence at Adrianople.

## THE BATTLE OF ADRIANOPLE

The annals of the later Roman Empire are scarred by the events that took place on the burning afternoon of 9 August 378. In a great battle, a Roman army was defeated near Adrianople in Thrace, an emperor died with tens of thousands of irreplaceable men, and the beginning was signalled of the collapse of the West's ability to resist external pressure and penetration of its defences (Ammianus XXXI 12–13).

The day before, the emperor Valens had received a report from his *procursatores*, the forward skirmishing cavalry, who had been carrying out an armed reconnaisance sweep beyond Adrianople. Their information was up to the minute and apparently correct. The large Gothic force encamped there now consisted of only 10,000 Visigothic infantry; and that meant the formidable Ostrogothic cavalry force was elsewhere, collecting food and plunder. Valens seized on this information and moved to Adrianople, aiming to deliver a decisive blow.

During the night, he called a planning meeting with his senior officers. Divisions emerged. The more cautious group centred on the *magister* Victor recommended that Valens wait before taking the Goths on, to allow time for the western emperor Gratian to arrive with his army and consolidate the Roman strength. Then they would move as a combined force to fight a safer battle and wipe out the whole Gothic threat. The western contingent was not many days away and already communication between the two armies had been established. The other group of officers urged an immediate action, led as they were by a general who knew what he was doing – Sebastianus had been appointed to overall command in the region about two months before, and in the previous week or so had adopted an aggressive guerrilla-style mode of campaigning. It had proved immensely successful. He had recovered very large amounts of plunder and a substantial number of prisoners, and his methods had forced the Goths to cease raiding in small bands and to coalesce into much bigger groups for their own protection: this way they were more vulnerable to large-scale Roman attack.

Valens' need for a final solution must be seen in its context. He had decided to intervene personally in the Gothic troubles, since problems associated with the handling of the peoples had steadily grown, and relations between them and the Roman administration had deteriorated ever since the Visigoths had been allowed to cross the Lower Danube in 375 and 376. The Ostrogoths and some other lesser tribes had been denied permission to enter the empire, but had crossed over anyway, taking advantage of the administration's preoccupation with the Visigoths. The influx of the Goths, the reception accorded them, and their responses to the abuses and negligence to which they were subjected over a period of more than twenty-two months, had created military and administrative chaos all over the region. Increasingly senior and experienced military men had been assigned to the region as the severity of the problem became more visible.

Despite all the disruptions, a comprehensive and accurate intelligence picture of where the various bands of Goths were and what they were doing was able to be developed and maintained throughout. We can, for example, see changes that reflect the needs of the moment being implemented in the strategic dispositions of Roman troops and in actual tactics, all based on appreciations of the situation. We know too that proper intelligence-collecting activity was being conducted by means of *exploratores* in several different areas at various stages of the crisis: for instance, the general Frigeridus was using them in northern Thrace in 377 and thus was able to avoid being confronted by a Gothic force (Ammianus XXXI 9.2); in a further notice, they were reporting direct to a campaign headquarters at Nice near Adrianople, where Sebastianus was organizing his guerrilla campaign (XXXI 11.2); and on yet another occasion, Gothic attempts to close essential supply routes immediately before Valens' move to Adrianople were closely monitored by them (XXXI 12.2). The intelligence side of the campaign was not marred by errors of information.

Valens had a further problem. It has been claimed that he did not want to share the credit for his victory over the Goths with his nephew Gratian, and thus he rushed into a battle. Psychological motivation such as this is notoriously difficult to prove. But Valens was, it seems, irritated by messages from Sebastianus reporting his successes, as well as by further reports from the West announcing Gratian's successes against the Germans. In the atmosphere of crisis surrounding the Adrianople campaign, such reports were a stimulant.

The battle-meeting achieved nothing. Valens' mind was made up, clearly locked into the error of interpretation that the information provided by his *procursatores* allowed. Their information covered what they saw, not what they did not see – an important distinction. They saw what they estimated as 10,000 infantry. It was not their function at that level to interpret their information, but solely to report it. So the mistake attributed to them is in fact one of subsequent interpretation, not of information. Interpretation was the responsibility of the higher-ranking officers associated with Valens' council. Indeed, if the attack planned by Valens had gone ahead at the time the decision was made, it is much more likely that his force would have put the Gothic infantry out of action before the cavalry was able to return. The cavalry did not reach the battlefield, where the fighting was just about to start, until the early afternoon, so the haste invoked by the emperor to start the fighting was justified: only that morning, *exploratores* working ahead of the army, as it moved the 12 or so km from Adrianople, had seen no changes in the numbers of Visigothic soldiers when they had reported the larger formation of the Goths' wagons.

One of the things that upset the emperor's calculations had nothing to do with intelligence: it was the temporization under the guise of last-minute negotiation exploited by the Gothic chieftain, Fritigern, on three occasions in the fifteen hours before the battle (Ammianus XXXI 12.8–15). We must assume that Valens was willing to enter negotiations at this very last moment in the hope of finding a solution to the Gothic problem by incorporating them into the empire without loss to Roman manpower, a practice he had adopted before (cf. Ammianus XXXI 4). In fact the negotiations provided the Goths with the vital few hours needed to get the Ostrogothic cavalry back to the scene, and so shift the balance of force in their favour at the very last moment. It also successfully distracted the emperor and his staff for a while from devoting their full attention to the oncoming battle.

But temporization, once recognized as such, would in itself have told the battle council that the intelligence reports they had been receiving were accurate – why else should Fritigern have been so desperate to put off the start of battle? By the early afternoon the case for striking before the Ostrogothic cavalry returned would have been overwhelming. Valens finally struck just too late.

The battle of Adrianople closed the era of Roman superiority on the battlefield. It was a defeat very serious in its long-term effects. But it cannot be ascribed to an intelligence failure. Intelligence collection had functioned in a normal and detailed way right up to the battle. The fault lay with the individuals concerned, who probably did not ask the right questions about the information they already possessed. What went wrong was the human factor, not the system.

# 10

# FULL CYCLE
## The development of Roman intelligence

We began this study with a number of questions: How did Roman military and political intelligence work? How effective was its contribution to Roman operations in the field? How was it linked to the formation of frontier policies? How did its structures develop and change? How good was it?

In tactical intelligence, we have been able to detect surprisingly little change. At the end of our period, cavalry troops – the *procursatores*, *exploratores*, *kataskopoi* – are still scouting ahead; the *speculatores* still have to operate covertly; commanders are still going to see for themselves, and sometimes, like Julian, paying the penalty; information still has to be extracted from prisoners, deserters, refugees and unhappy locals. The reason for this lack of significant development is not far to seek. The essential nature of warfare itself did not change through the six centuries we have surveyed. It is not until the introduction of new technologies from the mid-nineteenth century onwards that field intelligence moved beyond its solely human dimension (in the jargon, 'humint'). As we have argued (see pp. 65f.), signals intelligence ('sigint') hardly featured in the Roman world.

The artificiality of the division between tactical and strategic intelligence in ancient warfare which we adopted for convenience in chapters 2 and 3 must here be restated. When we came to consider how Roman intelligence developed in practice, the two shaded imperceptibly into each other. Nevertheless, it is clear that, by contrast with the uniformity of the tactical end of the spectrum, the strategic end showed considerable change over time. This reflects political rather than purely military changes in the Roman state and its neighbours over our period.

Under the Republic, the nature of Roman government ensured that control from the centre was weak. Furthermore, ill-defined provincial boundaries and areas of responsibility made it difficult even for commanders on the periphery to obtain strategic and other information. We have seen how even the methodical Julius Caesar had to be prepared to step into the unknown on occasion, while Cicero in Cilicia could have problems tracing some of his own troops. Limited experience, poor communications and personal rivalries combined to keep the Senate's understanding even hazier.

244

The move to one-man rule at the end of the first century BC brought much stronger central control. Frontier governors were now selected by the emperor, which may have produced an overall improvement in quality, but they were also constrained in their actions by their political subjugation to the emperor and by clearly defined provincial boundaries. Nevertheless, continued problems of communication made it difficult for that control to be exercised rapidly or in detail. At the same time, the very definition of boundaries and the gradual ossification of the frontiers permitted much more systematic and efficient collection of information and its archival retention.

The frontier line, despite widespread variation in its physical appearance and tactical operation, acted as a kind of permeable membrane around the empire at which a host of military installations automatically became sensors for intelligence. The line helped to make clear the peoples with whom the empire had to deal, and allowed for an accumulation of knowledge about them. The incoming governor could rapidly bring himself up to date through tours of inspection and the diplomatic meetings prompted by his arrival. A further corollary of the stabilization of the frontier was the development of permanent provincial capitals where the governor established his headquarters. The construction of governors' palaces which followed at last made provision for the housing of extensive archives, while the demands of administering large standing provincial armies created substantial and sophisticated provincial staffs. The archives and their staffs in turn became the nerve centre for the processing of information and the implementation of the intelligence cycle.

The system which evolved in this way was adequate to meet the low level of threat to the empire which obtained in the first two centuries of the Principate. The wars of the late second century and after changed all this. The reaction can be seen in piecemeal attempts to improve the acquisition and flow of information. Outpost forts are constructed, local scouting units are created, networks of staff-officers extend along some of the military roads of the empire. The variety of pressures on the frontiers meant that there could be no consistent response.

By far the most important development, however, was that the emperors could no longer afford to oversee the defence of the empire from its centre. In the North, movements of peoples from the steppes and from Scandinavia for reasons not fully understood prompted the formation of tribal coalitions amongst the peoples living along the Roman frontiers on a larger scale than had previously been experienced. These created zones of threat along fronts wider than individual provinces. In the East, the Arsacids and their successors the Sassanians adopted much more aggressive stances, and large amounts of Roman manpower were committed to a solution there. The co-ordination of the defence of these broader fronts now required the emperors to be present in person in the theatre where the threat was most active. The task could not be delegated because of the dangers inherent in the concentration of military power in the hands of a general who might become a rival. This fear prompted the further division of provincial commands by the Severi, which reduced the risk of rebellion but intensified the problem of co-ordination.

The enforced presence of the emperor on threatened sectors nevertheless produced real intelligence benefits. Apart from simple co-ordination, the emperor now saw for himself the terrain and the peoples with whom he was dealing, as did his *consilium* of high-ranking and experienced military advisers. This gave enormous advantages in the handling of foreign embassies and in playing one group off against the other. It also allowed immediate and informed decisions to be made and implemented over a much wider front than could be done by any individual provincial governor on his own.

The political problems were not solved, however, by these expedients, because continued threats on multiple fronts led to usurpation anyway; the emperor could not be in several places at once. Throughout the third century the emperors often took individual partners in power, but it was not until Diocletian set up the Tetrarchy that the political situation calmed for a while. A side-effect of the political turmoil was the building up for security reasons of central armies around the person of the emperor. This also provided a strategic reserve for the Roman army to back up the frontier garrisons. This process had been begun by Severus, was boosted by Gallienus and became a key feature of Constantine's military dispositions. The multiplication of emperors (both Augusti and Caesars) meant a multiplication of such armies and of their commanders, the *magistri militum*. As some of these began to operate independently in the fourth century, their operations enjoyed advantages similar to those conferred by the personal presence of an emperor. The overall effect of a system of defence which relied on frontier garrisons commanded by *duces*, backed up by the several mobile striking forces centred on *comites*, *magistri* or the emperors themselves, was to provide amongst other things a much denser coverage of intelligence-gathering and -processing than had ever been possible before.

It seems clear to us that Roman military and political intelligence improved as a whole over the period considered. In general terms that improvement was proportional to the external dangers faced by the empire. The improvements were not planned, but were usually side-effects of wider strategic developments. Nevertheless, those developments will have stuck in part because they offered intelligence advantages. If we compare the intelligence available to Caesar, to Marcus Aurelius and to Valens, it is easy to see the major advances that have taken place. By the end of our period, Roman intelligence, both tactical and strategic, was very good indeed. But, as Valens found out, military and political survival do not depend solely on good intelligence.

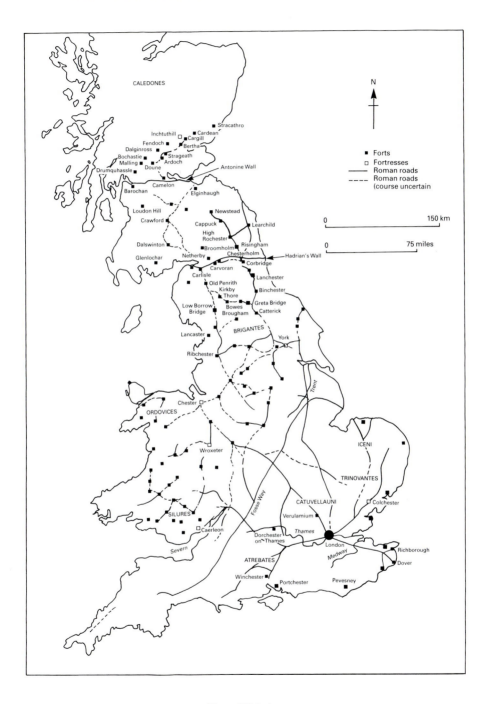

*Figure 6* Britain

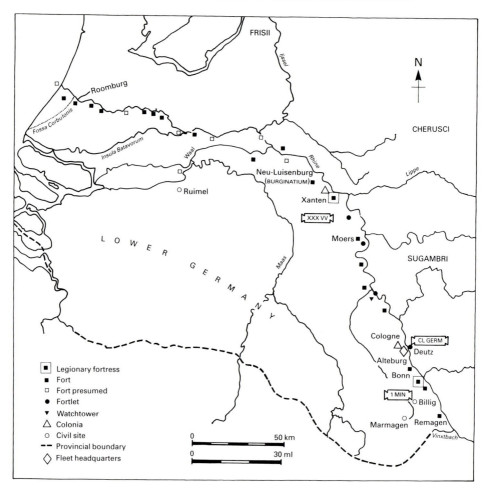

*Figure 7* The Lower German *limes*

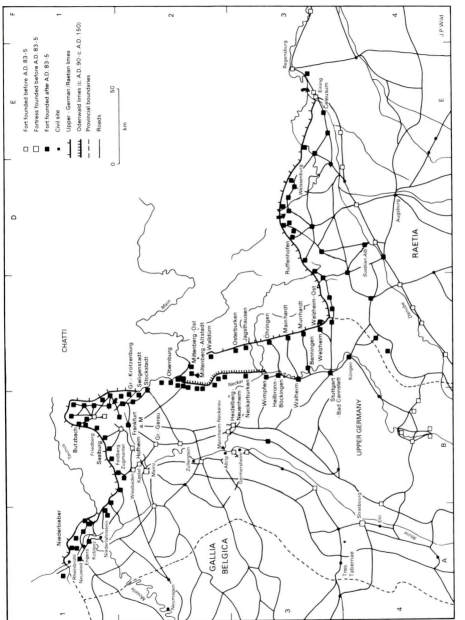

Fort founded before A.D. 83-5

Fortress founded before A.D. 83-5

Fort founded after A.D. 83-5

Civil site

Upper-German/Raetian limes

Odenwald limes (c. A.D. 90–c. A.D. 150)

Provincial boundaries

Roads

0   50

km

*Figure 8* The Rhine–Danube *limes*

J.P. Wild

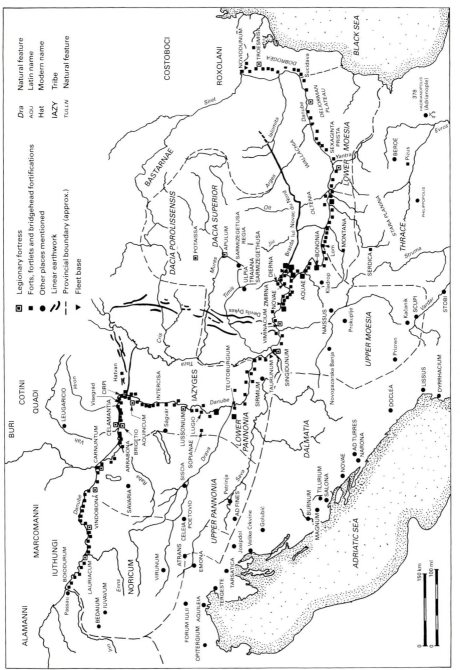

*Figure 9* The Danubian *limes*

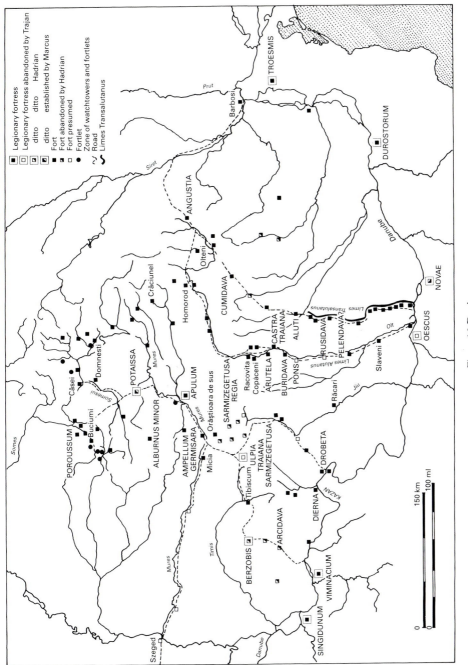

Figure 10 Dacia

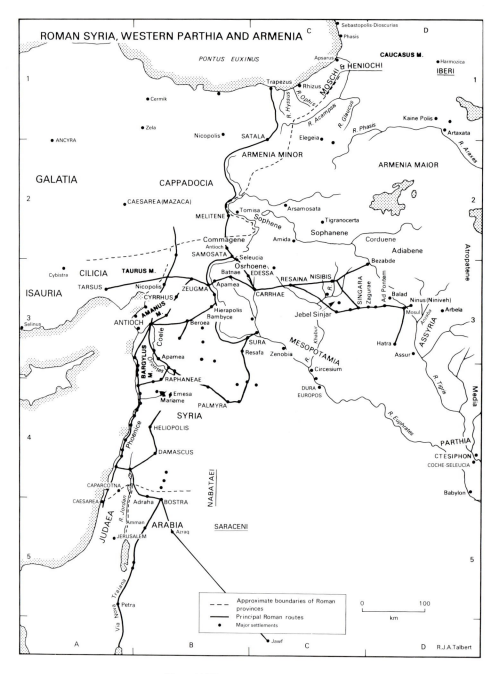

*Figure 11* The eastern frontier

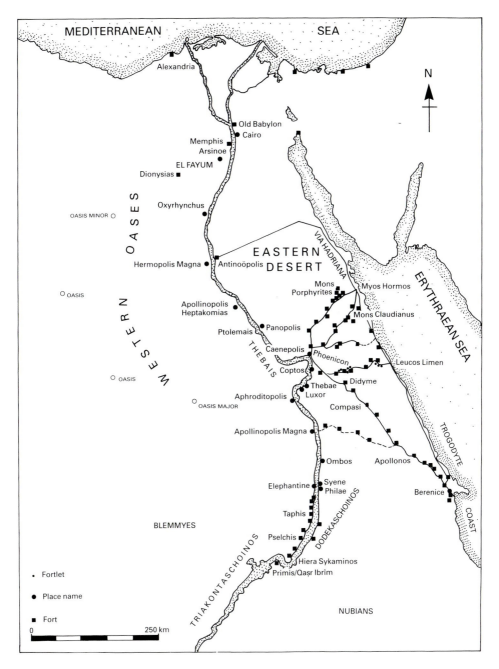

*Figure 12* Egypt

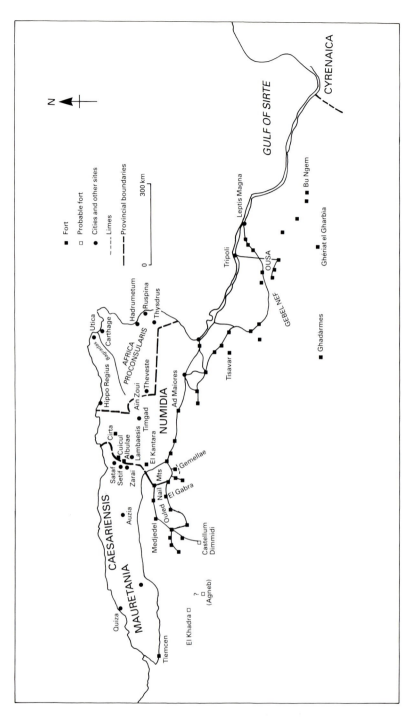

*Figure 13* Mauretania Caesariensis, Numidia and Africa Proconsularis

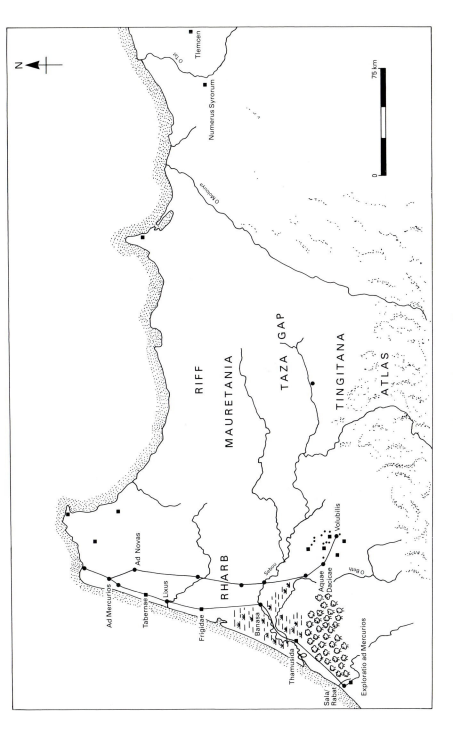

*Figure 14* Mauretania Tingitana

# NOTES

## 1 INTRODUCTION: THE OTHER SIDE OF THE HILL (pp. 1–11)

1 XII 28a.7–10: '[the historian without experience] naturally thinks that the collection of documents and the interviewing of those who know the facts are the most important and difficult aspects of history, when in reality they are the least significant and easiest. In this respect at least, the inexperienced will inevitably be misled. So how can he ask sensible questions about battlefield dispositions, or a siege, or a sea-fight – or understand the successive stages of an account, if he is ignorant of the basic principles? The interviewer contributes to the story no less than his informants, because when he is following up the events, the actual process of reminding conditions the informants' explanations of each incident. It is in this area that the inexperienced interrogator is inadequate when questioning eye-witnesses, and if he is present himself at an event, at understanding what is happening – in a way he is really absent even while present!' Cf. also Polybius' assertion of his qualifications at III 48.12: 'I can confidently speak on these issues, because I have questioned people who were present at the events, I have examined the [actual] sites and I have made the crossing of the Alps, in order to see and understand for myself.'

2 C.B.R. Pelling, 'Caesar's Battle Descriptions and the Defeat of Ariovistus', *Latomus* xl (1981), 741–66.

3 R. Syme, *Tacitus* (Oxford, 1958), 176f., 280, 288f., 291f., 296f.

4 F. Millar, *A Study of Cassius Dio* (Oxford, 1964); see also Z. Rubin, *Civil-War Propaganda and Historiography*, Collection Latomus 173 (Bruxelles, 1980).

5 N.J.E. Austin, *Ammianus on Warfare*, Collection Latomus 165 (Bruxelles 1979), now very substantially updated and developed by J.F. Matthews' magisterial *The Roman Empire of Ammianus* (London, 1989).

6 F.W. Walbank, *Polybius*, Sather Classical Lectures 42 (Berkeley, 1972); E.W. Marsden, 'Polybius as a Military Historian', in *Polybe*, Entretiens sur l'Antiquité Classique 20 (Vandoeuvres-Genève, 1974), 267–95.

7 Anon. Byz. *Peri strategikes*, in G.T. Dennis, *Three Byzantine Military Treatises*, Dumbarton Oaks Texts 9 (Washington DC, 1985). On the date of the work, see now B. Baldwin, 'On the Date of the Anonymous *Peri strategikes*', *Byzantinische Zeitschrift* lxxxi (1988), 290–3; A.D. Lee and J. Shepard, 'A Double Life: Placing the *Peri presbeon*', *Byzantinoslavica* lii (1991), 15–39, esp. 25–30.

8 *Jugurthine War* 88.2: 'But Marius acted with energy and discretion to survey with equal attention all aspects of his own and the enemy's situations. He set about finding out the strengths and weaknesses of the two sides, he reconnoitred the movements of the kings and anticipated their planning and traps [i.e. their attempts to induce him to make strategic mistakes], and he tolerated no slack on his side or security for theirs.'

## 2 THE HOSTILE HORIZON: STRATEGIC INTELLIGENCE (pp.12–38)

1 F. Millar, 'Emperors, Frontiers and Foreign Relations, 31 BC to AD 378', *Britannia* xiii (1982), 1–23 (on p. 21).

2 A fuller discussion of the strategic implications of this intelligence process can be found in N.J.E. Austin, *Ammianus on Warfare*, Collection Latomus 165 (Bruxelles, 1979), 22–7, with its supporting bibliography and references; see also now R.C. Blockley, 'The Coded Message in Amm. Marc. 18.6.17–19', *Échos du Monde Classique/Classical Views* xxx N.S. v.1 (1986), 63–5, who is more sceptical about the episode.

3 A complete list of the known refugee-leaders settled in the empire down to the Severan age can be found in D.C. Braund, *Rome and the Friendly King* (London, 1984), 165–80.

4 B. Isaac, 'The Meaning of the Terms Limes and Limitanei', *JRS* lxxviii (1988), 125–47.

5 Cf. F. Millar, op. cit. (n.1), 19 with n. 128.

6 For a general discussion of the important role of markets in frontier economies, see e.g. E.A. Thompson, 'Constantine, Constantius II and the Lower Danube Frontier', *Hermes* lxxxiv (1956), 372–81; *The Early Germans* (Oxford, 1965), 19ff.; *The Visigoths in the Time of Ulfila* (Oxford, 1966), 19f.; and more recently L.F. Pitts, 'Roman Style Buildings in Barbaricum (Moravia and NW Slovakia)', *Oxford Journal of Archaeology* vi, 2 (1987), 234–6; and B. Cunliffe, *Greeks, Romans and Barbarians* (London, 1988), 171–201.

7 C.M. Wells, *The German Policy of Augustus* (Oxford, 1972), 7.

8 See T. Kolnik, 'Q. Atilius Primus – interprex centurio und negotiator', *Acta Archaeologica Academiae Scientiarum Hungaricae* xxx (1978), 61–75.

9 S.S. Frere, *Britannia* (London, 3rd edn 1987), 167, 179 n.52.

10 Some further individuals with similar duties in frontier areas are attested: *CIL* V 1838 = *ILS* 1349 (Augustan); *AE* 1926.80 (Neronian, cf. P.A. Holder, *Studies in the Auxilia of the Roman Army*, BAR International Series 70 (Oxford, 1980), 76); R. Syme, *History in Ovid* (Oxford, 1978), 82 (Augustan); *CIL* IX 5363 = *ILS* 2737 (Augustan); similarly, internally, *CIL* III 14387ff. = *ILS* 9199 (Claudian); possibly *AE* 1972.572 (Domitianic).

11 For a detailed analysis of this and allied matters, A.B. Bosworth, 'Arrian and the Alani', *HSCP* lxxxi (1977), 217–55.

12 On Theodosius' methods, see E.A. Thompson, *The Historical Work of Ammianus Marcellinus* (Cambridge, 1947), 90–1; Austin, op. cit. (n.2), 36–9.

## 3 MAKING CONTACT: TACTICAL INTELLIGENCE (pp. 39–86)

1 C.B.R. Pelling, 'Caesar's Battle Descriptions and the Defeat of Ariovistus', *Latomus* xl (1981), 747.

2 These details were perhaps known to Tacitus from his acquaintance with the commanders' families and *commentarii*. See R. Syme, *Tacitus* (Oxford, 1958), 297, 303, 765.

3 The issues of signalling, the installations required to service it and the interpretation of the archaeological evidence provided by watch- and signal-towers, are well canvassed by G.H. Donaldson, 'Signalling Communications and the Roman Imperial Army', *Britannia* xix (1988), 349–56; P. Southern, 'Signals Versus Illumination on Roman Frontiers', *Britannia* xxi (1990), 233–42; P.R. Wilson, 'Aspects of the Yorkshire signal stations', in V.A. Maxfield and M.J. Dobson (eds), *Roman Frontier Studies 1989*, (Exeter, 1991), 142–7; D. Woolliscroft, 'Das Signalsystem an der Hadriansmauer und seine Auswirkungen auf dessen Aufbau', ibid., 148–52.

4 M.H. Dodgeon and S.N.C. Lieu, *The Roman Eastern Frontier and the Persian Wars AD 226–363* (London/New York, 1991), 386 nn. 22–5.

## 4 GROPING TOWARDS EMPIRE: THE REPUBLIC (pp. 87–108)

1 See A.H.M. Jones, 'The Roman Civil Service (Clerical and Sub-Clerical Grades)', *JRS* xxxix (1949), 38-42; N. Purcell, 'The Apparitores: A Study in Social Mobility', *PBSR* li N.S. xxxviii (1983), 125–73.

2 The fragments of Pytheas are collected by H.J. Mette, *Pytheas von Massalia* (Berlin, 1952).

3 See C. Cichorius, 'Panaitios und die attische Stoikerinschrift', *Rheinisches Museum für Philologie* N.F. lxiii (1908), 220–3.

4 On *commentarii* see A. von Premerstein, *RE* IV (1901), 757–9; F.E. Adcock, *Caesar as a Man of Letters* (Cambridge, 1956), 6–18.

5 On geographical and ethnographical writing in the late Republic, see now E. Rawson, *Intellectual Life in the Late Roman Republic* (London, 1985), 250–66; R. Syme, 'Military Geography at Rome', *Classical Antiquity* vii no. 2 (1988), 227–51.

6 On traders as a source of information for the Roman world see E. Norden, *Die germanische Urgeschichte in Tacitus Germania* (Leipzig/Berlin, 2nd edn 1922), 428–50.

7 See J.S. Richardson, *Hispaniae: Spain and the Development of Roman Imperialism, 218–82 BC* (Cambridge, 1986); A.M. Eckstein, *Senate and General: Individual Decision Making and Roman Foreign Relations, 264–194 BC* (Berkeley, 1987).

8 There is also much information to be gleaned from Caesar's *Commentarii* on the Civil War and the letters of Cicero for the period 49–43 BC, which is here mostly left out of account as relating to a highly abnormal situation from an intelligence viewpoint.

9 The fragments of Poseidonius are collected by L. Edelstein and R.G. Kidd, *Poseidonius I. The Fragments* (Cambridge, 1972).

10 See L.J.F. Keppie, *The Making of the Roman Army* (London, 1984), 79, 83–4.

11 On this aspect of senatorial procedure see R.J.A. Talbert, *The Senate of Imperial Rome* (Princeton, 1984), 240–8.

## 5 THE VIEW FROM ROME: THE EMPEROR'S PERSPECTIVE (pp. 109–41)

1 See J. Crook, *Consilium Principis* (Cambridge, 1955).

2 For an alternative view of this turning point, see J. Ober, 'Tiberius and the Political Testament of Augustus', *Historia* xxxi (1982), 306–28; T.J. Cornell, 'The End of Roman Imperial Expansion', in J. Rich and G. Shipley, (eds), *War and Society in the Roman World* (London/New York, 1993), 139–70.

3 On the nature of Roman frontiers, see A.W. Lintott, 'What was the "Imperium Romanum"?', *Greece and Rome* xxviii (1981), 53–67.

4 On the variability and significance of 'mental maps' in a military context, see P. Gould and R. White, *Mental Maps* (London, 2nd edn 1986), 140–5.

5 See further on the issue of the 'imageability' of trans-frontier phenomena: A.D. Lee, *Information and Frontiers: Roman Foreign Relations in Late Antiquity* (Cambridge, 1993), 90f.; N. Purcell, 'Maps, Lists, Money, Order and Power', *JRS* lxxx (1990), 178–82.

6 P.A. Brunt, review of H.D. Meyer, *Die Aussenpolitik des Augustus und die Augusteische Dichtung*, *JRS* liii (1963), 170–6 esp. 175–6.

7 The evidence for military surveyors is conveniently collected by R.K. Sherk, 'Roman Geographical Exploration and Military Maps', *ANRW* II Principat 1 (1974), 544–58.

8 On Roman maps in general see R.K. Sherk, op. cit. (n.7), 534–62; O.A.W. Dilke, *Greek and Roman Maps* (London, 1985), with the review by R.J.A. Talbert, *JRS* lxxvii (1987), 210–12.

9 On *periploi* see O.A.W. Dilke, op. cit. (n.8), 130–44.

10 On these itineraries see A.L.F. Rivet and C. Smith, *The Place-Names of Roman Britain* (London, 1979), 148–84.

11 On literary *commentarii* see A. von Premerstein, 'commentarii', *RE* IV (1901), 757–9; F.E. Adcock, *Caesar as a Man of Letters* (Cambridge, 1956), 6–18; E. Badian, 'The early historians', in T.A. Dorey (ed.), *Latin Historians* (London, 1966), 23–5; E. Rawson, *Intellectual Life in the Late Roman Republic* (London, 1985), 227–9.

12 However, see now P. Culham, 'Archives and Alternatives in Republican Rome', *Classical Philology* lxxxiv no.2 (1989), 100–15 on the restricted nature of the archives in the senatorial *tabularium*.

13 On communication between emperor and provincial governors see F. Millar, *The Emperor in the Roman World* (London, 1977), 313–28.

14 See A.N. Sherwin–White, *The Letters of Pliny. A Historical and Social Commentary* (Oxford, 1966), 554–5.

15 On the speed of the imperial posting system see W. Riepl, *Das Nachrichtenwesen des Altertums mit besonderer Rücksicht auf die Römer* (Leipzig, 1913), 123–240; W.M. Ramsay, 'The Speed of the Roman Imperial Post', *JRS* xv (1925), 60–74; M. Amit, 'Les moyens de communication et la défense de l'empire romain', *La Parola del Passato* xx (1965), 207–22; R. Chevallier, *Roman Roads* (London, 1976), 191–5; cf. F. Millar, *Britannia* xiii (1982), 9–10.

16 F. Millar, 'Emperors, Frontiers and Foreign Relations, 31 BC to AD 378', *Britannia* xiii (1982), 19, citing A. Alföldi, 'The Moral Barrier on Rhine and Danube', in E. Birley (ed.), *The Congress of Roman Frontier Studies, 1949* (Durham, 1952), 1–16.

17 R. Syme, *Cambridge Ancient History* X (Cambridge, 1934), 351–4, cf. 380; criticized by P.A. Brunt, op. cit. (n. 6), esp. 172–3; C.M. Wells, *The German Policy of Augustus* (Oxford, 1972).

18 See H. Schönberger, 'The Roman Frontier in Germany: An Archaeological Survey', *JRS* lix (1969), 144–64.

19 R. Syme, 'Military Geography at Rome', *Classical Antiquity* vii no.2 (1988), 249–50.

20 P.A. Brunt, op. cit. (n.6).

21 See chapter 2, n.3.

22 On the *frumentarii*, see P.K. Baillie Reynolds, 'The Troops Quartered in the Castra Peregrina', *JRS* xiii (1923), 168–89; W.G. Sinnigen, 'The Origins of the frumentarii', *MAAR* xxvii (1962), 213–24; M. Clauss, *Untersuchungen zu den principales des römischen Heeres von Augustus bis Diokletian. Cornicularii, speculatores, frumentarii* (Bochum, 1973), 82–109; F. Paschoud, 'Frumentarii, agentes in rebus, magistriani, curiosi, veredarii: problèmes de terminologie', *Bonner Historia-Augusta Colloquium 1979/81* (Bonn, 1983), 215–43; J.C. Mann, 'The Organization of the Frumentarii', *ZPE* lxxiv (1988), 149–50; N.B. Rankov, 'Frumentarii, the Castra Peregrina and the Provincial Officia', *ZPE* lxxx (1990), 176–82.

23 See N.B. Rankov, 'M. Oclatinius Adventus in Britain', *Britannia* xviii (1987), 243–9.

## 6 FACING FACTS: THE GOVERNOR AND HIS *OFFICIUM* (pp. 142–69)

1 On the senatorial career see A.R. Birley, *The Fasti of Roman Britain* (Oxford, 1981), 1–35, esp. 8–12, 15–32.

2 See G. P. Burton, 'Proconsuls, Assizes and the Administration of Justice under the Empire', *JRS* lxv (1975), 92–106.

3 A.R. Birley, 'Vindolanda: Notes on Some New Writing Tablets', *ZPE* lxxxviii (1991), 87–90.

4 C.D. Gordon, 'The Subsidization of Border Peoples as a Roman Policy in Imperial Defence' (unpublished doctoral thesis, Michigan 1948), summarized in 'Subsidies in Roman Imperial Defence', *Phoenix* iii (1949), 60–9.

5  See V.F. Gajdukevič, *Das Bosporanische Reich* (Berlin/Amsterdam, 1971), 348 with n.42.

6  M.P. Speidel and D.H. French, 'Bithynian Troops in the Kingdom of the Bosporus', *Epigraphica Anatolica* vi (1985), 97–102 (= M.P. Speidel, *Roman Army Studies II*, Mavors VIII (Stuttgart, 1992), 173–9); cf. W. Eck, 'Prokonsuln und militärisches Kommando. Folgerungen aus Diplomen für prokonsulare Provinzen', in W. Eck and H. Wolff (eds), *Heer und Integrationspolitik. Die römischen Militärdiplome als historische Quelle* (Köln/Wien, 1986), 518–34. On the garrisoning of Olbia and the Crimea, see V.F. Gajdukevič, op. cit. (n.5), 350.

7  A.H.M. Jones, 'The Roman Civil Service (Clerical and Sub-Clerical Grades)', *JRS* xxxix (1949), 41.

8  See V. Maxfield, *The Military Decorations of the Roman Army* (London, 1981), 97–9.

9  See M. Clauss, *Untersuchumgen zur den principales des römischen Heeres von Augustus bis Diokletian. Cornicularii, speculatores, frumentarii* (Bochum, 1973), 46–58 (*speculatores Augusti* – of the emperor), 59–77 (*speculatores* of the governor).

10  M.P. Speidel, *Guards of the Roman Armies: An Essay on the Singulares of the Provinces*, Antiquitas, Reihe I, Bd 28 (Bonn, 1978).

11  See Fink p. 13 and G.R. Watson, 'Theta Nigrum', *JRS* xlii (1952), 56–62; R.O. Fink, 'Hunt's Pridianum: British Museum Papyrus 2851', *JRS* xlviii (1958), 113 on col. ii, 3–12.

12  On the governor's archive, see now R. Haensch, 'Das Statthalterarchiv', *Zeitschrift der Savigny-Stiftung für Rechtsgeschichte* Bd. 109 Romanistische Abteilung (1992), 209–317. On the keeping of official documents in general, see E.G. Turner, *Greek Papyri. An Introduction* (Oxford, 1968), 136–46.

13  See Fink pp. 6–8.

14  London: P. Marsden, *Roman London* (London, 1980), 88–93; R. Merrifield, *London, City of the Romans* (London, 1983), 72–7. Cologne: G. Wolff, *Das römisch-germanische Köln* (Cologne, 1983), 160–5. Mainz: K.-V. Decker and W. Selzer, *ANRW* II Principat 5.1 (1976), 488–9; cf. H. Büsing, *Römische Militärarchitektur in Mainz*, Römisch-germanische Forschungen 40 (Mainz, 1982). Aquincum: I. Wellner, *Archaeologiai Értesítő* xcvii (1970), 116ff. Carnuntum: R. Egger, *Das Praetorium als Amtssitz und Quartier römischer Spitzenfunktionäre*, Österreichische Akademie. Sitzungsberichte ccl (Wien, 1966).

## 7 THE WATCH ON THE FRONTIER: THE GOVERNOR'S PERSPECTIVE
(pp. 170–84)

1  Convenience: J.C. Mann, 'The Frontiers of the Principate', *ANRW* II Principat 1 (1974), 513–14. Zone of control: C.R. Whittaker, *Les frontières de l'empire romain* (Besançon, 1989), 21–50. Ossified line of advance: B. Isaac, *The Limits of Empire. The Roman Army in the East* (Oxford, 2nd edn 1992), 416–18.

2  See M.P. Speidel, 'Swimming the Danube under Hadrian's Eyes. A Feat of the Emperors' Batavi Horse Guard', *Ancient Society* xxii (1991), 277–82; id., *Riding for Caesar. The Roman Emperors' Horse Guard* (London, 1994), 45–7.

3  On the bridges at Neuwied and Koblenz, see H. Cüppers, *Die Trierer Römerbrücken* (Mainz, 1969), 184–9; E. Mensching, 'Die Koblenzer Rheinbrücke, P. Pomponius Secundus und der Brückenbau am Rhein und Mosel', *Bonner Jahrbücher* clxxxi (1981), 325–54.

4  D. Baatz and F.R. Hermann, *Die Römer in Hessen* (Stuttgart, 1982), 369–72, cf. 350–7, 485–91; H. Schönberger 'Die römischen Truppenlager der frühen und mittleren Kaiserzeit zwischen Nordsee und Inn', *BRGK* lxvi (1985), 347–51, 432, 441–2, 451.

5  H. Cüppers, op. cit. (n.3), 189–93, esp. 190 on the absence of Roman bridges south of Gross-Krotzenburg noted during the dredging of the Main in 1885/6.

6  P. Filtzinger, D. Planck and B. Cämmerer (eds), *Die Römer in Baden-Württemberg* (Stuttgart, 2nd edn 1986), 73–4.

7  H. Cüppers, op. cit. (n.3).

8  Drobeta: D. Tudor, *Podurile Romane de la Dunărea de Jos* (Bucuresti, 1971) (= *Les ponts romains du Bas Danube* (Paris, 1974)), 53–153; see p. 177 below; Oescus: D. Tudor, op. cit.,17–31, assigning the bridge to the campaign of Cornelius Fuscus in AD 87, but cf. A.G. Poulter in A.G. Poulter (ed.), *Ancient Bulgaria* II (Nottingham, 1983), 76 with n.7, who suggests a Trajanic date based on its similarity to the Trajanic bridge at Drobeta; Transdierna: H. Cüppers, op. cit. (n.3), 197–8.

9  C.G. Starr, *The Roman Imperial Navy 31 BC–AD 324* (Cambridge/Ithaca, 1960), 129–52; H.D.L. Viereck, *Die römische Flotte* (Herford, 1975), 254–6; M. Reddé, *Mare Nostrum. Les infrastructures, le disposition et l'histoire de la marine militaire sous l'empire romain* (Paris, 1986), 290–307, 356–86.

10  Cf. A.D. Lee, *Information and Frontiers: Roman Foreign Relations in Late Antiquity* (Cambridge, 1993), 96–9.

11  Cf. A. Hyland, *Equus: The Horse in the Roman World* (London, 1990), 163.

12  A. Hyland, op. cit. (n.11), 87–94, 97.

13  On the German frontier in general see: H. Schönberger 'The Roman Frontier in Germany: An Archaeological Survey', *JRS* lix (1969), 144–97; id., 'Die römischen Truppenlager der frühen und mittleren Kaiserzeit zwischen Nordsee und Inn', *BRGK* lxvi (1985), 321–497; V.A. Maxfield in J. Wacher (ed.), *The Roman World* (London/New York, 1987), 140–71.

14  On the Dacian frontiers see: N. Gudea,'The Defensive System of Roman Dacia', *Britannia* x (1979), 63–87; V.A. Maxfield in J. Wacher, op. cit. (n.13), 179–87. On the *limes Alutanus* and *limes Transalutanus* see the summary of F.A. Lepper and S.S. Frere, *Trajan's Column* (Gloucester/Wolfboro, NH, 1988), 312.

15  Cf. E.N. Luttwak, *The Grand Strategy of the Roman Empire from the First Century AD to the Third* (Baltimore, 1976), esp. 51–126.

16  B. Isaac, op. cit. (n.1), 101–40.

## 8 BRIDGING THE GAP: EMPERORS ON THE FRONTIERS (pp. 185–213)

1  A. Mócsy, *Pannonia and Upper Moesia* (London/Boston, 1974), 110f; L.F. Pitts, 'Rome and the German Kings on the Middle Danube', *JRS* lxxix (1989), 50–1 with n.36.

2  B. Isaac, *The Limits of Empire: The Roman Army in the East* (Oxford, 2nd edn 1992), 126 (occupation of Azraq and Jawf), 131–4, 169–71, 213–18 (the role of the Arabian outposts).

3  M.P. Speidel, *Guards of the Roman Armies: An Essay on the Singulares of the Provinces*, Antiquitas, Reihe I, Bd 28 (Bonn, 1978), 6–11.

4  M.P. Speidel, op. cit. (n.3), 54–66, esp. 64–5.

5  M.P. Speidel, 'Exploratores. Mobile Élite Units of Roman Germany', *Epigraphische Studien 13. Sammelband.* (Köln/Bonn, 1983), 63–78; cf. P. Southern, 'The Numeri of the Roman Imperial Army', *Britannia* xx (1989), 110–14.

6  On *exploratores* in Germany, see E. Stein, *Die kaiserlichen Beamten und Truppenkörper im römischen Deutschland unter dem Prinzipat* (Wien, 1932), 260–8.

7  N.B. Rankov, 'M. Oclatinius Adventus in Britain', *Britannia* xviii (1987), 243–9.

8  See N.B. Rankov, 'The Beneficiarii Consularis in the Western Provinces of the Roman Empire' (Unpublished D.Phil. Thesis, Oxford, 1986). The inscriptions recording *beneficiarii* of all kinds have now been collected together in E. Schallmayer *et al.* (eds), *Der römische Weihebezirk von Osterburken I. Corpus der griechischen und lateinischen Beneficiarier-Inschriften des römischen Reiches*, Forschungen und Berichte zur Vor- und Frühgeschichte in Baden-Württemberg, Bd 40 (Stuttgart, 1991); the evidence for *stationes* mentioned by place-name in this section may be sought in this *Corpus* by reference to the indexed maps between pages 743 and 773.

9   O. Hirschfeld, 'Die Sicherheitspolizei im römischen Kaiserreich', *Sitzungsberichte der Berliner Akademie* (1891), 862–3 = *Kleine Schriften* (Berlin, 1913), 594–6; A. von Domaszewski, 'Die Beneficiarierposten und die römischen Strassennetze', *Westdeutsche Zeitschrift* xxii (1902), 158–211.

10  R.W. Davies, 'The Investigation of Some Crimes in Roman Egypt', *Ancient Society* iv (1973), 199–212; N.B. Rankov, 'Die Beneficiarier in den literarischen und papyrologischen Texten', in *Der römische Weihebezirk von Osterburken II. Kolloquium 1990 und paläobotanische–osteologische Untersuchungen*, Forschungen und Berichte zur Vor- und Frühgeschichte in Baden-Württemberg, Bd 49 (Stuttgart, 1994), 219–32.

11  N.B. Rankov, 'A Contribution to the Military and Administrative History of Montana', in A.G. Poulter (ed.), *Ancient Bulgaria. Papers Presented to the International Symposium on the Ancient History and Archaeology of Bulgaria, University of Nottingham, 1981*, Part 2 (Nottingham, 1983), 40–73, esp. 49–51; cf. M.P. Speidel, 'Regionarii in Lower Moesia', *ZPE* lvii (1984), 185–8.

12  S.J. de Laet, *Portorium: étude sur l'organisation douanière chez les Romains, surtout à l'époque du haut-empire* (Bruges, 1949), 140, 208, 266, 268, 307, 337, 376, 417, 449.

13  M. Mirković in V.A. Maxfield and M.J. Dobson (eds), *Roman Frontier Studies 1989. Proceedings of the XVth International Congress of Roman Frontier Studies* (Exeter, 1991), 252–5; id., 'Beneficiarii consularis in Sirmium', in *Der römische Weihebezirk von Osterburken II. Kolloquium 1990 und pabäobotanische-osteologische Untersuchungen* Forschungen und Berichte zur Vor- und Frühgeschichte in Baden-Württemberg, Bd 49 (Stuttgart, 1994), 193–8.

14  See n.11.

15  See n.10.

16  See N.B. Rankov, op. cit. (n.8), 100–15; K. Eibl in *Der römische Weihebezirk von Osterburken II* (Stuttgart, 1994), 278–97.

17  H. Lieb, 'Expleta Statione' in M.G. Jarrett and B. Dobson, *Britain and Rome. Essays Presented to E. Birley on his Sixtieth Birthday* (Kendal, 1965), 139–44; P. Herz, 'Neue Benefiziarier-Altäre aus Mainz', *ZPE* xxii (1976), 191–9; N.B. Rankov, op. cit. (n.8), 243–50; M. Mirković in V.A. Maxfield and M.J. Dobson (eds), op. cit. (n.13), 252–4.

18  D. Tsontchev, 'La voie romaine Philippopolis–Sub Radice', *Latomus* xviii (1959), 154–70.

19  See L.F. Pitts, 'Roman Style Buildings in Barbaricum (Moravia and SW Slovakia)', *Oxford Journal of Archaeology* vi, 2 (1987), 219–36.

20  A.D. Lee, *Information and Frontiers. Roman Foreign Relations in Late Antiquity* (Cambridge, 1993).

21  See D.L. Kennedy, 'Some Observations on the Praetorian Guard', *Ancient Society* ix (1978), 275–301.

22  H.-J. Diesner, *RE Suppl.* XI (1968), 1113–23 esp. 1115–6 s.v. *protectores*.

## 9 HIERARCHIES OF INTELLIGENCE: THE FOURTH CENTURY (pp. 214–43)

1   *Contra*, A.D. Lee, *Information and Frontiers. Roman Foreign Relations in Late Antiquity* (Cambridge, 1993), 33–40.

2   Cf. R.S.O. Tomlin, 'Notitia Dignitatum Omnium, Tam Civilium Quam Militarium', in R. Goodburn and P. Bartholomew (eds), *Aspects of the Notitia Dignitatum*, BAR Supplementary Series 15 (Oxford, 1976), 189–209.

3   O. Höckmann, 'Late Roman Rhine Vessels from Mainz, Germany', *International Journal of Nautical Archaeology* xxii no.2 (May 1993), 125–35; P. Marsden, 'A Hydrostatic Study of a Reconstruction of Mainz Roman Ship 9', *ibid.*, 137–41.

4   See S. Johnson, *Late Roman Fortifications* (London, 1983).

5   A. Mócsy, *Pannonia and Upper Moesia* (London/Boston, 1974), 280–1.

6   Cf. A.H.M. Jones, *The Later Roman Empire 284–602* (Oxford, 1964), 610.

# BIBLIOGRAPHY

Adcock, F.E., *Caesar as a Man of Letters* (Cambridge, 1956).

Alföldi, A., 'The moral barrier on Rhine and Danube', in E. Birley (ed.), *Congress of Roman Frontier Studies, 1949* (Durham, 1952).

Amit, M., 'Les moyens de communication et la défense de l'empire romain', *La Parola del Passato* xx (1965), 207–22.

Austin, N.J.E., 'Investigations into the military knowledge of Ammianus Marcellinus' (Unpublished Dissertation, University of London, 1971–2).

—— 'Ammianus' account of Adrianople: some strategic observations', *Acta Classica. Proceedings of the Classical Association of South Africa* xv (1972), 77–83.

—— 'Julian at Ctesiphon: a fresh look at Ammianus' account', *Athenaeum* l (1972), 301–9.

—— *Ammianus on Warfare*, Collection Latomus 165 (Bruxelles, 1979).

Baatz, D. and Hermann, F.-R., *Die Römer in Hessen* (Stuttgart, 1982).

Badian, E., 'The early historians', in T.A. Dorey (ed.), *Latin Historians* (London, 1966), 1–38.

Baillie Reynolds, P.K., 'The troops quartered in the Castra Peregrina', *JRS* xiii (1923), 168–89.

Baldwin, B., 'On the date of the anonymous *Peri strategikes*', *Byzantinische Zeitschrift* lxxxi (1988), 290–3.

Birley, A.R., *Marcus Aurelius: A Biography* (London, 1966, 2nd edn 1987).

—— *The African Emperor. Septimius Severus* (London, 1972, 2nd edn 1988).

—— *The Fasti of Roman Britain* (Oxford, 1981).

—— 'Vindolanda: notes on some new writing tablets', *ZPE* lxxxviii (1991), 87–90.

Blockley, R.C. 'The coded message in Amm. Marc. 18.6.17–19', *Échos du monde classique/Classical Views* xxx NS v.1 (1986), 63–5.

—— *East Roman Frontier Policy: Formation and Conduct from Diocletian to Anastasius*, ARCA, Classical and Medieval Texts, Papers and Monographs 30 (Leeds, 1992)

Boak, A.E.R., *The Master of the Offices in the Late Roman and Byzantine Empires* (New York, 1919).

Bosworth, A.B., 'Arrian and the Alani', *HSCP* lxxxi (1977), 217–55.

Braund, D.C., *Rome and the Friendly King* (London, 1984).

Breeze, D.J. and Dobson, J., *Hadrian's Wall* (London, 3rd edn 1987).

Brennan, P., 'Combined legionary detachments as artillery units in late-Roman Danubian bridgehead positions', *Chiron* x (1980), 553–67.

Brunt, P.A., review of H.D. Meyer, *Die Aussenpolitik des Augustus und die Augusteische Dichtung*, *JRS* liii (1963), 170–6.

—— *Italian Manpower 225 BC–AD 14* (Oxford, 1971).

Burton, G.P., 'Proconsuls, assizes and the administration of justice under the Empire',

*JRS* lxv (1975), 92–106.

Büsing, H., *Römische Militärarchitektur in Mainz*, Römisch–Germanische Forschungen 40 (Mainz, 1982).

Chapot, V., *La frontière de l'Euphrate de Pompée à la conquête arabe* (Paris, 1907).

Chevallier, R., *Roman Roads* (London, 1976).

Cichorius, C., 'Panaitios und die attische Stoikerinschrift', *Rheinisches Museum für Philologie* NF lxiii (1908), 220–3.

Clauss, M., *Untersuchungen zu den principales des römischen Heeres von Augustus bis Diokletian. Cornicularii, speculatores, frumentarii* (Bochum, 1973).

—— *Der Magister Officiorum in der Spätantike, 4.–6. Jahrhundert: das Amt und sein Einfluss auf die kaiserliche Politik* (München, 1980).

Cockle, W.E.H., 'State archives in Graeco-Roman Egypt from 30 BC to the reign of Septimius Severus', *Journal of Egyptian Archaeology* lxx (1984), 106–22.

Cornell, T.J., 'The end of Roman imperial expansion', in J. Rich and G. Shipley (eds), *War and Society in the Roman World* (London/New York, 1993), 138–70.

Crook, J., *Consilium Principis* (Cambridge, 1955).

Culham, P., 'Archives and alternatives in Republican Rome', *Classical Philology* lxxxiv no.2 (1989), 100–15.

Cunliffe, B., *Greeks, Romans and Barbarians* (London, 1988).

Cüppers, H., *Die Trierer Römerbrücken* (Mainz, 1969).

Davies, R.W., 'The investigation of some crimes in Roman Egypt', *Ancient Society* iv (1973), 199–212 (= *Service in the Roman Army* (Oxford, 1989), 175–85).

Decker, K.V. and Selzer, W., 'Moguntiacum: Mainz von der Zeit des Augustus bis zum Ende der römischen Herrschaft', *ANRW* II Principat 5.1 (1976), 457–559.

Demandt, A., 'Magister militum', *RE Suppl.* XII (1970), 553–790.

Dennis, G.T., *Three Byzantine Military Treatises*, Dumbarton Oaks Texts 9 (Washington, DC, 1985).

Diesner, H.-J., 'Protectores', *RE Suppl.* XI (1968), 1113–23.

Dilke, O.A.W., *Greek and Roman Maps* (London, 1985).

Dodgeon, M.H. and Lieu, S.N.C., *The Roman Eastern Frontier and the Persian Wars AD 226–363* (London, 1991).

Domaszewski, A. von, 'Die Beneficiarierposten und die römischen Strassennetze', *Westdeutsche Zeitschrift* xxii (1902), 158–211.

—— *Die Rangordnung des römischen Heeres* (Bonn, 1908) (= *Bonner Jahrbücher* cxvii (1908), 1–278); 2nd edn by B. Dobson (Köln, 1967).

Donaldson, G.H., 'Signalling communications and the Roman imperial army', *Britannia* xix (1988), 349–56.

Dvornik, F., *Origins of Intelligence Services* (New Brunswick, NJ, 1974).

Eck, W., 'Proconsuln und militärische Kommando. Folgerungen aus Diplomen für prokonsulare Provinzen', in W. Eck and H. Wolff (eds), *Heer und Integrationspolitik. Die römischen Militärdiplome als historische Quelle* (Köln/Wien, 1986), 518–34.

Eckstein, A.M., *Senate and General: individual Decision Making and Roman Foreign Relations, 264–194 BC* (Berkeley, 1987).

Edelstein, L. and Kidd, R.G., *Poseidonius. I. The Fragments* (Cambridge, 1972).

Egger, R., *Das Praetorium als Amtssitz und Quartier römischer Spitzenfunktionäre*, Österreichische Akademie. Sitzungsberichte ccl (Wien, 1966).

Eibl, K., 'Gibt es eine spezifische Ausrüstung der Beneficiarier?' in *Der römische Weihebezirk von Osterburken II. Kolloquium 1990 und paläobotanische-osteologische Untersuchungen*, Forschungen und Berichte zur Vor- und Frühgeschichte in Baden-Württemberg, Bd 49 (Stuttgart, 1994), 273–98.

Engels, D.W., *Alexander the Great and the Logistics of the Macedonian Army* (Berkeley, 1978).

Fiebiger, H.O., 'Exploratores', *RE* VI (1909), 122–5.

—— 'Frumentarii', *RE* VII (1912), 1690–3.

Filtzinger, P., Planck, D. and Cämmerer, B., *Die Römer in Baden-Württemberg* (Stuttgart, 2nd edn 1986).

Fink, R.O., 'Hunt's Pridianum: British Museum Papyrus 2851', *JRS* xlviii (1958), 102–16.

—— *Roman Military Records on Papyrus*, American Philological Association Monograph 26 (Cleveland, 1971).

Frere, S.S., *Britannia* (London, 3rd edn 1987).

Gajdukevič, V.F., *Das Bosporanische Reich* (Berlin/Amsterdam, 1971).

Gichon, M., 'Military intelligence in the Roman army', in H.E. Herzig and F. Frei-Stolba, (eds), *Labor omnibus unus: Gerold Walser zum 70. Geburtstag dargebracht von Freunden, Kollegen und Schülern*, Historia Einzelschriften 60 (Stuttgart, 1989), 154–70.

Gordon, C.D., 'The subsidization of border peoples as a Roman policy in imperial defence' (Unpublished Dissertation, University of Michigan, 1948).

—— 'Subsidies in Roman imperial defence', *Phoenix* iii (1949), 60–9.

Gould, P. and White, R., *Mental Maps* (London, 2nd edn 1986).

Gudea, N., 'The defensive system of Roman Dacia', *Britannia* x (1979), 63–87.

Haensch, R., 'Das Statthalterarchiv', *Zeitschrift der Savigny-Stiftung für Rechtsgeschichte*, Bd 109 Romanistische Abteilung (1992), 209–317.

Heather, P. and Matthews, J.F., *The Goths in the Fourth Century* (Liverpool, 1991).

Herz, P., 'Neue Benefiziarier-Altäre aus Mainz', *ZPE* xxii (1976), 191–9.

Hirschfeld, O., 'Die Sicherheitspolizei im römischen Kaiserreich', *Sitzungsberichte der Berliner Akademie* (1891), 845–877 (= *Kleine Schriften* (Berlin, 1913), 576–612).

Höckmann, O., 'Late Roman Rhine vessels from Mainz, Germany', *International Journal of Nautical Archaeology* xxii no.2 (May 1993) 125–35.

Holder, P.A., *Studies in the Auxilia of the Roman Army*, BAR International Series 70 (Oxford, 1980).

Hyland, A., *Equus: The Horse in the Roman World* (London, 1990).

Isaac, B., 'The meaning of the terms limes and limitanei', *JRS* lxxviii (1988), 125–47.

—— *The Limits of Empire. The Roman Army in the East* (Oxford, 1990, 2nd edn 1992).

Janni, P., *La mappa e il periplo. Cartografia antica e spazio odologico* (Rome, 1984).

Johnson, S., *Late Roman Fortifications* (London, 1983).

Jones, A.H.M., 'The Roman civil service (clerical and sub-clerical grades)', *JRS* xxxix (1949), 38–55.

—— *The Later Roman Empire 284–602* (Oxford, 1964).

Keil, J. and Premerstein, A. von, *Bericht über eine dritte Reise in Lydien und den angrenzenden Gebieten Ioniens, ausgeführt 1911* (Wien, 1914).

Kennedy, D.L., 'Some observations on the Praetorian Guard', *Ancient Society* ix (1978), 275–301.

—— 'A lost Latin inscription from the banks of the Tigris', *ZPE* lxxiii (1988), 101–3.

Keppie, L.J.F., *The Making of the Roman Army* (London, 1984).

Kolnik, T., 'Q. Atilius Primus – interprex centurio und negotiator', *Acta Archaeologica Academiae Scientiarum Hungaricae* xxx (1978), 61–75.

Laet, S.J. de, *Portorium: Étude sur l'organisation douanière chez les Romains, surtout à l'époque du Haut Empire* (Bruges, 1949).

Lammert, F., 'Speculatores', *RE* III A (1929), 1583–6.

Le Bohec, Y., *La troisième légion Auguste* (Aix/Marseille/Paris, 1989).

Lee, A.D., 'Embassies as evidence for the movement of military intelligence between the Roman and Sasanian empires', in P.M. Freeman and D.L. Kennedy (eds), *The Defence of the Roman and Byzantine East*, BAR Supplementary Series 297 (Oxford, 1986), 257–65.

—— 'Procopius, Justinian and the kataskopoi', *Classical Quarterly* xxix (1989), 569–72.

—— *Information and Frontiers. Roman Foreign Relations in Late Antiquity* (Cambridge, 1993).

—— and Shepard, J., 'A double life: placing the *Peri presbeon*', *Byzantinoslavica* lii (1991), 15–39.

Lepper, F.A. and Frere, S.S., *Trajan's Column* (Gloucester/Wolfboro, NH, 1988).

Lieb, H.J., 'Expleta statione', in M.G. Jarrett and B. Dobson (eds), *Britain and Rome. Essays Presented to E. Birley on his Sixtieth Birthday* (Kendal, 1965), 139–44.

Lieu, S.N.C., 'Captives, refugees and exiles: a study of cross-frontier civilian movements and contacts between Rome and Persia from Valerian to Jovian', in P.M. Freeman and D.L. Kennedy (eds), *The Defence of the Roman and Byzantine East*, BAR Supplementary Series 297 (Oxford, 1986), 475–505.

Lintott, A.W., 'What was the "Imperium Romanum"?', *Greece and Rome* xxviii (1981), 53–67.

Luttwak, E.N., *The Grand Strategy of the Roman Empire from the First Century AD to the Third* (Baltimore, 1976).

Mann, J.C., 'The frontiers of the Principate', *ANRW* II Principat 1 (1974), 508–33.

—— 'The organization of the frumentarii', *ZPE* lxxiv (1988), 149–50.

Marsden, P., 'A hydrostatic study of a reconstruction of Mainz Roman Ship 9', *International Journal of Nautical Archaeology* xxii no.2 (May 1993), 137–41.

—— 'Polybius as a military historian', in *Polybe*, Entretiens sur l'Antiquité Classique 20, Fondation Hardt (Vandoeuvres-Genève, 1974) .

—— *Roman London* (London, 1980).

Matthews, J.F., *The Roman World of Ammianus* (London, 1989).

Maxfield, V., *The Military Decorations of the Roman Army* (London, 1981).

—— 'The frontiers. Mainland Europe', in J. Wacher (ed.), *The Roman World* Vol. I (London, 1987), 139–97.

Mensching, E., 'Die Koblenzer Rheinbrücke, P. Pomponius Secundus und der Brückenbau am Rhein und Mosel', *Bonner Jahrbücher* clxxxi (1981), 325–54.

Merrifield, R., *London, City of the Romans* (London, 1983).

Mette, H.J., *Pytheas von Massalia* (Berlin, 1952).

Millar, F., *A Study of Cassius Dio* (Oxford, 1964).

—— *The Roman Empire and its Neighbours* (London, 1966).

—— *The Emperor in the Roman World* (London, 1977).

—— 'Emperors, frontiers and foreign relations', *Britannia* xiii (1982), 1–23.

—— 'Government and diplomacy in the Roman Empire during the first three centuries', *The International History Review* x (1988), 345–77.

Mirković, M., 'Beneficiarii consularis and the new outpost in Sirmium', in V.A. Maxfield and M.J. Dobson (eds), *Roman Frontier Studies 1989. Proceedings of the XVth International Congress of Roman Frontier Studies* (Exeter, 1991), 252–6.

—— 'Beneficiarii consularis in Sirmium', in *Der römische Weihebezirk von Osterburken II. Kolloquium 1990 und paläobotanische-osteologische Untersuchungen* (Stuttgart, 1994), 193–8.

Mócsy, A., *Pannonia* (Stuttgart, 1962).

—— *Pannonia and Upper Moesia* (London/Boston, 1974).

Norden, E., *Die germanische Urgeschichte in Tacitus Germania* (Leipzig/Berlin, 2nd edn 1922).

Ober, J., 'Tiberius and the political testament of Augustus', *Historia* xxxi (1982), 306–28.

Paschoud, F., 'Frumentarii, agentes in rebus, magistriani, curiosi, veredarii: problèmes de terminologie', in *Bonner Historia-Augusta-Colloquium 1979/81* (Bonn, 1983), 215–43.

Pelling, C.B.R., 'Caesar's battle descriptions and the defeat of Ariovistus', *Latomus* xl (1981), 741–66.

Pitts, L.F., 'Roman style buildings in Barbaricum (Moravia and NW Slovakia)', *Oxford Journal of Archaeology* vi, 2 (1987), 219–36.

—— 'Relations between Rome and the German "kings" on the Middle Danube in the first to fourth centuries AD', *JRS* lxxix (1989), 45–58.

Poulter, A.G., 'Town and country in Moesia Inferior', in A.G. Poulter (ed.), *Ancient Bulgaria*.

*Papers Presented to the International Symposium on the Ancient History and Archaeology of Bulgaria, University of Nottingham, 1981* Part 2 (Nottingham, 1983), 74–118.

Premerstein, A. von, 'Commentarii', *RE* IV (1901), 726–59.

Purcell, N., 'The apparitores: a study in social mobility', *PBSR* li NS xxxviii (1983), 125–73.

—— 'Maps, lists, money, order and power', *JRS* lxxx (1990), 178–82.

Ramsay, W.M., 'The speed of the Roman imperial post', *JRS* xv (1925), 60–74 .

Rankov, N.B., 'A contribution to the military and administrative history of Montana', in A.G. Poulter (ed.), *Ancient Bulgaria. Papers Presented to the International Symposium on the Ancient History and Archaeology of Bulgaria, University of Nottingham, 1981*, Part 2 (Nottingham, 1983), 40–73.

—— 'The beneficiarii consularis in the western provinces of the Roman Empire', (Unpublished Dissertation, University of Oxford, 1986).

—— 'M. Oclatinius Adventus in Britain', *Britannia* xviii (1987), 243–9.

—— 'Frumentarii, the Castra Peregrina and the provincial officia', *ZPE* lxxix (1990), 176–82.

—— 'Die Beneficiarier in den literarischen und papyrologischen Texten', in *Der römische Weihebezirk von Osterburken II. Kolloquium 1990 und paläobotanische-osteologische Untersuchungen* (Stuttgart, 1994), 219–32.

Rawson, E., *Intellectual Life in the Late Roman Republic* (London, 1985).

Rebuffat, R. and Marichal, R., 'Les ostraca de Bu Ngem', *REL* li (1973), 281–6.

Reddé, M., *Mare nostrum. Les infrastructures, le disposition et l'histoire de la marine militaire sous l'empire romain* (Paris, 1986).

Reincke, G., 'Nachrichtenwesen', *RE* XVI (1935), 1496–541.

Richardson, J.S., *Hispaniae: Spain and the Development of Roman Imperialism, 218–82 BC* (Cambridge, 1986).

Riepl, W., *Das Nachrichtenwesen des Altertums mit besonderer Rücksicht auf die Römer* (Leipzig, 1913).

Rivet, A.L.F. and Smith, C., *The Place-Names of Roman Britain* (London, 1979).

Rubin, Z., *Civil-War Propaganda and Historiography*, Collection Latomus 173 (Bruxelles, 1980).

Schallmayer, E., *et al.* (eds), *Der römische Weihebezirk von Osterburken I. Corpus der griechischen und lateinischen Beneficiarier-Inschriften des römischen Reiches*, Forschungen und Berichte zur Vor- und Frühgeschichte in Baden-Württemberg Bd 40 (Stuttgart, 1991).

Schönberger, H., 'The Roman frontier in Germany: an archaeological survey', *JRS* lix (1969), 144–97.

—— 'Die römischen Truppenlager der frühen und mittleren Kaiserzeit zwischen Nordsee und Inn', *BRGK* lxvi (1985), 321–497.

Seeck, O., 'Agentes in rebus', *RE* I (1893), 776–9.

Sheldon, R.M., *Tinker, Tailor, Caesar, Spy: Espionage in Ancient Rome* (Michigan, 1987; on microfilm).

Sherk, R.K., 'Roman geographical exploration and military maps', *ANRW* II Principat 1 (1974), 534–62.

Sherwin-White, A.N., *The Letters of Pliny. A Historical and Social Commentary* (Oxford, 1966).

Sinnigen, W., 'The origins of the frumentarii', *Memoirs of the American Academy in Rome* xxvii (1962), 213–24.

Southern, P., 'The numeri of the Roman imperial army', *Britannia* xx (1989), 81–140.

—— 'Signals versus illumination on Roman frontiers', *Britannia* xxi (1990), 233–42.

Speidel, M.P., 'The captor of Decebalus, a new inscription from Philippi', *JRS* lx (1970), 142–53.

—— *Guards of the Roman Armies: An Essay on the Singulares of the Provinces*, Antiquitas, Reihe I, Bd 28 (Bonn, 1978).

—— 'Exploratores. Mobile élite units of Roman Germany', *Epigraphische Studien 13. Sammelband* (Köln/Bonn, 1983), 63–78.

—— 'Regionarii in Lower Moesia', *ZPE* lvii (1984), 185–8.

—— 'The Roman road to Dumata (Jawf in Saudi Arabia) and the frontier strategy of praetensione colligare', *Historia* xxxvi (1987), 213–21.

—— 'Swimming the Danube under Hadrian's eyes. A feat of the emperor's Batavi horse guard', *Ancient Society* xxii (1991), 227–82.

—— *Riding for Caesar. The Roman Emperors' Horse Guard* (London, 1994).

—— and French, D.H., 'Bithynian troops in the kingdom of the Bosporus', *Epigraphica Anatolica* vi (1985), 97–102 (= M.P. Speidel, *Roman Army Studies II*, Mavors VIII (Stuttgart, 1992), 173–9).

Starr, C.G., *The Roman Imperial Navy 31 BC–AD 324* (Cambridge/Ithaca, 1960).

Stein, E., *Die kaiserlichen Beamten und Truppenkörper im römischen Deutschland unter dem Prinzipat* (Wien, 1932).

Syme, R., 'The Northern frontiers under Augustus', in *Cambridge Ancient History* X (Cambridge, 1934), 340–81.

—— *Tacitus* (Oxford, 1958).

—— *History in Ovid* (Oxford, 1978).

—— 'Military geography at Rome', *Classical Antiquity* vii no.2 (1988), 227–51.

Talbert, R.J.A., *The Senate of Imperial Rome* (Princeton, 1984).

—— Review of O.A.W. Dilke, *Greek and Roman Maps*, *JRS* lxxvii (1987), 210–12.

—— 'Commodus as diplomat in an extract from the Acta Senatus', *ZPE* lxxi (1988), 137–47.

Thompson, E.A., *The Historical Work of Ammianus Marcellinus* (Cambridge, 1947).

—— 'Constantine, Constantius II and the Lower Danube frontier', *Hermes* lxxxiv (1956), 372–81.

—— *The Early Germans* (Oxford, 1965).

—— *The Visigoths in the Time of Ulfila* (Oxford, 1966).

Tomlin, R.S.O, 'Notitia dignitatum omnium, tam civilium quam militarium', in R. Goodburn and P. Bartholomew (eds), *Aspects of the Notitia Dignitatum*, BAR Supplementary Series 15 (Oxford, 1976), 189–209.

Tsontchev, D., 'La voie romaine Philippopolis–Sub Radice', *Latomus* xviii (1959), 154–70.

Tudor, D., *Podurile Romane de la Dunărea de Jos* (Bucureşti, 1971) (= *Les Ponts romains du Bas Danube* (Paris, 1974).

Turner, E.G., *Greek Papyri. An Introduction* (Oxford, 1968).

Viereck, H.D.L., *Die römische Flotte* (Herford, 1975).

Wacher, J., (ed.), *The Roman World* (London/New York, 1987).

Walbank, F., *Polybius*, Sather Classical Lectures 42 (Berkeley, 1972).

Watson, G.R, 'Theta nigrum', *JRS* xlii (1952), 56–62.

Wellner, I., 'Az Aquincumi helyartói palota építésének kora (Zur Frage der Bauzeit des Statthalterpalastes von Aquincum)', *Archaeologiai Értesító* xcvii (1970), 116–25.

Wells, C.M., *The German Policy of Augustus* (Oxford, 1972).

Whittaker, C.R., *Les frontières de l'empire romain* (Besançon, 1989).

Wilson, P.R., 'Aspects of the Yorkshire signal stations' in V.A. Maxfield and M.J. Dobson (eds), *Roman Frontier Studies 1989. Proceedings of the XVth International Congress of Roman Frontier Studies* (Exeter, 1991), 142–7.

Wolff, G., *Das römisch–germanische Köln* (Köln, 1983).

Wooliscroft, D., 'Das Signalsystem an der Hadriansmauer und seine Auswirkungen auf dessen Aufbau', in V.A. Maxfield and M.J. Dobson (eds), *Roman Frontier Studies 1989. Proceedings of the XVth International Congress of Roman Frontier Studies* (Exeter, 1991) 148–52.

# GENERAL INDEX

# INDEX OF SOURCES

## PAPYRI AND
## PALAEOGRAPHICAL
## SOURCES

## COINS

## OTHER SOURCES